Hans-Georg Fill

Visualisation for Semantic Information Systems

Hans-Georg Fill

Visualisation for Semantic Information Systems

GABLER EDITION WISSENSCHAFT

Bibliographic information published by the Deutsche Nationalbibliothek
The Deutsche Nationalbibliothek lists this publication in the Deutsche Nationalbibliografie;
detailed bibliographic data are available in the Internet at http://dnb.d-nb.de.

1st Edition 2009

Editorial Office: Frauke Schindler / Anita Wilke

Gabler is part of the specialist publishing group Springer Science+Business Media.
www.gabler.de

Cover design: Regine Zimmer, Dipl.-Designerin, Frankfurt/Main
Printed on acid-free paper
Printed in Germany

ISBN 978-3-8349-1534-4

Preface

The topic of visualisation is today apparent in many areas of science. Visualisation in general uses graphical representations in order to amplify human cognition. It is thus more formal than artistic visual representations. These may leave it entirely to the artist and the beholder to infer the 'correct' interpretation from a graphical composition. At the same time visualisation is less focused on technical aspects than for example computer graphics that primarily deals with algorithms and technologies to realise graphics on technical devices. A central aspect of visualisation as it is seen here, is its orientation towards solutions for particular agents performing tasks in specific domains. In contrast to the often technical discussions on visualisation, this perspective promotes the explicit consideration of domain specific and contextual factors.

This book contains the core parts of my dissertation that has been completed in 2006. The domain of business informatics is considered as the core field of analysis. By building upon the view of *semantic information systems*, a basis is formed for developing both a conceptual and technical framework for visualisation in IT-based management. The results presented in the following represent the state of discussion at the end of the year 2006. Despite this limitation it can be stated that the findings are still applicable and the analyses well characterise the state-of-the-art.

The central propositions in this book have been reviewed and published at international conferences in the context of business informatics, visualisation, and computer science. Also, in the areas of legal informatics and legal visualisation particular interest could be drawn. At the ongoing annual meetings of the Munich Legal Visualisation Convention (Münchener Tagung zur Rechtsvisualisierung) and the session on legal visualisation at the IRIS conference some fruitful and inspiring discussions on the approach of semantic visualisation have been raised in the last years.

The future of the visualisation in business informatics is seen in a combination of both a very focused view on the use of semantic visualisation for specific domain-dependent issues as well as an open-minded approach towards new and innovative concepts of visualisations. This open-mindedness encompasses conceptual and technical views on visualisation. Recent developments start to take this into account and several big players of the IT industry begin to provide corresponding solutions. Examples include aproaches such as IBM Many Eyes, Google SketchUp or the XAML and XUL specifications. Similar to the developement of standards for the interoperability of IT systems it is envisaged that visualisation functionalities will require a common conceptual and technical basis to gain momentum on a larger scale. The approach described in the following is seen as a first step in this direction.

The work on this book has been conducted during my employment at the Institute of Knowledge and Business Engineering of the University of Vienna. During the research for this book several people have supported me in my work with discussions, helpful advice and valuable feedback on the topic.

First of all, I want to thank the supervisor of my dissertation Prof. Dr. Dimitris Karagiannis for his continuous support and inspiring discussions on the topic of visualisation as well as for the possibility to participate in international conferences and projects for presenting the first conceptions of the approach and receiving professional feedback. Furthermore, from my work at the University of Vienna which has been conducted under his guidance I could gain both theorectical and practical experiences in business informatics that have been fundamental to the development of this book.

Secondly, I want to thank Prof. Dr. Erich Schikuta for being the co-promoter of my dissertation and for his support and very valuable feedback during the doctorate programme.

A special thanks goes to Prof. Dr. Friedrich Lachmayer for his advice on the topic of visualisation and semiotics and the fruitful discussions.

Finally, I want to thank all colleagues from the Institute of Knowledge and Business Engineering at the University of Vienna as well as the management team of BOC for the great discussions in the context of visualisation throughout the last few years.

Hans-Georg Fill

Contents

List of Figures

List of Tables

1 Introduction

When starting to perform scientific research on the role of visualisation in regard to semantic information systems it seems at first necessary to describe the intention and context of this undertaking. This includes not only the positioning of the topic itself but also the consideration of the level of scientific research.

The overall goals of scientific work stem to a great extent from philosophical considerations which provide the fundament for every level of scientic work [Pos04]. More specifically this concerns the procedures and applied methods for investigating a topic, which sources of knowledge are taken into consideration and how these factors are influenced by the scientific community. Every branch of science has a slightly different view on these aspects and the methods how scientific work is performed greatly differ from purely mental thinking to actual physical implementations. The central goals that can be found in many scientific fields are however the *classification* of the work in relation to already existing findings, the definition of the *applied methods* and the provision of exact *references* to allow for the comprehension, reproduction, and inspection by other researchers.

Therefore, a classification of the types of research that can be undertaken is necessary to primarily explain the choice of methods. Three areas have been identified as a basis for this classification:

- Fundamental or Basic Research
- Applied Research
- Visionary Research

The goal of *fundamental research* is to build theories about the core relationships of a research area independent of any specific requirements. The theories can either be based on empirical observations or on *ideas* that cannot be directly related to an empirically observable fact but that originate in the mind of the researcher in the course of his interaction with the world. The results of this type of research are in general not directly applicable to practical problems but are rather investigations of fundamental principles.

In *applied research* the insights gained in fundamental research are applied to questions arising in practical scenarios. The input from practice is required for the successful application. The goal is to solve problems arising in practice with the help of scientific methods and by developing specifically shaped methods for a concrete task. Unlike fundamental research applied research is only concerned with fundamental principles of a science to the level it requires to solve a practical problem.

The third area is here denoted as *visionary research*. By this term the research on practical applications is encompassed that is not directly related to a current practical scenario as applied research but on a visionary scenario of the researcher. In relation to the previously two areas visionary research is regarded as the most creative but at the same also the least well founded form of research. It makes assumptions about the world in the near and far future and descibes scenarios under these assumptions. Its goal is primarily seen in the widening of the point of view of other researchers that may have been narrowed in the course of basic and applied research.

According to this classification the following work is positioned in the area of fundamental research of business informatics. To show the possibility for a concrete application a practical scenario is also included. The core parts of this work have been reviewed by the international scientific community in the following publications:

- Fill, H.-G., Karagiannis, D. (2006): Semantic Visualisation for Business Process Models, in: Proceedings of the Twelth International Conference on Distributed Multimedia Systems - International Workshop on Visual Languages and Computing 2006, Knowledge Systems Institute, Grand Canyon, USA, 168–173 [Fil06b].
- Fill, Hans-Georg (2006): Semantic Visualization of Heterogenous Knowledge Sources, in: Hinkelmann, K., Reimer, U. (2006): Modellierung für Wissensmanagement - Workshop im Rahmen der Modellierung 2006, Sonderdrucke der Fachhochschule Nordwestschweiz 2006-W01, 17–27 [Fil06a].
- Fill, H.-G., Höfferer, P. (2006): Visual Enhancements of Enterprise Models, in: Lehner, F., Nösekabel, H., Kleinschmidt, P. (2006): Multikonferenz Wirtschaftsinformatik 2006, GITO-Verlag, 541–550 [FH06].
- Fill, H.-G. (2005): UML Statechart Diagrams on the ADONIS Metamodeling Platform, Proceedings of the International Workshop on Graph-Based Tools (GraBaTs 2004), Electronic Notes in Theoretical Computer Science, Vol.127(1), Elsevier, 27–36 [Fil04].

With these fundamental descriptions semantic information systems and business informatics as the science that studies these systems can now be regarded in more detail. After this positioning of the work in regard to the scientific fields the motivation for the research on visualisation will then be elaborated in the following.

1.1 Semantic Information Systems and Visualisation

The term *semantic information system* as it will be used in the context of this work describes a system that is built upon information technology for the purpose of a business task. More precisely an information system can be defined as "a set of interrelated components that collect (or retrieve), process, store, and distribute information to support decision making and control in an organisation" [LL96](p.9). Information systems are therefore used for analysing problems, visualising complex subjects, and creating new products [LL96]. This view positions information systems in an organisational context where not only the pure technical realisation is required as it is addressed in computer science but where also the requirements and dependencies of an application domain have to be considered.

The addition of the term *semantic* signifies that the system is able to take into account the meaning of the information being processed. Therefore it can for example differentiate between human resource, financial, and logistical information. This is in contrast to other types of information systems that are only concerned with the processing of information independent of its meaning as e.g. a spreadsheet application that is able to perform certain arithmetic operations on data or a database application which provides certain types of reports created from user-defined queries on a given set of data. Although the support of decision making and control in an organisation can also be successfully realised by non-semantic information systems the inclusion of semantics can be regarded as a further attempt to ease the interaction with the large amounts of information that occur in today's business operations.

In particular this influences not only the way how these systems have to be designed but also their implementation and running. The first approaches for realising information systems that take into account semantics can be found in the area of artificial intelligence where several types of expert systems have been conceived that allow for the processing of semantic information (cf. [RN04, KT01]). However, these approaches are only one direction of how semantics can be dealt with. Other examples include the approaches for defining common semantic schemata that are used as references for information systems in an enterprise (cf. [Fox92, BKM01]) as well as the concepts developed in the area of conceptual and meta modelling that focus to a large extent on the human interaction for the purpose of communication and understanding (cf. [Myl92, Str98, KK02]).

The role of visualisations in the area of semantic information systems is manifold: As will be shown in the subsequent parts of this work – in particular in chapter 3 on page 39 – several types of visualisations can be found that are related to the aspects of semantic information systems. To clarify the general relation be-

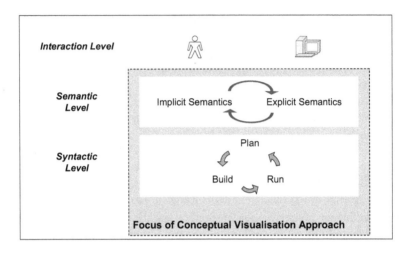

Figure 1.1: Visualisation and Semantic Information Systems

tween visualisations and semantic information systems a structural concept will be presented in the following (see figure 1.1).

Derived from the general differentiation between a *world perspective* and a *system perspective* of an information system [Jar92b] three areas are introduced for discussing the aspect of visualisation in semantic information systems (see figure 1.1): These are denoted as the *Interaction Level*, the *Semantic Level*, and the *Syntactic Level*. The Interaction Level stands for aspects of the world perspective and requirements that have to be met to allow for an interaction with entities external to the system. These entities may comprise human actors working with the information system as well as other information systems – this is depicted by the two symbols in figure 1.1. The Semantic Level acts as the mediator between the interaction and the Syntactic Level. It addresses the different properties of the Syntactic level as well as the requirements and constraints imposed by the interaction level.

A further distinction is therefore made between *explicit* and *implicit* semantics. By implicit semantics it is denoted that the meaning of terms and concepts is not available in a machine processable schema but is rather specified informally. In contrast, explicit semantics denotes the existence of one or several formally defined schemata. The degree of formality of this schema is nevertheless not predetermined by this classification. Depending on the requirements of the interaction level and the aspects of the underlying system it may span from schemas that are oriented towards syntactic structuring as it is e.g. valid for bare XML schemas [FW04] to schemas that include sets of formal axioms allowing for deductive and reasoning capabilities [FG97, W3C04, AL04]. This directly corresponds to the amount of semantic expressiveness that can be achieved through the usage of these schemas: Whereas schemas that do not include any pre-defined axioms only permit the "looking-up" of answers explicitly represented by the schema – in the sense of an SQL query of a database – axiom-enriched schemata allow for the application of reasoning mechanisms which are built upon these axioms for constraining the interpretation and well formed use of the terms, e.g. for specifying inheritance relationships [FG97, GGKZ85].

When regarding the properties of the Syntactic Level these can be detailed by reverting to a framework from the area of IT management (cf. [ZB03, ZB04] cit. [Mol94]) that differentiates between the *plan*, the *build* and the *run* aspects of an information system. As the plan and build aspects will be discussed in more detail in chapter 3 on page 39 they will only be shortly characterised in the following. On the other hand the run aspects which are partly taken up in section 3.3 on page 156 will be more concretely explained below.

With the *plan aspects* a holistic, business oriented view on the use of information systems is taken. This includes the use of different types of analyses and modelling methods[1]. Typical examples are the various enterprise modelling languages as will be outlined in section 2.3 on page 31 and in section 3.3 on page 111 that act as the mediators between the requirements of the interaction level and the technical infrastructure. It has to be remarked that the view on the planning of information systems is broader than the design level mentioned in other elaborations (cf. [LL96]): Not only the logical and physical aspects that are immediately relevant for the implementation of an information system (e.g. concerning the available infrastructure and technologies) are considered but also the organisational factors accompanying the information system. This concerns especially the IT-based approaches in strategic and business process management (see section 3.3 on page 111) where an information system such as a process modelling tool is not primarily oriented towards a technical implementation but rather on the representation of domain specific knowledge.

The *build aspect* of information systems addresses the technological implementation of the plan aspects. Technical opportunities and constraints have to be balanced with the design requirements in order to optimally meet the intended use of the system. The focus on is therefore put on the actual creation of an information system respectively its configuration and adaptation – also see section 3.2

---

[1] Also see section 4.2 on page 164 for a further discussion.

on page 64. To achieve consistency between the design aspects and the implementation not only syntactical and notational issues have to be aligned but also the semantics of the terms and entities that interface the two aspects. The discussion in the scientific community in this regard is currently centered around the orchestration and choreography of *services* as independently developed and operated applications that may be interconnected with one another using standardised protocols and languages [DSW06]. Especially the alignment between domain conceptualisations such as business process models and their IT based execution has been discussed for quite some time in the area of business process and workflow management [Jab95, Sch96, Jun01]. Through the integration of service based approaches and the upcoming of internet technologies these aspects have recently gained new importance [KZA06, TP06]. The current achievements are marked by the availability of standards such as the Business Process Execution Language for Web Services (BPEL4WS) [JMS04] and the XML Process Definition Language (XPDL) [Coa05] for specifying the execution flow of services and the corresponding modelling languages such as BPMN [BPM04].

With the *run aspects* of information systems the actual deployment of technology is taken into consideration. This includes the accompanying technical and organisational issues such as the provision of appropriate IT infrastructure, i.e. the actual hardware for running the services, and the aspects of managing the infrastructure. Again, the semantic consistency is required in relation to the other aspects: For the execution of the services and applications it is essential to respect the requirements that each service demands in terms of technical properties (e.g. the type of operating system, the needed interfaces to networks and other applications, the required security level etc.) as well as in terms of usage oriented aspects such as the preservation of service level agreements and the associated organisational measures. The field that is concerned with run aspects is therefore – as the fields above – of considerable size and complexity. For this purpose a range of frameworks is currently discussed. The most prominent ones in this area are at present the IT Infrastructure Library (ITIL)[2] [oGCO] and the Control Objectives for Information and related Technology (COBIT)[3] [Ins05, Ins00] frameworks. Whereas ITIL consists of a set of best practice process descriptions for IT Service Management, COBIT aims to "meet the multiple needs of management by bridging the gaps between business risks, control needs and technical issues" [Ins00](p.5).

The emphasis of the risk and control aspect in COBIT has its roots in its historic evolution: The increased legal obligations for enterprises – especially in

---

[2]ITIL is a Registered Trade Mark, and a Registered Community Trade Mark of the Office of Government Commerce, and is registered in the U.S. Patent and Trademark Office.

[3]COBIT is a registered trademark of the IT Governance Institute.

the United States – to comply to financial reporting demands for risk assessment (cf. [FB05, oC02]) have also influenced the view on the execution of IT based enterprise functions. As a considerable amount of the internal control structures and procedures in large enterprises is today represented by information systems their correct functioning is essential for ensuring the running of the whole business. Therefore, not only the mere 'running' of the information systems but also the compliance to service level agreements and risk control obligations is of high importance today on this level. Approaches for the semantic description of these aspects can be found in the area of IT architecture and IT service management modelling (cf. [BKM04, MB05]).

Based on this structural concept it can now be investigated what kinds of approaches can be found and how they influence the conceptions of visualisations. Most information systems can be classified in regard to their exposure and treatment of semantic issues in the following four major approaches: *Traditional, Data-based Modelling, Meta Model*, and *Integrated Approaches*.

Traditional Approaches

The characteristic of *traditional approaches* is that they are not based on explicit semantics as stated above. This leads to a problem that has been described as the *correspondence problem* (cf. [FG97] p.2): Although several terms refer to the same concepts they are denoted differently. Nevertheless they may be built according to a common model for defining the systems' properties and functionalities. However, this model is only implicit and may therefore lead to inconsistent interpretations and uses. On the interaction level the description of the system is oriented towards human usage, e.g. in the form of natural language in a documentation for describing its use.

Despite the many pitfalls that this approach may have it is still in use in some areas. This applies in particular to large legacy information systems where the costs for a re-implementation exceed the benefits that would arise from the availability of an explicit semantic schema. Nevertheless the required alignment to new technologies such as web-based functionalities often necessitates a migration of these systems [SS03]: The challenge that has to be faced in this case is to investigate the implicit semantics of the functions of the system.

Data-Based Modelling Approaches

In contrast to traditional approaches the case of *data-based modelling approaches* can be identified. The idea behind this type is to provide a common explicit semantics that can be be used as reference by all involved information systems. The problem that occurs in this approach is that the creation and maintenance of a common semantic schema for the whole enterprise is a costly and cumbersome undertaking: Not only the choice which concepts are to be included in the schema but also their updating and quality assurance requires a lot of organisational as well as technical effort. The solutions that have been developed are therefore based on the provision of generic enterprise schemata: These are pre-defined semantic schemata that aim to cover classes of objects and relationships that are generic across certain types of enterprises or branches. Examples for such approaches include the generic enterprise model by Fox et al. [FG97, FG98] as well as several approaches for defining enterprise ontologies, e.g. [Fox92, Gor02, BKM01, Par06].

Fox et al. list six categories for which enterprise ontologies have been developed in the past: *Process and Activities*, *Resources and Inventory*, *Organisation Structure*, *Product Structure and Requirements*, *Quality*, and *Cost* [FG97](p.7). From this classification it can be derived that the use of a generic enterprise schema already presupposes the definition of its purpose of application. Even though very general schemata are available (cf. [Fox92, UKMZ98]) they might still lack specific characteristics required in a particular application scenario. Hence the main benefit of these approaches is regarded to lie in a *shared* standardisation of terms and their relationships that is useful for distinct solutions.

Overall seen the focus of of these approaches is mainly put on the aspects of data and data schemata. They are not oriented towards the end-users of an information system but rather towards specialists that have an in-depth knowledge both of the language of the schema as well as the large number of concepts contained in the schema. Especially the language of explicit semantic schemas that are used in these approaches sometimes requires extensive knowledge about formal mathematical relationships.

An example for an application of the Data-based Modelling Approaches can be found in the area of information systems interoperability. The goal is to enable the communication between different data schemata by using common ontological concepts. Park et al. [Par04] describe a number of semantic conflicts that can be resolved by their approach of using an ontology as a top-level reference: On the level of data these are data value, data representation, data-unit, and data precision conflicts and on the level of schemas they describe naming conflicts, schema-isomorphism conflicts, generalisation conflicts, aggregation conflicts and schematic discrepancies (see [Par04] for an in-depth discussion). As shown in figure 1.2 on page 10 by the mapping of several local to a federated schema (i.e. an ontology respectively parts of ontologies) these conflicts can be effectively resolved. For example the data-unit conflict that occurs when one local schema refers to *acres* for the *gross-size* of *CITY-SIZE* and another one refers to *square meter* for the *area* attribute of *COUNTY-AREA* can be resolved by mapping them to the semantic concept *Area* and its descendents. From this it follows that through the *total 1-1* relationship between the semantic concepts *Square Meter* and *Acre* the different data units can be transformed to each other. Furthermore the descendent relationship implies that the concepts are synonyms. Thereby also the inherent naming conflict is resolved.

Whereas the goal of data-based modelling approaches is to provide one common semantic schema the following approach goes a different way for defining explicit semantics for the aspects of information systems.

Meta Model Approaches

The *meta model approaches* have to be regarded from two pragmatic perspectives: On the one hand meta modelling as a *concept* and on the other hand meta modelling as a *technical* approach. With the first perspective it is expressed that the aim of these approaches is to provide a high level of abstraction of real world relationships for the purpose of a specific user based on semi-formal definitions. The result of this abstraction is an easier understanding and better manageability by domain experts. In contrast to the approaches described in the section of data-based modelling approaches it is not intended to provide a global semantic reference for all types of information systems but rather individually tailored solutions. This view is for example taken in the publications of [Küh04, KK02, TK04] as well as by the Unified Modelling Language (UML) [OMG04a]. In this regard the high level of abstraction does not imply that the created conceptions (i.e. the models) cannot be used as a basis for direct code generations or other deployments (e.g. the IT based calculation of performance indicators[4]). It rather concerns the way how the interaction with the user is established, e.g. in the form of symbolic visual languages as well as domain specific adaptations.

The second perspective of meta model approaches is the technical aspect: Several implementations have been described in the literature as well as by the Object Management Group (OMG) as an international standard organisation to realise the definition of modelling languages by meta models (cf. [Jab95, Kel05]) respectively hierarchies of meta models (cf. [OMG02, KK02, Str98]). The purpose of these undertakings is to define a common set of objects and relationships that can be re-used in several modelling languages. The semantic consistency between the separately derived modelling languages is thereby not a priori ensured.

---

[4] Also see section 3.3 on page 119 for further elaborations in the context of performance indicator models (see figure 3.53 on page 124).

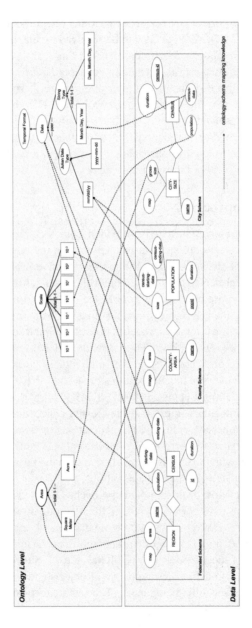

Figure 1.2: Data-Oriented ontological interoperability (redrawn and modified after [Par04])

What has not been considered with these two perspectives so far is the aspect of the semantic descriptions of meta models as well as their own semantic expressiveness. In contrast to ontologies the high level of abstraction for the purpose of simplicity that is inherent in the meta model approach does not allow for the same semantic expressiveness as a formally defined ontology in the data-based modelling approaches. Meta model approaches are therefore not based on formal semantics that would allow for direct inferences based on the exactly defined axioms. Instead they require particularly defined algorithms and mechanisms that can either be based on a specific meta model or the common meta meta model (also see section 4.2 on page 175) [KK02].

Examples for meta model approaches in regard to the Syntactic Level of information systems can be found for the plan, build and run aspects. The focus of meta model approaches towards the interaction with end-users – in the sense of non-experts of the creation, updating or modification of meta models – has led to a number of visualisation approaches based on meta models. This will therefore be taken up in chapter 3 on page 39.

Integrated Approaches

The last type that has been found are *integrated approaches*. Their characteristic is a combination of the properties of data-based modelling approaches and meta model approaches: Meta models are employed for several information systems and their aspects. Instead of describing them informally as in the meta model approaches a global formal description for example in the form of an ontology is used. Thereby the advantages of both approaches can be gained: The meta models can be highly abstract and do not need to be formally specified. By mapping the elements of the meta models to a formal description their semantics can be exactly described. Inference mechanisms working on these formal descriptions can thus also be applied to the meta models and in turn to the model instances. At the same time the benefits of the meta model approach can be preserved: Meta models can be based on meta meta models to allow for an easy creation as well as the re-use of generic mechanisms and algorithms. A "side effect" of this proceeding is that the effort for mappings between different meta models described by the formal descriptions can be reduced from $O(n^2)$ to $O(n)$ [KKK$^+$06].

Two examples for this approach can currently be found in the literature: The first has been described in the context of method engineering by Kühn [Küh04] and Karagiannis [KK02] and will be taken up again in section 4.2 on page 183. The second is referred to as meta model lifting [KKK$^+$06] and shall be shortly outlined in the following.

The approach by Kappel et al. reverts to a set of tool ontologies used to describe the meta models (i.e. the actual lifiting). These tool ontologies in turn are themselves related to a generic ontology from which also the mappings between the tool ontologies are derived. Through the alignment of the meta models to ontologies and the common generic ontology the semantic consistency between all participants can be ensured: A common terminology for the concepts in the different meta models is established so that relations between the different tools can be deduced. The example given by Kappel et al. [KKK+06] assumes that the concepts of a meta model of BPEL are mapped (resp. lifted) to the semantically appropriate classes of a generic workflow ontology. In parallel the elements of a UML activity diagram meta model are mapped to the workflow ontology as well. By employing structural reasoning it can thus be derived which elements in BPEL correspond to which elements in the UML activity diagram meta model. This derivation is denoted as *bridging* between meta models. It can be further extended to the level of models so that executable *transformations* between different meta models are generated.

Implications for the Conceptual Level of Visualisations

The four different approaches shown in the previous sections can now be analysed in regard to their particular implications for the conception of visualisations. For the traditional approaches visualisations are used without an alignment to a common semantics. This is either reflected by the use of a kind of drawing tool such as Microsoft PowerPoint, Microsoft Visio or Smartdraw. Although these kinds of tools may comprise large sets of visual elements for depicting various diagram types they are not aligned to an explicit, i.e. computer processable, semantic schema. A user creating visualisations may therefore deviate from the implicit semantics another user would apply to the same graphical representation. Furthermore, the creation of a visualisation corresponds only to a drawing that cannot be analysed or consistency-checked. Even though the lack of an explicit semantic schema constrains the use of visualisations in certain aspects it has to be remarked that it is nevertheless still used for many purposes. This concerns especially the plan and build phases of semantic information systems: When new systems are conceptualised there may not exist a referencable semantic schema at first. The first sketches may include notes on paper sheets or rough drawings in PowerPoint. To make use of this type of visualisations in the same way as the subsequent approaches with explicit semantics one solution would be the application of pattern based picture recognition algorithms to transform a set of graphical elements into machine processable visualisations. In section 4.2 on page 183 related scientific work from the area of visual languages will be outlined that partly addresses these challenges.

The second type of data-based modelling approaches provides a common semantic schema that can be referenced also by visualisations. Therefore visualisation applications contain mechanisms to associate the graphical representations with a machine processable schema. Examples for this approach will be shown e.g. in section 3.2 on page 106 with the visualisation of ontologies. Other examples would include different tools for modelling semantic schemata such as Kaon[5] or OntoStudio[6]. Although the availability of an organisation wide semantic schema allows for a semantically exact description many of the visualisations that can be found do not make full use of these opportunities: The visualisation of ontologies is for example often constrained to very uniform symbols that do not take into account the meaning of the concepts contained in the ontology. This would however greatly ease the user interaction with the information systems: A user could then directly perceive the meaning through a semantically coherent visualisation. Examples where this is successfully done – although without the consideration of an explicit semantic schema – can be found in the area of user interface design (see again section 3.2 on page 106).

The meta model approaches provide the opportunity to define explicit semantics for a specific domain or a particular aspect of a semantic information system. This influences the Conceptual Level of Visualisation in the way that a specific graphical representation may be used with different meanings according to the meta model that it refers to. From the viewpoint of visualisation this semantic adaptability corresponds to an individualisation of the graphical representations: Depending on the type of domain and even on the type of user interacting with the information system a specific visualisation can be defined. At the same time however also the semantic consistency and machine processability is ensured. This stands in contrast to the previously discussed approaches and is the basis for a large number of visualisation approaches that can be found in relation to semantic information systems. Nevertheless a certain drawback persists through this tailoring to specific domains or users: The exchange of information and therefore also of the visualisations between different meta model based applications still requires manual adaptations. As there does not exist a common semantic reference the visualisations of each domain have for example to be evaluated for their compatibility when being used together.

The aim of the integrated approaches presents a recent effort that claims to overcome this deficiency and thus provides new opportunities for the conception of vi-

---

[5]See http://kaon.semanticweb.org/ (accessed 15-10-2006)
[6]See http://www.ontoprise.de/

sualisations. Here, not only an explicit semantic schema is available as a reference but also the individually tailorable meta models for particular domains. This permits to conceive visualisations which are both adapted to specific requirements but satisfy at the same time the global constraints imposed by the commonly agreed semantics. So far, no proposals have been found on how visualisations have to be designed for using this type. The approach developed in this work will focus in particular on this aspect.

Apart from these very specific elaborations on semantic information systems a broader view can be taken on these relationships. This concerns in particular not only the technical but also the organisational issues that have to be taken into account when dealing with semantic information systems in concrete application scenarios. In the german speaking area a specific branch of science has evolved that studies these aspects both from a scientific/theoretical as well as a practical and implementation oriented view: This branch is denoted in this work as *business informatics*[7] and shall serve in the following for detailing the fields involved in the development and deployment of semantic information systems.

1.2 Business Informatics

The organisational environment of enterprises is today characterised by the economic factors of globalisation, increasing competition, and the availability of cheap and easily accessible information technology. In this context new strategies for enterprises have been formulated that have led in the past to a variety of innovative, IT based business models and rapidly changing business types (cf. [LW05]). Not all of these innovative approaches have been successful. More and more decision makers in business demand measures for assessing the efficiency of information technology and its contribution to a corporation's benefit[8].

With the availability of global markets and internet technologies the worldwide distribution of IT activities has therefore gained importance in the last years. The outsourcing of IT functions to other countries is a common practice for many enterprises today and spans countries around the globe [Mer05]. What results from these developments is a high complexity of the structure and processes performed in an enterprise. Whereas enterprises in the 'old economy' had a defined set of locations and only slowly changing business processes, enterprises of the 'new economy', as it is still often denoted, are faced with the challenge of quickly adapting to new environments, global competition and the worldwide exchange of informa-

---

[7] German equivalent: Wirtschaftsinformatik.
[8] See also the discussion in economics on this subject [DGK03].

tion and services. This complexity requires particular attention and is addressed by business informatics as an interface between the business requirements and the technical possibilities.

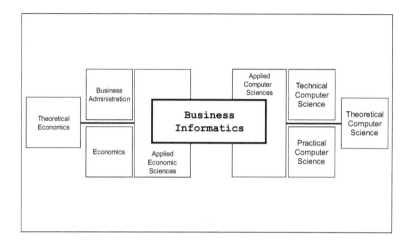

Figure 1.3: Classification of the Field Business Informatics

The upcoming of the research field of business informatics can be dated back to 1970-ies when the first study programmes for this subject were introduced. The main goal of business informatics as defined here is to provide an interface for the purely technically oriented field of computer science and the practically oriented parts of the economic sciences in particular the area of business administration and management. Both fields rely on theoretical foundations: The theoretical background of the economic sciences can be seen for example in formal-theoretical models that are leveraged for applications in business administration as well as in economic research.

The research field of business administration encompasses in this context areas such as production, logistics, finance, marketing, organisation or accounting or certain parts of sociology. The field of economics on the other side is more closely related to theories and formal models and aims to extend and empirically prove the therein proposed assumptions.

When investigating both fields further towards practical applications they meet in a sector that can be entitled as applied economic sciences. The main goal of this part is to prepare the theoretical developments for practical use. Typical subjects are the various types of management approaches (finance management, human resource management, marketing management, etc.), the foundations for business modelling (workflow modelling, business process modelling, supply chain modeling, etc.), or the provision of the economic basis for the evaluation of information systems.

The same considerations can be applied vice versa to computer science. Based on theoretical foundations including formal language theory, theories of automata and complexity theory, logic or formal semantics two practically oriented fields can be identified: Technical and practical computer science. These two topics deal with the technical realisation of circuits and architectures of computer systems (technical computer science) and the practical realisation of computer applications in the form of algorithms, data-structures etc.

Again a practically oriented field can be defined out of these two: Applied computer science. It investigates how the hardware- and software related insights can be transfered to concrete application scenarios. It includes subjects such as the provision of theoretically developed technologies for the deployment in concrete application scenarios (e.g. semantic web technologies and webservices, techniques from knowledge engineering and knowledge management etc.).

Business informatics lies in the middle of the two practically oriented fields of applied economic sciences and applied computer science. It brings together the two fields by acting as a broker and offering solutions from computer science to concrete scenarios in the practical economic sciences. This view is depcited in figure 1.3 where business informatics spans the blue part in the middle. In the following it will be discussed which particular role visualisation plays in business informatics.

1.3 Motivation for the Research in Visualisation

In today's businesses information technology is used on all management layers, ranging from applications for strategic management, business process management to the management of IT-architectures and -systems themselves. By *IT-based management approaches* a variety of management methods can be subsumed which are based on specific paradigms supported by information technology. An example would be IT-based performance management with the paradigm of the Balanced Scorecard by Kaplan and Norton [KN96]. Typically these methods make use of models as a way to represent fragments of reality by reducing complexity without altering the underlying facts. This enables users of these models to manage complex issues such as for example the analysis of cause effect relationships of strategic goals, the re-engineering of interconnected business processes and assigned organisational structures or the realisation and control of IT service level agreements.

To graphically represent these models and their properties and to ease the interaction with them *visualisation* plays a major role. For showing qualitative relationships most approaches make use of graph diagrams in line with different types of charts to show quantitative characteristics. The type of visualisation is often specifically adapted to the underlying models. To apply the visualisation to a concrete model in the way defined by the particular approach and to later understand the graphical models expert knowledge is required.

In the last years IT-based management approaches have been successfully used in many companies. The widespread deployment in practice has nevertheless shown some deficiencies of these concepts, especially from the viewpoint of visualisation, that need to be addressed by scientific research:

– Although it is one of the basic intentions of IT-based management approaches to reduce complexity by using models the graphical models themselves become very complex when practically applied. It is therefore of high importance not only to further develop and adapt the models but also to conduct research from the area of visualisation to make this complexity better manageable.

– The assignment of visual representations to the models is today a complex task that requires both design and domain knowledge as well as (in some case) programming skills. To support and facilitate this assignment would therefore greatly ease the design of new models.

– Not all visual representations of models are equally suited for different users or groups of users. The adaptation to these human diversities, preferably supported by information technology, would make the visualisations even more useful and easier perceivable by a larger community of users.

– And finally, the generation of visualisations is today often bound to specific software tools that require themselves particular knowledge. To abstract from these tools in a way that visualisations become uniformely accessible would make visualisations easier accessible and applicable.

In the following section the approach applied in this work for developing solutions to these open issues is outlined.

1.4 Chosen Approach

The approach taken in this work reflects the cognitive process that the author has undergone during the last three years focusing on the aspects of visualisation in the field of business informatics.

Several paths could be chosen for approaching the subject of visualisation in business informatics, from purely theoretical considerations, philosophical reflections to core technical discussions. The path that has been chosen for this work is grounded on a pragmatic approach. The reason for this decision is a result of the many aspects that have been discovered by the author in regard to visualisation and the notion that the field of business informatics is itself characterised as being highly pragmatic in the way that it strives for practically implementable and usable solutions. This does not in any way speak against the requirement for a sound theoretical foundation and the many advantages that stem thereof.

The work is therefore structured according to the following considerations: The introduction has outlined the field of business informatics and thereby defined the major fields that have to considered. Therefore, at first the scientific fields that are seen as related to visualisation in business informatics are shortly outlined and their relevance to this work is established to motivate and position the subsequent elaborations.

Subsequently a survey of existing visualisation approaches in the field of business informatics is elaborated to take into account the pragmatic aspect as remarked above: By reverting to a framework based analysis the fields of business, computer science, and business informatics are investigated for different types of visualisations that are used for the augmentation of human understanding, according to the working definition of visualisation as presented in the next section.

On the basis of this survey different approaches for the specification of visualisations are discussed to illustrate the current state of the art. To conclude the analysis, possible extensions for the investigated visualisations are given based on a theoretical derivation.

As a result of this analysis a framework for visualisation is presented which is the basis for the newly developed approach of *Semantic visualisation*.

Prior to the evaluation of the results of the work, a usage scenario for Semantic Visualisation is given as well as details on a prototypical implementation.

1.5 Definition of Terms

As will be shown in the subsequent chapters a number of different views on visualisation currently exist. So far, in the field of business informatics visualisation has not been specifically described, so that a definition for *business informatics visualisation* would exist, but it is rather integrated in many approaches as a supportive technique - these findings will be underpinned by the analysis of existing approaches of visualisations in chapter 3 on page 39ff. Therefore, when aiming to clarify the term *visualisation* one has to revert to a number of related scientific fields as laid out in chapter 2 on page 21ff.

From a scientific point of view it is nevertheless necessary to give a first "working definition" of the core terms that are used so that further elaborations can be carried out. As a consequence, visualisation in the field of business informatics within the scope of this work shall be defined as *"the use of graphical representations to amplify human cognition"*. This definition will be used as a hypothetical construct that shall be tested for compatibility and consistency against definitions and views that will be presented successively in the following.

In some sections of this work *formal* descriptions will be presented. To differentiate between formal, semi-formal and non-formal descriptions it is reverted to a definition given by Mosses in the context of programming languages: "Descriptions are called formal when written in a notation that already has a precise meaning." [Mos04](p.133). The "precise meaning" is thereby understood to comprise a precise structure and precise semantics. If only the structure of the used notation is precisely defined and the semantics has to be additionally specified the description is defined as *semi-formal*.

2 Related Fields

The term *visualisation* turns up in many research fields each of which has a slightly different understanding of what the term stands for. Based on the definition that is used in this work (as described on page 19) possible domains of visualisations range from *artistic* sciences and methods (e.g. design, aesthetics), over the art and science of manually, semi-automatically or automatically created *diagrams* (as e.g. apparent in descriptive and analytical geometry, visual languages, technical illustrations, and descriptive statistics), to the *technical* areas of knowledge, information, and scientific visualisation and computer graphics. Close to these main areas reside a variety of research fields that are not entirely focused on an idiosyncratic view of visualisation but provide additional methods, insights, and guidelines that influence and are influenced by the core domains. Among these would be *psychology* – especially in regard to the physiological and cognitive theories of visual perception – *sociology and semiotics* – with respect to different perceptions of visualisations due to cultural factors – and *mathematics* – regarding the provision of calculus apart from the geometry for different types of visualisation.

2.1 Applied Method

To narrow down this wide range of scientific fields concerned with visualisation and identify those fields that are of interest for the research in business informatics, a first approach has been taken by focusing on the role of information technology as a central concept. Thereby it is estimated to gain the insight necessary for relating the approach developed in this work to existing research results that make use of IT for creating visualisations. In figure 2.1 eight major areas are listed which have been selected based on a literature survey for visualisations in the libraries of the University of Vienna[1], the Technical University of Vienna[2], the IEEE[3] and ACM[4] online publications and the online archive of the German Wirtschaftsinfor-

---

[1] Online search via: http://aleph.univie.ac.at
[2] Online search via: http://aleph.tuwien.ac.at
[3] Online search via: http://ieeexplore.ieee.org/
[4] Online search via: http://portal.acm.org

matik journal[5]. The wide range of scientific fields that is covered by the University of Vienna as the largest university in the German speaking area is considered to be of particular importance to capture views on visualisation from different fields.

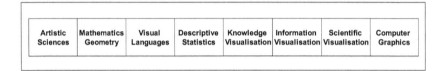

Artistic Sciences	Mathematics Geometry	Visual Languages	Descriptive Statistics	Knowledge Visualisation	Information Visualisation	Scientific Visualisation	Computer Graphics

Figure 2.1: Major Scientific Areas Dealing with Visualisation

Three functions of information technology in regard to visualisation have been looked at within these eight fields to estimate the influence of IT:

- IT as an *enabler* of scientific and practical advancement for visualisations in a field.
- IT as a *trigger* of new theories and *responsible factor* for a change of paradigms of visualisation.
- IT as a *supportive* technology for creating visualisations.

The *artistic sciences* have treated aspects of visualisations for a long time before information technology has occurred. From prehistoric cave paintings to current representations of industrial design IT has not changed the theories and paradigms of art significantly. Although some areas that also belong to artistic sciences make intensive use of IT (e.g. in computer aided design) the overwhelming influence of purely artistic concepts and techniques outshines the importance of IT in these areas. So, the main influence of IT here is as a supportive technology for producing visualisations. Nevertheless artistic sciences provide important insights into the composition of graphical representations, specifically in relation to aspects of human aesthetical perception. The concepts of the golden ratio or sectio divina and the application of colours for creating specific sentiments cf. [Itt00] evidently illustrate the potential of these fields for visualisations. Usually these aspects are not laid down in a computer processable way[6] and not particularly considered in other areas of visualisation.

In *mathematics and geometry* information technology plays an important role for the creation of visualisations today. Especially in descriptive geometry, as it is

---

[5]Online search via: http://www.wirtschaftsinformatik.de
[6]An approach in this direction is discussed in [Lie95]

used for technical[7] and architectural design[8], computer-based visualisations mark
an important and almost indispensable method for managing the inherent complexity. In these fields visualisations also constitute an important economic benefit, in
the way that virtual product models and simulations are less cost-intensive than
their real counterparts. Also, the understanding of the behaviour of mathematical formulae can be greatly enhanced by visualisations, some of which would be
very hard to construct manually: E.g. three dimensional representations of complex functions as shown in figure 2.2). Comprehensive software packages such
as the commercial toolkit Mathematica [WJ94] or the open source implementation Gnuplot [WK04] as well as a number of CAD tools provide today appropriate
functionality for the realisation of such visualisations.

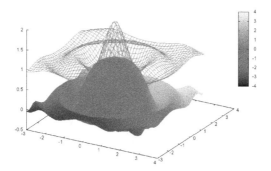

Figure 2.2: Visualisation of the Mathematical Function $f(z) = 1 + \frac{\sin\sqrt{16(x^2+y^2)}}{\sqrt{16(x^2+y^2)}}$ (generated
with Gnuplot)

The field of *visual languages* and especially the field of visual language theory as it presents itself today is strongly related to information technology (cf. the
publications of the IEEE visual language symposia in this regard [BG04, ES05]).
However, it has to be remarked that the term "visual language" is not exclusively
used by this community but also turns up in other contexts, e.g. in the field of
design [Bon99], that have to be taken into consideration as well. Although the
fundamental concepts of visual language theory claim to be universally applicable to every type of visual language, many publications in this community focus on visual languages that are closely related to representing concepts of information technology itself, such as for example the Universal Modelling Language

---

[7] Also denoted as mechnical CAD (MCAD).
[8] Also denoted as computer-aided architectural design (CAAD)

(UML) [OMG04a] or approaches in enterprise modelling (eg [Fra99, FH06]). It can thus be concluded that this scientific field is of major importance for visualisations in business informatics. It will therefore be looked at in more detail on page 33.

Although the formalisation and practical creation of diagrams is also a part of visual language theory (see [DFM93, Gur99] the area of *descriptive statistics* has been included in this listing as a distinct field due to its specific focus on diagrams and their importance in business environments. The use of statistical charts is a common method in many fields of business, spanning from operational functions to strategic management. Information technology has contributed a lot to this widespread use as it allows for an easy and fast creation of complex visual representations based on large data sets.

The areas of *knowledge visualisation*, *information visualisation* and *scientific visualisation* all have a strong focus on information technology [SGR05, RTW04, Bur04a] as their methods and techniques as used today depend largely on the availability of computers. Nevertheless also earlier approaches can be found that have been developed without the use of electronic data processing (cf. [Tuf83]). The basic definitions and contributions relevant for this work are discussed on pages 26ff. and 36ff. Also included in this field is the area of *geovisualisation* which can be classified as a sub-field of information visualisation which is not directly related to business informatics but also provides valuable insights for designing visualisations [MKN04].

The field of *computer graphics* provides the technical and theoretical basis for realising visualisations with information technology [HB97]. On the one hand computer graphics has developed theoretical concepts and algorithms and on the other hand there are several technologies and technical standards available today that ease the generation of graphics via IT. These include interfaces for programming languages to specialised software components, e.g. the APIs[9] for realising two and three dimensional graphics such as Java Swing and Java2D [LEW02], the OpenGL Utility Toolkit GLUT [SWND05] or the recently developed and not yet released Windows Presentation Foundation by Microsoft [Cor05]) as well as open accessible representation formats such as SVG (Scalable Vector Graphics) [FFJ03] for 2D graphics, X3D [Con05] for 3D and SMIL (Synchronised Multimedia Language) [BGJ+05] for integrating different media formats and authoring of interactive audiovisual presentations.

Other related technologies which shall be included in the field of computer graphics would be the standards of the MPEG (Moving Picture Experts Group)

---

[9]Application Programming Interface

which is concerned with the "standardisation of all technologies that are required for interoperable multimedia" (MPEG Homepage[10]), with the latest developments in MPEG-7 [MKP02] and MPEG-21 [BdWH+03]. Although they include approaches for semantic specifications of digital resources – as described by the metadata framework in MPEG-7 – they mainly focus on multimedia compositions.

Included in computer graphics are also aspects of virtual reality techniques used in several areas and branches of science and industry, e.g. in scientific and information visualisation [RBdBT94, Bry96, Che99], manufacturing [CB01] or life sciences [SAKW02].

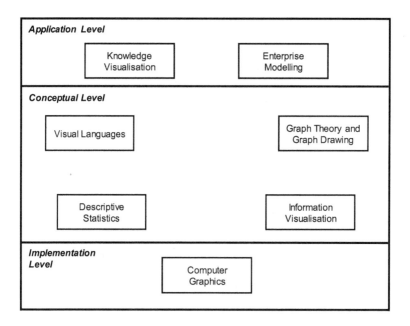

Figure 2.3: Overview of the Fields related to this Work

Not all of the above mentioned areas have a direct relation to the concept that is developed in this work. Therefore a specifically shaped selection of fields has been elaborated which is derived from the main areas. It focuses on the specific relations in which the concepts of visualisation in business informatics and the approach of this work – see chapter 5 on page 223 – are embedded (see figure 2.3).

---

[10]http://www.chiariglione.org/mpeg/technologies/

The areas have been classified into the three categories *Application Level, Conceptual Level*, and *Implementation Level*.

On the application level the areas of *Knowledge Visualisation* and *Enterprise Modelling* are positioned. In the selection of the core areas Enterprise Modelling has not been chosen as a distinct field but has been implicitly included in the general field of Visual Languages in regard to its visualisation aspects. From the viewpoint of business informatics the methods and techniques as circumscribed by Enterprise Modelling are of high importance for today's business applications. Nevertheless the field of *Visual Languages* is still included as the basis for formal definitions of visualisations. Another field that has previously not been presented is *Graph Theory and Graph Drawing*. Graph Theory is usually assigned to the field of mathematics, aspects of Graph Drawing often occur in relation to information visualisation. The reason for pointing out this field is on the one hand its relevance for enterprise modelling where a considerable amount of methods revert to graphs and the underlying theories and on the other hand the description of layout algorithms as they have been developed in the area of graph drawing that are required for the arrangement of graphical objects. The remaining fields have been directly taken over from the core fields, whereas scientific visualisation has been left out as it is largely focused on physics based data (see also the definitions in table 2.7 on page 37).

2.2 Knowledge Visualisation

The field of *knowledge visualisation* is a comparatively new research area which has evolved from information visualisation. It "..examines the use of visual representations to improve the transfer of knowledge between at least two persons or a group of persons" [Bur04a]. In the last years a range of publications have been issued that build on this definition [Bur04a, Bur04b, Epp04, Epp03]. Also included in knowledge visualisation are the approaches for creating the various types of knowledge maps [Noh00].

When regarding the definition of knowledge visualisation in more detail it becomes apparent that it does not further specify the term *knowledge*. For the relation to the approach developed in this work (see chapter 5) it is however necessary to further specify what is understood by knowledge and which technical concepts are required for the expression and processing of knowledge.

Without going into a detailed philosophical discussion of the origins of knowledge it can be reverted to the area of knowledge management as the scientific field that is concerned with the generation and acquisition, the identification and transparency, and the distribution and usage of knowledge [Noh00]. In knowledge management two major directions can be identified: On the one hand *organisational* approaches and on the other hand *technical* approaches. The organisational approaches generally take the view that knowledge is something that persists in the minds of people and requires human oriented measures for its management, e.g. by encouraging employees to share their knowledge so that they can engage in learning from each other. The technical approaches take the view that knowledge can to a certain degree be expressed by representation formalisms which can in turn be implemented as computer systems.

The view on knowledge visualisation as used in this work is concerned with the technical approaches for managing knowledge, i.e. how visualisations can be used to express knowledge in visual form. It is further distinguished between knowledge that cannot be transfered to a visual format (implicit knowledge) and knowledge that can be handled in this way (explicit knowledge). This view is distinguished from an organisational view on knowledge visualisation where for example a visual representation may increase the motivation of employees and thereby improve the transfer of knowledge.

Directly related to knowledge visualisation as it is understood in this work is the concept of the Semantic Web and in particular the role of ontologies. These concepts are regarded as the main factors today in the area of the technical representation of knowledge and the corresponding machine processing. The approach for Semantic Visualisations developed in in chapter 5.2ff. will follow a similar structure as Semantic Web. Therefore an overview of these topics is given in the following.

Relation to Semantic Web

The vision of a *Semantic Web* [BLHL01] and the technologies and standards that have been developed for its realisation are largely based on approaches from artificial intelligence and especially the area of decription logics (cf. [SS04, BHS04]). The theories which have been elaborated in these fields are used for the enabling of machines to process information on a semantic level and conduct inferences from this semantic information. Although artificial intelligence once had the goal of designing machines that can act in the same way as humans this view is not taken up any more today (cf. [KT01] p.24). The current development of AI technologies is rather directed towards narrowly focused applications such as expert systems and information retrieval [KT01].

The origin of Semantic Web is seen in the need to make the vast amounts of information available on the world wide web today better accessible and usable.

The handling of the information shall thereby primarily be performed by machines but with the goal of improving the support of the information needs of humans. This view is reflected by the basic article by Berners-Lee et al. [BLHL01] who defines the Semantic Web as "(..)not a separate Web but an extension of the current one, in which information is given welldefined meaning, better enabling computers and people to work in cooperation." [BLHL01](p.2).

Although the scientific concepts that are inherent in Semantic Web have been developed much longer before the internet in its current form has come to life it can be regarded as the first attempt to internationally align and standardise the often very heterogenous approaches for knowledge representation techniques. Therefore its main contribution is not seen in the invention of semantic annotations, thesauri or ontologies but as a way to align the various efforts for these functionalities just as the world-wide-web has been for presenting information. The goal of Semantic Web is not – as may be assumed due to its roots in AI – to make the computer fully understand all information but to "manipulate the terms much more effectively in ways that are useful and meaningful to the human user." [BLHL01](p.4)

For this purpose information resources that adhere to the Semantic Web approach have to be built upon a common syntax basis for describing the syntax of the information itself and the semantic annotations (metadata) for the information. Currently several international standards exist that enable this proceeding: Unicode [AAB+03] as the common international set for signs, URI[11] to uniquely reference resources, XML[12] [BPSM+04] for the syntax and RDF[13] [BM04a], RDFS[14] [Bri04] and OWL[15] [MH05] for the semantics.

The *Unicode* standard is a universal character encoding scheme which treats alphabetic characters, ideographic characters, and symbols equivalently [AAB+03]. In its current version it contains more than 96.000 characters (with the major part of approx. 70.000 symbols from the unified Han subset for East Asian sign languages such as in Chinese and Japanese). Unicode does not specify the representation of the signs (glyphs[16]) but only deals with character codes. The glyphs are specified by fonts which can vary in their graphical attributes (e.g. by shape, colour, size etc.).

---

[11]URI: Unique Resource Identifier

[12]XML: Extensible Markup Language

[13]RDF: Resource Description Framework

[14]RDFS: RDF Schema

[15]OWL: Web Ontology Language

[16]Unicode makes a distinction between characters and glyphs: *Characters* "are the abstract representations of the smallest components of written language that have semantic value" [AAB+03](p.15) whereas *Glyphs* "represent the shapes that characters can have when they are rendered or displayed" [AAB+03](p.15).

Unique Resource Identifiers (URI) are compact sequences of characters that are used to identify an abstract or a physical resource [BLFM05]. URIs have a distinct syntax that has evolved from previous standards for addressing resources on the world wide web. The resources that may be referenced by URIs can be information resources (e.g. documents, images, services or web pages) as well as physical objects (e.g. human beings or corporations).

The *eXtended Markup Language* (XML) is a subset of the more general ISO[17] standard 8879:1986 for a Standard Generalized Markup Language (SGML). XML is formally specified by production rules [18] which are built upon the Unicode standard. Markup languages belong to the family of meta-languages, i.e. languages that can be used to specify other languages. They contain markup, which encodes the description of the document's storage layout and logical structure, and character data, i.e. the actual information of a document. By specifying the meta-structure of a document in XML, constraints on the storage layout and the logical structure can be imposed [BPSM+04]. XML therefore represents the syntax layer in the Semantic Web Stack. The structure of an XML document is defined via a Document Type Definition or an XML Schema [FW04]. An XML schema and the containing elements are in turn identified by URIs.

To extend the syntactic descriptions semantics can be added. The standards that are used for this purpose in the context of Semantic Web are RDF, RDFS and OWL. By RDF basic semantic relationships between resources (identified by URIs) can be expressed. The so-called *RDF triples* consist of a subject, a predicate and an object. Predicates define the relationships between an object and a subject node. As the core RDF vocabulary is however restricted to describing resources in this way (e.g. by their description, author, content) the vocabulary can be defined by the according RDF schema (RDFS). An RDF schema defines classes, properties and additional elements (e.g. lists, bags and collections). With the properties of RDFS the relationships between classes can be further detailed. This concerns the definition of ranges of property values and type definitions as well as sub class relationships. The resulting schema can be instantiated to a concrete resource description. Thereby for example the syntactic elements of an XML schema (as being URI described resources) can be semantically described.

The Web Ontology Language (OWL) extends RDFS and provides additional mechanisms for defining the relationships between resources. This includes additional relations between classes (e.g. disjointness), cardinalities for relations, equality definitions between classes or enumerated classes. OWL has three sub-languages with increasing expressiveness: OWL Lite, OWL DL, and OWL Full.

---

[17] See http://www.iso.org

[18] See http://www.w3.org/TR/2004/REC-xml-20040204/#NT-document (accessed 03-01-2006)

As one of the main concepts of Semantic Web is to enable machines to perform automated reasoning tasks the conception of OWL is mainly directed towards this possibility. Therefore the semantics of OWL itself are formally defined and several software applications are available that implement reasoners on these semantics[19].

Both with RDFS and OWL *ontologies* can be created. An ontology in the context of computer science "..defines the basic terms and relations comprising the vocabulary of a topic area as well as the rules for combining terms and relations to define extensions to the vocabulary" [NFF+91](p.40). An even more and today widely cited definition of ontologies regards them as "explicit specification(s) of a conceptualisation" [Gru93](p.2). A conceptualisation in this definition is seen as an "abstract simplified view of the world that we wish to represent" [Gru93](p.2). With this definition ontologies are leveraged from a purely vocabulary oriented view to a type of domain model. This aspect will be particulary discussed in section 4.2 on page 164 and also in the context of the visualisation framework (section 5 on page 223).

Ontologies can be classified according to their purpose as: *Top-level Ontologies* describing very general concepts independent of a specific domain or task, *Domain Ontologies* describing the basic vocabulary of a generic domain and specialise the concepts of a Top-Level ontology, *Task Ontologies* describing the fundamental terms of a concrete activity or task, and *Application Ontologies* that are descriptions for a specific domain or task and that further specialise a domain or task ontology.

Furthermore Obrst introduced an approach to distinguish ontologies on the basis of their expressiveness, from weak to strong semantics [Obr03] (see figure 2.4 on the next page). His approach implies that the possibility for conducting reasoning is not a necessary requirement for an ontology. The approach for the functionalities of Semantic Visualisation and in particular Ontological Visualisation Patterns is based on a similar view in the way that ontologies are regarded as a semantic reference schema without the explicit need of conducting inferences (see section 5.3 on page 245).

For the purposes of this work it is further distinguished according to the availability of ontologies: *General ontologies* are ontologies that can be accessed by everyone on the internet (commercially or non-commercially) and *Individual ontologies* are ontologies that are only available to a restricted user or group of users. This may also include large user groups such as an enterprise or a specific branch.

The top layers of the Semantic Web Stack finally represent the aspects of reasoning by *Logic*, the concrete application for deriving *proofs* and the resulting *trust* in

---

[19]E.g. Racer (See http://www.sts.tu-harburg.de/~r.f.moeller/racer/) or Fact++ (See http://owl.man.ac. uk/factplusplus/ last accessed 21-06-2006)

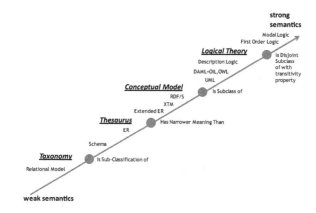

Figure 2.4: Ontology Spectrum by Obrst (Redrawn after: [Obr03])

the thus generated conclusions. Apart from Logic the top layers of Semantic Web are however not yet available in the form of standards.

The technologies used on the bottom layer of Semantic Web (Unicode, URI, XML) have also been used to realise concepts of service oriented architectures as will be discussed in sections 4.3 and 6.4 on page 287. More specifically, the three main standards for web services SOAP [Mit03], WSDL [CCMW01], and UDDI [CHRR04]) also build upon these base technologies. This common basis also allows to create semantically defined services [BFM02] which are however so far not officially standardised[20].

2.3 Enterprise Modelling

In today's companies large amounts of information are processed and have to be successfullay managed. This concerns the core operative levels in the same way as strategic levels. Still very often this information is not made explicit but persists in the head of the people executing the various activities in an enterprise. From the viewpoint of knowledge management this would be termed as tacit procedural knowledge [Dal05](p. 82). To be effective it is necessary for the management and the workforce of an enterprise to be able to access and transfer the knowledge how the business processes are performed, how they relate to strategic

---

[20]For the current developments see the web site of the Semantic Web Services Interest Group http: //www.w3.org/2002/ws/swsig/

objectives and what kinds of technology are required for their successful accomplishment [JOO01, Fra99]. This allows for a qualitative analysis of the causes and effects that influence the performance of the business.

One of the key success factors in this regard is the provision of appropriate methods to represent this knowledge to allow for its documentation respectively its externalisation [NT95]. By *enterprise modelling* a range of IT-based management approaches are understood here to represent this organisational knowledge in the form of (graphical) models that are based either on a user-defined or standardised schema (cf. [Fra99]). Included in this definition would be models of cause-effect relationships of strategic goals as used in balanced scorecards [LKK02, Wef00], business process and workflow models [Cor01, Jun00b, KNS92] as well as models of IT services and their implementation [OMG04a, BKM04]. They span from strategic to operational issues of an enterprise and abstract from the real world in varying degrees.

The unification of a *human and a technically oriented* view on enterprise models is regarded as an essential characteristic of the field of business informatics: The models used in enterprise modelling are therefore directed towards an IT implementation. This requires the formal or semi-formal definition of the applied modelling method, the according modelling languages and the representation of the models (see also figure 4.5 on page 175). Enterprise models as a basis for the design of information systems have therefore also been compared to the plans of architects for designing and constructing of buildings [Zac87] (see section 3.3 on page 113). The view taken here is however particularly focussed on the knowledge representation aspect of enterprise modelling.

For the creation of enterprise models it can be reverted to a variety of standards: These concern either the *content* of the models, e.g. as available by the IT Infrastructure Library (ITIL)[21] and the Supply-Chain Operations Reference model (SCOR) [SCC05] or the *meta approaches* for defining models. The standards for meta approaches to specify enterprise models can again be divided into *syntactic standards* such as the Meta Object Facility [OMG02] or UML [OMG04a] and *semantic standards* such as the Business Process Modelling Notation [BPM04]. Whereas the standards for the contents prescribe how a particular aspect that is represented by a model has to be implemented also in the real world, the standards for the meta approaches either only provide the syntactic structure for defining models – also denoted as the meta meta level see figure 4.16 on page 198 – or a basic semantic meta structure which is equivalently denoted as a meta model.

---

[21] See http://www.itil.org/

An essential characteristic of many approaches in enterprise modelling is the visualisation of the elements and relations. It enables users to easily understand a model and to interact with it as well as it supports the knowledge transfer between individuals.

The survey of existing visualisation approaches in chapter 3 and in particular the visualisations in section 3.3 on page 111 show the currently used types of representations for this purpose.

2.4 Visual Languages

The discussion of *visual languages* in the scientific literature can be divided into a *formal* and an *artistic* view on this field. The formal view on visual languages is concerned with the exact, mathematical definition of visual representations [Haa95, Erw98]. This includes the formal definition of syntactic and semantic relationships between visual elements based on the requirements of a specific application domain (cf. [MM98, NH98]) as well as the application of these definitions to a concrete task. Although publications in the field of visual language theory position visual languages in specific application domains [NH98] the majority of approaches found in this field do not explicitly differentiate between the aspects of the application domain and the applied visual language but rather integrate both views in one theory. This will become apparent especially by the discussion of meta approaches for specifying visualisations in section 4.2 on page 179.

The second view on visual languages is in the sense of a *means of communication* in the area of applied arts and design [Bon99, Sta94]. Here the focus is not on the mathematical definition of a visual representation but rather on the informative, emotional, and cultural effects that are expressed by a visualisation and its graphical attributes (e.g. by the use of colour [Itt00]). At first sight it might seem inappropriate to mention artistic aspects in a work that is directed towards semantic information systems and business informatics. However, it can be stated that the visualisations in the area of information systems have so far mostly not been regarded from this viewpoint. Although visual language theory for example addresses the semantics of visual languages this is only done up to a formal theoretical level that does not take into cultural or emotional implications. This is seen as a major shortcoming of these approaches as especially in a business setting not only the technical exactness but also the consideration of the contextual embedding play an important role.

Research on such aspects is done in the field of *semiotics* (cf. [Ber95, Kaz95, War00]) and in the area of cross-cultural user interface design [Mar01]. In general semiotics studies the meanings of signs, which encompasses both visual as well as textual aspects. Even though this field provides valuable insights in this regard it is not directly concerned with the IT based processing of such aspects. For textual data the approaches related to Semantic Web as discussed above are a first attempt to take the IT processing into consideration, e.g. by referencing terms to shared ontologies. Depending on the design of the ontology also cultural aspects can thereby be integrated in the semantic definition of a term. For visualisations the field of user interface design in general considers the *adaptation to human diversity* [Shn93], spanning from physiological to cognitive aspects. However, also here no standard is currently available to semantically define a visual representation and consider its relation to a shared set of terms.

To overcome these deficiencies is one of the goals of this work. Therefore in chapter 5 on page 223 a framework for visualisation is presented that takes into account contextual factors already on a conceptual level. The following techniques elaborated in section 5.2 and 5.3 then found the basis for a syntactical as well as a semantical specification of visualisations. These are regarded as a first attempt to standardise the design of visualisations and their meaning.

2.5 Graph Theory and Graph Drawing

The field of *graph theory* and more specifically *graph drawing* underlies many approaches for visualisations in business informatics. Graphs are primarily a mathematical construct that can also be treated without any visual representation. However, as Battista et al. state "the geometric representations of graphs have been investigated by mathematicians for centuries, for visualisation and intuition, as well as for the pure beauty of the interplay between graph theory and geometry" [BETT99](p.vii). Therefore the basic terms and main ideas of this big branch of science shall be briefly discussed. For further details it is referred to the specialised literature [Wes96, BETT99, Die00].

The formal description of a graph in mathematics is independent from its graphical representation and can be described as follows [Die00]: A Graph is a pair of disjoint sets $G = (V, E)$ with $E \subseteq [V]^2$ which signifies that the set E is a subset of V containing two elements. V are denoted as vertices and E as edges which leads to the common representations as shown in figure 2.5.

Graph theory in general studies the properties of these constructs and their relationships among each other. This includes for example the description of various types of graphs, the calculation of the shortest paths between two vertices, the comparison of graphs to each other or the optimal labelling (colouring) of graphs

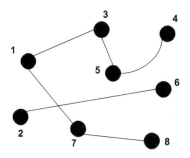

Figure 2.5: Basic Graph Representation G with $V = \{1,2...8\}$ and $E = \{\{1,3\},\{3,5\},\{5,4\},\{2,6\},\{1,7\},\{7,8\}\}$

that concerns the aggregation of sets of nodes and edges of a graph (see [Wes96] p.173). The nodes and edges of a graph can be further detailed which leads to the following extended types of graphs: *Directed* graphs (or digraphs) where the direction of an edge is determined, *labelled* graphs where either the edges or the nodes or both of them are assigned an additional value (e.g. a text label or a numerical value) and *multigraphs* where more than one edge can defined between two nodes.

Based on these theoretical fundaments the field of graph drawing is concerned with the development of algorithms for visualising graphs. This implies a largely automated layout of graphs based on a computer processable definiton (e.g. by adjacency matrices that contain the node and edge definitions). For this purpose it takes into account *aesthetics criteria* (cf. [WPCM02, BETT99, Pur97] such as the *size* of the total graph, the *minimisation of crossings* for a clear visual structure, the number of *bendpoints* or the *angles* of edges between bendpoints. Furthermore also the use of animations [ECH97, BRB03] as well as the drawing of graphs in three dimensional space [ARR$^+$97] are discussed.

The relation of graph drawing to this work will become apparent particularly by the conception of multi-object Ontological Visualisation Patterns (see section 5.4 on page 262) that refer to the layouting of visual objects. Additionally, several diagram types shown in chapter 3 are graph based. The layout of these diagrams is however mostly human based in contrast to the approach of graph drawing that is largely focused on automatic layout techniques.

2.6 Descriptive Statistics

The field of *descriptive statistics* is of high importance for many applications in business and business informatics. It is concerned with "describing the observed set of data, be it a sample or a polpulation" [SA95](p.8). Descriptive statistics has a long tradition in using visualisations for analysing the characteristics of data, both from a qualitative as well as quantiative point of view (see also the citation in [Shn01][22]).

For this purpose several types of diagrams are used that plot the set of data. Thereby absolute and relative comparisons, time series developments as well as the identification of dependencies in the data can be derived. This enables a user to formulate hypotheses about the data which can then in turned be mathematically checked with the means of inferential statistics. The graphing of data in this way is today provided by many standard software packages and is also widely known to many users. This aspect renders these types of diagrams especially useful for many visualisation needs.

In section 3.1 on page 45 several examples for visualisations will be shown that have their origin in descriptive statistics. Directly related to descriptive statistics is the field of information visualisation as discussed in the following that takes a broader view and makes use, in contrast to descriptive statistics, of visualisations that are specifically shaped to a concrete task or domain.

2.7 Information Visualisation

Also the field of *information visualisation* has a long historic tradition [Tuf83]. As already mentioned in the previous section it makes to a large extent use of specialised types of graphical representations. In contrast to visualisation methods in descriptive statistics the representations in information visualisation therefore often require specific knowledge about the elements and the meaning of a visualisation. The orientation of information visualisation as it is described in the current international literature of this field is strongly directed towards a data based, computer-supported view. This is reflected by the common definition of information visualisation [War00, CMS99] as "the use of computer-supported, interactive, visual representations of abstract data to amplify cognition" [CMS99](p. 7).

---

[22]"The invention of times-series plots and statistical graphics for economic data is usually attributed to William Playfair (1759-1823) who published The Commercial and Political Atlas in 1786 in London." [Shn01](p.18)

The relation of this view to definitions of visualisation, information design and in particular scientific visualisation is given in table 2.7 [CMS99].

Term	Definition
External Cognition	Use of the external world to accomplish cognition.
Information Design	Design of external representations to amplify cognition.
Data Graphics	Use of abstract, nonrepresentational visual representations of data to amplify cognition.
Visualisation	Use of computer-based, interactive visual representations of data to amplify cognition.
Scientific Visualisation	Use of interactive visual representations of scientific data, typically physically based, to amplify cognition.
Information Visualisation	Use of interactive visual representations of abstract, nonphysically based data to amplify cognition.

Table 2.1: Definitions in the Area of Information Visualisation

Also included in the tasks of information visualisation are the preparation of the data as well as statistics-based procedures to preprocess the data [Hib99]. Particular attention is given to the aspect that information visualisations provides possibilities for the analysis of data. This results from high-dimensional, very large datasets where the generation of hypotheses about the characteristics of the data (e.g. to identify a pattern) is difficult to be performed by traditional mathematical methods [GKW04]. Similar to the approach in descriptive statistics several branches in information visualisation aim to create visual representations of the data that facilitate such analyses. Examples are shown by the visualisations in section 3.2 on page 106.

Furthermore, attempts have been made in information visualisation to automate the design of visualisations [Mac86, Cas91, Gra01]. The procedure used in these approaches is to analyse the input data (e.g. resulting from a database query) and generate a specific visualisation for optimally representing the data. However, two major drawbacks can be identified in these approaches: The first is that the generation is directed towards a data oriented view in correspondance to the direction of the field of information visualisation. This leads to the problem of not being able to take into account the semantics of the data but only the semantics of the data structure, e.g. whether the data is ordinal or nominal. For simple representations of charts this approach seems partially satisfying but for more complex visualisations as surveyed in chapter 3 it is not appropriate due to the complex models underlying the visualisation (cf. section 4.2 on page 164). The second criticism that can be mentioned is that the approaches elaborated so far are built on a finite number of available definitions for graphical representations. This significantly limits the potentials of systems built on these approaches. By the approach discussed in this work (see chapter 5 on page 223) the problem of semantically describing visualisations is solved in the way that a general or an individual semantic schema can be related to a visualisation (also see section 6.3 on page 279). Additionally, due to the conception of open accessible visualisation services (see section 4.3 on page 218) a large number of adequate visualisations can be accessed.

2.8 Computer Graphics

As has already been mentioned above the field of *computer graphics* provides the necessary technical foundations for realising visualisation on computer hardware. Therefore the specific relations of this field to the conceptions in this work shall be highlighted.

Besides the foundation for the realisation of the prototype discussed in chapter 7 on page 291 computer graphics is also related to the concept of Semantic Visualisation (see section 5.2 on page 231ff). The technical requirement of transforming graphical representations into arrays of points to enable the display on rasterised displays [HB97] has additionally inspired the choice for points as the basic graphical primitive. Furthermore, the definition of graphical representations in computer language is directly related to the specification of visual objects.

After the analysis of the related scientific fields a survey on existing visualisation approaches in business informatics will be presented in the next chapter. Thereby it will become visible which types of visualisations represented the current state-of-the-art in this field.

3 Survey of Existing Visualisation Approaches

In this chapter selected approaches for visualisations shall be discussed that exist today in the area of business informatics to give an overview of the current state of the art and to provide the basis for the following elaborations. Despite the limitation of the analysis to the field of business informatics the number of different attempts is still very large. As a consequence further structuring and classification is necessary.

For a scientifically sound structuring it seems indispensable to provide a comprehensible method that allows for a clear justification of the inclusion or exclusion of a specific approach. Furthermore, this procedure gives an overview of the whole field that is taken into consideration to show possible focal points for visualisations or points where visualisation is not yet employed. Therefore, a methodology has been chosen that builds upon different frameworks in the areas of concern.

The term *framework* is commonly used and describes the nature of a domain of discourse by attempting to capture its broad characteristics, relationships to other fields and a view on the inner structure. As has been shown in section 1.2 on page 14 business informatics is positioned as an interface between the area of economics respectively management and computer science. This definition already gives a broad overview of the relevant topics but is still very general and thus does not permit to identify relevant groups of interest that can be analysed in depth in regard to visualisations.

Both in the area of economics and management as well as in computer science efforts have been made to structure the particular field further than is shown in figure 1.3 on page 15. Business informatics itself has developed specific frameworks that focus on the integration of business requirements and technical possibilities. In the following five frameworks are presented that are related to management, computer science and business informatics:

- Porter's Value Chain
- Amarel's Framework
- Rosenbloom's Framework
- The Business Engineering Model

- Zachman's Framework
- The BPMS Paradigm

The value chain model by Porter [Por85] belongs to the area of business and the theory of organisations, Amarel [Ama71] describes an approach for a conceptual framework for curriculum planning in computer science that structures the major areas of activity and application areas, Rosenbloom [Ros04] presents a recent view on computing studies from the viewpoint of science and the viewpoint of engineering, the framework by Zachman [Zac87, SZ92] focuses on enterprise modelling and combines organisational and technical aspects and is therefore assigned to business informatics. Similarly assigned to business informatics are the Business Engineering Model and BPMS (Business Process Management Systems) paradigm [Kar95] that originates from the financial services sector and integrates strategic, operational, and performance measurement issues.

3.1 Business Frameworks

In his often cited book "Competitive advantage - creating and sustaining superior performance" [Por85] Michael Porter describes a systematic way of examining the activities of a firm. The basic approach thereby is to disaggregate a firm into its strategic activities. Porter assumes that competitive advantage can be gained when a firm manages to perform these activities in a better or cheaper way than its competitors.

Porter's Value Chain

The value chain of a single firm is embedded in a value system with the value chains of suppliers lying before and the value chains of the (distribution) channels and the buyer value chains after (see figure 3.1). In the case of a diversified firm the value chain of a firm spans several business units located in different parts of the value system (as shown in figure 3.2 on the next page).

Figure 3.1: Value System for a Single-Industry Firm (redrawn after [Por85])

Closely related to the concept of the value chain is the field of *supply chain management* that aims to holistically consider the creation of goods whereas the organ-

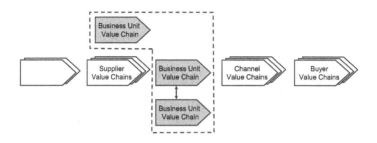

Figure 3.2: Value System for a Diversified Firm (redrawn after [Por85])

isational embedding is also considered (in contrary to pure logistics). An approach for a concrete structuring of supply chains is given by the SCOR[1] model [SCC05]. A reference model in the context of SCOR is defined as a framework that provides standard descriptions of management processes and their interrelations as well as standard metrics to measure process performance and suggestions for management practices to achieve optimum results [SCC05]. It has to be noted that reference modelling itself is also a distinguished field of research that encompasses various approaches for the exact definition of a reference model and the resulting implications that are not investigated here in detail[2]. Substantial similarity to reference modelling is apparent in the field of meta-modelling that will be discussed in 4.2 on page 196.

The SCOR framework spans [SCC05](p. 3):

- All customer interactions, from order entry through paid invoice.
- All product (physical material and service) transactions, from your supplier's supplier to your customer's customer, including equipment, supplies, spare parts, bulk product, software, etc.
- All market interactions, from the understanding of aggregate demand to the fulfillment of each order.

SCOR therefore strongly resembles the concept of Porter's value chain which can be easily perceived by comparing the basic structure of Porter's value system (supplier value chains - firm value chain - channel value chain - buyer value chain as depicted in figure 3.1 on the preceding page) with the sequence of the main actors (supplier's supplier - supplier - company - customer - customer's customer in SCOR.

---

[1] Supply Chain Operation Reference
[2] For an outline of the current state-of-the-art in reference modelling see [FL04, BDK04]

In contrary to the value chain SCOR defines four layers that represent different aggregation levels of firm operations and five distinct management processes. As described for the latest version of SCOR [SCC05] the top level defines the scope of the SCOR model with the basics for competition performance targets. Level II that is also named the Configuration Level contains the process categories. These are chosen from a selection of 30 standard categories (grouped under planning, execution, and enable processes) which are used to implement the operations strategy of a company. On the third layer the concrete integration of a company into its market environment is considered. For each process category from level two detailed process element definitions are given including input and output information for each element, process performance metrics, best practices, required system capabilities etc. The bottom level is the implementation level and is not treated explicitly by SCOR. It defines the concrete processes of a company to achieve competitive advantage and represents the highest level of detail. Here the actual processes have to be modelled (a discussion of process modelling will follow in 3.3 on page 129).

From the viewpoint of visualisation there exist several ways of representing the relationships of SCOR graphically. Apart from the illustrations in [SCC05] SCOR is also integrated in professional business software toolkits such as the ADONIS plattform [JKSK00][3] or ARIS[4] where the SCOR levels are represented in the form of process landscapes that permit a direct linkage to business process models. In figure 3.3 the top level of SCOR is shown as it is used in the ADOlog[5] supply-chain-management toolkit.

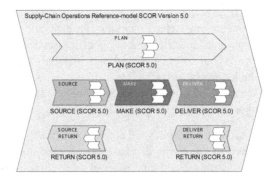

Figure 3.3: ADOlog SCOR Model Level I

---

[3]ADONIS is a commmercial product and registered trademark of BOC AG.

[4]ARIS is a commercial product and registered trademark of IDS Scheer AG.

[5]ADOlog is a commerical product and registered trademark of BOC AG.

In the following Porter's concept of the value chain will be analysed in detail as it provides (in comparison to the SCOR model) a more detailed way of classifying the activities in a firm as well as an overview of the different functions that occur. It is therefore estimated to be more useful for identifying the various types of visualisations that are used in business.

A value chain as defined by Porter consists of a collection of activities that are performed by a firm to design, produce, market, deliver, and support its product (see figure 3.4 on the following page). These activities may differ within a branch and reflect the strategy of a firm to compete with others. The difference between the cost of the activities and the total (market) value of the product is denoted as *margin*. Porter divides the activities into two types: *primary* and *support* activities. The primary activities (inbound logistics - operations - outbound logistics - marketing and sales - service) contain all actions that have to be taken to create the physical product, to sale it and to transfer it to the buyer. The support activities (firm infrastructure - human resource management - technology development - procurement) support the primary activities and include the provision of purchased inputs, technology development, human resources and other firmwide functions.

The primary activities in the area of *inbound logistics* concern everything that is related to receiving, storing, and disseminating inputs to a product. This includes material handling, warehousing, inventory control etc. Through *operation* activities inputs are transformed into a product (e.g. through machining, assembly, and facility operations. With *outbound logistics* all activities are summed up that are associated with collecting, storing, and distributing the product to buyers (e.g. warehousing of finished goods, material handling etc.). The *marketing and sales* activities include the provision of means so that a buyer can actually purchase a product as well as the activities that induce him to do so (e.g. the often referred to 4Ps of marketing: product, price, promotion, place[6]). *Service* activities span all activities that enhance or maintain the value of a product (e.g. installation, repair, training etc.).

Procurement refers to all activities that are necessary for acquiring the inputs (i.e. the function of purchasing) that are needed for a firm's value chain (e.g. raw materials, office supplies, machinery or laboratory equipment, consulting or accounting services). Procurement is usually distributed throughout a firm from the traditional purchasing department to office managers and probably even the chief executive officer (e.g. for strategic consulting). Notable in this context are the substantial efforts for the creation of electronic marketplaces and the spread of e-procurement that provides methods to realise economic gains by linking the

---

[6]For a review and discussion on this classification see [WdB92].

different procurement undertakings in a company electronically and achieving economies of scale due to higher purchasing amounts (e.g. due to high rebates the bulk purchasing of office supplies).

By *technology development* Porter broadly classifies all activities that are related to the improvement of the product and the processes in a firm. He conciously does not employ the term "research and development" for these activities as he estimates it to be too narrow. He assumes that technology development takes place in many parts of the firm and not only the ones that are directly linked to the creation of the end product (e.g. also in process equipment design or service procedures). Since the writing of Porter's book this area has obviously gained in importance as will be shown by the currently used IT-based management approaches that are discussed in 3.3 on page 111.

The activities of *human resource management* consist according to Porter of "recruiting, hiring, training, development, and compensation of all types of personnel" [Por85]. Human resource management plays an important role in all sections of the value chain (primary as well as support activities) and can therefore turn out as competitive advantage in many ways.

The *firm infrastructure* contains activities such as general management, accounting or finance and usually supports the entire value chain. Porter also includes the area of management information systems in this section of activities.

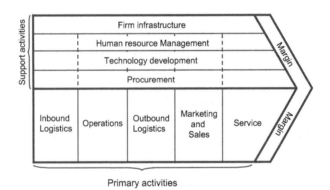

Figure 3.4: Michael Porter's Value Chain (redrawn after [Por85])

Relation to Visualisation

Based on the framework that is outlined by the value chain it shall now be investigated what types of visualisations play major roles in each field of activity. Although there might be highly innovative and specialised types of visualisations for the use in a firm it is assumed that there exists a kind of standard and established set of visualisations that are used to perform or support various activities in a firm.

It has to be remarked that the discussion of some activity fields is deferred to succeeding sections (especially for visualisations in business informatics) as these have been strongly influenced by the availability of IT-based management methods: This applies in particular to the field of operations which are today highly influenced by business process management as well as to all activities that make use of process management techniques.

Apart from the activities that will be covered later on, two major fields can be derived from the concept of the value chain that make use of quite distinct types of visualisations. The first field concerns logistics, production and project management and the second marketing and sales and finance: As will be shown the main focus in the first field are operations that deal to a great extent with the scheduling of activities and their dependencies[7] whereas the second field concentrates on the analysis of external and internal data such as financial figures, market data etc.[8].

Logistics, Production and Project Management

In the area of inbound and outbound logistics as well as in production management various types of visualisations can be found that are used to support decision makers in finding solutions as well as to illustrate relationships and communicate intended plans to the workforce that executes them. Included in this section is the area of project management - that can of course not only be found in logistics or production but also in many other functions of an enterprise - but that has its origins in these methods, e.g. for the scheduling of activities. Many of the visualisations found in these areas are related to the field of network planning although there also exist approaches that go beyond traditional network planning methods, e.g. by using virtual reality techniques. At first traditional visualisations in network planning shall be discussed, followed by an outlook to recent developments of visualisations especially in logistics and production planning.

---

[7]Which could also be classified as *qualitative* issues in the sense that it is investigated how things are related.

[8]Which can be regarded as *quantitative* issues, i.e. the focus is to analyse amounts of things (which can also be of a qualitative nature in some cases, e.g. for ratios).

Production can be briefly characterised as a process of adding value by transforming simple or complex inputs into outputs of higher value. Today this process is distributed world-wide and the number of people involved continually decreases whereas the employment of capital increases due to mechanisation and automation. Critical factors for successful production include: time, flexibility, quality and profitability [GT97](p. 1ff). Production management as a business discipline is mainly concerned with the production of material goods (and not services) [GT97](p. 7ff).

Logistics is closely related to production and is defined as a "holistic approach spanning all functional areas of an enterprise that aims to optimise the flow of material and products by taking into account the interrelated flows of information" [GT97](p. 8). It is therefore regarded as an integrating function.

In both production and logistics graphs (also see section 2.5 on page 34) play an important role. One common application of graphs are network planning graphs for structuring projects. These shall be discussed in the following.

Network planning graphs   Network planning techniques comprise methods for the structuring, planning, control, and monitoring of the operation of large and complex projects on the basis of graph theory [Alt96]. Projects in this context are separate, self-contained tasks that are unique in regard to their specific realisation and that require the involvement of many different actors. One major characteristic of network planning is the splitting of a project in a number of sub-tasks (activities) and the identification of temporal and functional dependencies.

Altrogge emphasises the advantage of network planning techniques in regard to previous techniques such as bar chart diagrams and thus directly relates to the aspect of visualisations in this field [Alt96] (p.1). He states that network planning separates the structuring of a project from the temporal planning which has not been possible by the use of Gantt diagrams. Nevertheless Gantt diagrams can still be found in current project management tools as e.g. in Microsoft Project and shall therefore be shortly discussed subsequently to network planning.

Network planning techniques can be applied to *time planning* (e.g. for the estimation of project durations, the identification of time-critical activities, the definition of the begin and end times of activities for a timely execution of the entire project or the analysis of effects of temporal adjustments), *capacity planning* (e.g. to investigate at what time and how long resources are required for a project, how a balanced utilisation of resources can be achieved or to calculate the minimum project duration with a given set of resources), and *cost planning* (e.g. to calculate total project costs, the cost effects of a change in project time etc). Domains that use network planning are apart from project management in general production and logistics [GT97] or also other areas such as software engineering [Bal98]. The later discussed aproaches grouped under the field of business informatics such as business process management or performance management are very similar to the principles of network planning.

Usually three types of network plans (see figure 3.5 on the next page for simple examples) can be distinguished (as for example laid out in [Bal98, Alt96]):

- *Activity Node Network Plan*[9]: Activities are represented by nodes, the arrows between the nodes define a precedence relationship. Altrogge states that this type of network is not considered to be a valid graph as the nodes have a temporal dimension which does not allow for direct temporal analyses of the graph. By using visualisations that are different from the common node representation (e.g. in the form of a circle or square with a label inside) temporal aspects can be re-integrated in the graphical representation [Alt96](p.166).

- *Activity Arrow Network Plan*[10]: Here the activities are depicted by arrows and the logical sequence is defined by the order of the nodes. A node symbolizes an event, every arrow is bordered by a start and an end event. An event can only occur if all activities have been finished, i.e. the condition for the execution of the next activity is fulfilled. The labels of the nodes represent descriptions of the events (again in the standard form as described in [Alt96](p.18)).

- *Event Node Network Plan*[11]: This type of network plan only shows events and their chronological dependency. A method that uses this type of charts is PERT[12] developed in 1958 in the USA (for a detailed discussion of this method see [Alt96]).

All three types of network plans are not practically used in their original way but enriched with additional information. This can either concern the type of nodes or edges, as well as their labelling and the rules for defining loops and multiple edges of the same type between two nodes. Very often additional information about the activities, events and dependencies is integrated (e.g. earliest start and endpoints, activity duration etc.). It will be shown in the following that the practical use of network planning principles has led to a variety of graph types that are in use today.

---

[9]German: Vorgangsknoten-Netzplan
[10]German: Vorgangspfeil-Netzplan
[11]German: Ereignisknoten-Netzplan
[12]PERT: Program Evaluation and Review Technique.

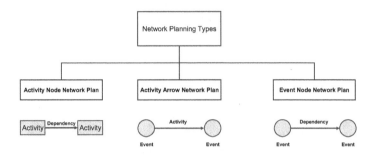

Figure 3.5: Overview of Major Types of Network Planning (redrawn after [Bal98])

Gozinto graphs   Another type of graph that is commonly used in production management are *gozintographs* as described e.g. in [GT97](p. 170). It describes how different parts have to be assembled to create a product. The parts i.e. the input can be raw materials, half-finished or finished parts. The nodes symbolize the parts and the directed, labelled edges define how many units of a part have to be included for production of the next part. The graph directly corresponds to a system of linear equations which can also be solved mathematically and yields the required inputs and the resulting outputs. An example for a gozintograph is shown in figure 3.6 on the facing page. The endproducts in this example are A,B, and C. The logic is as follows: To produce one item of A one item of D and one item of E are required, for one item of E two items of I, five items of J and two items of K are needed and so on[13].

Gantt charts   As has been mentioned above *Gantt charts* are not as powerful for a detailed analysis as graphs used for network planning but are still used for giving an overview of the project activities and their duration. As shown in figure 3.7 on page 50 for a Gantt chart the activities are listed on the vertical axis and the timeline of the project on the horizontal axis. The duration of each activity is marked by a bar. The total project duration as well as overlapping activities can thus be easily identified. The disadvantages of Gantt charts mentioned in [Alt96] are that possible changes in the duration of activities and the implications for the overall project duration are difficult to monitor and that the updating of the Gantt diagrams is often not done in practice. With the wide spread of project management software

---

[13]The term *gozintograph* has been coined by the mathematician Andrew Vazsonyi who had cited as the author of this representation the Italian mathematician Zepartzat Gozinto - which is nothing else as a malapropism of "the part that goes into" that exactly describes the purpose of this graph

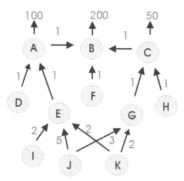

Figure 3.6: Example for a Gozintograph (Source: http://de.wikipedia.org/wiki/Gozintograph)

that can perform such updates automatically this argument has though become less important. It is assumed that in many cases a combination of network planning techniques and charts is used.

Another type of diagrams that is sometimes used to represent flows (e.g. for the identification of bottlenecks) are Sankey diagrams. These diagrams also occur in eMPlant which will be discussed below. An example for a Sankey Diagram is shown in figure 3.8 on page 51. It can be directly perceived by this type of diagram how a kind of flow is composed and what the proportions of these compositions are.

Three dimensional representations   The most advanced visualisations that are estimated to be available for production and logistics management are three dimensional, interactive representations of production and logistics flows. As will be shown in the following for these new types of visualisation no kind of standard currently exist which makes it difficult to compare them to each other. Due to their high level of reality they cannot be regarded as visual models as the various types of graphs shown above (which need an explicit definition of their meaning to be comprehensible) but are rather self-explaining almost reality-like visualisations.

Two examples for software tools that support such visualisations are *eM-Plant*[14] and *CASUS*. eM-Plant supports the modelling, simulation and visualisation of production facilities. For this purpose it provides object libraries for specific subdomains of production management (e.g. for assembly processes or the automo-

---

[14]see http://www.emplant.de

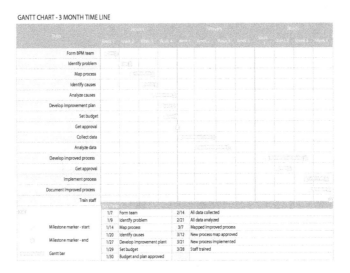

Figure 3.7: Example for a Gantt-Chart (created with SmartDraw.com)

tive industry). Although no academic publications nor a software license has been available to the author it is estimated based on the screenshots and product descriptions on the company website that the basic tool functionalities are also graph based with a possibility to automatically create interactive 3D visualisations that can be animated, see figure 3.9 on page 52. As far as can be derived from the available information the creation of three dimensional objects by the user is not possible, instead pre-compiled extensive object libraries have to be used.

The acronym *CASUS* stands for Computer Animation of Simulation Traces. CASUS is a tool for the generation of three-dimensional animations and visualisations on the basis of simulation data. It has been developed as part of the project "Simulation Demonstration Centre for Production and Logistics"[15] and is therefore also discussed in this section. Its functionalities are well described on the corresponding project website[16] as well as publicly accessible publications [MWJ02, LB97] which allow for a deeper investigation than has been possible with eMPlant.

CASUS supports interactive three-dimensional visualisations of simulation data including animations and interactive "walk-throughs". Based on a proprietary in-

---

[15]Translated from German: Demonstrationszentrum Simulation in Produktion und Logistik
[16]http://www.igd.fhg.de/CASUS/

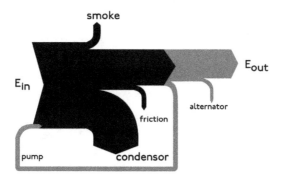

Figure 3.8: Example for a Sankey-Diagram (Source: http://en.wikipedia.org/wiki/Sankey_diagram)

terface format external simulation tools can be linked to CASUS. The main intention of CASUS is the support of immediate and three-dimensional visualisation of industrial equipment and processes ("virtual factories"). An adoption for the use in service industries appears to be possible.

CASUS is entirely based on an object-oriented architecture. The single animation elements therefore contain for example their own methods for animation sequences which ensures the correct usage of the contained behavioural functionalities and the interaction of multiple objects can be realised in a very simple way (e.g. the necessary transformations such as rotation or scaling are performed automatically when objects are arranged).

For the visualisation of processes and operations with CASUS the data that are provided by a simulation tool have to be converted to a CASUS specific format by the use of a normalizer. Out of this the CASUS translator creates an animation script that relates the simulation objects or components with the animation elements that are stored in the CASUS element library. The animation elements can be created on the basis of existing CAD[17] data.

In the following the animation system processes the animation script. The results is a playback script that is based on parameter configurations of an individual user and the underlying visualisation system. It contains all necessary information for a three dimensional animation [Krö02]. Possible parameters for the playback that can be interactively defined are camera position, camera target, light sources and the background. For the future the development of a VRML [18] driver is en-

---

[17]Computer Aided Design
[18]Virtual Reality Markup Language

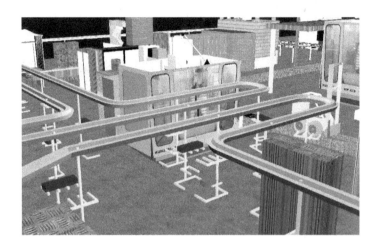

Figure 3.9: eM-Plant 3D Visualisation (Source: http://www.emplant.de)

visaged to enable internet access to the animations as well as an extension of the library of animation elements such as realistic human figures.

The graphical representation of animation elements in CASUS is as can be seen by figures 3.1 on page 54 and figure 3.1 on page 54 fully three-dimensional in the sense that a user of the system can navigate through the virtual space as well as modify animation parameters online. By the introduction of VRML these possibilities will even be enhanced and will also be available for a distributed environment. The interaction with the objects is however not complete which means that they can only be manipulated indirectly in the three-dimensional environment. The level of detail in CASUS is in the high-level-detail mode already very close to reality as shown in figure 3.1 on page 54 the user can choose from different abstraction levels. The degree of animation in CASUS is high which follows from its aim to directly represent real operations.

When evaluating the cost/benefit aspects of the different visualisations for production and logistics the following points have to be considered: A clear advantage of tools like eMPlant and CASUS is the realistic visualisation of processes, actors and their behaviour. This permits an intuitive understanding of relationships that would have to be expressed in a very complex manner with for example a network plan (e.g. for a process with a lot of activities that are performed shortly after another). Despite the visual details that are present in both CASUS and eMPlant an analysis of the process details such as an exact determination of waiting times, precedence or dependency relationships is not possible with these types of visual-

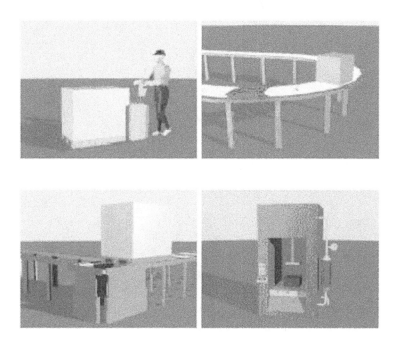

Figure 3.10: Examples for CASUS Animation Elements (Source: http://www.igd.fhg.de/CASUS/)

isations. In the case of eMPlant a combination of Gantt charts, bar charts and pie charts is used to compensate for the particular disadvantages.

The major difference between the tools CASUS and eMPlant is that CASUS offers mainly visualisation functionalities whereas eMPlant also provides mechanisms for altering and manipulating data and simulations i.e. the process structures underlying the visualisations. CASUS instead received the data for the visualisation from simulation tools[19].

Both CASUS and eMPlant are of great advantage concerning the expression and naturalness of the three dimensional visualisations. Reality is rebuilt with a high degree of detail that enables an intuitive understanding of the relationships, dependencies and processes. Especially the animation and interaction functionalities in the 3D environment open possibilities for a quick understanding of the visualisa-

---

[19]No hint could be found in the relevant publications that mention CASUS about what types of formats or standards are supported.

Figure 3.11: Example of a Model Element in CASUS in High-detail Representation (Source: http://www.igd.fhg.de/CASUS/)

Figure 3.12: Example of a Model Element in CASUS in Low-detail Representation (Source: http://www.igd.fhg.de/CASUS/)

tion - in contrast to the very specialised charts that require an in-depth study of the symbols and captions that are employed.

Despite these great benefits major problems of the 3D visualisations of this type are the high effort for the generation of new visual elements (e.g. when a new machine that is not part of the standard library should be added) as well as difficulties that arise when a detailed analysis of the relationships is demanded. Although the barrier of becoming familiar with specialised types of charts (e.g. a PERT chart) might be high, their abstract representation of specific facts permits a faster and more accurate analysis of specific details. It is evident that for example a difference in the timing of an activity (e.g. duration, transport time, waiting time) is easier to recognize by a visualisation that is specifically adapted to highlighting the timing than one that is very close to reality and does not allow for a direct inspection of these details. The generation of new 3D elements that exactly represent the appearance and behaviour of the real counterparts is still a very complex undertaking and often requires the use of CAD and professional 3D animation tools. Besides the technician who might already have the 3D (CAD) data available a graphics specialist might be needed to adapt the animations, surface appearances, lightings etc. that lead to the impression of a visualisation that is close to reality. Therefore, the cost aspects of the use of 3D visualisations could be considerable - in contrast to abstract representations where the graphical symbols do not have to be tailored in this laborious way.

Marketing and Sales - Finance

The area of marketing and sales and the area of finance probably do not seem to fit in a common group as one might state that the tasks performed in each of the two fields are indeed very heterogenous. Nevertheless from the viewpoint of visualisation it is estimated that these two fields actually share quite a lot when it comes to the analysis of data and decisions that are based on this data. To underpin this argument a short description of the two fields shall be given which enables to identify the common visualisation basis which will be found in the area of descriptive statistics.

To shortly describe the field of marketing it shall be referred to the introductory book by Armstrong and Kotler [AK00]. They describe marketing as "..a social and managerial process by which individuals and groups obtain what they need and want through creating and exchanging products and value with others" [AK00](p.5) (a similar basic approach in this area can be found in [Mef00][20] or as given by the American Marketing Association[21]).

Apart from the many processes and theories that can be built upon this definition to accurately describe the methods and tasks in marketing - which would go beyond the scope of this work - one aspect shall be highlighted that seems to be essential when searching for visualisations in this field: As [AK00] outline in their chapter about Marketing Research[22] and Information Systems that compa-

---

[20]Meffert defines marketing as "..every form of exchange between two counterparts.." [Mef00](p.9)

[21]"Marketing is the process of planning and executing the conception, pricing, promotion and distribution of ideas, goods, and services to create exchanges that satisfy individual and organisational objectives" (Definition from 1985 as in [Mef00]) and the recently adapted definition "Marketing is an organisational function and a set of processes for creating, communicating, and delivering value to customers and for managing customer relationships in ways that benefit the organization and its stakeholders" (Definition from 2004 from http://www.marketingpower.com/content4620.php)

[22]Definition Marketing Research by AMA: "Marketing research is the function that links the consumer, customer, and public to the marketer through information - information used to identify and define marketing opportunities and problems; generate, refine, and evaluate marketing actions; monitor marketing performance; and improve understanding of marketing as a process. Marketing research specifies the information required to address these issues, designs the method for collecting

nies need information at almost every turn in order to produce superior value for customers.

As in other fields of empirical social science research – of which marketing can be regarded to be a part of in the sense of a social process when following the definition by [AK00]) – the objects of study that generate this information can be analysed based on attributes that are associated with them. These attributes can either be of a qualitative or a quantitative type [Fri90](p. 86). It shall be remarked that the meaning of quantitative and qualitative in relation to the type of attributes is different to the connotation of the terms in relation to quantitative and qualitative social science research. In quantitative social science research data are usually acquired by measurement or counting and are then analysed with statistical methods. In qualitative research in contrast data is usually acquired by using not standardized methods (e.g. interviews, narrations) and then analysed without mathematical/statistical methods but with 'qualitative methods' (e.g. by creating hypotheses about certain types of behaviour) [Laa93](p. 11f). It is however possible to process qualitative data that has been gained by not standardized means in a quantitative way by applying a coding technique (e.g. by identifying the occurence of certain words in a not standardized interview). The same is possible the other way round i.e. to treat quantitative data in a qualitative way (e.g. for the generation of hypotheses based on quantitative facts) [Laa93].

When combining the statements about qualitative and quantitative attributes with the two types of social science research it becomes evident that the two types of data attributes can be classified under quantitative social science research (as depicted in figure 3.13 on the next page). This view of qualitative and quantitative attributes corresponds to views expressed in statistics when dealing with data: Nominal and ordinal scales therefore reveal qualitative relationships, interval and ratio scales represent quantitative relationships (which can be converted to qualitative scales but not the other way round).

Visualisations used in marketing   Coming back to the area of marketing and relating it to the statements about social science research the following examples can be given to illustrate the differences of qualitative and quantitative attributes in a practical context: A typical quantitative attribute in marketing are sales figures, whereas the information to what degree each product contributes to the overall sales as a percentage would be a qualitative attribute. As examples for aspects of qualitative social science research Meffert lists attitudes, motives or satisfac-

---

information, manages and implements the data collection process, analyzes the results, and communicates the findings and their implications"(http://www.marketingpower.com/content4620.php)

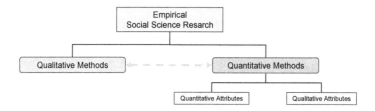

Figure 3.13: Overview Empirical Social Science Research

tion [Mef00] for which no generally accepted, reliable benchmarks or instruments exist. As these aspects are nevertheless important for making decisions in marketing ways have to be found to allow for an operationalisation of these theoretical constructs (e.g. by using standardized interviews). After a suitable operational measurement has been found visualisations can be used to graphically represent the findings (e.g. as shown in figures 3.14 (qualitative data showing the proportion of people with a certain knowledge in different geographical regions)).

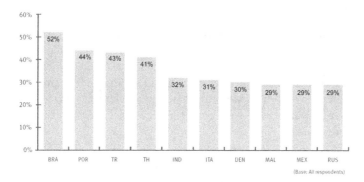

Figure 3.14: Barchart illustration taken from a report of the marketing research company ACNielsen [ACN05] about consumer attitudes in food packaging (Original question: When you are buying packaged food, when would you check the nutritional information on the package?; Proportions of respondents for 'Always')

Besides these classical chart types (that will be further discussed below) two specialised types of visualisations shall be discussed that are also related to marketing: The first is from the area of information visualisation and relates geographical data directly to other data such as sales (figure 3.15 on the next page).

Figure 3.15: Example for a Geochart depicting the Sales Information of a US company (Source: http://www.map-engine.com)

Another visualisation application in marketing that makes use of virtual reality technology and three dimensional displays is the virtual presentation of product prototypes for the evaluation by marketeers and customers prior to the start of production (discussed for example by [HF02, KS00, AK00, Hol97]) as well as for a virtual product preview on a website (e.g. as often used in a simple form by car manufacturers to illustrate possible product configurations). Evidence for positive effects of such virtual product demonstrations for e-commerce applications has been shown by [HF02]. More sophisticated applications also integrate haptic devices into the virtual reality environment to complete the simulation by adding tactile impressions.

Visualisations used in finance The field of finance in an enterprise comprises a variety of functions and shall therefore be structured according to a model laid out by Fischer [Fis96]. He divides the theory of finance into two parts: The managerial capital theory[23] and the capital market theory[24]. The first investigates the capital allocation decisions of private investors (portfolio theory) and of enterprises (investment and financing decisions - which are also subsumed under the term corporate finance), the latter describes the financial securities that occur on financial markets[25] and aims to develop models and hypotheses for an empirical verification

---

[23]German: Betriebswirtschaftliche Kapitaltheorie
[24]German: Kapitalmarkttheorie
[25]Denoted by Fischer as traditional capital market theory or instrumental approach [Fis96](p. XI)

of the conditions on capital markets[26]. Although graphical representations can be found in many of these sub-fields, from the viewpoint of visualisation especially the area of capital market theory and descriptions of market progression are of relevance. In these areas visualisations are used to present continously changing data such as stock prices, trading volumes, interest and exchange rates etc. in compact and easily comprehensible charts. Besides the plain visualisation of stock prices (e.g. in the form of a simple line chart) it is common to add statistical indicators to the representation. These shall aid in predicting the future trend of the stock price (e.g. by integrating moving averages) based on historical data.

This *technical analysis* that only takes into account past prices (and not the fundamental figures of enterprises) to find patterns that predict future stock prices [Hel01], [Mon00], [Sch00], [Mur97] is sometimes regarded to be of minor importance by the field of academia [LeB99, FB66] - for a short discussion of the arguments and recent developments based on the use of technical analysis see [PSV04]. Despite a number of criticisms that can be mentioned applied finance seems to make use of charting techniques as an additional source of information [LM98, TA92] so that the field is worth looking at from a visualisation perspective. Therefore, a selected number of charts used in technical analyses are be presented in the following.

The first chart (see figure 3.16 on page 60) consists of lines representing the minimum and maximum stock price on each trading day with the average price marked by a small horizontal attached line. Dividend payments are denoted by a 'D' and a graphical symbol indicates when shares have been split. Around the stock price movements the so-called *Bollinger-bands* are drawn. These are constructed by adding and subtracting the standard deviation to the moving average of a certain period. The combined diagram shows the trend of the stock price per traded volume as a line chart and the intra-day volumes that have been traded as a column chart.

The Renko chart in figure 3.17 on page 61 orginates from Japan. The speciality of this type of chart is that the temporal information usually assigned to stock prices plays a minor role. The name *Renko* is related to the Japanese word for bricks (*Renga*) and characterises the typical representation in the form of small boxes. The method for drawing a Renko chart is very straightforward: If the stockprice at the end of a day has changed by an amount greater of lesser than a pre-defined value a new brick is drawn, independent of the time interval. If the stock price has risen the brick is drawn in yellow, if it has fallen in blue. A Renko chart therefore only depicts the current trend of a stock price but does not allow

---

[26]Classified by Fischer as modern capital market theory or market approach [Fis96](p. XI)

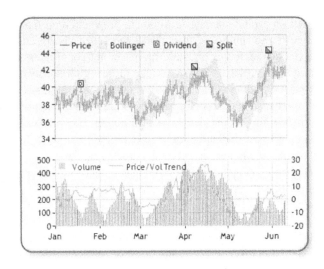

Figure 3.16: Example for a Stock Chart using Bollinger Bands (Source: Dundas Chart for .NET)

judgement about the past as it is not known which time span is represented by each brick.

In general, both the field of finance and the field of marketing are strongly related to statistics as a part of mathematics that deals with collecting, organizing, and analyzing data. Statistics is, has been mentioned in the introduction to this sub-chapter the basis that unites marketing and finance in regard to visualisation. More specifically it is *descriptive statistics*, which can be characterised by the goal "to describe a set of data." [SA95](p.9), in contrast to inferential statistics that aims to "make a statement about a population based on the information available in a sample." [SA95](p.10)). Besides mathematical methods descriptive statistics provides several means and methods to visually explore the different kinds of data that can occur. It is therefore related to the field of information visualisation that focuses solely on the aspect of the visualisation of data and usually deals with large, high dimensional data sets that cannot be analysed efficiently by traditional mathematical methods (see section 3.2 on page 106).

To structure the basic types of statistical charts that are currently practically used in business it can be referred to a model set up by Gene Zelazny [Zel92] which is shown in figure 3.18 on page 62. He lists on the horizontal axis the basic types of comparisons that shall be expressed and on the vertical axis the basic chart types

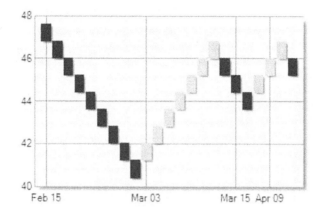

Figure 3.17: Example for a Renko Chart (Source: Dundas Chart for .NET)

that are suited for each particular comparison. Although it is not a scientifcally elaborated model it is very intuitive and well argumented for selecting appropriate chart types based on the underlying comparison requirements.

The comparison of the components of a whole in percentages is therefore best visualised by a *pie chart* (e.g. the sales percentages of the products of a company). When discussing the various chart types Zelazny also gives advice in regard to their actual usage: For the pie chart for example he suggests not to show more than six components. In case there are more components he proposes to show five and merge the remaining components in one category.

To compare the ranking of items he advocates a *vertical bar* chart where the vertical axis is not scaled but only contains the labels of the categories (e.g. for a comparison between different companies based on their sales volumes). The ordering of the bars should follow a distinct logic (e.g. from best to worst, alphabetically, based on temporal relationships etc.) to ease the visual comprehension of the diagram. Furthermore the scales shown in the diagram should contain "round" values without decimals (if not required). Detailed figures accompanying each bar should be omitted if only an overview of the relationships is given.

For time series comparisons that show how positions have changed over time Zelazny recommends either *column* or *line charts*. In case only a few points (seven to eight) in time have to be compared the column chart is best suited and for more items (as it occurred in the cases of stock prices as shown above) the line chart is the optimum representation. Additonally, Zelazny also stresses semiotic aspects of these two chart types: The column chart gives an impression of height and order of

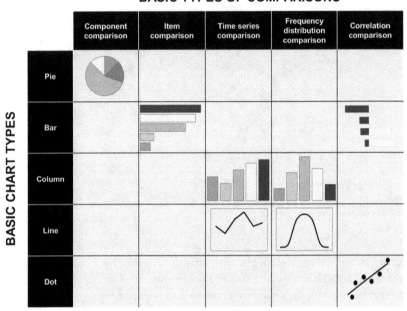

Figure 3.18: Basic Chart Types and Types of Comparisons (redrawn and adapted after [Zel92])

magnitude which is appropriate for activities that are terminated within a specific time period or start from the beginning in every period (e.g. for production data) while the line chart symbolises the continuity and the degree of change which fits better for data that is continued over time (e.g. the history of inventory stock data).

The frequency distribution comparison shows how often an object occurs in a series of sequential categories of magnitude. Zelazny suggests either *histograms* or *curve diagrams*. Zelazny does not give detailed arguments for their usage but it seems that histograms are better used for categorial distributions and curve diagrams for continuous distributions.

The last type discussed by Zelazny are correlation comparisons that can either be expressed by *double bar charts* or *scatter plots*. They show whether the correlation between two variables follows a pattern or not. Especially the scatter plots are a widely used technique in statistics for finding hypotheses about the correlation of data. This includes not only the detection of linear correlations as shown in figure 3.18 but also of polynomial correlations and clusters.

Figure 3.19: Conception of NYSE MarkeTrac (Source: http://www.asymptote.net)

To round up the chapter of visualisations in business a last example from the area of finance shall be presented. In contrast to the other approaches shown for visualisations used in finance it does not build upon classical or extended chart types but relies on an innovative three dimensional visualisation approach that depicts the floor of the New York Stock Exchange (NYSE) in an abstracted style which corresponds to the physical layout [Del99] (see figure 3.19). Although it has been originally invented for the operations staff at NYSE to oversee the developments taking place on the trading floor it is now also available to the public on the internet[27]. The interactive visualisation is capable of giving an overview of major events on the trading floor. By navigating through the posts in the web based interface (see figure 3.19) the user can both gain an insight as to where a particular stock is traded as well as oversee the changes in stock prices and then drill down to investigate the details of a particular post or stock. The approach can therefore be regarded as outstanding either in regard to the amount of data that can be visualised at the same time as well as the successful web based implementation.

---

[27] See http://marketrac.nyse.com/. MarkeTrac is a registered trademark.

3.2 Computer Science Frameworks

The second section of the this chapter will now review the visualisation approaches in the field of computer science as the second major basis for business informatics.

Amarel's Framework

Although the publication by Saul Amarel [Ama71] from Rutgers University already dates back to the beginning of the 1970-ies it still seems to be appropriate to be mentioned when trying to outline the major fields in computer science[28]. The aim of Amarel is to clarify the nature of computer science for the development of sound computer science programmes at universities. Based on the consideration that a computer science programme should guide new entrants to the field in a manner that will, besides their personal interest and development, empower them to engage in later scientific activities the discussion of the planning of curricula reflects the essential pillars of a specific field of science.

Amarel in his work considers two views: a *global* view that is concerned with 'the kind of objects, phenomena, and concepts that form the domain of discourse in computer science, and also with the pattern of relationships between this domain and other domains of study' [Ama71, p.391] and a *local* view that examines the type of knowledge, problems, and activities in computer science as well as their interrelations. Even though the discipline of computer science presents itself at a highly dynamic stage (which has already been apparent in 1971) and new technologies, concepts, and applications are developed in evidently diminishing cycles the fundamental questions have not changed much since then.

In his elaborations on the global view of computer science Amarel states that computer science is concerned with *information processes*. That is with the procedures and information structures of such processes and their implementation in machines. Furthermore he stresses the relationship between classes of problems that necessitate information processes and the solution of such problems by information processing machines. It is worth remarking that in the German speaking world computer science has for a long time been denoted as *electronic data processing*[29] and that not until recently the term has in many publications been replaced by *information technology (IT)* - a fact highlights the anticipatory character of Amarel's thoughts in regard to the importance of the semantic description of data. For the implementation flexible schemes are needed to transform the abstract

---

[28] Also the more recent publication by Rosenbloom [Ros04] that will be discussed later refers to Amarel's concepts.

[29] In German: Elektronische Datenverarbeitung (EDV)

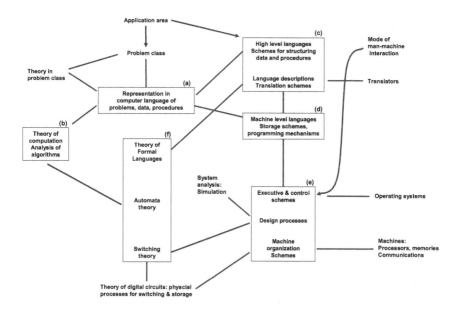

Figure 3.20: Structure of Major Areas of Activity in Computer Science (redrawn after [Ama71])

specification of an information process into an operating machine. Amarel assigns a central role to the digital computer that enables humans to build any number of information processing machines - a fundamental property of universality. From a global perspective Amarel defines two major components of activity in computer science: a *synthesis* component that is oriented towards exploration and innovation and an *analysis* component that regards the search for fundamental principles and the formulation of theories. To achieve progress in the field a continuous interaction between these two components is essential from Amarel's point of view.

When investigating the local view of computer science, i.e. its inner structure Amarel identifies six major areas of activity and certain relationships between them (depicted in figure 3.20):

(a.) Representations in computer language of problems, data, and procedures in an application area
(b.) Theory of computation; analysis of algorithms
(c.) High level languages for different application areas; schemes for structuring data and procedures; language descriptions; translation schemes

(d.) Machine level languages; storage schemes and programming mechanisms

(e.) Machine organisation schemes; executive and control schemes; design processes

(f.) Theory of formal languages; automata theory; switching theory.

The first area (a) can be seen as a mediating function between application areas and the area of computer science: 'Real-life' tasks, as Amarel states, have to be decomposed in various ways and represented in a form that is appropriate for computer-processing, i.e. a computer language. The cooperation between specialists in the relevant area of application and specialists in computer science is essential for the generation of new and better solutions. Amarel presents a set of eight major application areas (see figure 3.21 on page 68) that he considers relevant from the viewpoint of computer science. The application areas are classified by 'the kinds of problem solving methods, information structures, and procedures that are characteristic of the problems in the application' [Ama71](p.396). As Amarel already envisaged the successful solution of problems often requires the combination of several of the major application areas.

Directly related to the language based representation of problems is the theory of computation and the analysis of algorithms (b). Stemming from theories in mathematical logic this area is concerned with the investigation of processes that can compute certain classes of functions (e.g. sorting a set of numbers effectively) and the estimation of the complexity of such processes. Further questions in this area include the evaluation of termination conditions (i.e. whether a process ever terminates under specified conditions) and the research in regard to the semantics of languages in which algorithms can be formulated.

For a better direct support of specialists of an application domain high level languages (c) have been developed that allow for a convenient and natural expression of concepts and methods. This results in the provision of flexible means for writing and testing complex procedures within a reasonable amount of time. The availability of application programming interfaces (API)[30] and software development kits (SDK)[31] that can act as further abstractions of technical relationships as well as advanced integrated development environments (IDE) that include functions for the semi-automatic generation of source code. In this context also the latest developments in regard to the model-driven-architecture [MM05, FL03] have to be mentioned that aims to abstract application logic from technological platforms and

---

[30] APIs are interfaces that include commands, routines or macros which are provided by an operating system or an extension of an operating system (e.g. for using a network). Applications can access the interfaces to execute actions on the operating system that are pro

[31] Software Developments Kits (SDK): A collection of programs and documentation for a specific software that shall ease the use of that software by providing interfaces and exemplary implmentations.

thus presents a meta-approach to the traditional high level languages. Further major fields of high level languages include specialised languages for data base design and query or meta data languages (e.g. the family of XML languages).

The machine level languages, storage schemes and programming mechanisms are subsumed under the fouth area (d). These fields are strongly dependent on the physical mechanisms and organisation of the computer and are therefore also sometimes denoted as low level programming languages. The specification of such languages requires a tight cooperation between software and hardware designers. Already in the 1970-ies it was apparent to Amarel that programming in machine level languages will be mostly limited to systems software and that in most areas high level languages will be developed. Nevertheless, in some areas machine level languages are still important also for the development of applications (e.g. for certain three dimensional graphics operations specialised hardware oriented languages are used).

The fifth major area that is defined by Amarel are machine organisation schemes, executive and control schemes, and design processes (e). It deals with the overall organisation of the digital computer that executes the commands and performs the computations. Today this field is strongly supported by methods of computer aided design (CAD), system analysis and simulation to manage the complexity inherent in the currently used highly integrated circuits [Moo03, Gee05]. As will be shown later in this section this area has an impact on visualisation that is not to be underestimated (in regard to computer graphics hardware).

The last area is the theory of formal languages, automata theory, and switching theory (f). It investigates the theoretical properties of computer languages, computer mechanisms and their realisations. It is strongly related to linguistics and provides the foundations for the definition of syntax, semantics and pragmatics. The work in switching theory is concerned with the logical design of computer systems (elementary logic gates and storage elements). Although the prominence of this area has declined in the last decades the developments e.g. in the area of optical switching technology [MK03] have a direct impact on possible applications that are based on high bandwidth and processing power (e.g. in supercomputing or gridcomputing).

Rosenbloom's framework

Another more recent framework for computer science is described out by Paul Rosenbloom [Ros04]. He sees computer science as being traditionally composed of two partitions: science and engineering. After Rosenbloom the two fields are separated by a line approximately at the computer architecture level with computer

Figure 3.21: Application Areas from the Viewpoint of Computer Science (redrawn after [Ama71])

science being above the line and computer engineering below. With his framework he aims for an reaggregation of the two fields and a repartitioning of the resulting single field into an analysis and a synthesis component (a view that has also been taken by Amarel [Ama71]). Shortly put Rosenbloom sees the science part as dissecting and understanding the nature of computing and its relationship to other sciences and the engineering part as envisioning and building real computer systems.

The first part of Rosenbloom's framework is dominated by the concept of *binary computer science* (see figure 3.22 on the facing page). Stemming from the assumption that computer science can either be seen as a self-standing science (*unary computer science*) or as an interdisciplinary field that interacts with the other scientific domains of physical sciences (P) (concerned with nonliving matters), life sciences (L) (concerned with living matters) and social sciences (S) (concerned with humans and their societies) Rosenbloom has classified these possible combinations as binary computer science.

As this work is primarily directed to the field of business informatics only the C+S and C+C fields in Rosenbloom's framework will be further examined in detail. Nevertheless it is estimated that the analysis procedure taken for these two

	C + P	C + L	C + S	C + C
C/*	C/P: Silicon and quantum computing	C/L: Biological and neural computing	C/S: Wizard of Oz	C/C: Languages, compilers, operating systems, emulation
*/C	P/C: Modelling and simulation, data/information systems	L/C: Artificial life, biomimetics, systems biology	S/C: Artificial intelligence	
C •* and * • C	C•P and P•C: Sensors, effectors, robots, peripherals	C•L and L•C: Biosensors	C•S and S•C: Human-computer interaction, authorization	C•C: Networking, security, parallel computing, grids
C[*]	C[P]: Analog computing	C[L]: Autonomic systems	C[S]: Immersion	C[C]: Embedded monitoring and testing
*[C]	P[C]: Embedded computing	L[C]: Cyborgs	S[C]: Cognitive prostheses	

Implementation (A/B): Technology from field A is used to implement computation B or computation A is used to implement an aspect of domain B

Interaction (A•B): The domain A,B interact in a symmetric relationship as peers

Embedding (A[B]): Some fragment of domain B is embedded in domain A

Figure 3.22: Sub-Areas of Binary Computer Science (after Rosenbloom [Ros04])

fields is in principle also applicable to the others. The concrete subareas for the combinations that are given by Rosenbloom (also depicted in figure 3.22) can only be seen as examples as e.g. 'modelling and simulation, data/information systems' does obviously not only occur in the area of physical sciences (for representing physical phenomena) but also in the area of social sciences (for representing social phenomena, e.g. the model of a business process in an organisation).

Rosenbloom defines three relationships that can occur when combining a scientific domain with computer science:

- implementation (denoted by /)
- interaction (denoted by •)
- embedding (denoted by [])

An *implementation* relationship occurs when one domain makes use of technology from another domain to implement computation. The Wizard of Oz experiments (mentioned in the third row first line) represent humans that implement computer functionality[32] - the technology from the field of computer science is

---

[32] "...Wizard of Oz techniques, i.e. studies where subjects are told that they are interacting with a computer system through a natural-language interface, though in fact they are not. Instead the interaction is mediated by a human operator, the wizard, with the consequence that the subject can be given more freedom of expression, or be constrained in more systematic ways..." [DJA93]

used for the field of social sciences in the form of a computation. Opposite to the Wizard of Oz experiments Rosenbloom denotes the field of Artificial Intelligence (i.e. an implementation relationship where technology from the social sciences is used for creating computations in computer science S/C). An implementation relationship where computer science technology is used to realise computations in computer science (C/C relation) is illustrated by the field of computer languages, compilers, operating systems etc.

Interaction relationships are used to express domain combinations where both act as peers (i.e. the relationship is of symmetric nature). Examples given by Rosenbloom for this combination in computer and social science (C•S) are human-computer interaction (e.g. user interfaces) and authorization processes that allow people to access computational resources. For the C•C area Rosenbloom lists networking (i.e. the communication between computers themselves) as well as parallel and distributed computing (groups of computers working together).

In *embedding* relationships one domain surrounds the other in the way that a fragment of the embedded domain becomes a part of the embedding domain and does not maintain its own identity as in a peer relationship. Examples brought up for this type are immersion (i.e. the integration of a human in a computational/virtual environment), cognitive prostheses (i.e. systems that support or augment the abilities of people who suffer cognitive deficits[33]. The example give for embedding in the C+C area is embedded monitoring and testing where the (computational) control systems are directly embedded in the actual system[34].

The second part of Rosenbloom's approach is dedicated to the structuring of the field of computer engineering to provide the basis for a synthesized view of computer science. He assumes therefore that computer systems are built from technology layers where one layer embodies a coherent *technology thrust* that contributes certain, critical capabilities to the layers above. As shown in figure 3.23 on page 72 there are six layers:

The *platform* layer represents the computational hardware. Lower levels such as a microsystems layer or a layer representing fundamental physics exist theoretically but are not part of the framework. Rosenbloom mentions among others computers, personal digital assistants (PDAs), mobile phone, satellites, and cars as examples for platforms. It thus becomes apparent that he not solely classifies the pure hardware as a platform but actually the combination of different hardware components to a basic operating environment on which other applications can be built.

---

[33]For a detailed explanation see [AAW99].
[34]Concrete applications of this approach can be found e.g. in network management [Lin01] or in the area of intelligent robots [HH93].

For providing connectivity among different platforms Rosenbloom defines the *network* layer as the subsequent layer on top of the platform layer. Under this item he includes the challenge to ensure universal connectivity among several different types of platforms regardless of their location, security issues, and the dynamic creation and management of large-scale networks.

On the *grid* layer networks of platforms are combined to establish shared resource pools that yield uniform access across all resources despite of their geographical or organisational location[35]. The term 'grid computing' originally stems from the analogy of a power grid where heterogenous, distributed resources can be uniformly accessed on demand. The challenges in this field include among many others the provision of cross-domain authorizations[36], the interoperability between resources and workflow management[37].

Through the support of the technology of the grid layer the creation of *environments* becomes possible that contain data, information, knowledge, and models of a domain. By the specification of processes that operate on such environments additional content in the form of insights, calculation, reasoning or simulation can be created. Current research issues on this layer include the ways of organising resources over entire domains (e.g. a science discipline), multiscale systems (e.g. the human body in the area of life sciences) or geographical regions (e.g. for a whole city) and how to acquire and manage conclusions for relating them to the underlying real-world system. Similar considerations can also be made for enterprise environments where again many different types of (sometimes world-wide distributed) resources, data and knowledge have to be processed, analysed and the results be transfered back to the original sources - ideally in real-time.

The access of users to the environments is realised through *interfaces*. For an effective use of the content of the environments this access should be possible in an easy and intuitive way. The solutions currently offered include speech interaction as well as specific visualisations especially in the area of user interfaces or the visual treatment of very large datasets.

The top layer is the *organisation* layer. The challenge here includes the support of groups of people and goal-oriented systems such as agents and robots as well as how to dynamically create such organisations and enabling their effective work.

---

[35]Or as Foster et al. phrase it in the context of virtual organisations: "The real and specific problem that underlies the Grid concept is coordinated resource sharing and problem solving in dynamic, multi-institutional virtual organizations." [FKT01]

[36]For example on the basis of the concept of a single-sign log-on where a user or application only needs to identify itself against the grid once and the corresponding rights are handed on across the resources automatically.

[37]For the foundations on the research field of grid computing as well as detailed elaborations on the current discussions of frameworks and structures for grid computing see [FKT01, FKNT02]

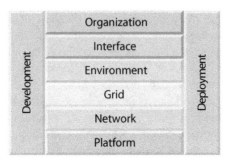

Figure 3.23: Rosenbloom Framework for Computer Science (after Rosenbloom [Ros04])

Integrated Computer Science Framework

The two frameworks which have been used to gain insights into the structure and major fields of computer science have a number of common aspects. Amarel iden-tied the relevant fields of action in computer science, Rosenbloom showed with the concept of binary computer science the possible interdisciplinary character - which is also relevant for business informatics that can be regarded as an instance of binary CS.

Rosenbloom's framework is strongly oriented towards an application perspec-tive in computer science, whereas the first part of Amarael's framework (as shown in figure 3.21 on page 68) can be regarded as similar to a procedure model for developing solutions for an application area by the use of the various computer science techniques and methods[38].

It is thus obvious to integrate the central ideas of both frameworks which has been done as shown in figure 3.24 on the facing page. This three dimensional, in-tegrated view lists on the depth axis the major fields of activity in computer science as described by Amarel (in a slightly changed order), the six technology layers by Rosenbloom on the vertical axis and on the horizontal axis the six relationships of computer science and the social sciences as described in the approach of binary computer science by Rosenbloom (exemplary for one application field).

The resulting cubic representation allows for the classification of a large number of methods, technologies, and applications in computer science: It considers both the different abstraction levels of representations in computer language (from the basic choice of a representation in computer language, over the underlying theoret-

---

[38] As the framework does not contain definite paths relating the areas it cannot be regarded as a com-plete procedure model.

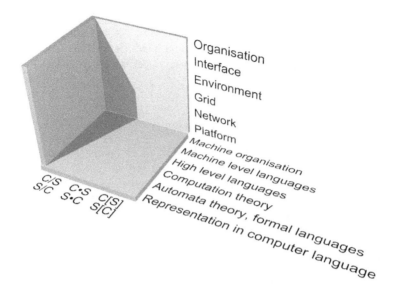

Figure 3.24: Integrated Computer Science Framework

ical conceptions by automata theory and formal languages, computation theory to the actual implementation by using high level languages, machine level languages and finally the hardware level of machine organisation), as well as the technological application levels for employing these languages (on the platform, network, grid, environment, interface, and organisation level). The combination of these two dimensions permits e.g. the positioning of aspects of formal conceptions for networks as well as low level implementations for graphical user interfaces (as often used in computer graphics to achieve high performance). The integration of the third dimension adds information about where the examined part of computer science is located in regard to the interdisciplinary character of the field. For a focus on the relations of computer sciences and the social sciences only the implementation, interaction, and embedding relationships for computer science and the social sciences are depicted on the third axis in figure 3.24.

Relation to Visualisation

The abovely described integrated framework for computer science can now be applied to classify a number of selected visualisation approaches that are in use in computer science. Although a complete quotation of examples for every possible position in the three dimensional framework would go beyond the scope of this work the following selection of visualisation approaches is estimated to cover a wide range of the principal methods and techniques which are practically used in the field.

Hardware Level and Machine Organisation

Starting on the lowest levels of the framework which corresponds to the strongly hardware related areas of machine organisation and the platform level a number of visualisations can be found that support the design and understanding of hardware engineering. For the design of highly integrated electronic circuits which are the basis of every microprocessor and memory unit examples can be found for visualisations of voltage and current analyses, noise analyses or circuit tuning (for a detailed enumeration of examples and their discussion see [Res01]). Although relations to computer science obviously exist the main target group of these visualisations are electrical engineers and neither computer or business computer scientists.

Circuit Board Visualisations   An area that is also part of machine organisation and hardware engineering and that is closer related to computer science is the representation of printed circuit boards and their elements. One common task that shall be mentioned in this regard is the layout of circuit boards which is - in the case of electronic circuits as used in today's computer hardware - a complex undertaking that involves the optimal multi-layered arrangement of a large number of electronic components on a limited surface area and by taking into account the satisfaction of electrical engineering principles such as electromagnetic compatibility (EMC) restrictions [HGD+93].

An approach that makes use of visualisations for this field is available by the implementation of the electronics design and simulation tool Electronics Workbench with the corresponding Electronics Workbench Layout tool as described by Waite et al. [WB99]. The latest version of the layout tool is the UltiBoard printed circuit board layout (PCB) software which supports either the traditional two dimensional layouting of components as well as it provides a three dimensional visualisation of the board and the the deployed components (figure 3.25 on the facing page). The three dimensional visualisation gives a realistic impression of the actual result of the layouting process and can be used to ensure that the component heights fits the enclosure.

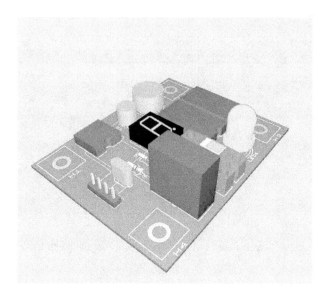

Figure 3.25: UltiBoard Circuit Layout Software 3D View (created with NI UltiBoard)

Virtual Instrument Visualisation in LabVIEW   Another example for a visualisation on the level of electronics and machine organisation is the visual language (and software application) LabVIEW [JW95]. The fundamental metaphor that LabVIEW is built on stems from a laboratory setting: LabVIEW programs symbolise a hierarchy of instrument-like moduls which are called *virtual instruments* (VI). Virtual instruments contain interactive *front-panel* controls which provide input and display output and an interior *block diagrams* that determines the instrument's functionality. VIs can be connected to data sources lying on the PC or in a database as well as to sensors and input signals that are connected to the PC (via specialised hardware components). The VIs can be assembled and configured graphically and then used immediately without additional programming effort. In its recent versions the LabVIEW software is also capable of publishing and subscribing data on the internet. This includes the possibility of distributing VIs via the web and using them remotely. The current version no.8 of LabVIEW is available as an online version (via a terminal interface) and could therefore also be investigated practically.

When creating a new LabVIEW project the two windows for editing the front-panel and the block diagram immediately become apparent (see figure 3.27 on page 77 and figure 3.27 on page 77). Even when not being familiar with the de-

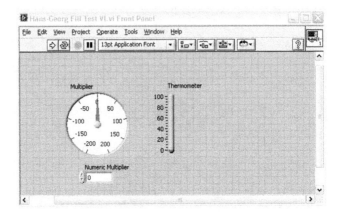

Figure 3.26: Screenshot of Labview Front-Panel (created with LabVIEW)

tails of electronic circuits the visual environment of LabVIEW is very intuitive
and allows for the fast achievement of results. In figure 3.27 on the next page
the wire connections between a user input field, a numeric constant (labelled 'Numeric Mulitplier'), a multiplier operator and a gauge and thermometer are shown.
Corresponding to this inner structure of the virtual instrument is the view of the
front-panel (figure 3.26) that shows the visual representation of the gauge and the
thermometer as well as an input field for the numeric constant. When running the
virtual instrument in this setting at first an input dialogue comes up that asks for a
number. When a number is entered and the dialogue is closed the value is multiplied by the numeric constant (which is displayed by the gauge) and assigned to the
thermometer. Although this a very simple example (in respect of the capabilities
of LabVIEW) it clearly shows the basics approach.

Besides the large library of electronical and logical elements that is contained in
LabVIEW it also allows for a reciprocal use of virtual instruments, i.e. the use of
VIs as elements in other VIs. This permits to offer elements that embody complex
functionality such as for example the representation of three dimensional diagrams
or mathematical calculations. By linking gauges to external data, e.g. to XML,
which is possible in LabVIEW also applications for the use in business engineering
as shown in section 3.3 on page 119 would be possible.

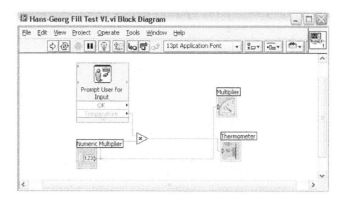

Figure 3.27: Screenshot of Labview Block Diagram (created with LabVIEW)

Network Level

On the network layer specialised frameworks (such as the ISO/OSI reference model as it is e.g. described in [SH02](p. 97ff)) can be consulted that provide detailed information on the structure and major concepts of this field. From the viewpoint of visualisation the nature of networks – as being constructs that consist of collections of nodes and links between these nodes – almost directly leads to representations as graphs or graph-like structures. To show specific requirements and concepts for visualisations of computer networks the field of network protocol visualisation has been selected to act as a representative.

Network Protocol Visualisation   The visualisation of network protocols is used to support network protocol designers in understanding and analysing complex message exchanges and monitoring the state of potentially large numbers of nodes in a network. Traditionally these tasks have been accomplished by the utilisation of packet traces (log files), i.e. recordings of the state and operations occurring in a network in textual form. The drawbacks of using packet traces are that they are very detailed and therefore difficult to comprehend and that they only provide a static view of the protocol behaviours [EHH+00].

The visualisation of the network activities in contrast allows for a graphical representation of the acquired data as well as the representation of dynamic aspects e.g. by animations. The goal is to enable network protocol designers to quickly comprehend large amounts of information, visually identify patterns in communi-

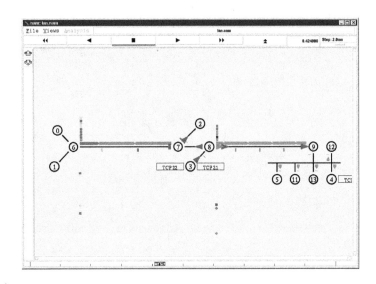

Figure 3.28: NAM Network Animator (Source: http://www.isi.edu/nsnam/nam/)

cation, and better understand causality and interaction [EHH$^+$00]. An example for a network visualisation is given in figure 3.28. Through the coupling of the visualisation to network simulators further insights into the network functionality can be gained such as the a-priori identification of possible congestions, the effects of router queuing policies, the analysis of the reliability of network protocols under different settings (assurance of quality-of-service) or the responses of protocols to changes in the topology (for a detailed discussion see [BEF$^+$00]).

High Level Languages

When stepping up the layers of the integrated computer science framework the importance of high level languages that abstract from the machine organisation rises. This abstraction concerns data as well as data processing aspects which becomes manifest by the corresponding paradigms in this field that have evolved during the last thirty years. From the data side the abstraction has developed from the identification of common data types which are still in use as core entities of every programming language such as integer, float or strings to the semantic modelling and description of the problem domain as apparent by semantic information models and further from methods of functional programming and separate data modelling to object oriented modelling and programming (with its bases in the Object Modelling Technique [RBP⁺91]). From the perspective of visualisation it is revealing that both semantic information modelling and object oriented methods have since their introduction relied strongly on distinct visual notations [Che76, RBP⁺91] whereas for the representation of algorithms visual representation techniques such as flow diagrams have, although being in use for a much longer time, not been theoretically founded and standardised until the mid-1960ies (cf. [BJ66] and the standards DIN66001-1966 and DIN66001-1983[39] as well as ISO5807:1985[40]).

The field of *programme visualisation* which encompasses static and dynamic illustrations of code, data, and algorithms [Mye90] has been identified as relevant in this context. Therefore, examples for the visualisations of *code and algorithms* and their latest extensions in regard to web-based applications as well visualisations for *data and data structures* and the Unified Modelling Language, as the main representative for visual representations in object oriented programming, shall be discussed in the following. Additional aspects of modelling languages, especially domain specific languages (DSL) will be discussed in relation to visualisations in business informatics on page 111ff.

As stated above the visual representation of algorithms has a long tradition. Although modern high level programming languages such as C++, Java or C# are already very close to natural human expressions of algorithmic structures, visual representations provide means to illustrate algorithms in a general way, independent of a specific implementation or textual syntax and in an intuitive format. Two forms of algorithm visualisations have been selected to show the basic conceptions: Flowcharts and Nassi-Shneiderman diagrams (or structograms). Although there exist systematic approaches for defining flowcharts (as mentioned above) many different forms can be found today in practice (also certain forms for business process representations build upon flowchart-like notations as discussed in section 3.3 on page 111 on page 111ff.).

Flowchart Diagrams   According to [SH02] two versions of flow diagrams are specified: *Data flow charts* and *program flow charts*. Data flow charts show the flow of data through a system that processes information, program flow charts de-

---

[39] Standards issued by the German industry standard forum (Deutsches Institut für Normung - DIN). An original source of the (not freely accessible) DIN standard documents was not available to the author but besides two (untrustworthy, since not official) internet sources that claim to offer the original documents [Deu66, Deu83] references to the standards can be found in secondary literature, e.g. in [SH02].

[40] Standard issued by the International Standards Organisation (ISO) on "Information processing - Documentation symbols and conventions for data, program and system flowcharts, program network charts and system resources charts" (http://www.iso.org) where the original document is available for purchase. Also this document was not available to the author.

Symbol	Meaning	Symbol	Meaning
	Process / Processing unit		Data / Data medium unit
	Manual operation / Point of manual operation		Data on Document / Input,Output unit for documents
	Decision / Selection unit		Data on sequential access storage / Sequential access storage unit
	Comment, annotation		Data on direct access storage / Direct storage access unit
	Flow / Connection line		Data in internal storage / Processor storage
	Communication link		Displayed or accoustical output data/unit
	Terminal, Interrupt		Manual input data/unit
	Connector		

Figure 3.29: Excerpt of symbols of DIN66001 (adapted and translated from [SH02])

scribe the sequence of operations in an information processing system subject to the available data. It has to be noted that the term "information processing system" in this context does not only refer to a single computing or data processing unit but that such a system can also be composed of multiple units. Furthermore tasks that have to be accomplished by humans can be included. In figure 3.29 an excerpt of the symbols described in DIN6001 is shown which has been created after the illustrations in [SH02]. These symbols can be arranged in diagrams according to predefined rules which corresponds to the syntax of the thereby defined visual language. The symbols *process, manual operation, decision, comment, flow line, communication link, terminal,* and *connector* are used in program flow charts, *process, manual operation, comment, flow line, communication link, terminal, connector, data, data on document, data on sequential access storage, data on direct access storage, data in internal storage, displayed or accoustical output data,* and *manual input data* are used in data flow diagrams.

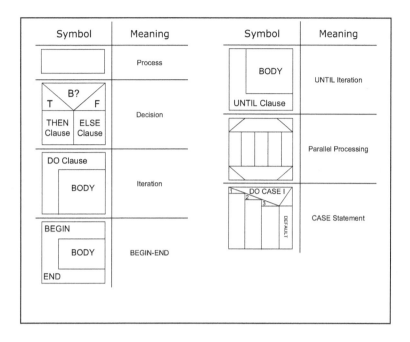

Figure 3.30: Symbols and Meaning of Nassi-Shneiderman Diagrams (cf. [NS73]

Nassi-Shneiderman diagrams   Another method to represent program flows are Nassi-Shneiderman[41] diagrams which are also defined in a DIN (DIN66261-1985-11) and an ISO (ISO/IEC 8631:1989) standard. The intention of Nassi-Shneiderman diagrams, as expressed by their inventors [NS73], is to provide a more restrictive control structure than flow charts and to better represent constructs such as iterations and loops. In the visual language of flowcharts as shown above iterations are not explicitly defined but have to be built from simpler control structures such as decision elements. This possibility for "unrestricted GOTOs" [NS73](p.13) in flowcharts as Nassi and Shneiderman denote it, leads to problems in the translation of the diagrams to concrete source code in programming languages, especially in the logical analysis of programs and program verification, optimisation, and debugging because the mapping of the diagram constructs to the constructs of a programming language is a one to many relationship where only one solution might be

---

[41] Also referred to as structograms or program structure diagrams (PSD).

legible, concise and efficient [NS73][42]. In the light of the paradigm of structured programming Nassi-Shneiderman diagrams therefore have a well-defined and visible scope of iterations and IF-THEN-ELSE clauses, explicitly show the scope of local and global variables, have a trivial representation for recursion and are in general very compact [NS73].

The set of symbols for Nassi-Shneiderman diagrams and their meaning is depicted in figure 3.30 on the previous page. Similar to flowcharts Nassi-Shneiderman diagrams contain basic elements for the representation of processes and control structures whereas the degree of freedom for the arrangement and usage of control structure elements is limited compared to flowcharts. The first major difference in regard to flowcharts becomes apparent by the *decision* element that contains besides the string for a boolean expression (symbolised by "B?" in figure 3.30 on the preceding page) only two paths for subsequent processes (according to the two results of a boolean expression "T" - true and "F" - false) whereas in the flowchart notation it would also be correct to have decisions with more than one result path. For expressions with multiple results the *CASE Statement* element is given where a default process and several alternative processes are chosen based on the value of a variable "I". Another difference is the existence of special elements for the definition of iterations. Nassi-Shneiderman diagrams in their original form provide two iteration elements: An exclusive *iteration* where the iteration clause is tested before the first run of the iteration and a non-exclusive *UNTIL iteration* where the clause is tested after the first run. The designer of a diagram (and thereby also the programmer who has to code the information of the diagram) are therefore forced to use these four concepts to represent control structures. The consequence is the prevention of arbitrary GOTO expressions and a clearly traceable program structure.

In contrast to flowcharts Nassi-Shneiderman diagrams do not build upon a graph-based representation for the arrangement of the elements but enforce a hierarchical structure where the symbols either directly follow each other or are nested within other symbols. An example for a Nassi-Shneiderman diagram is shown in 3.31 on the next page which represents the same Straight Selection Sort algorithm that was used for the example of the program flow chart. The diagram in figure 3.31 on the facing page has been created with a freely available structogram editor[43] and therefore does not correspond exactly to the original symbols as defined by Nassi

---

[42]For a discussion of the first considerations why GOTO statements are undesirable in source code see [Dij68].

[43]The Nassi-Shneiderman Diagram-Editor which has been developed in a student project by Marcel Kalt - see http://diuf.unifr.ch/softeng/student-projects/completed/kalt/NSD.html accessed 10-04-2006.

et al. [NS73][44]. Nevertheless it gives a good impression of the design and basic principles of the arrangement of symbols for Nassi-Shneiderman diagrams.

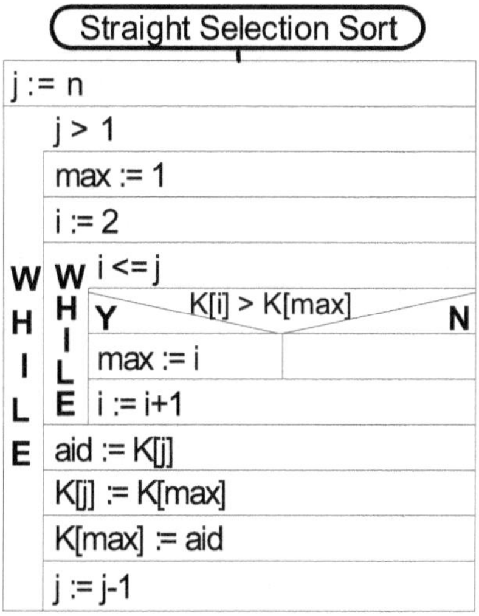

Figure 3.31: Example of a Nassi-Shneiderman Diagram

By the visualisations of algorithms as exemplarily shown by flowcharts and Nassi-Shneiderman diagrams the understanding of complex processes can already be performed visually and the exchange of algorithmic knowledge is theoretically founded through a distinct notation and application procedure. Besides these traditional approaches, new methods for visually explainining the functioning of algorithms have been developed. Here, especially the advent of animation functionalities on standard PCs and not specific graphics workstations [BS84] has had much influence in the last twenty years that becomes apparent by various publications that discuss the explanation of algorithms with means of animations [BS84, Sta90, BCLT96b, CS01, Naj01, Tud03].

Algorithm animation The term *algorithm animation* can be characterised as "attempts to explain an algorithm by visualising interesting events of the execution of the implemented algorithm on some sample input" [BW00](p.1). Therefore, the

---

[44]The only deviations from the original symbols are the additional "WHILE" label for the non-exclusive iteration, the swap of the true and false paths of the IF-clause and their labelling as well as the addition of a diagram label at the top.

difference to the above shown methods for visualising algorithms lies in the different application purposes: Whereas diagrams of algorithms such as flowcharts and structograms have the intention to support the design as well as the understanding of algorithms (which may also by denoted as "code visualisation" [Mye90] since it refers to the original source code), algorithm visualisation uses graphics to show abstractly how a program operates [Mye90]. Its aim is to understand the inner workings of programs, to evaluate existing programs, and to develop new programs based on the findings gained by debugging algorithms and analysing their behaviour and characteristics [Sta90]. Algorithm animation assumes the existence of an algorithm or a program and abstracts from its data, operations and semantics to create dynamical views of these abstractions. Thereby the visualisation does not have to correspond directly to a program's data or execution units but rather presents abstractions that shall illustrate the semantics of the program [Sta90]. Thus, pictures in an algorithm visualisation may not correspond to the actual data and changes in the graphical representation might not correspond to changes in the actual code [Mye90].

To realise algorithm animations a wide range of systems has been developed (e.g. BALSA [BS84], Tango [Sta90], Zeus [Bro91], Polka [SM96], Polka/Eliot [LSTT97][45]) - a good review of animation systems for algorithms until 1996 is given by [WAK96] - with the latest developments in the direction of web-based animation systems [BCLT96a] (e.g. JCAT [Naj01], Mocha [BCLT96b]) and including three dimensional visualisations [OST04, Tud03]. Sometimes only purely animation systems are also discussed under the term "algorithm animation systems" (e.g. the Animal system [RF02]). Despite their high practicability for visually explaining algorithms – on the Animal website a large number of freely available algorithm animations is available[46] – these systems, as well as other commonly used animation systems such as Macromedia Flash or animated GIF images[47], are not included in this discussion here. The reason is that their visual representations do not contain a linkage to an actual algorithm (i.e. the mapping between an algorithm and an animation component as will described below)[48].

---

[45] Due to the large number of available system for algorithm animation this enumeration is only exemplary. A comprehensive collection of algorithm animation systems is maintained by the computer science department of Hope College, Michigan, USA http://www.cs.hope.edu/~alganim/ccaa/index.html.

[46] See http://www.animal.ahrgr.de/.

[47] See the website of Macromedia Flash http://www.macromedia.com/software/flash/; GIF (Graphics Interchange Format) is a common commerical graphic standard owned by Compuserve Corporation that can be used for displaying animations.

[48] Of course such a linkage could be established in some of these animation systems, but only with additional programming effort.

For the goal of analysing the pragmatic character of visualisations as well as the underlying concepts and methods for their composition the field of algorithm animation is particularly valuable due to the following aspects:

- The design, understanding and use of algorithms concerns a core aspect of computer science and business informatics.
- Due to its existence for more than twenty years it can be regarded as a well researched field with a large range of available practical implementations that allow for detailed insights into the concepts.
- And finally, the concepts developed in algorithm animation are of particular interest because of their inherent explicit separation of content and visualisation (to achieve the goal of multiple application possibilities) - which does not apply to other visualisation approaches.

Therefore, the functional requirements and the often cited conceptual framework for algorithm animation by John Stasko [Sta90] shall be illustrated in the following to highlight the key considerations for creating visualisations based on algorithms. In the introduction to his approach Stasko defines general functional requirements for algorithm animation systems by four groups of features: The first group contains features that all systems should support (minimal requirements, denoted as *kernel* by Stasko), the second group comprises desirable features (denoted as *shell*), the third group (*fringe*) are features that may be evident in some systems and the fourth group (*future*) specifies features that were beyond the capabilities of hardware at the time when the artical was published (1990).

In detail, the *kernel* requirements include the availability of two-dimensional black and white objects (lines, rectangles, circles, and text), the possibility for program-driven changes of the position, size, visibility, and fill-style of the objects, sequential and simultaneous multiobject modifications, bounding-box-oriented geometric alignment, simple coordinate-based graphical input and the control for the relative animation-speed.

Desired but not necessary (*shell*) features for algorithm animation systems are the extension of the available graphical primitives (to polylines, polygons, ellipses, arcs, and splines), the possibility for changes in the highlighting or colour of the objects, the line style and thickness and functionalities for arbitrary scaling and rotation. Furthermore, Stasko describes desirable features for the user control of the windows views such as panning and zooming, multiple concurrent views, and postexecution forward and reverse playback of varying speed.

As *future* features Stasko listed the real-time control of actions and motions, the arbitrary geometric alignment and collision detection by the definition of object-to-object relationships and constraints for such mappings, the mapping of the animation to its driving programme to enable the user to visually modify a programme's data and execution and the provision of three-dimensional graphic animation facilities.

The requirements described by Stasko in 1990, including the future features, can today all be realised by standard programming languages such as C++ or Java and (in the case of visualisations as used traditionally in algorithm animation) also on standard hardware components. The requirement for special graphic workstations as expressed by Stasko can therefore be neglected due to the rapid advancements in computer hardware in the last sixteen years. But even so, these functional specifications provide insights that can be consulted for future developments, especially for the design of (semantic) web enabled visualisation functionalities and services as will be shown later in this work.

Besides the requirements, Stasko also describes a conceptual framework for a systematic approach to algorithm animation. The framework consists of three primary components: Algorithm, Mapping and Animation. In the *Algorithm component* a designer identifies key positions (resp. interesting events) in a programme that correspond to operations that are important to the programme's semantics. The name and parameters of these "algorithm operations", as Stasko denotes them, are forwarded to the mapping component and then further to the animation component. In the *animation component* the graphical objects are contained. These object can change their location, size, and colour throughout the frames of an animation. Stasko also specified a formal model for the component that consists of four abstract datatypes: The graphical images (i.e. the primary images[49] lines, rectangles, circles, and text and composite images that are collections of primary images which are geometrically related to each other), locations (i.e. positions described by (x,y)-coordinate pairs for 2D views), paths (i.e. the magnitude of change in one or more image attributes from one frame to the next), and transitions (i.e. the actual modification of an image's position or appearance based on a path parameter; transition types include e.g. move, resize, colour, fill or alter visibility actions). The *Mapping component* contains the mappings from an algorithm to the animation. By the use of associations (i.e. general mechanisms for storage and retrieval) data objects (images, locations or data values) can be connected to a set of parameters that are received from the Algorithm component.

The conceptual framework has been implemented in the Tango algorithm animation system [Sta90]. In Tango programmes can either be annotated directly in their source code or with the support of a special editor. Algorithm animations are defined via code definitions in the C programming language and on the basis of

---

[49]Sometimes also denoted as graphical primitives

user-defined data types (for images, locations, paths, and transitions). The mapping between the operations and the animation scenes is defined in a separate control file. When all components have been defined that animation and the algorithm execution can be started and the algorithm operations are visualised accordingly.

The visualisations of the example for an algorithm animation in figure 3.32 have been created using a JCAT web applet. Figure 3.32 shows three steps (start, intermediate, and final stage) of an animation of an algorithm for determining the convex hull[50] of a set of points. When the animation is started the virtual "rubber band" continuously spans around the outer points until the polygon that equaly the convex hull is reached.

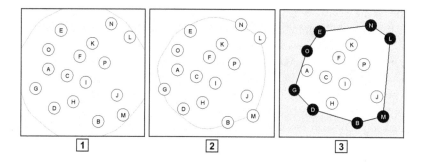

Figure 3.32: Screenshot of an Algorithm Animation for Determining the Convex Hull in JCAT (Source: http://www-cg-hci.informatik.uni-oldenburg.de/)

Finally, a three dimensional algorithm animation is shown in figure 3.33 on page 89, created with the Zeus system [BN93]. It represents the procedure of a shortest path algorithm for a directed graph. Shortest path algorithms are used to "find the shortest paths from one specified vertex to all other vertices in a weighted graph, where the edge weights correspond to nonnegative distances between junctions" [Wes96](p.76) and the length of a path is defined as the sum of the weights of the edges along the path. This corresponds to the problem of finding the shortest way on a map from a particular location to another location on the map where the lengths of the streets that can be taken corresponds to the weights of a graph. One common algorithm to solve this problem (for the case of non-negative weights) is Dijkstra's shortest path algorithm [Dij59] which could be used as a basis for the algorithm animation in figure 3.33 on page 89 ((although not explicitly mentioned in the corresponding article [BN93]).

---

[50]The convex hull of a set of points is defined as the smallest convex polygon containing the points.

The animation shows the directed graph in a three dimensional environment (frame 1 in figure 3.33 on the next page). In the second frame a copy of the directed graph is shown with green columns on top of each vertex. The height of the column represents the cost (i.e. the length of the shortest path found so far) for reaching that vertex from the root vertex, which is set to infinite at the initial stage of the algorithm. The algorithm then repeatedly examines whether one of the neighbouring vertices can lower the cost of that vertex. If a vertex is found that can do so, the edge leading to that vertex is coloured red and the height of the column of that vertex is adjusted to represent its cost, otherwise the edge is hidden (or previously found edges that led to higher costs of the vertex). The tip of the three dimensional edge is then raised to the top of the column (see frame 3 in figure 3.33 on the facing page). When the algorithm has terminated the unused edges of the three dimensional representation are removed so that the shortest paths from the root to all vertices are shown by the red coloured three dimensional sub graph (frame 4 in figure 3.33 on the next page[51].

Basically, the same output of showing the evolution of the algorithm could have also been shown by a two dimensional represenation, the three dimensional view however permits to directly visually identify additional characteristics of the calculated subgraph as for example the longest path of all shortest paths and the comparison of the relative steepness of the paths.

As has been outlined above programme visualisation also comprises the representation of data and data structures. To subdivide the large field of data visualisation - which has already been partly covered in section 3.1 on page 45 with the discussion of the various diagramme types as used in descriptive statistics and will be further brought up later in this chapter for the discussion of information visualisation on the user interface level - it shall now be focused on aspects of data modelling and in the following on the latest developments in regard to the visual representations of ontologies.

Entity Relationship diagrams   For setting the boundaries of conceptual versus data models and to take into account the various views on the representation of data it can be reverted to the ANSI/SPARC architectural model for database systems that defines a conceptual, internal, and external data view [SH02][52]: The conceptual view determines the logical data structure, independent of specific implementations or application purposes. The logical data structure is described in a *semantical data model* that is then transformed into a *logical database model*. The

---

[51]Due to the unavailability of the original website it has been referred to the website of http://web.archive.org

[52]Also denoted as conceptual - physical - view, e.g. [Ull82]

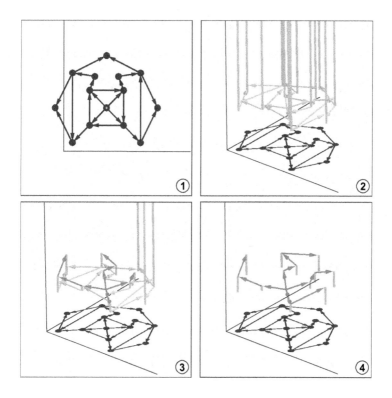

Figure 3.33: Shortest Path Algorithm Animation in Zeus (Source: http://web.archive.org/)

internal view is concerned with the *physical storage* of the data structures elaborated in the database model. The external view (also denoted as the *user's view*)
describes which parts of the database system are available to the user and which
restrictions and access rights have to be imposed.

Various approaches have been developed for these views with the most established and widely taught and used being the entity-relationship model by Chen
[Che76] for the semantic data model and the relational model by Codd [Cod70]
for the logical database model. Other models that have been developed in the past
such as the hierarchical or the network data model may still persist in legacy systems today but are in general not considered for the development of new database
applications any more (cf. [LLS06]). An extension to the relational database model
are object oriented databases which is also denoted as object-relational model, see
cf. [EN94](p.663ff.) for an overview. that builds upon the concepts of object orientation.

As mentioned already above visualisations have been used for a long time in
the area of semantical data modelling and some approaches have even incorporated distinct visual representations from their very beginning (with the first one
usually ascribed to Bachman in 1969 [Bac69]). The Entity-Relationship model
and the corresponding Entity-Relationship diagrams by Chen [Che76] are a well-
known example for a visual data modelling language. In figure 3.34 on the next
page the symbol set for creating basic Entity-Relationship (ER) diagrams and their
meanings is depicted. The following explanation of the semantics of ER diagrams is restricted to the core concepts, further elaborations can be found e.g.
in [EN94, Ull82] and in the original publication [Che76]. The remarks given here
are based on the statements in [EN94].

Basically, ER diagrams consist of *entities* that represents things of the real world
with an independent existence and *relationships* between the entities [EN94].

Therefore, an entity could be a physical object (e.g. a person, car or house) or an
object with a conceptual existence (e.g. an institute, a company or a course). Entities are further described by their properties which are denoted as *attributes*. An
entity type describes the schema for a set of entities that share the common characteristics and structure. The entity sets are also called extensions of the entity
type. A *relationship type* between a number of entity types defines a set of associations among entities of this type. The degree of a relationship is the number
of the entity types that participate in the relationship. Relationships may also be
further characterised by attributes attached to them, their links to the entity types
are described by *roles* which are especially important for recursive relationships to
distinguish the meanings of each participation. Furthermore, structural constraints
can be imposed upon relationship types: The *cardinality ratio* defines the amount

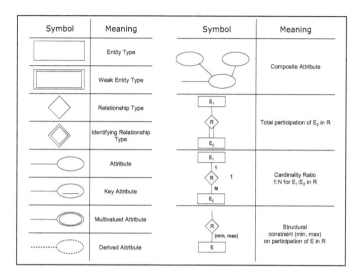

Figure 3.34: Symbols and Meanings of the Symbol Set for ER Diagrams (after [EN94](p.59))

of relationship instances that an entity type can participate in and the *participation constraint* specifies if the existence of the entity that participates in the relationship depends on the relation to another entity type (a *total participation* constraint implies that every participating entity must be related, a *partial participation* constraint means that it does not necessarily have to be related). *Weak entity types* are entity types that do not have key attributes themselves and therefore depend on the existence of another entity (they must therefore always be related with a total participation constraint and the relationship type that relates a weak entity type to its owner has to be an *Identifying Relationship Type*).

The concept of entity relationship models has been enhanced by additional semantic concepts of *specialisation, generalisation, inheritance,* and *categories* to take into account new requirements that have been developed in the course of the research on semantic data models [EN94]. The terminology for Enhanced Entity Relationship (EER) models has not been standardised but is derived from a number of approaches, therefore it is reverted here to the remarks in [EN94](p.611ff). The

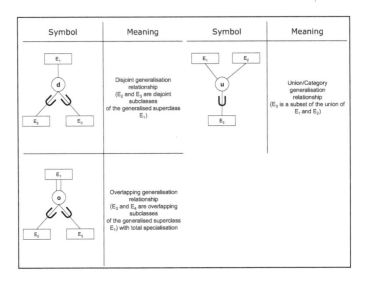

Figure 3.35: Symbols and Meanings for Enhanced Entity-Relationship Diagrams (cf. [EN94])

concepts of specialisation and generalisation allow to define subclass respectively superclass relationships between entities[53].

A subclass is used to explicitly express additional, meaningful subgroupings of an entity type thereby specialising the entity type by different distinguishing characteristics. The process of generalisation can be seen as the reverse process of an abstraction: Differences between entity types are neglected and a common superclass is defined, of which the previous entity types are subclasses. The processes of generalisation and specialisation may also be applied several times thereby creating subclass/superclass lattices. For the notation as shown in figure 3.35 a differentiation between generalisation and specialisation relationships has not been included. In line with these concepts goes the concept of *attribute inheritance* from which follows that a subclass possesses, additional to its own attributes and participations in relationship types, all attributes and relationship instances of the superclass. The definition of subclasses and superclasses can be constrained in the following ways: By the specification of *disjointness* respectively *overlap* of

---

[53]The first proposals for the technical as well as philosophical concepts of generalisation and abstraction can be found in [SS77], the extensions regarding additional predicates for subclass definitions (e.g. the intersection, union and difference predicates) in [HM81].

classes, which signifies that an entity can either belong to at most one of the subclasses of the specialisation (i.e. disjoint subclasses) or that the sets of entities can overlap. And furthermore completeness constraints can be defined, i.e. whether every entity in a superclass must be a member of some subclass in the specialisation (*total specialisation* or whether an entity may not belong to any of the subclasses (*partial specialisation*, which is the standard case). For the possibility to depict subclass/superclass relationships with more than one superclass the concept of *categories* is provided. Therefore, the union of the two or more classes can be specified.

Apart from the traditional notations for Entity Relationship diagrams several alternative representations can be found today. In figure 3.36 two common notations for the visual representation of cardinalities are depicted. On the left side the so called "chicken-feet" notation is shown, on the right side the "Bachman" notation (cf. [EN94](p.801ff.)). Both notations have the same expressiveness as the traditional number and character based notations and are used in a variety of tools that implement the modelling of Entity Relationship diagrams.

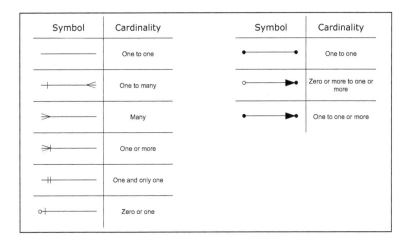

Symbol	Cardinality	Symbol	Cardinality
———————	One to one	•———————•	One to one
─┼──────<	One to many	o────────▶•	Zero or more to one or more
>──────	Many	•────────▶•	One to one or more
>┼──────	One or more		
─┼┼──────	One and only one		
o┼──────	Zero or one		

Figure 3.36: Alternative Notations for Cardinality in Entity Relationship Diagrams

In the last years the vision of a *Semantic Web* [BLHL01] that basically aims to enable software agents to semantically understand and act upon information on the world wide web has considerably influenced the discussions on the definition of data semantics and its possible applications in a web setting. To position these views in relation to the historical discussion about how to express semantics when conceiving data structures and their repositories and then to look for specific types of visualisations in this area the following distinctive characteristics of *semantic data modelling, knowledge representation* and *conceptual modelling* shall be highlighted (cf. [Myl92]): Whereas semantic data modelling establishes, due to its roots in the database communities, a close relationship to actual implementations of the created models, conceptual modelling can be generally described as "the activity of formally describing some aspects of the physical and social world around us for purposes of understanding and communication" [Myl92](p.52) by human users, therefore being much more open and independent from actual implementation considerations (in line with the views expressed in the ANSI/SPARC model as has been outlined above) although not necessarily being less formal or less well-defined.

The area of knowledge representation which strives, just as semantic data modelling and conceptual modelling, for the capturing of knowledge of a specific domain or subject matter focuses on the joint application of theories and techniqes from logic, ontologies and computation to enable systems to perform "intelligent" tasks (cf. [Sow00]), as e.g. apparent in expert systems. Whereas conceptual modelling and semantic data modelling share the requirement to allow for a human interaction with their abstractions from the real world, knowledge representation assumes that the abstractions generated by its methods and tools will be primarily dealt with by machines and not by humans [Myl92]. This view is supported by the obvious varying semantic richness and complexity (cf. based on the framework of the Ontology Spectrum by [Obr03]): While the standard Entity Relationship model only contains some basic semantic constructs, the Enhanced Entity Relationship model and further approaches such as the Unified Modelling Language (UML), the Resource Description Framework and its schema (RDF, RDFS), the Web Ontology Language (OWL) in line with description logics have a much stronger semantic expressiveness to enable machine understanding. This aspect has to be taken into account when examining visualisations of ontologies, thesauri and other representations discussed in the context of semantic web technologies.

Before turning to the discussion of visualisations of approaches built on rich semantic models, especially for the visualisation of ontologies, a widely discussed visualisation approach shall now be drafted. It is positioned in the Ontology Spectrum by Obrst at a medium semantic expressiveness: The Unified Modelling Language (UML).

The Unified Modelling Language (UML)   The Unified Modelling Language has evolved from the paradigm of object orientation that dominates today's programming languages. The aim of *object orientation* is to represent objects of the real world in an abstract and manageable form but with all attributes and behaviours that are necessary to accomplish a specific task (cf. [Oes04]). Object orientation therefore directly refers to the semantic data models that have been described above and makes use of many of the concepts that have evolved in this field (e.g. the concept of abstraction, classes, subclasses and the inheritance of attributes, the associations between classes etc.). What differentiates of object orientation from semantic data models is on the one hand the inclusion of operations, i.e. dynamic behaviour, into the models and on the other hand the concepts that result from this combined view of data and behaviour (cf. the concepts of *encapsulation* and *polymorphism*[54]) as well as very detailed assertions on the usage of the constructs (cf. [RBP+91, RJB99, HK99, Oes04]). The symbols of the Unified Modelling Language have evolved out of the first notations for object oriented modelling with many similarities to notations in semantic data modelling.

The UML can be defined as "a visual language for specifying, constructing and documenting the artifacts of systems." [OMG04b](p.10). It is not restricted to a specific purpose but is "a modelling language that can be used with all major object and component methods, and that can be applied to all application domains (e.g. health, finance, telecom, aerospace) and implementation platforms (e.g. J2EE, .NET)." [OMG04b](p.10). It can therefore be used for conceptual models as well as strongly implementation oriented models as it is today realised by the concepts of the Model Driven Architecture (MDA) [MM05] that differentiates between plattform independent models (PIM) and plattform specific models (PSM), both of which can be created in UML [FL03]. The official current specification of the UML version 2.0 is laid down in the UML Infrastructure [OMG04b] and and the UML Superstructure[OMG04a] documents which are published by the Object Management Group (OMG), a non-profit organisation that is open to small and large companies and which "produces and maintains computer industry specifications for interoperable enterprise applications" [55].

Due to the open accessibility of the UML specification documents and the wide acceptance of its approach as a general-purpose modelling language UML has been intensively researched and used in academia and industry (c.f. the sections in the IEEE Symposia on Visual Languages and Human Centric Computing focusing on aspects of UML [BG04](p.235ff.), [ES05](p.109ff.) and specific conferences focusing on UML such as the ACM/IEEE International Conferences on Model Driven Engineering Languages and Systems). The discussion of UML shall here be restricted to an overview of the main visual aspects of the language and will not focus in detail on the specific concepts underlying the language constructs such

---

[54]For a discussuion of these specific concepts see e.g. [RBP+91, Oes04].
[55]See http://www.omg.org/gettingstarted/gettingstartedindex.htm

as the principles of object orientation underlying class and object diagrams or behaviour representation in e.g. statechart diagrams (cf. [Har87]) which have, as will
be illustrated in the following, comparatively similar forms of visual representations. The UML is divided into two types of diagrams: *Structure* and *behaviour*
diagrams. UML structure diagrams represent the static structure of objects in a
system whereas behaviour diagrams contain information about the the dynamic
behaviour of objects, i.e. a series of changes to the system over time. In the following an overview of the diagram types in UML2.0, their basic intentions and
elements is given (closely based on the elaborations by [Oes04](p.211ff.) and the
official UML2.0 documents [OMG04a, OMG04b][56]). For component, deployment, activity, and sequence diagrams the actual notations and their meaning as
well as an example are shown[57].

A UML *Class diagram* describes the existing classes and their relationships.
Class diagrams can be used for different purposes e.g. to depict models of business terms or the structure of concepts. Class diagrams can be based on specific
programming code and can be used to generate code or visualise existing code
structures in the sense of reverse engineering. A class in UML represents the
definition of the attributes, operations and semantics of a number of objects and
participates in inheritance hierarchies. *Attributes* are data elements contained in
every object (instance) of that class and hold an individual value in every object.
A special case are class attributes that do not belong to a single object but are attributes of a class whose values can be accessed by every instance of that class (e.g.
for counting the number of instances of a class). *Operations* are services which
can be requested of an object and are described by their signature (operation name,
parameters and an optional return value). They can be invoked on any object that
is directly or indirectly an instance of the class.

Classes, attributes, and operations can be further detailed to describe specific
behaviours or properties, e.g. in inheritance hierarchies. Between classes the following relationships can be defined: *Inheritance relationships* define a relation
between a superclass and a subclass (as discussed above for Enhanced Entity Relationship diagrams) where attributes and operations of the superclass are made
available to one or more subclasses and a*ssociation relationships* show the common semantics and structure of links between objects. Associations may be defined for one or more objects (thereby including recursive relationships) and can
be further specialised by directions (directed association), attributes (attributed as-

---

[56]Not covered here are the additional documents for the specification of the UML Object Constraint
Language (OCL) and the UML Diagram Interchange format.

[57]The selection of these diagram types is based on their perceived high attraction from the viewpoint
of visualisation.

sociation - the attributes may also be classes themselves), qualifications (where the multiplicity of objects that participate in the association is limitied by qualification attributes), and n-ary associations (similar to ternary or higher dimensional relationships in ER diagrams). Furthermore, three special subtypes of associations are available: *Aggregations*, which extend associations by defining a whole/part relationship between classes, *compositions* as the strict form of an aggregation where the existence of the parts depends on the whole and the instances of the parts cannot be shared with other objects, and *dependency relationships* that state that a change in the independent model element necessitates a change in the dependent model element.

Object diagrams have a similar structure as class diagrams but represent instead of classes a selection of objects (instances) and their current values at a specific point in time. It can therefore be used to visualise the state of objects at runtime.

With *Composite structure diagrams* (or collaboration diagrams) design patterns (cf. [GHJV95]) can be specified that describe which classes and components are part of a pattern, thereby stressing the fact that a specific behaviour results from the collaboration of multiple elements. The UML Superstructure defines that elements of composite structure diagrams may be used in all other structure diagrams [OMG04a](p.188).

In *Component diagrams* the structure of components, i.e. executable and exchangeable software units with defined interfaces and an individual identiy, as well as the relations between components can be represented. The elements that can be used in component diagrams include Component, Interface, Realization, Interface Realization, Usage Dependency, Class, Artifact and Port. Artifacts are defined by the user and represent concrete elements in the physical world (e.g. a document or files), ports specify distinct interaction points between a classifier (e.g. a component) and its environment or between the classifier and its internal parts [OMG04a]. In figure 3.37 on the following page the symbols for component diagrams and their meanings are shown.

The goal of *Deployment diagrams* it to illustrate which software (components and objects) is executed on which nodes (i.e. physical computing units). Deployment diagrams may contain the elements: Artifact, Node, Artifact deployed on Node, Node with deployed Artifacts, Deployment specification, Deployment specification - with properties, Deployment specification - with property values, Artifact with annotated deployment properties and the relations Association, Dependency, Generalization, Deployment, and Manifestation.

In figure 3.38 on page 99 the notations for the elements and relations in UML deployment diagrams are presented as they are outlined in the UML Superstructure

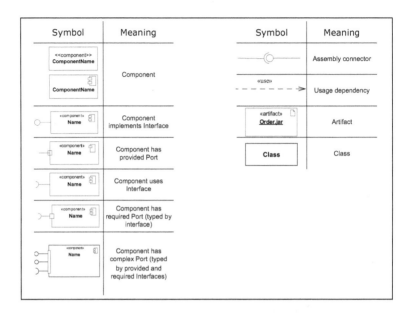

Figure 3.37: Symbols for UML Component Diagrams (Source [OMG04a])

specification. It is worth remarking that the relations for Association, Dependency, and Generalization are the same as in the remaining structure diagrams.

Pakckage diagrams are collections of model elements of arbitrary type that are used to structure the overall model into manageable sub-units. A package defines a namespace which implies that elements within a package must have unique names. Every element may be referenced in other packages but only belongs to one specific package. The top most package contains the complete system.

After the discussion of the UML2.0 structure diagrams it will now be focussed on the seven behaviour diagrams: Activity, Use case, State machine, Sequence, Communication, Interaction Overview, and Timing diagram.

The UML *Activity diagrams* are very similar to the abovely discussed flowchart diagrams and equally describe a flow of actions. They consist of different node types (action, object, and control nodes) as well as object and control flows that connect the nodes. The whole diagram is named an *activity* and contains a start (InitialNode) and an end node (ActivityFinal). Activities can be nested in action nodes, thereby defining hierarchies of interleaved activity diagrams. In figure 3.39 on page 100 an excerpt of the most important elements of activity diagrams is

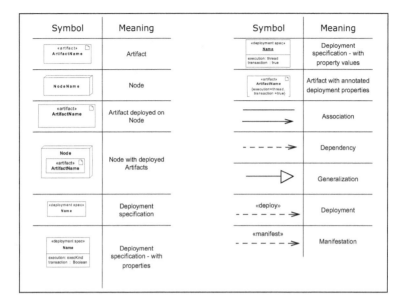

Figure 3.38: Symbols for UML Deployment Diagrams (Source [OMG04a])

shown (the total set of elements according to the UML Superstructure contains 25 elements [OMG04a](p.402–406)). Besides the standard elements for the definition of decisions (DecisionNode and MergeNode) and the the merging of different flows that does not affect the following executions of actions, activity diagrams also contain control elements to define parallel executions (ForkNode) and synchronisations (JoinNode) where the control flow is delayed until all incoming flows have been accomplished. Instead of action nodes it is also possible to model object nodes that symbolise that an object or a set of objects exists. An object flow defines that the particular objects are required by the following actions or that they are created or modified by the actions. For the graphical representation of objects two possible notations are shown in figure 3.39 on the next page. In the case of an interruption within a set of actions special areas and signals can be defined to take into account the steps that shall follow an interruption.

Figure 3.40 on page 101 shows an example for an activity diagram. The activity starts with Step 1 which is together with the following decision and Step 2 within the interruptable area "parallel" (shown by the dotted line) that contains a signal that is connected to an ActivityFinal node by an interrupt connector. One path

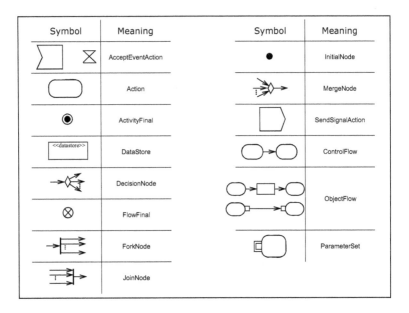

Symbol	Meaning	Symbol	Meaning
	AcceptEventAction	●	InitialNode
	Action		MergeNode
◉	ActivityFinal		SendSignalAction
<<datastore>>	DataStore		ControlFlow
	DecisionNode		ObjectFlow
⊗	FlowFinal		
	ForkNode		ParameterSet
	JoinNode		

Figure 3.39: Excerpt of Symbols for UML Activity Diagrams (Source [OMG04a])

after the decision leads to a ForkNode, indicating the parallel execution of the subsequent flows. Step 4 is represented as an action node containing a nested activity diagram, which is shown below the main diagram.

Activity diagrams can be used to describe the dynamic behaviour of use cases and may also be used for general flow representations, for example they would also be suitable for a simplified representation of business processes.

Use case diagrams show actors, use cases and the relations between them. They show the context of a business case and shall support the communication with the future users or customers of the system by describing the external behaviour of the system and the interaction with the external actors (who need not be human actors but could also be other computer systems which becomes apparent by the free choice of symbols for the actor entity cf. [OMG04a](p.583)). Use case diagrams themselves do not describe the behaviour and processes of the system but are only an aid for the identification and management of the system requirements.

A *State machine diagram* shows a sequence of states which an object can adopt during its lifetime and which events (actions) trigger the result of changes (transitions) in the states. It consists of an initial state, a finite, non-empty set of states, a

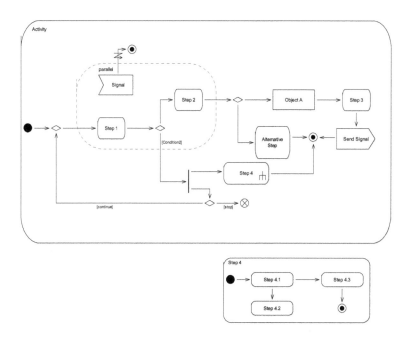

Figure 3.40: Example for a UML2.0 Activity Diagram (created with Adonis UML2.0 Library)

finite, non-empty set of events, state transitions and a set of final states. An example for the definition of state machine diagrams based on meta-modelling concepts can be found in [Fil04]. Finally the four types of interaction diagrams as sub-types of behaviour diagrams shall be illustrated: The *Communication diagram* presents a set of interactions between distinct objects in a specific context. Similar to the subsequently discussed Sequence diagram, Communication diagrams show objects and their interactions but do not focus on the temporal relationships (which can nevertheless be integrated). For the precise and complete definition of behaviour state machine and activity diagrams are to be preferred due to their higher expressiveness [Oes04]. Nevertheless Communication diagrams can be used for simple interaction representations as illustrations.

The *Sequence diagram* shows a set of messages that are exchanged between participating entities (which may be objects or actors) in a temporally limited situation with a focus on the intertemporal flow [Oes04](p.329). Sequence diagrams extend the ideas of Communication diagrams by explicitly showing the temporal

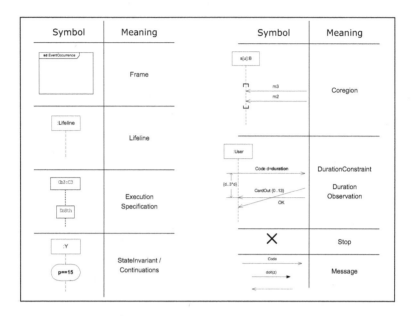

Figure 3.41: Excerpt of Symbols for UML Sequence Diagrams (Source [OMG04a])

relations of messages in the lifetime of objects. This is symbolised by Lifeline elements that show the progress of time for a specific object in the vertical direction from top to bottom (see figure 3.41 for the excerpt of the most important symbols for Sequence diagrams). On these lifelines the activity of objects is marked by the Execution Specification elements from which messages may be sent to other active objects. The construction of objects is marked by a message arrow directed to the Execution Specification of that object, the destruction of objects is shown by a Stop element on a lifeline. With Frame objects that are specified by an additional "ref" attribute references to nested Sequence diagrams can be established. Furthermore alternative flows can be defined by an "alt" Frame and intertemporal relationships between messages can be defined via Duration Constraint elements. State Invariants define invariant values that are evaluated prior to whatever event occurs during execution time.

Interaction Overview diagram is basically an activity diagram where parts of the flow are represented by nested or referenced Sequence diagrams. Oestereich states that the usage of this diagram is unclear [Oes04](p.333) as it does not provide additional information to activity or sequence diagrams themselves. The last diagram of UML2.0 is the *Timing diagram*. It describes the temporal conditions of state changes of multiple related objects. Therefore, it permits to define exact temporal requirements and dependencies and may be used to meet the requirements of real-time systems.

To conclude the section of the discussion of the diagrams of the Unified Modelling Language another visual representation for a UML class diagram shall be presented that constitutes one of the few approaches that are discussed in the literature that propose variations for the very strict and exactly defined UML notation[58]. In figure 3.42 on the left hand side a traditional UML class diagram is shown and on the right hand side the new version which is based on "geons" (which stands for geometrical icons) that form the graphical primitives. On the basis of a perception theory and experiments that have been performed with these forms of representations it is stated that the geon diagrams are easier and faster to interpret than traditional 2D UML diagrams [IW00].

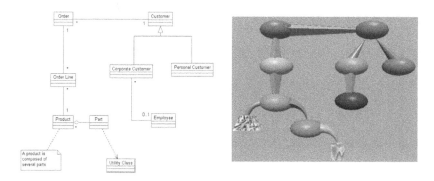

Figure 3.42: Example for a Three-Dimensional UML Geon Diagram (Source: [IW00])

Interface Level

On the highest levels of the integrated computer science framework resides the interaction of computer science with the environment, i.e. the user and the organisation. Especially the area of user interface design contains important aspects when examining visualisations in computer science. Since the early conceptions for user interfaces the field has been particularly influenced by the availability of personal

---

[58]Two approaches have been found [Dwy01] and [CE03, IW00] from which the second was selected to be shown here as the quality of the pictures in the first approach was not sufficient.

computers with enough graphical power to realise complex graphical interfaces. The upcoming of techniques based on the *desktop metaphor*, i.e. the provision of a graphical interaction environment that resembles a conventional desktop has considerably eased the human-machine interaction and is still the basis for today's user interfaces. The accomodation to human diversity which includes physical, intellectual, and personality differences [Shn93] has always been a central goal in user interface design that has gained new importance for web based interactions where the human-computer interaction is not apriori determined by specific programming standards but rather depends on the conceptions of the individual designer of an application. Therefore, efforts have been made to define standards for a barrier-free access to web ressources, as e.g. laid out by Web Accessibility Initiative of the World-Wide-Web Consortium (see http://www.w3.org/WAI/).

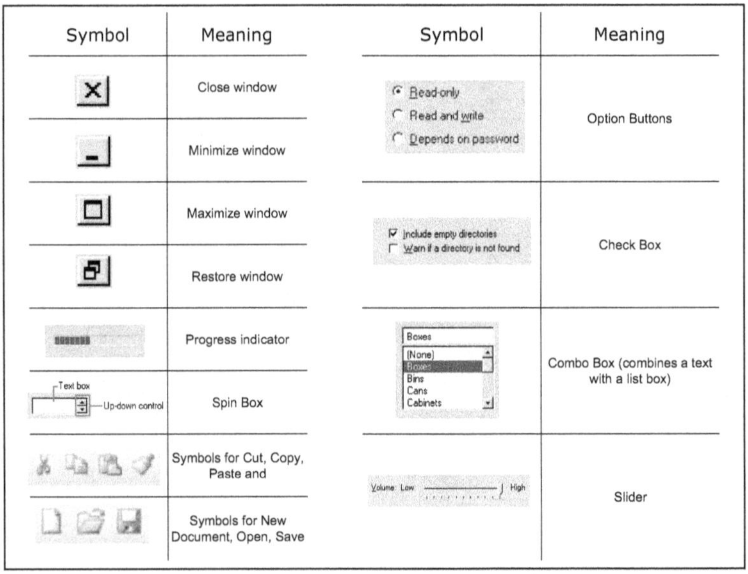

Symbol	Meaning	Symbol	Meaning
✕	Close window	● Read-only ○ Read and write ○ Depends on password	Option Buttons
_	Minimize window		
▢	Maximize window	☑ Include empty directories ☐ Warn if a directory is not found	Check Box
⧉	Restore window		
▬▬▬▬	Progress indicator	Boxes / [None] / Boxes / Bins / Cans / Cabinets	Combo Box (combines a text with a list box)
Text box / Up-down control	Spin Box		
✂ ⬚ ⬚ ✔	Symbols for Cut, Copy, Paste and	Volume: Low —————┤ High	Slider
⬚ ⬚ ⬚	Symbols for New Document, Open, Save		

Figure 3.43: Examples for Common User Interface Components in the Microsoft Windows Environment (Source:http://msdn.microsoft.com)

User interface design   Taking the perspective of visualisation in regard to user interfaces a large number of graphical representations with sometimes very specific meanings can be detected. However, due to the high coherence of the meanings of these visual representations, which is unquestionably caused by the dominance of the Microsoft Windows operating system and its standardisation efforts, most of the representations are fairly easily understandable to the average PC user. This is illustrated by figure 3.43 on the preceding page that shows an excerpt of user interface components used by various applications based on the Windows operating system. To employ the shown components in an application, programming effort is required which comprises the positioning of the components, the definition of possible interactions with the component, and linkage to an underlying data model that supplies the values used to display the state of the component[59].

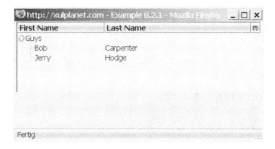

Figure 3.44: Example for a XUL-Based User Interface Showing a Tree Component (Source: http://xulplanet.org)

An alternative approach for the definition of user interfaces has recently come up with XML languages for defining user interfaces, first in the open source community but then also taken up in a different format by Microsoft. It builds upon the requirement of making user interfaces independent of their actual implementation to ease their portability between different plattforms and programming languages. The two markup languages that are currently in use for this purpose are XUL[60], which has been developed in the course of the Mozilla open source project and XAML[61] which is part of the new Windows Presentation Foundation framework that will be integrated in Microsoft's next generation operating system Windows Vista (scheduled for 2006). Although a full documentation for XAML is not yet available from the hints accessible on the Microsoft Developer Network it can be assumed that XAML will be of higher expressiveness and able to include procedural code as well as vector graphics and animations. Furthermore it is stated that XAML descriptions including procedural statements will have to be com-

---

[59] In line with the common model-view-controller design pattern [GHJV95].
[60] See http://xulplanet.com/ accessed 11-05-2006.
[61] See http://msdn.microsoft.com/winfx accessed 11-05-2006.

piled whereas XUL descriptions are always interpreted, which may result in performance differences. Nevertheless at this point of time it is too early to compare both technologies.

To illustrate the basic idea of XUL a code example is shown in listing 3.1 and the according representation in figure 3.44 on the previous page. It describes a hierarchical tree as it is common in many applications for displaying hierarchical structures (e.g. a file system). When dealing with large datasets it would be necessary in XUL to separate the data structure (model) and the view (which has not been done for the example) as it is common also for other user interface implementations. Additionally, to take into account the interaction with a user, the scripting language JavaScript can be used to add event handling and processing in XUL.

Listing 3.1: XML Source Code for the XUL Example in Figure 3.44 on the previous page (Source:http://xulplanet.org)

```
<?xml version="1.0"?>
  . . .
<tree rows="6">
  <treecols>
      <treecol id="firstname" label="
          First Name" primary="true"
          flex="3"/>
      <treecol id="lastname" label="
          Last Name" flex="7"/>
  </treecols>
  <treechildren>
    <treeitem container="true" open="
        true">
      <treerow>
        <treecell label="Guys"/>
      </treerow>
      <treechildren>
  . . .
          <treerow>
            <treecell label="Jerry"/>
            <treecell label="Hodge"/>
  . . .
  </window>
```

Information Visualisations - Visual Data Mining To conclude the chapter of visualisations in computer science a selection of visualisations coming the large field of information visualisation shall be analysed. Information visualisation can be regarded as a special category of user-interface design [Mar06](p.42). In contrast to the abovely discussed approaches of data modelling that take an apriori view on the conception of data models, the tasks in information visualisation build upon the existence of a concrete data set that is to be analysed.

The basic concept of information visualisation without information technology has a long historical tradition and several methods for explaining and analysing data visually have been invented before the advent of computers (for an overview see [Tuf83]). Today information visualisation is concerned with the visual representation of large, high-dimensional data sets[62]. Modern information visualisation techniques allow for visually mining data, identifying structures and relationships in the data and thereby supporting not only the mere presentation but also a confirmatory analysis of hypotheses as well as an exploratory analysis to develop hypotheses [GKW04].

Information visualisation therefore operates tightly with the application fields that generate the underlying data sets but is actually a distinct field with its own methods. It is closely related to descriptive statistics but actually goes far beyond the traditional chart techniques - the 3D trading room shown on page 63 could in this regard also be classified as an information visualization. Due to the large number of visualisation approaches in this field only some selected examples for typical representatives of this field will be shown in the following.

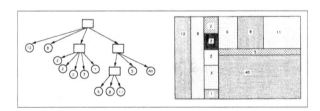

Figure 3.45: Original Conception of the Tree Map and the corresponding Graph Structure (Source: [Shn92])

The first prominent example for an information visualisation that shall be discussed are *tree maps* which have been conceived in 1992 by Shneiderman [Shn92].

---

[62]Grinstein et al. define large data sets to contain more than 10^7 entries and high dimensional by up to 1000 parameters [GKW04].

The approach presents an innovative view on hierarchically structured, quantitative data and can be extended to additionally show the different types of data. The basic concept of the underlying algorithm is to partition a given rectangle subject to the number and size of the subsequent nodes and rotating the partition by 90° when an additional level in the tree is reached. Thereby at even levels nodes are partitioned vertically and at odd levels horizontally. In figure 3.45 on the preceding page the original conception by Shneiderman and the corresponding hierarchical tree are shown.

The second example for a typical information visualisation are *parallel coordinates*. For the creation of a parallel coordinates visualistion each data dimension is represented as a horizontal (or vertical) axis and the resulting number N of axes are organised as uniformly spaces lines. A data element in an N-dimensional space is then mapped to a polyline that traverses across all of the axes and crosses each axis at a position that is proportional to its value for the specific dimension [FWR99]. The approach of hierarchical parallel coordinates extends the basic approach by applying a hierarchical algorithm to the data in the phase of exploratory data analysis. Thereby, data clusters, with specific minimum and maximum bounds and the cluster means are identified and can be additionally encoded visually [FWR99]. Parallel coordinates facilitate the exploration of large multivariate data sets [FWR99] and can be used as a basis for hypothesis generation about data relationships.

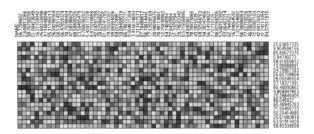

Figure 3.46: Example of a Heatmap (created with Heatmapbuilder)

Another example for the identification of clusters by means of information visualisation techniques is the approach of heatmaps (cf. [Sii04, GKW04]). A heatmap is generated from a data table where data records are represented in the rows and the different dimensions of a data set by columns. The values of a dimension are then classified into categories (e.g. categories for low, medium and high values). By using a colour coding scheme the type of category is assigned to the values of a dimension (see figure 3.46 on the preceding page). To support the detection of clusters the dimensions and records can be sorted and re-organised thereby changing the visual representation.

Finally, an information visualisation example shall be presented that is concerned with the representation of the semantics of data as it has been announced above: In the field of knowledge representation considerable attention has been paid in the last years to the vision of a Semantic Web that shall basically enable machines to collaborate automatically and without prior bilateral adjustments on the web based on a user query [BLHL01]. A central concept of Semantic Web are *ontologies* which are required to set up "the basic terms and relations comprising the vocabulary of a topic area as well as the rules for combining terms and relations to define extensions to the vocabulary" [NFF+91](p.40) and that can be processed by machines and shared on the web (cf. also the elaborations by [Gru93, BA97]). Currently, several definitions exist in the scientific literature as to what exactly constitutes an ontology, which semantic expressiveness it should have (e.g. whether a taxonomy, an ER model or a UML model may also be considered as an ontology - cf. the concept of the ontoloy spectrum [Obr03]) and whether it is only conceived for machine usage or might also be used by humans.

Based on the earlier elaborations in regard to semantic models and the UML the view on ontologies that shall be taken here is that ontologies are, due to their roots in the area of knowledge representation which is concerned with models for the usage by machines [Myl92], primarily directed to machine and not human processing. Nevertheless, it shall be stressed that this approach of a *pragmatic differentiation* does not exclude a human interaction with ontologies but only refers to the processing aspect.

Taking the perspective of visualisation in regard to ontologies two theoretical approaches can be considered based on human interfaces to ontologies: The first approach concerns the *design of ontologies* where the input of users may be required to create or modify the contents of an ontology and visualisation could be employed to support this interaction. A second aspect where visualisations might come into play is the human interaction with an existing ontology for *analyses and evaluations* of their properties, e.g. to assess the scope of the ontology. Whereas the first aspect can be resolved by visual modelling techniques (cf. in this context the recently issued meta model for the web ontology language by OMG [OMG05]) the second approach may necessitate techniques from information visualisation as the number of instances and relationships in an ontology can become considerably large (e.g. the wordnet database by Princeton University that can be considered as a generic ontology for the English language currently contains some hundred

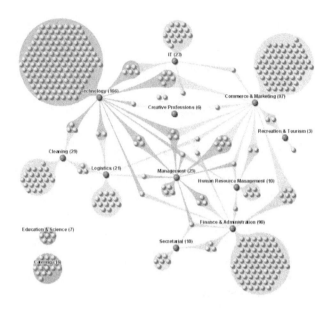

Figure 3.47: Cluster Map Visualisation for Job Vacancies (Source: [FSH03])

thousand entries[63]). In figure 3.47 an information visualisation is shown that visualises the number of instances for the concepts in an ontology, thereby allowing for an assessment of the relative size of the instance space. Apart from a pure size comparision the figure also gives an impression of possible qualitative conclusions that can be derived: The visualisation shows a set of job offers from the perspective of different economic sectors. The added value of using an ontology for the semantic description of the underlying data results in the possibility to visually depict similarity relationships between the different concepts (e.g. to assess that few vacancies exist in the mediating field between human resource management and finance& administration but several vacancies exist in the mediating field between technology and commerce& marketing).

---

[63]See http://wordnet.princeton.edu/ accessed 12-05-2006.

3.3 Business Informatics Frameworks

After having outlined various approaches for visualisations in the areas of business and computer science the focus shall now be put on the field of business informatics as the mediating function between these two fields. The positioning and structure of business informatics as described on page 14ff can be further detailed by using the same considerations as for the previously discussed fields, namely to revert to frameworks that classify the major elements and relationships of a science.

Several frameworks have been described in the business informatics literature and related areas that can be used for this purpose. Among these are the Business Engineering Model by Österle and Blessing [sB00], the CIMOSA framework [KVZ99], [Kos95], [ZVK95], the ARIS House of Business Engineering by Scheer [Sch96], the Zachman Framework [SZ92], [Zac87], the Business Process Management Systems (BPMS) Paradigm by Karagiannis [Kar95], MEMO by Frank [Fra99], and the Semantic Object Model by Ferstl and Sinz [FS93]. All of these frameworks belong to business informatics in the way that they propose approaches for linking the views on the management of businesses with the technical possibilities provided by information technology.

In the following three of these frameworks shall be discussed in detail to highlight the main concepts and thoughts in business informatics and again provide a foundation for classifying visualisation approaches in this field.

Business Engineering Model

The Business Engineering Model [sB00] achieves this challenge by decomposing the transformation of enterprises into manageable steps, giving directives for the treatment of the individual steps and combining them to procedure models for projects. The model structures the transformation by three layers (strategy, process, and system).

In detail the Business Engineering Model builds upon the foundations of method engineering (for a comprehensive discussion of method engineering in the context of business engineering see [Küh04]) with the following basic assumptions [sB00] (pp.12): It is oriented towards *results*, the execution of activities alone does not lead to success - each activity must have a defined outcome (e.g. a document). *Techniques* support the business engineer in the generation of the results and focus on critical questions in a project. A project consists of a sequence of *activities* which are laid out in a project or activity plan. Techniques support the execution of activities. The *stakeholder value* is seen as the criterion for every business solution: On the strategic level the business logic determines success factors which have to be drawn on on all levels for measuring the success of the project and the business. One important part of the stakeholder value is the economic assessment (e.g. by the Return on Investment (ROI) performance indicator). The participants in a project take over specific *roles* which have to be equipped with assignments, expertise, and responsibilities. In the *meta model* of Business Engineering (see figure 3.48) the entities of business engineering and their relations as well as the data model are described. On the strategy level it is determined how the market influences the strategic business segment that is taken into consideration and which market services are offered. The strategic business segment uses processes that either consume or produce services (that may be offered to the market as market services). The processes are composed of assignments which are supported by functions on the system level. Applications that execute these functions revert to data repositories and run on IT components.

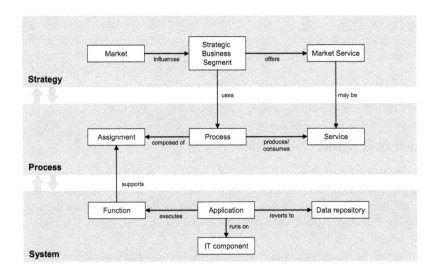

Figure 3.48: Meta Model of Business Engineering (translated from [sB00])

The Business Engineering Model does not specify concrete model definitions, procedure models or specific tools but is open for various different instantiations of the proposed framework. Although it might be implied by the conception of the meta model Business Engineering is not restricted to top-down procedure models but can also be used for bottom up solutions that are conceived on the system level [sB00](p.10).

Zachman Framework

The framework for information systems architecture by Zachman – first presented in [Zac87], extended and formalised in [SZ92] – presents a logical construct (also termed as a descriptive framework) for managing the complexity of the implementations of information systems by defining and controlling the interfaces and the integration of all components of a system [Zac87]. The framework focuses on a rationalisation of various architectural concepts and specifications for the purpose of professional communication, the improvement and integration of development methodologies and tools. It is thereby envisaged to enhance credibility and confidence in the investment of IT systems. It explicitly does not cover the relation of information systems to strategic methodologies.

In analogy to the procedures used in classical architecture[64] the Zachman framework has in its original form been based on seven layers or phases (see table 3.1 on page 159).

The first layer (*Bubble charts* in the case of classical architecture, *Scope/objectives* in the case of information systems) contains a conceptual representation which shows the basic intent of the final outcome in a highly abstract format. It results from the communciation of the architect and the customer and contains requirements and constraints of the intended product (in the case of a house this might be the approximate size required for a specific number of people or the limitations imposed by the real estate).

Based on these conceptions the architect transcribes the perceptual requirements of the customer to architectural drawings from which the customer can conclude how the final product will look like and which modifications he would like to be made (*Architect's drawings* and *Model of the business*). Zachman also stresses the importance of the agreement on the price of the conceived product between the architect and the customer in these phases.

The next step is the translation of the owner's perception of the final product into a detailed designer's representation (*Architect's plans* and *Model of the information system*). These plans provide detailed information on the material relationships and bills-of-materials and are the final deliverable of the architect. The owner can use them for negotiations with a contractor to build the final product.

---

[64]The etymological foundation for the term *Business Engineering* actually results from a similar analogy as it stands for the application of engineering and architectural principles to business tasks.

Modifications because of costs and price can still occur at this stage but in general the architect's plans serve as the basis of the final construction.

For the realisation of a complex engineering product such as a building or an information system the contractor has to redraw the architect's plans for his own purposes, i.e. the builder's perspective (*Contractor's plans* and *Technology model*). This includes the ordering of the operational steps for the creation of the parts of the product (e.g. the foundation, then the first floor) as well as the consideration of possible constraints (e.g. natural or logistical constrainsts).

The actual creation of the components or parts of the total structure is then performed by sub-contractors who again require a representation for their purposes (*Shop plans* and *Detailed description*). In contrast to the architect and the contractor they are not concerned with the overall structure of the product but with particular stand-alone solutions.

In manufacturing and information system development an additional phase is needed (which does not occur in classical architecture) that contains a machine language representation (*Machine language description/Object code*). This is required for production of parts by computer controlled equipment. The final outcome is the *Building* respectively the *Information System*.

An important aspect of this architectural approach is that the plans used by the different actors do not merely differ in their degree of abstraction (e.g. from conceptual to a detailed design level) but that they are different in nature, content, and semantics as they represent different perspectives for different users.

In the current version of the *Zachman Framework for Enterprise Architectures* as it is named today [Zac06, Zac98] there are six layers (scope, business model, system model, technology model, detailed representations, and functioning enterprise) which are directly related to the original layers. Furthermore six dimensions have been added to the framework: Data, Function, Network, People, Time, and Motivation.

According to a publication by the Zachman Institute [Zac98] the *Data* column describes the universe of discourse of the enterprise, the semantic relationships of things in an enterprise (also termed as business rules), the logical representation of the things, the physical (technology constrained) representation and the data definition language required for an implementation.

The *Function* (or Process) column contains a list of the processes a business performs on the highest level, concrete models of the business process which are independent of any implementation considerations or organisational constraints, models of the logical (but technology neutral) manual or automated systems that support the business processes, design diagrams that constitute the implementation of the logical systems and finally the specifications for the actual implementation (e.g. based on pre-fabricated components). The third column is denoted as *Network* and encompasses information about where the company operates (i.e. the universe of discourse in relation to location), models of the locations of an enterprise and their connections (business logistics), logical models (again technology neutral) that show the types of system facilities and software in the system, physical depictions of technology environment for the enterprise and the specific definition of the node addresses and protocols between the links.

In the following column, *People*, the aspects concerning the organisation of the business are described. This includes the list of organisations that are important to the business, models of the allocation of responsibilities and specifications of work products, including the identification of the originating and receiving units, the logical expression of the work flow by the roles of the responsible parties and the logical specification of the work products, the physical expression of the work flow (including ergonomic requirements and the presentation format of the work product) and specifications of the access of people to systems and their authorities.

By the *Time* column it is described to which events in time the enterprise responds, which business cycles the enterprise faces (in regard to initiating events and elapsed time), how transitions from one valid state (point in time) to another are triggered and what dynamics these transitions have (in relative or absolute time respect), how the physical expression of system events and physical processing cycles is expressed and how interrupts and machine cycles are defined.

The last column *Motivation* treats the objectives, strategies and critical success factors for an enterprise, how these business objectives and strategies can be modelled, how logical models (business rules) can be derived and physically specified (indepdent from data and logic) and how the business rules can be specified generally (out-of-context).

Especially the last column (Motivation) together with the Time and People column are major extensions to the original framework where strategic aspects have been explicitly left out. In the publications describing the Zachman framework there are several references for the cells of the framework to (standardized) modelling approaches and thus already some hints which types of visualisations may be used in the various contexts.

BPMS Paradigm

The third framework that shall be pointed out it the BPMS[65] paradigm. BPMS is a business engineering framework which has been conceptualised for the design

---

[65]Business Process Management Systems

of information systems dealing with the definition, administration, customization and evaluation of tasks evolving from business processes as well as from organizational structures" [Kar95](p.10). It assumes a process oriented view of the different activities that take place to support the modelling, analysis, design, simulation, evaluation and redesign of BPMS applications. In contrast to other approaches in this area (e.g. Petri nets [LSW97], the Semantic Object Model [FS93] or the ARIS approach [Sch96]) the BPMS paradigm not only aims to reduce the complexity which results from the various management requirements, technical and organisational constraints and environmental conditions that are prevalent in business informatics but also takes into account the interrelation and continuous improvement of strategic, tactical, and operational/technical activities. This is achieved by dividing the necessary tasks into a closed loop of five sub-processes thereby providing a holistic view from organisational to technical aspects: A Strategic Decision Process, a Re-Engineering Process, a Resource Allocation Process, a Workflow Management Process and a Performance Evaluation Process (also cf. [Jun00b]).

The *Strategic Decision Process* starts after a decision has been taken to reengineer a business. It takes into consideration global objectives, constraints and success factors and identifies the business processes that are relevant for reengineering. Furthermore the methodology for reengineering is chosen.

In accordance with the assigned methodology detailed insights of the determined business processes are constructed in the *Re-Engineering Process*. This comprises the modelling of process activities, their links and relationships as well as involved persons and interfaces to the external environment.

Within the *Resource Allocation Process* the view of business processes is extended from the mostly organisational, cost and time view that has been taken in the reengineering process. Informational and other resources as well as IT related issues are considered in this stage of the implementation of business processes. Later publications taking up the BPMS concept divide the Resource Allocation Process into an information technology oriented part and and organisational part, thereby relocating the treatment of the organisational embedding of a business process from the Re-Engineering process to the underlying layer (cf. [Jun00b]) - a modification that probably stems from the increased importance of fully automated processes in the last years, especially with the upcoming of e-business scenarios.

The *Workflow Management Process* characterises the real-time and -location execution of the business process including test runs and potential corrective actions. As a result of this process data is generated that is necessary for the subsequent evaluation.

The *Performance Evaluation Process* describes the structuring, analysis and evaluation of the acquired quantitative and qualitative data. The results of this data processing are input to adaptions in the Strategic Decision Process as well as the Re-Engineering Process - the consequence is a closed loop of activities that permits a continuous improvement of the business processes (see figure 3.49).

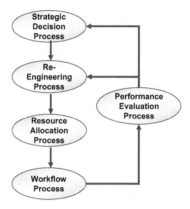

Figure 3.49: Business Process Management Systems Paradigm [Jun00b, Kar95]

When comparing the three frameworks for business informatics (the Business Engineering Model, the Zachman Framework for Enterprise Architectures and the Business Process Management Systems Paradigm) a number of similarities for all frameworks are apparent. Firstly, all three approaches have incorporated a *layered view* on the functioning of an enterprise from strategic issues over considerations concerning the design of conceptual and logical processes to actual IT implementations. This is in line with common views in business where management tasks are often divided into *strategic*, *tactical* and *operational* issues. Furthermore all three frameworks propose a top-down procedure - although for the Business Engineering Model it is stated that also a bottom approach is possible, the conception as laid out in the meta model seems to favor a top-down thinking. Only the BPMS paradigm incorporates the concept of a *loop cycle* to take into account a continuous improvement of all layers. On the other hand the *mutual diffusion between the layers* to allow for top-down as well as bottom-up approaches is only realised in the Business Engineering Model.

Relation to Visualisation

On the basis of the three selected frameworks for business informatics it can now be investigated which kinds of visualisations currently dominate in this area. For this purpose the discovered visualisation approaches have been classified by their affiliation to three levels: *strategic level, business process level,* and *information technology level* to reflect a view on business informatics that is expressed by all three frameworks.

To convey the principal considerations that influence visualisations in business informatics it seems necessary to shortly point out the environment in which businesses that make use of information technology operate today: When looking at the economic environment of businesses two essential factors currently dominate: The globalisation of business activities that presently takes place in almost every economic sector leads decision makers to shift their attention from a sometimes purely national to an international range which increases the amount and complexity of information that has to be processed. On the other side this abolition of the traditional borders between countries enables foreign firms to operate on national markets and thus causes higher competition in the before sometimes strongly protected markets. The management of enterprises therefore faces the challenge to align and redesign all business activities towards maximum efficiency to ensure the survival of the organisation in an internationalised environment. To allow for a successful handling of the complexity that is inherent in such an undertaking well structured and effective approaches are mandatory.

One way to reduce this complexity and therefore facilitate decision making arises in the generation of models. The method of modelling that stems from various fields in scientific research (cf. the various types of models for computer science discussed in section 3.2 on page 64 and the discussion of general model theory in section 4.2 on page 164) can be used to represent parts of real-world relationships and behaviours for the purpose of a subject. These models can either serve for the explanation of current states of a system or as a basis for the (re-)design of operations, in the sense of *descriptive* or *prescriptive models*. When translating this idea to enterprises several types of models can be envisaged, ranging from the strategic level to the level of IT systems. This aspect of the usage of models strongly influences the types of visualisations and their underlying concepts in business informatics.

The use of visualisation concepts for these models provides several advantages for the creators and users in comparison e.g. to text-based methods: As images carry a greater charge of meaning than words they have the ability to make huge amounts of (textual) data comprehensible in a faster way [Kaz95, War00]. Visualization can be further used to identify patterns and features that might have previously not been apparent as well as to facilitate the formulation of hypotheses about underlying facts. It can therefore also serve as an aid in quality control activities by highlighting errors and artificats that had not been recognized before by other means [War00]. To achieve an easy understanding of the visualisation – which is of primary importance for the use in enterprises as decisions usually have to be taken within short spans of time – the low semantic precision of pictures has to be compensated either by the addition of glossaries that explain the meaning by discursive language or by the use of familiar visual codes that are pertinent in a certain semantic domain [Kaz95]. For the application in IT-based management several visual approaches in this field are largely based on abstract symbols combined with a glossary for their semantic definition. Examples will be shown by the different visual languages in strategic management, for workflow and business process representations as well as on the level of IT systems management.

A second aspect that shall be used for a classification of the visualisation approaches in business informatics originates from the visualisation approaches discussed so far in the areas of business and computer science. Although there are many similiarities between the visualisations in these two fields it can already at this point be recognised that in the business world quantitative data play a slightly more important role than in the technical world of computer science. This becomes apparent by the range of different types of charts that are used in the areas of business whereas in computer science the use of graphs indicating relationships between entities clearly dominates. Therefore, another criterion for differentiation for visualisations in business informatics can be based on the underlying information of a visualisation, i.e.

- qualitative information
- or quantitative information.

The view on qualitative and quantitative information corresponds to the view described for social sciences in general, i.e. the differentiation between qualitative and quantitative methods (as outlined in the context of figure 3.13 on page 57).

When applying these views especially to business informatics and bringing them together with the technical concepts of this field a possible classification for visualisations becomes apparent: By the term *qualitative visualisations* all visual representations will be denoted that represent relationships between entities and their attributes whereas by *quantitative visualisations* those representations are subsumed that display amounts of entities or attributes (which may be traditional charts but also other types of visualisations).

Strategic Level

Within the area of IT based strategic management a large number of methodologies is currently available. Approaches may be identified in the area of quality management (cf. the standards by ISO or the EFQM excellence model[66] and corresponding IT solutions, e.g. based on IT supported business process modelling), performance management (in the sense of a holistic view on the management of enterprises that strongly focuses on the measurement of performance [Ron05b]) as well as in business intelligence (which denotes systems that support management on the basis of external and internal data [CG04]). Besides specific IT implementations for strategic management that originate from these or other fields[67] also standard software applications may be used (e.g. based on spreadsheets or reports).

For the discussion of visualisations on the strategic level it is focused on three approaches in the area of strategic management that are currently widely used and offer interesting examples for visualisations: *Balanced Scorecard* approaches and the closely related *Enterprise Cockpits* as well as visualisations in the area of knowledge management, denoted as *knowledge visualisations*.

Balanced Scorecard Visualisations   The concept of a balanced scorecard (BSC)) has originally been proposed by Kaplan and Norton in 1996 [KN96]. It can be shortly characterised by the attempt to provide a concept that unites the aspects of a traditional financial, resp. monetary orientation, in strategic management with non-monetary indicators. These non-monetary indicators, also denoted as *soft factors*, shall raise the classical strategic process (of setting goals, applying measures directed towards these goals and evaluating the achievement of the goals) to a holistic level that incorporates multiple perspectives of an enterprise.

Based on the definition of a vision and a mission for an enterprise four classical perspectives have been defined by Kaplan/Norton for balanced scorecards: The *Financial*, *Customer*, *Business Process*, and *Learning and Growth* perspective. On the basis of these perspectives strategic goals can be determined that indicate the specific directions in each perspective. By assigning performance indicators to the strategic goals the achievement of the goals can be evaluated. Besides classical financial goals (e.g. increase the return on investment, increase market share etc.) the BSC approach also permits to integrate "soft-factor" goals, e.g. directed towards employee and customer satisfaction, that cannot be measured by hard financial indicators. To weight the importance of the strategic goals and describe dependencies between the goals, cause-effect relationships are determined between the goals. Although approaches exist that propose an automatic determination of these dependencies (cf. [Hil03]) they are usually based on the subjective assessment of management.

---

[66]European Foundation for Quality Management

[67]For a recent scientific discussion of the various approaches see [Ron05b] and [Ron05a] for an integrated meta model for performance management.

For visualisations for balanced scorecards two principal directions can be identified: On the one hand the representation of strategic goals and the corresponding cause effect relationships, which is in most cases done by directed graphs, and on the other hand the visual depiction of the current achievement of the goals based on the assigned performance indicators. The latter is either integrated directly into the cause-effect graphs and/or available in the form of enterprise cockpits (discussed in the subsequent section). The following five approaches for visualisations of balanced scorecards have been selected to highlight the key aspects[68]:

- ADOscore[69]
- Oracle PeopleSoft Customer Scorecard[70]
- Procos Strat&Go Balanced Scorecard[71]
- Hyperion Scorecard[72]
- Business Objects Scorecard[73]

The approach taken in *ADOscore* for defining balanced scorecards (as described in [LKK02]) is based on a meta model approach and consists of nine graphical models: A BSC map model, a strategy model, a success-factor model, a cause-effect model, a performance indicator model, a measures model, an organisational model and an optional data structure model (which is a simplified Entity relationship model). To exemplify the visual realisation of these diagrams three diagram types shall be discussed in detail. The core symbols of ADOscore and their meanings are shown in figure 3.50 on the next page.

The *success factor model* serves as a kind of virtual blackboard that is used to group the different success factors to the perspectives of the BSC and aggregate them to strategic goals. The perspectives are represented by colored parallel rectangles that show the name of the perspective and can contain other objects. Success factors are visualised by visual objects that resemble commonly known post-it notes. Success factors are aggregated to strategic goals by the placement

---

[68] As will be apparent by the following elaborations the shown visualisations all stem from commercial tools. This results from the fact that in the scientific literature only few examples of visualisations for balanced scorecards are discussed, cf. the representations in [Ron05b, JLMM04, LKK02, Wef00], and that very often the quality of the graphical representations in these sources is not sufficient for a discussion of the visual aspects. The commercial aspect also results in the lack of appropriate documentation, therefore for some visualisations the meaning of the represented symbols and their relationships had to be derived from the theoretical principles of the balanced scorecard.

[69] ADOscore is a registered trademark of BOC GmbH.

[70] See http://www.oracle.com

[71] See http://www.procos.com

[72] See http://www.hyperion.com

[73] See http://www.businessobjects.com

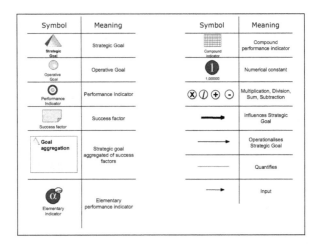

Figure 3.50: Symbols for ADOscore for Cause-Effect, Success Factor and Performance Indicator Models

inside another rectangle with a pyramid at the top left corner and the name of the strategic goal (fig. 3.51).

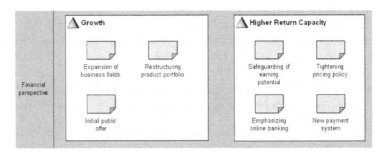

Figure 3.51: Example for a Success Factor Model with one Perspective, two Strategic Goals, and seven Success Factors

The *cause-effect model* relates the strategic goals to each other. Each strategic goal can be influenced by one or more other strategic goals. These relationships are visualised in the form of directed graphs with the nodes being the strategic goals (small blue pyramids) and the edges expressing the dependencies (see figure 3.52 on the next page). In ADOscore the thickness of the edges can be adjusted based

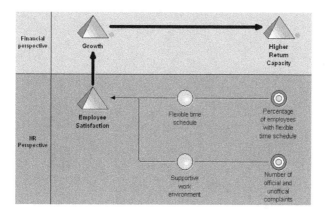

Figure 3.52: Example for a Cause-effect Model with two Perspectives, three Strategic and two Operative Goals and two Performance Indicators

on the degree of dependency. Strategic goals can be detailed by linking them to one or more operative goals. Operative goals are symbolized by orange circles. As specified by the requirements for the BSC all goals have to be measurable by performance indicators. Therefore performance indicators are integrated in the model visualised as small dartboards.

Performance indicators can be basic indicators that directly relate to a specific numeric expression or can be composed of other indicators by the use of simple arithmetic expressions. The *performance indicator model* visualises mathematical expressions by defining visual objects for the four basic arithmetic operations (summation, subtraction, multiplication, division) that can be applied to basic performance indicators by linking them through directed edges (figure 3.53 on the following page). Furthermore, constants can be integrated into the model and also linked by arithmetic operations.

The visualisation used in the *Oracle Peoplesoft Customer Scorecard* combines a quantitative and a qualitative part (as shown in figure 3.54 on page 125). The strategic goals are aligned in a tree structure on the left hand side (the yellow triangle and red square symbols indicate the achievement resp. under-achievement of a strategic goal), together with the key performance indicators (which are symbolised by small keys in front of the label). The proportions of the number of strategic goals in all perspectives is visualised by a pie chart.

From the approach of the *Procos Strat&Go Balanced Scorecard* at first the cause effect relationship diagram is shown in figure 3.55 on page 126. Similar

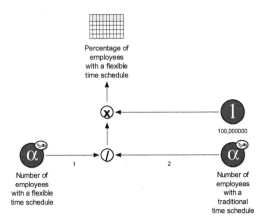

Figure 3.53: Example for a Performance Indicator Model for the Composition of Performance Indicators

to the cause effect model in ADOscore it shows the dependencies between strategic goals (represented by rectangles) that are arranged on the four perspectives (financial, customer, processes, and learning). The affiliation to a perspective is indicated by the four different colours of the strategic goal rectangles. Attached to the strategic goals are the values of indicators for measuring the achievement of the strategic goal (which are assumed to be percentages of actual values in relation to target values). Additional symbols in the bottom left corner of the strategic goal objects indicate the degree of achievement of the strategic goal (green squares seem to indicate full achievement, yellow triangles partly achievement and red circles under-achievement).

A very similar approach to the Procos approach is the visualisation of the cause effect relationships in the *Hyperion Scorecard* (shown in figure 3.56 on page 127). Even the symbolic coding of the goal achievement in the Hyperion approach is similar to the Procos approach. The only visible difference in the two approaches is that the strategic goals in the Hyperion Scorecard are not coloured but that the assignment to perspectives is only based on the spatial arrangement and that the relative achievement of the goal is visualised additionally by a blue progress bar.

In the balanced scorecard visualisation of the *Business Objects Scorecard* the strategic goals are represented by ellipses that are coloured based on the achievement of the particular goal (green, yellow, and red). The assignment of the goals to the perspectives is again realised by spatial arrangement and for each strate-

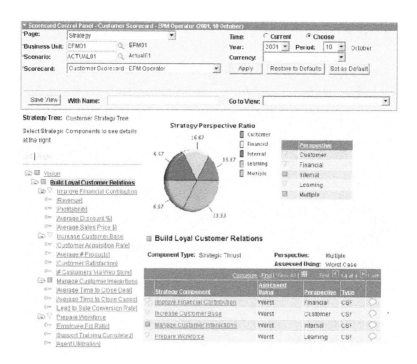

Figure 3.54: Screenshot Oracle Peoplesoft Customer Scorecard (Source: [Ent06])

gic goal additional textual labels are included, showing the name of the goal as well as actual and target values (either as percentage or absolute values). An interesting detail is the integration of operational goals into the description of the strategic goals (e.g. "improve cross sell-ratio to *3.5*"), which is for example in the ADOscore approach methodologically separated from the strategic goals by an extra visual object. The symbols indicating the achievement of a strategic goal (additional to the colour coding) are all of the same circular shape and their colour matches the colour of the ellipses.

Enterprise Cockpit Visualisations For the illustration of enterprise cockpit visualisations that can either be derived from balanced scorecards or act as stand alone applications showing the values and achievements of performance indicators three approaches have been selected:

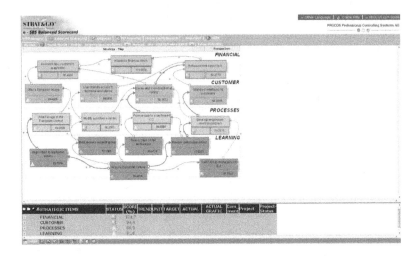

Figure 3.55: Cause Effect Diagram in Procos Strat&Go (Source: http://www.procos.com)

- The Management Cockpit[74] [Geo00]
- Cognos Dashboard[75]
- ADOscore Cockpit

All approaches of enterprise cockpits share the goal to communicate complex business information (especially the values of performance indicators) in an efficient and visually intuitive way. They therefore rely largely on chart based representations to show the change of indicator values over time and include specialised visualisations (often based on metaphoric images as e.g. of speedometers or thermometers) to illustrate the current positions in the achievement of goals.

The first approach of an enterprise cockpit is the *Management Cockpit* which has been theoretically described in [Geo00]. It is conceived as a specialised human-computer interface integrated in a special meeting room. It originates from research in the area of human intelligence management which can be defined as "the knowledge enabling amplification of the intellectual capacities of people at work" [Geo00](p.131). The basic idea was to create a cockpit solution that has been designed by managers themselves (and not technicians) and is therefore more intuitive to handle. The key characteristics that have been identified in this research process are as follows [Geo00](p.134): To work optimally together in teams the

---

[74]The Management Cockpit is a trademark of SAP.
[75]See http://www.cognos.com

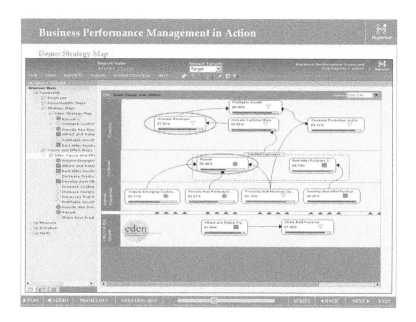

Figure 3.56: Hyperion Cause Effect Diagram (Source: http://www.hyperion.com)

interface should be three dimensional (in a material, not virtual sense) instead of a two dimensional computer screen. The information in the interface should have been pre-processed by experts and only showing the status and trends, not online figures. The interface should be visual and be able to answer questions in natural language. The interface should have functionalities for providing information for decisions, assisting in decisions, and helping with decision implementations. Traditional means of input to a computer have been identified as not being appropriate for the kind of team work, and e-mail and artificial intelligence should be provided by the management software.

The walls in the cockpit can be assigned to different functions in the decision process of managers (e.g. to represent opportunities/possible paths, current status etc.) and the screens on the walls provide the necessary figures for the decision steps. Although the approach seems to be very complex and costly (as a whole room has to be adapted), the website[76] related to the concept presents example installation e.g. at SAP, Unilever, Siemens, Thai Airways and others. From the viewpoint of visualisation especially the interaction aspects of the Manage-

---

[76]See http://management-cockpit.net

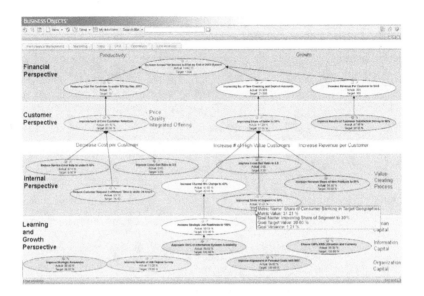

Figure 3.57: Business Objects Scorecard (Source: http://www.businessobjects.com/)

ment Cockpit are interesting, as they constitute a new way of dealing with large sets of data. The visual representations themselves on the screens of the Management Cockpit (as is assumed from the available pictures) do not seem to deviate much from the standard chart representations of other cockpit solutions (e.g. also speedometer representations can be recognised).

The second example for an enterprise cockpit is the *Cognos Dashboard* approach. As apparent by figure 3.58 on the facing page it is a web based application (in contrast to the location dependent Management Cockpit) that uses traditional vertical bar chart visualisations, geocharts, tables and speedometer representations. As Cognos also provides an approach for balanced scorecards it can be assumed that the Dashboard could also be linked to the strategic goal and performance indicator information from a BSC.

For the third example of an enterprise cockpit it is again turned to the ADOscore toolkit. For the distribution of user centric business information as required to control the individual achievements of the goals of balanced scorecards a cockpit component is integrated in ADOscore. This component is implemented in Java and receives the relevant data via an XML interface from the ADOscore core component storing the models and assigning data from various data sources to the models. It offers visualisation functionalities for the display of the current sta-

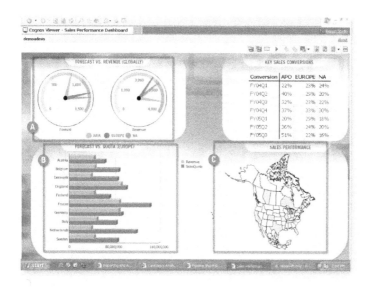

Figure 3.58: Cognos Dashboard (Source: http://www.cognos.com)

tus of strategic goals and performance indicators (by thermometer and traffic light visualisations) and permits a drill-down of performance indicators to investigate their change over time.

The visualisation of the achievements of goals is realised by the use of two types of visual objects (traffic lights and thermometers) for the representation of the current state of a strategic goal or performance indicator (red, green or blue) and several types of charts that are used to enable a drill down to the details of the data. The advantage of this approach is on the one hand the high level of aggregation of the relevant information by allowing immediate insight whether the relevant figure is in a positive, average or negative range through the traffic light/thermometer representation (fig. 3.59 on the next page) and on the other hand the high familiarity of potential users in business with the visualization of detailed numerical information in the form of charts.

Business Process Level

The second level which is analysed in regard to visualisation in business informatics is the level of business processes. It subsumes aspects of the re-engineering process, the resource allocation and the workflow management process of BPMS,

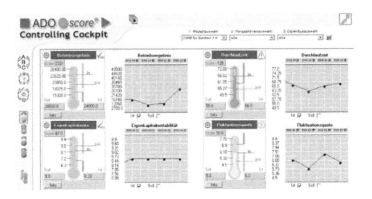

Figure 3.59: The ADOscore Cockpit

the business model layer in the Zachman framework and the process level of the Business Engineering framework. As the concept of representing business processes constitutes not only a core function of today's enterprises[77] but has also influenced many other approaches in the field of enterprise modelling[78] it will be given special attention in the following. Besides three notations (BPMN, EPC, Adonis Standard Method) that are widely regarded as standards for the graphical representation of business processes a special focus will be put on innovative visualisation approaches.

Among the many definitions that can be found for the term *business process* the following has been selected to reflect an all-embracing as possible view: "A business process is a set of activities, actors, artefacts, resources, and relations between these elements for the creation or development of one or more products" [Jun00b](p.8). Several approaches exist how business processes can be represented by models. Usually different model types (as being subsets of the original business process, cf. the discussion concerning general model theory in 4.2 on page 164) for focusing on specific aspects are derived (e.g. for the documentation of processes for presentation and training purposes, for analysis and enhancement approaches or for workflow management, i.e. the definition of the execution of processes [GW00]). Most commonly this includes models for the sequence of business activities (process models) and models of the organisational structure

---

[77]Cf. the market trend analyses by Forrester research for 2005 and 2006 indicating a focus on the modelling of business processes and the necessity for business process optimisation [Vol05, PPL04].

[78]Cf. for example the approaches adopting process oriented views in knowledge management [Woi04], in IT service management [MB05] or for instruction design [BK05].

(standard organisational charts) as well as resource models (e.g. document models).

When merging the approach of representing different views on business processes as models with the facilities that are offered by computer science, software applications can be developed that support the generation, editing and analysis of these models. By the availability of such software the creation of models is highly simplified which allows for the deployment of the method at a large scale. The technical support by computer science often includes the collection of process data and their analysis and evaluation as well as the design of the processes and the corresponding organisational structures.

A core element of most approaches in business process modelling is a *visual notation* (cf. the details on components of explicit models in section 4.2 on page 175) for the models to illustrate the relationships and properties of process elements (e.g. activities, decisions, actors etc.) in a graphcial way. Although textual descriptions of business processes may also be sufficient for some scenarios, graphical representations in general greatly facilitate the understanding of models and ease modelling itself. Especially the sequence of elements can be well depicted in graphical form (e.g. by attributed directed graphs) and possible changes in this sequence can be quickly performed and immediately detected.

Since the upcoming of the first apporaches in the area of business process modelling in the mid-1990ies several methods have been developed and used in many business sectors. The practical application of the concepts showed that the models sometimes became highly detailed and thus very complex. The graphical representation often reached the limits of usability with the grand number of models and modelling elements that a user had to handle. Highly nested process structures became very difficult to understand and the orginal idea of a simplified and easily manageable illustration faded away that gives an impression of the large number of relations underlying today's business process models). Solutions to this problem that exist can be classified in two categories: On the one hand the the modelling method can be altered in such a way that the resulting models are of a lower complexity. On the other hand the visualisation of the model can be enhanced so that even highly complex models can be easily handled by the user.

In the last years the technical possibilities in the area of computer graphics have undergone tremendous changes. The availability of high-performance computer graphics hardware not only for professional users but also in the consumer markets has given rise to new visualisation applications. Sophisticated animation and video sequences as well as three dimensional representations can today also be executed on average consumer PCs. As business process modelling is in practice often performed by employees that do not have access to specialised computer hardware a direct impact of these technical developments is obvious: Instead of simple visualisations that dominated most business process modelling tools in the beginning the latest developments in this area make extensive use of animated and/or three-dimensional representations or even virtual reality techniques.

To give an overview and compare traditional visualisations of business process with the currently existing innovative visualisation approaches a classification scheme has been set up that permits to evaluate the visualisations functionalities of the particular attempt. After a review of several approaches four criteria have been identified that allow for a differentiation between the various solutions in regard to their visualisation capabilities (see figure 3.60 on the facing page for an overview):

- – Dimensionality
- – Level of Detail
- – Level of Animation
- – Level of Interaction

The criterion *Dimensionality* contains three parameter values: The lowest level stands for *two-dimensional* representations of objects and the highest for *three-dimensional* occurences. In between lie so called *2 1/2-D* illustrations where objects are only perceived to be of a three-dimensional nature (e.g. through shadings, distortions etc.).

The *level of detail* describes how close to reality the graphical representations of the particular approach are. Again there are three parameter values: The lowest level of detail is applied if the graphics are only made up of *abstract symbols* such as basic graphical primitives. The highest level of detail is assigned to representations that are close to *photorealistic* illustrations (e.g. when presenting virtual characters that can hardly be differentiated from real human beings). The value in the middle (*partly abstract*) characterises illustrations that lie in the middle, i.e. a graphical representation that is not photorealistic but does not only contain abstract symbols.

Regarding the *level of animation* the possible values are set as: *static, animated,* and *reality-ident animation*. The top value stands for animations that are close to movements in reality (as the highest level of detail) e.g. a virtual human actor performs human-like movements or a fully animated representation of a machine that can virtually show the same movements as in reality. The value *partly animated* comprises animations that are used e.g. to show the conceptual flow of activities in an abstract representation.

By the *level of interaction* it is expressed to which degree a user can interact with a graphical representation. The values here are *no interaction, partly interaction,* and *full interaction* with all elements.

When assigning the maximum values to all levels the resulting visualisation would theoretically be a virtual world that has the same behaviours as objects in the real-world. Very close to this maximum would be for example a CAVE[79] that shows a virtual world. Although this theoretical possibility fully utilises all possible visualisation capabilities that are available today this does not mean that it is also the most desirable solution in terms of a cost, effort/benefit ratio. Sometimes also simpler representations can be very effective (as it is apparent in the case of the traditional process graphs that do not make use of the new visualisation possibilities). It seems therefore essential to evaluate the effort and costs that are needed for a particular approach in relation to the benefits that arise.

Dimensionality	*2D*	*2 1/2-D*	*3D*
Level of detail	*abstract*	*partly abstract*	*photorealistic*
Level of animation	*static*	*animated*	*reality-ident animation*
Level of interaction	*no interaction*	*partly interaction*	*full interaction*

Figure 3.60: Classification for Innovative Business Process Visualisations

As a basis for the comparison of the benefits of the visualisations of business process models it can be reverted to a systematic approach for assessing the quality of notations as outlined by the *Generally accepted modelling principles*[80] by Becker et al. [BRS95](pp 435-445) (also cf. [SB98]). These method-independent guidelines have been developed for the evaluation of the notation of models that are adequate to specific professional requirements. The principles consist of three necessary and three additional guidelines. The necessary principles are:

- Accurateness
- Relevance
- Economic efficiency

The additional principles are:

- Clarity
- Comparability

---

[79] CAVE stands for Cave Automatic Virtual Environment and denotes an immersive virtual reality facility where pictures are projected on the walls of a room that can be perceived as three dimensional by special viewing devices (e.g. shutter glasses).

[80] translated from German: Grundsätze ordnungsmässiger Modellierung

– Systematic structure

The *prinicple of accurateness* relates either to the syntactical correctness of a model, that means the formal correctness in regard to the underlying meta-model[81], as well as to the semantical correctness, that is a correct reproduction in terms of the structure and behaviour of the underlying system of objects, the logical conditions and relationships.

The *principle of relevance* states that, based on the goals of modelling as much information as necessary and as little information as possible shall be used in the models. That means that the right level of abstraction of the model is found when the benefit of the model would decrease with additional model information. Becker et al. define two dimensions that have to be considered for this principle: The first is how the part of the real world that is depicted in the model corresponds to the intended purpose of the subject (i.e. the user of the model). The second is the relation between the level of abstraction and the goal of the model.

The *principle of economic efficiency* aims to apply economical and managerial concepts to the area of modelling. Although there currently does not exist a specific cost/benefit theory for modelling, this principle limits the intensity of modelling according to Becker et al.. Furthermore the expenditures for the use of a special modelling toolkit would have to be taken into considerations under this point (e.g. costs for software licenses, additional hardware or training costs).

The *principle of clarity* shall ensure the understandability and readability of a model. Models shall be designed in such a way that they are clear to third persons. As Becker et al. state clarity is determined besides other factors by the graphical layout of the information objects. They therefore demand guidelines that explicitly define the graphical layout of objects to each other. Conflicts may arise due to the interference with the principle of accurateness: Although the principle of accurateness might be improved by methodological additions to the model that allow for a semantically enriched representation the principle of clarity might stand in contrast to these enhancements if the transparency of the model is thereby decreased.

According to the *principle of comparability* IS- and SHOULD-models as well as IS- and reference models have to be comparable. This principle is not a property that can be evaluated for one model autonomously but only in relation to other models.

The *principle of systematic structure* includes the instances of models as well as the underlying meta-models and aims to ease the re-use of model elements or parts of model structures to further the ability of models to be integrated with others.

---

[81] Also see section 4.2 on page 196.

Although in the orginal version by Becker et al. only the principle of clarity directly relates to visualisation aspects it will be outlined in the course of the discussion of the visualisation approaches how all six priniciples of proper modelling can be used for evaluating the visualisation of business process models.

The evaluation is carried out by comparing the models in the three standard notations to the new forms of visual models or visualisation on the basis of the principles of proper process modelling. In the case of an improvement in one of the principles that only stems from the change in the visual representation the new visualisation is estimated to be of higher value to a potential user. This rating is also possible in the opposite direction: In case a visualisation leads to a worsening in a principle the value is rated lower. It might be the case that a new form of visualisation leads to improvements in some principles and to worsenings in others so that the overall gain is neutral. For example if a three dimensional representation leads to an improvement in clarity as it allows to better understand the model but increases the costs for the visualisation (e.g. through the need of new hardware) and thus diminuishes the profitability the positive and negatives effects might outweigh.

To illustrate the current status in the visualisation of business process models at first the three standard approaches of the Business Process Modelling Notation (BPMN), Event Driven Process Chains (EPC) and the Adonis Standard Method are discussed. It is acknowledged that there exist also other forms of business process representations that could have been included in the discussion (e.g. Petrinets [LSW97], the IDEF standards[82] or from the area of workflow management [Cor01]), nevertheless the primary focus is seen in the visualisations that deviate from the traditional representations. Therefore, subsequently a selection of innovative approaches for business process visualisation is presented. Most of the tools underlying the innovative approaches have not been available to the author and could only be analysed based on different literature sources. This limits of course the possibilities for an investigation of the features, especially as the visualisations are not specifically described but rather shown in screenshots. Based on this information the visualisation functionalities of the particular tool will be related to the abovely described classification model and a (theoretical) evaluation of the expected effort and benefit of the approach shall be given.

Business Process Modelling Notation   The *BPMN (Business Process Modelling Notation)* specification is issued by the non profit organisation Business Process Management Initiative which is now joined with the Object Management Group in

---

[82]See http://www.idef.com/.

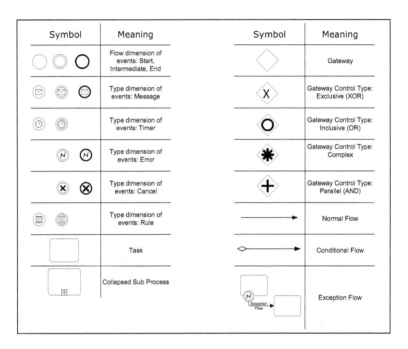

Figure 3.61: Excerpt of Symbols of the BPMN (Source: [BPM04])

the Business Modeling & Integration Domain Task Force. The goal of the BPMN is to provide a graphical notation for expressing business processes in Business Process Diagrams and is directed towards technical and business users [BPM04]. The specification also provides a mapping between the graphical representations and underlying constructs of execution languages. More specifically, the BPMN specification recognises the gap that currently exists between formal/mathematical approaches for defining the execution of business processes in a technical environment and the approach of business people preferring simple flow-chart like notations to study the way how enteprises work. By providing both an intuitive visualisation format to ease human interoperability as well as a formal mapping to execution specifications for satisfying formal technial requirements BPMN is envisaged to close or at least significantly diminish this gap. Furthermore, the open access policy for the specification documents and the expected resulting adoption by tool designers may further the evolution of a commonly accepted standard and thus lead to additional benefits (e.g. in regard to less training for employees that are not required to understand multiple representations of business processes when moving from one company to another) [BPM04].

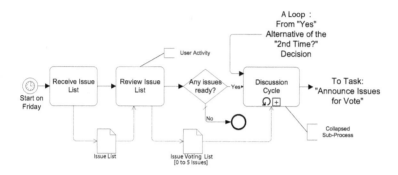

Figure 3.62: Example for a Business Process in BPMN (Source: [BPM04])

The scope of BPMN is restricted to the concepts applicable to the process view of business processes and does not include e.g. organisational structures and resources, functional breakdowns, data and information models, strategy or business rules [BPM04](p.22). This is in contrast to other approaches in business process modelling as will be outlined by the subsequent approaches of EPCs and the Adonis Standard Method. To give an overview of the main elements of the notation in BPMN figure 3.61 on the facing page lists an excerpt of the central symbols and concepts of BPMN.

Modelling objects in BPMN are divided into flow objects (events, activities and gateways), connecting objects (e.g. the normal and conditional flow objects), swimlanes (for grouping elements) and artifacts (for providing additional information about a process, e.g. data objects or annotations). As shown by figure 3.61 on the preceding page elements may have additional dimensions that have corresponding graphical representations and can be combined to describe multiple semantic properties of one element. The basic symbol for an event that stands for something that happens during the business process and affects its flow is detailed by the *flow dimension* which differentiates between start, intermediate and end events. To integrate a type dimension into events several *triggers* can be added to define the cause for an event (shown here are message, timer, error, cancel and rule triggers). Activities represent work that a company performs and may be atomic or compound. An activity can stand for a whole process, a sub-process or a task. A *task* is an atomic activity that is used for work that is not broken down to a finer level of detail. The element for a *collapsed sub-process* indicates that this activity stands for a more detailed version. *Gateways* function as control elements for the divergence and convergence of control flows. They can be detailed by internal markers that define the type of behaviour control (see the symbols for gateway control types in figure 3.61 on page 136). The syntactic arrangement of the elements of BPMN is restricted by sets of application rules, e.g. to define valid sequence flows.

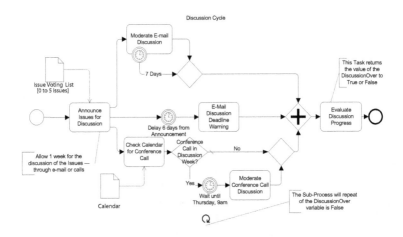

Figure 3.63: Example for a Sub Process in BPMN (Source: [BPM04])

A notable aspect of the BPMN notation from the viewpoint of visualisation is that the use of specific line styles and colour is explicitly allowed as long as they do not conflict with other defined styles in the BPMN specification [BPM04](p.38). Therefore, additional information can be coded into the graphical representation. The application of such possibilities has been discussed in [Fil06a] and will be taken up again in chapter 6 on page 269).

In figures 3.62 on the preceding page and 3.63 process diagrams according to the BPMN notation are shown. Figure 3.62 depicts a business process that starts with an event of the type timer. In the following a sequence of tasks is executed, including a gateway and an activity linked to a collapsed sub process. The elements contain labels and are partly supplemented by comments (denoted by specific symbols, as e.g. the one close to the label "User Activity"). In parallel to the sequence of the tasks a flow of data objects is shown (e.g. by the document "Issue List"). The second business process in figure 3.63 is the detailed version of collapsed sub process "Discussion Cycle". Worth mentioning here in regard to the visualisation are the exception flow "Moderate E-mail Discussion" and the inclusion of timer events in the sequence flow. The first has a timer intermediate event attached to it which signifies together with the labelled edge "7 days" that an event is triggered at most seven days after the start of the task. The latter are intermediate timer events indicating delays in the sequence flow, e.g. the element "Delay 6 days from Announcement".

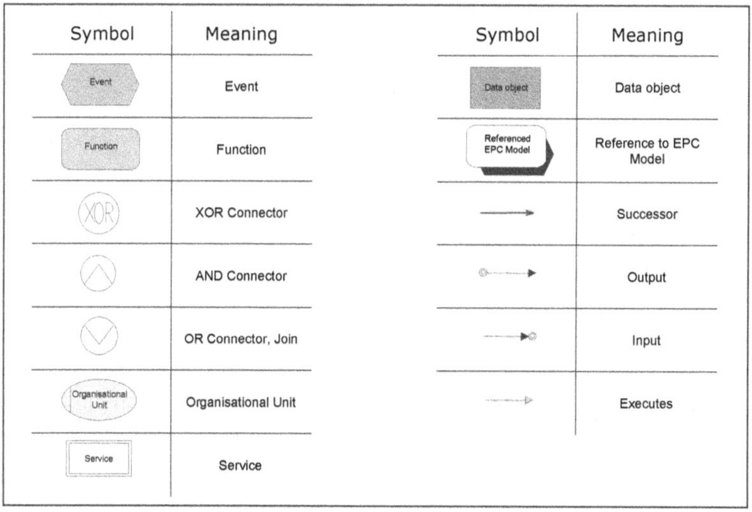

Symbol	Meaning	Symbol	Meaning
Event	Event	Data object	Data object
Function	Function	Referenced EPC Model	Reference to EPC Model
XOR	XOR Connector	⟶	Successor
AND	AND Connector	⊙┄┄➤	Output
OR	OR Connector, Join	┄┄➤⊙	Input
Organisational Unit	Organisational Unit	┄┄▷	Executes
Service	Service		

Figure 3.64: Symbols for Extended Event Driven Process Chains (notation as implemented in Adonis Student version)

Event Driven Process Chains   The concept for *Event driven process chains* is based on the theory of semantic process modelling by Keller et al. [KNS92]. The view taken in this model regards information models of an enterprise as a form of representation of the operational business respectively an ideal, prescriptive plan for the realisation of an enterprise information system. The views taken in the information model may concern data, functional or organisational aspects. The different views are integrated by a control view. Furthermore, views are structured by three layers of abstraction (cf. also [Sch91]): On top resides the *functional specification*, followed by a platform indepdent *IT concept* and finally the concrete technical, platform specific *implementation*. Semantic process modelling is positioned on the level of a functional specification in the control view. Its goal is to characterise the functional specifications of a business in a description language that is formal enough to be translated into an IT concept. The elements of process models according to these theoretical foundations are divided into active and passive components. Business *functions* which are defined as tasks, i.e. a target value that is to be accomplished by physical or cognitive activities [KNS92](p.10), is presented as an active component. Functions transform input data into output data by reading, modifying, deleting or creating objects. *Events* are passive components that are defined as entered states which cause a sequence of activities. The following rules apply to events and functions: Events can trigger functions, functions are triggered by events, events represent an entered business state, events server to specify business conditions, and events can reference information objects in the data (model) view.

Models of event driven process chains (EPC) describe the dynamic view in an information model. Events and functions as described above are abstracted to *event types* and *function types*. An event type is a distinct collection of events that can be merged on the basis of the same attribute values. The same applies to function types. A process model based on EPC is a sequence of events that trigger functions which in turn create events. Thereby a chain is defined that can be complemented by connectors (AND, OR, XOR) for imposing control structures. In figure 3.64 on the preceding page the basic symbols for event driven process chains are shown (in an extended version as available for the Adonis meta modelling plattform).

Adonis Standard Method   The third approach for the visual representation of business processes that is also part of the group of traditional approaches is the Adonis Standard Method. It originates from the business process management toolkit Adonis [Jun00b] and is similar to the abovely described BPMN notation as well as certain aspects of EPCs. To take into account the different views on information models in a business Adonis makes use of five model types: Process landscapes, business process models, organisational models, document models, and use case diagrams. Apart from the use case diagram (which is taken from UML) all model types are derived from specifically elaborated meta models (excerpts of the meta models are published in [Jun00b]). The Adonis approach is similar to BPMN in the respect that it is both intuitive to business users familiar with traditional flow chart diagrams as well it can be used for deriving technical models for implementations (see e.g. [KJS96] for the formalisation of business graphs as used in Adonis and their mapping to workflow graphs[83]).

---

[83]The formal aspects will be again considered in chapter 6 on page 269.

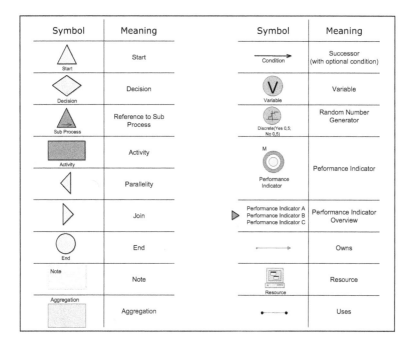

Figure 3.65: Symbols for Adonis Business Process Models

In the following, the visualisations of Adonis business process and organisational models will be further examined. Adonis business process models are graph based and build upon a flow chart like notation as BPMN, consisting of flow, connector and additional elements. The symbol set for business process models is shown in figure 3.65. The core set of symbols contains the *Start, Decision, Reference to Sub Process, Activity, Parallelity, Join, Successor,* and *End* symbols. The control elements are coloured in yellow, the task elements in blue. The core set of elements can be extended by *Variable* symbols together with *Random Number Generator* symbols. These are required to allow for the simulation of business processes and may be integrated into the sequence flow of the process. Additionally, *performance indicators* (and special *performance indicator overview elements*) can be included in the process and linked to the flow elements by the *owns* connector. The relation of activity elements to *resources* is realised by the *uses* connector. Just as in BPMN also the elements of Adonis business processes can be grouped by swimlanes.

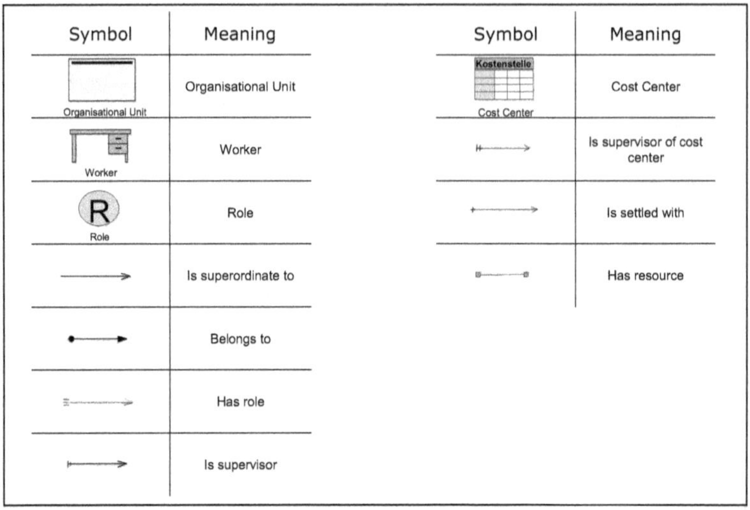

Symbol	Meaning	Symbol	Meaning
Organisational Unit	Organisational Unit	Kostenstelle / Cost Center	Cost Center
Worker	Worker	⊢⎯⎯⎯→	Is supervisor of cost center
R / Role	Role	•⎯⎯⎯→	Is settled with
⎯⎯⎯→	Is superordinate to	▫⎯⎯⎯▫	Has resource
•⎯⎯⎯▸	Belongs to		
⋮⎯⎯⎯→	Has role		
⊢⎯⎯⎯→	Is supervisor		

Figure 3.66: Symbols for Adonis Organisational Models

The example process also reveals a specific feature of the Adonis notation: The status and values of attributes of the model elements can be integrated in the visual notation. This allows for the representation of relationships that could otherwise be perceived only upon an investigation of the underlying (non-visual) model structure. In Activity I and II the working role related to the activity (from the subsequently discussed organisational model) is printed in the lower half of the activity rectangle. In Activity I and II the standard graphical representation is complemented by symbols indicating the manual and automated execution of activities. As shown on the bottom swimlane the symbol of the resource element can also be changed according to the type attribute of the resource.

The *organisational models* in the Adonis Standard Method represent the organisational structure of enterprises. The symbol set is shown in figure 3.66. In contrast to conventional organisation charts Adonis organisational models not only allow for the representation of hierarchies of organisational units and the allocated employees but also of *roles*. These roles are used to specify the functional allocation of employees and can be referenced by the process models. These basic skill profiles can then be used as well in simulations (e.g. to assess the required number and qualifications of employees for a process).

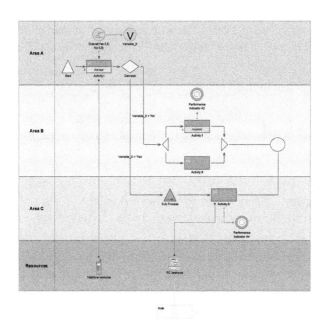

Figure 3.67: Example for an ADONIS Business Process Model

Following the traditional approaches of visualising business processes it will now be turned to a selection of innovative approaches in this field. Starting with ProVision3D the approaches of 3D business process gadgets, the Interactive Process Modeller, and GRADE-3D will be discussed.

ProVision3D   *ProVision3D* (Process Visualization in 3-Dimensions) has been developed in the course of a research project at the Institute of Business Informatics of the Technical University Berlin. The goal of the developement was to find out, how virtual reality technologies can be used for the accomplishment of complex organisational tasks. For this purpose a so-called "Virtual Reality Workbench" has been created based on the following requirements (cf. [KGM99]) that the new approach should fulfill:

- A three-dimensional visualisation of business process and other organisational models.
- The modelling of business processes in virtual space.
- The developement of animation functionalities for supporting the simulation of process runs.
- The possibility for a control and manipulation of process runs in virtual space.
- The support for cooperative work in virtual space.
- The availability of open interfaces to commercial organisational tools.

ProVision3D is built upon a meta-model which formally describes process and organisational models. The models can either be directly created in ProVision3D or imported from other modelling tools (which interface formats are supported is not explicitly stated in the publication that describes the tool [KGM99]). In the same way possibilities for the exchange of data with workflow management systems are mentioned. ProVision3D possesses a metaphor library which contains abstract graphical object for the visualisation of structures and scenarios in virtual space.

These metaphors are visualised in ProVision3D based on the DOI (Degree Of Interest) method: This method shows objects that are closer to the position of the viewer in higher details and objects that are further away in a more abstract (and thus computable) simpler representation. At the same time a 3D layout is applied to the process models so that a differentiation between diverse process levels (e.g. main and sub process level) can also be directly visualised.

The *Graph in Graph* method as described by Krallmann et al. [KGM99] unites DOI and 3D layout. At first the user only sees the topmost process layer. When he moves forward in virtual space the sub-process models lying behind the main process become visible and the level of detail of the objects increases. For the visualisation of organisational models ProVision3D reverts to Cone Tree representations (cf. [RMC91]). In this method the hierarchical structures which typically occur in organisational models are visualised with cones that lie on top of each other, as shown exemplarily in figure 3.3.

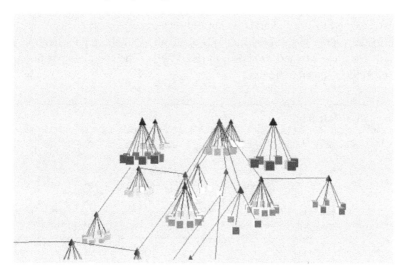

Figure 3.68: Example for a Cone-Tree Representation (Source: http://www.cs.wpi.edu/)

Generally seen, only very vague assertions can be made regarding the capabilities and usage scenarios of ProVision3D as the only available publication [KGM99] does not contain further details about the actual implementation of the described concepts and their effectiveness. So far (by 2006), still only a prototype of the software seems to exist that does not contain all envisaged functionalities.

This lack of information and the unavailability of a tryout software version makes it difficult to assess the value of ProVision3D on the dimensions in the above proposed classification model. Nevertheless an attempt shall be made for the positioning of ProVision3D in the classification model.

In regard to dimensionality ProVision3D operates completely in three dimensional space (as can be derived from the available screenshots and descriptions). The user interacts with the software in a 3D environment through 3D mice (bats), sensor pens and shutter-glasses with tracking systems. According to the article the prototype also provides possibilities for the manipulation of the components, but altogether it seems to focus on the visualisation of the views as defined by the meta-model and the connected graphical metaphors. Therefore, the value for in-teraction is set to average, which means partly interaction. Although the usage of animations for the support of process runs is mentioned as a developement goal of ProVision3D the concrete realisation is not described and is neither apparent from the representations of the prototype. Therefore, the value for the animation dimension is set to the lowest magnitude. In regard to the level of detail an average value can be assigned to ProVision3D as not only abstract geometric shapes are used but also (according to the DOI method) detailed, symbolic representations (e.g. symbols for filing cabinets as shown in [KGM99]). The complete positioning of ProVision3D is shown in figure 3.3.

ProVision3D			
Dimensionality	2D	2 1/2-D	3D
Level of detail	abstract	partly abstract	Photorealistic
Level of animation	static	animated	reality-ident animation
Level of interaction	no interaction	partly interaction	full interaction

Figure 3.69: Classification of ProVision3D

To evaluate the advantages that can be achieved and the effort that has to be invested when using ProVision3D instead of traditional approaches it has again to be reverted to theoretical considerations. The accurateness of the models is satisfied by the systematic definition and the use of the graphical metaphors which are based on the ProVision3D meta-model, resp. the models that have been imported via the interfaces. The aspect of the relevance of the visualised model content is supported by the DOI method - in comparison to other tools this method allows to mask less relevant parts of a model without completely hiding them. Other approaches solely use abstract symbols which have to be further described by additional information. However, the recognition of abstract model elements seems to be easier especially in complex models than the visual comprehension of detailed symbols. The DOI method is therefore seen as one way to unite the advantages of abstract and highly detailed representations which can lead to an increased clarity of the models. The understanding of the systematic structure is well supported in ProVision3D by the use of 3D layouts: The relations of different model types (e.g. a business process model and a work environment model) can thus be directly detected, which leads to an added value as the relationships can now be detected more quickly. The principle of economic efficiency is ambivalent in regard to ProVision3D: On the one hand benefits may arise due to the faster understanding of complex models due to the advanced visualisation methods, but on the other hand the three dimensional representation requires additional investments in hardware (shutter glasses, special input devices) as well as the (personal) ability of the user to find one's way in the virtual environment. This ability is also questioned in the literature (for discussions on this point see for example [Coc04, CM01, WOCD97, MS95, SVM+99]) and it can be easily shown by simple three dimensional, abstract games that the interaction with three dimensional objects usually requires a lot of training to be effective. From an economic point of view this training is equal to additional costs and thus limits the benefits of such approaches.

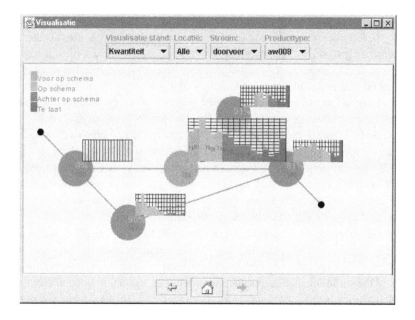

Figure 3.70: 2D Visualisation of Process Throughput (Source: [SBE00])

3D Business Process Gadgets The approach taken for the *3D business process gadgets* has been described in the course of a case study [SBE00]. The goal as described in the case study was to optimise the business processes of the Dutch social security provider GAK NL. Therefore, at first bottlenecks in the business processes had to be identified. In the second stage also simulations of the processes were performed. For the first task the data of process measurements which were available in a data base had to be visualised. Figure 3.70 on the preceding page shows the 2D visualisation that has been created for this purpose. It combines a graph based process structure and related histograms to help managers identify the bottlenecks in the execution of the process. Although Schoenhage et al. acknowledge certain difficulties that are related to three dimensional visualisations (as already remarked above in the context of ProVision3D) they mainly revert these difficulties to the non familiarity of users with 3D interaction devices. In their opinion the interaction with 3D visualisations will add value due to the larger amounts of presentable information as soon as the technical problems (in regard to cheaper input devices and faster hardware) of interaction are solved. Therefore they describe how they have shifted the approach of 2D business process visualisations to a three dimensional environment by using *visualisation gadgets*.

These gadgets are based on the Java3D library and consist of two types of primitives: *Behaviours* that are required for the interaction with a visualisation and *visualisation primitives* that can display information by means of 3D graphical representations. Behaviours can be of five different types: Brushing behaviours that reveal additional information about an object that the input device points at, Key behaviours to move objects upon the pressing of a key, Menu behaviours to display context sensitive menus for 3D objects, Modify behaviours to rotate, translate, scale and iconify three dimensional objects, Translate behaviours to translate 3D objects along the screen's x- and y-axis (instead of the object's axes). The visualisation primitives that have been implemented are cone trees, 3D histograms and 3D graphs. Figure 3.71 on the next page gives an impression of the final visualisation including the representation of a 3D business process together with 3D histograms showing the corresponding waiting times in the process.

The classification of the approach is therefore as follows: On the dimensionality scale the highest value is assigned, the level of detail receives the lowest value as the representations only show abstract graphical primitives, the animation scale is set to the middle value due to the mentioning of animation capabilities for the simulation of processes, and the level of interaction is set to the highest value as the user can fully interact with all objects as described by the behaviour primitives, see figure 3.72 on page 150 for a summary.

For comparing the approach of the 3D business process gadgets in relation to traditional visualisation approaches the following remarks can be made: As the exact meaning of the symbols used in the graph representation is not stated an assessment of the principle of accurateness cannot be seriously made. The principle of relevance is better satisfied by 3D business process gadgets in case the goal of

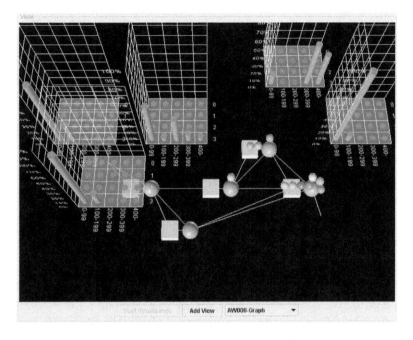

Figure 3.71: 3D Business Process Gadgets (Source: [SBE00])

the visualisation is the identification of bottlenecks in the business process. In the traditional approaches (BPMN, EPC and Adonis) additional mechanisms would be necessary for this purpose. The economic efficiency is again hard to evaluate as it is not exactly described how the modelling takes place in the approach. However, based on the statement in the publication it can be assumed that for an optimal use of the approach additional investments in hardware equipment are necessary thereby reducing the economic efficiency in relation to the traditional approaches. The clarity of the models again depends on the purpose of the visualisation. For the identification of bottlenecks the visualisations proposed in this approach are more clearly understandable than in the traditional approaches (merely due to the integration of the histogram representations in the model that are estimated to be commonly known). Theoretically, the comparability of the 3D visualisations with other modelling approaches is given, although the meaning of the symbols would then need additional explanation (e.g. to be able to identify tasks, decisions etc. in the graph model). Also the systematic structuring can therefore only be regarded

3D Business Process Gadgets			
Dimensionality	2D	2 1/2-D	3D
Level of detail	abstract	partly abstract	Photorealistic
Level of animation	static	animated	reality-ident animation
Level of interaction	no interaction	partly interaction	full interaction

Figure 3.72: Classification 3D Business Process Gadgets

from a theoretical point of view. Nevertheless due to the data base underlying the visualisations a certain structure can be assumed.

Interactive Process Modeller   The approach that is taken in the concept of the *Interactive Process Modeller* is a concrete implementation of a theory that has been set up in the PhD thesis by Leinenbach [Lei00]. The quintessence of this theory is that the description of business processes is performed in a new way by the employees of an enterprise. Instead of arranging abstract graphical objects the users can interact with realistically designed objects in a virtual environment and thus effectively re-enact the sequences of activities which occur in the real world. This interaction is recorded and translated into formal process models. The main idea is that it is not necessary anymore to utilise abstract elements and formal methods that require intensive courses of instructions and highly paid specialists. It is further assumed that by using this approach the direct involvement of the employees, as the knowledge sources of an enterprise, in the creation of the process models is increased which may lead to a better quality of the resulting models. Furthemore, by using the Interactive Process Modeller, the processes can be modelled in distributed environments, e.g. over an intranet. The Interactive Process Visualiser is a documentation component which also works in distributed environments. It can be used to make existing process models available to third parties and is also built upon virtual reality techniques.

By the screenshot shown in figure 3.3 on the next page the concept is directly understandable: In the left frame an event driven process chain (EPC) is depicted and in the right frame the corresponding virtual reality environment is shown. By selecting a state or an event in the EPC the related animations in the virtual world are triggered so that it can be understood which consequences the formal process

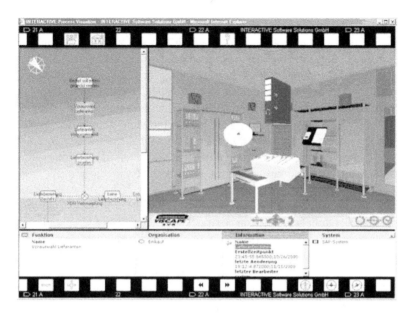

Figure 3.73: Screenshot Interactive Process Modeler I (Source: http://www. interactive-software.de)

descriptions would have in the real world. For the definition of processes with the Interactive Process Modeller various virtual environments are presented to the user in which he/she has to explain how the processes are performed.

An example that is taken from [Lei00] would be as follows: At the beginning the user chooses a virtual character (avatar) that symbolises him/herself and which serves as an interface for the direct communication between the employees in the virtual world. If the employee wants to represent a process that has to performed by using a telephone he/she chooses a telephone symbol in the virtual world and thus triggers the modelling. In the following several pop-up windows are presented to him/her in which he/she can choose and enter the conversational partner, the type of telephone conversation (incoming or outgoing), a short description as well as the content of the conversation. Additionally dialogues are available for defining which documents the employee needs for the particular activity, which activities are related and which IT applications are required. Based on this information a process model is generated and represented as an EPC. This EPC can then be imported into other process modelling tools or processed by other software. Although at the end a formal process definition is available the employee was at no point in the modelling process required to get in touch with the EPC method. The functionalities of the Interactive Process Modeller resp. Visualiser encompass the creation and documentation of process models. Thereby a real three dimensional representation is continuously employed (for the representation of the EPCs as well as the virtual environment). The user can interact with the objects in such a way that he/she can view them in the virtual space from every perspective and start new definition sequences by selecting objects. However it is not possible to define new objects or arrange the objects in three dimensional space. Therefore, for the degree of interaction only the average value is assigned. In regard to animation capabilities no functionalities became apparent when trying out a locally installed demonstration version of the Interactive Process Visualiser. Only the transitions between different process models were animated, yet the single visual elements do not posess animation facilities – in contrast to the approach of CASUS for example. The representation of the objects in the Interactive software applications are very detailed (in regard to the virtual reality representations). The classification for Interactive Process Modeller and Visualiser is therefore as depicted in figure 3.74.

Interactive Process Modeller			
Dimensionality	2D	2 1/2-D	3D
Level of detail	abstract	partly abstract	Photorealistic
Level of animation	static	animated	reality-ident animation
Level of interaction	no interaction	partly interaction	full interaction

Figure 3.74: Classification Interactive Process Modeler

The benefit that can be achieved by Interactive Process Modeller and Visualiser lies on the one hand clearly in the simplified creation of formal business process models, on the other hand in the possibility for a better understanding of modelled processes. In regard to the principles of accurateness, the principle of comparability and the principle of systematic structure similar assessments have to be made as to any application that makes use of event driven process chains because the basic method is not altered through the use of the visualisation functionalities in the Interactive software applications (the formal representation of EPCs is displayed three dimensionally and the user can move along this 3D representation).

Concerning the clarity of the models Interactive Process Modeller and Visualiser combine the formal representation with visualisations that are very close to reality. Thereby the advantages of both approaches can be gained: Both the simple manipulation and fast comprehension of the overall process by the EPC representation as well as the realistic and therefore intuitive incorporation of relationships in the virtual world are possible. What does not seem to have been taken into account is the fact that in the case of very complex and nested models resp. models with many interrelations difficulties may arise when using the standard visual representations of the models (e.g. in the case of EPCs that are linked to organisational models). As shown above in the ProVision3D approach this can be taken into account by making use of the 3D layout technique - which would in principle also feasible in the Interactive applications. As one of the probably most important aspects in regard to virtual reality techniques lies in the adapted user input and display devices it seems remarkable that although Leinenbach discusses these technologies [Lei00](p.27–42) it cannot be inferred from the screenshots of the software applications as well as the elaborations on the distributed, internet based modelling that these technologies are actively used for the approach. Instead most of the screenshots and the hardware requirements lead to the conclusion that the approach reverts to internet browser plugins for three dimensional representations - which has also been detected when evaluating the available trial versions[84]. If this is effectively the case in practice it would be seen as a major shortcoming.

With respect to the principle of economic efficiency Interactive Process Modeller breaks new ground: The training of employees for the understanding of formal process modelling languages can be at least reduced to a major extent or maybe even completely substituted which clearly leads to cost and efficiency advantages. However, these benefits may be outweighed partly by the expenses for specialists who might be required for the developement of the virtual worlds (similar to the problem of the creation of the elements in the CASUS approach).

All in all the approach of interactive process modelling based on virtual reality techniques is an interesting attempt to leave the traditional formal process modelling languages aside at the stage of modelling but still integrate their advantages through an automatic generation of the formal models. In the case of simple process structures the advantages seem to prevail (even with the requirements of additional hardware and software investments for displaying virtual environments) but for complex models it is estimated that the effort for defining process models in the virtual reality may be higher than with traditional modelling approaches that allow for very short creation times if the user has been trained well enough.

---

[84]Of course this cannot be regarded as a proof for the non-existence nor the usage of these technologies as no full version and documentation where available.

GRADE-3D   *GRADE-3D* is a visualisation tool that is based on the GRAPES (Graphical Engineering Language[85]) language which has been developed by Siemens Nixdorf for the modelling of information systems [SLB97]. The language elements of GRAPES are documents and symbols. A document can either be a table or a diagram, whereby seven types of documents exist: Communication diagrams, interface tables, process diagrams, data tables, specification diagrams, data structure diagrams, and hierarchy diagrams. The different diagram types contain symbols which determine the nature of the diagram and form the basis for the relation of diagrams. In the case of large processes the GRAPES approach leads to complex representations with many interrelations.

The acronym GRADE stands for tools that support GRAPES. The tool GRADE-3D allows for the graphical representations of models described in GRAPES and provides computer-graphical methods for the reduction of the model complexity. This is achieved by the use of 3D layout techniques (as described above) in combination with virtual reality input devices. For the representation of business process models GRADE-3D uses a 3D layout approach where the user has the possibility to edit objects and interact with the models. For this purpose he/she can change the view by using a data glove[86], select individual objects and move inter-connected parts of a document. As animation functionalities are not apparent in GRADE-3D (based on the available literature sources) and mainly abstract symbols without any detailing are used the classification for this tool is as shown in figure 3.75.

Grade-3D			
Dimensionality	*2D*	*2 1/2-D*	*3D*
Level of detail	*abstract*	*partly abstract*	*Photorealistic*
Level of animation	*static*	*animated*	*reality-ident animation*
Level of interaction	*no interaction*	*partly interaction*	*full interaction*

Figure 3.75: Classification Grade-3D

In relation to other tools – such as the traditional business process modelling tools – GRADE-3D offers the possibility to graphically represent relationships

---

[85]Translated from German: 'Graphische Engineering Sprache'

[86]A specialised input device that is worn like a glove and records the movements of the hand as well as the fingers which can then be processed electronically.

between different models. Additionally to the 3D layout the DOI and the Fish-Eye method (see figure 3.76)) have been integrated in GRADE-3D which causes that only the currently relevant facts of a model are displayed to the user and therefore an increase in the principles of clarity and relevance is achieved. Generally seen GRADE-3D seems to be outstanding mainly in regard to its three dimensional representations as the graphical modelling of processes with abstract symbols and different model types also occurs in more traditional visualisation approaches of business process modelling.

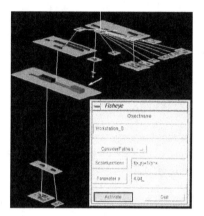 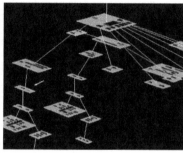

Figure 3.76: GRADE-3D representation with (left) and without (right) Fish-Eye view (Source: [SLB97])

When comparing the approaches for innovative visualisations in the area of business process management it becomes apparent that despite the differences in the approaches some similar functionalities occur in several of them: This incluces the technique of 3D layouts that has been mentioned in ProVision3D and GRADE-3D and which seems to provide a good possibility for giving an overview of complex, highly nested models and their relationships. This applies as well to the Degree-of-Interest method and the Fish-Eye method that enables to focus on relevant parts of models. The integration of virtual reality technologies as done in ProVision3D or the Interactive Process Modeler might offer advantages for specific use cases but the cost/benefit ratio of such systems – when deployed professionally in an immersive 3D environment – might not be favourable for simple modelling tasks. If the technical requirements are on the other hand reduced for VR systems the interaction might suffer (e.g. as assumed for the Interactive Process Modeller where only a 3D plugin is used for a traditional 2D webbrowser).

By applying these insights to the classification model that has been used to compare the characteristics of the approaches a first attempt for the overall guidelines of a visualisation procedure in business process management can be drafted: Along with an increasing model complexity the advantages of three dimensional representations (e.g. the 3D layout) become apparent whereas the benefits of detailed virtual reality techniques diminuish. At the same time the full interaction of a user with highly complex models does not seem to be convenient if the models are not visually preprocessed (e.g. by using a Fish-Eye view or DOI method). For complex model representations the degree of detail should be reduced, when showing parts of a model it should increase to further the intuitive understanding (e.g. through a transition from abstract to concrete symbols). Although animation functionalities could not be assessed for the abovely outlined approaches they might provide advantages for the understanding of global relationships in complex models.

Information Technology Level

The bottom layer as it has been derived from the three business informatics frameworks constitutes the system or information technology level that is responsible for the actual execution of the IT services required by the layers above. This execution comprises both the manual (human) execution as well as the automated execution of IT services. The aspect of IT as a service provider to other enterprise functions is of critical importance to the continuity of the business today as many key processes, especially in large enterprises, depend on the well functioning of the underlying information technology. It is therefore a great concern to establish methods and mechanisms to ensure the professional management of a corporation's IT services and evaluate the proper functioning of the IT as well as identify and remedy potential risks that might have impacts on business processes. Besides these service aspects of information technology, all methods discussed in section 3.2 on page 64 in relation to computer science are applicable on this level (e.g. for hardware and software implementations, user interface design etc.). Therefore, only the specific business informatics aspect is highlighted here.

The area that addresses these needs and provides basic concepts and methods for resolution can be characterised by *IT Governance* [MZK03]. Several approaches currently exist that mainly stem from the practical needs of enterprises to meet regulatory requirements that are imposed by government legislation (e.g. by the recently introduced Sarbanes-Oxley Act in the USA). They range from the management of IT service processes to the holistic management of an enterprise's IT activities and are characterised by the treatment of aspects of value added by the use of IT, the enabling of new business models through IT (top-down) and the requirements to IT due to new processes (bottom-up), the orientation towards IT as a service function and the risk management in regard to IT [MZK03].

Symbol	Meaning	Symbol	Meaning
Server	Infrastructure Element, Type: Server	Switch	Communication Element, Type: Switch
Tower	Infrastructure Element, Type: Tower	Communication element	Communication Element, Type: Data Connection
Plotter	Infrastructure Element, Type: Plotter	Bridge Router	Communication Element, Type: Bridge Router
Projector	Infrastructure Element, Type: Projector	Performance Indicator	Performance Indicator
			Evaluates
Printer	Infrastructure Element, Type: Printer		Is connected to
			Is logically connected to

Figure 3.77: Excerpt of Symbols for ADOit Production Architecture Models

From the viewpoint of visualisation several of the previously approaches could be used to meet these requirements on the IT level. This includes the different diagram types for depicting quantitative figures as well as the representations of business processes that can (and have already been) applied to IT service processes. An approach that is particularly interesting in this context is the representation of IT architectures as the basis for assessments on the IT level. The meta model based IT management software ADOit [BKM04, MB05] provides a comprehensive solution for these representations as well as for the evaluation and analysis of IT management in general. In figure 3.77 an excerpt of the symbols used in ADOit for the representation of Production Architecture Models is shown. The main elements of the model are *infrastructure* and *communication* elements that can be physically and logically related to each other. Both elements can have a range of different types to represent various hardware devices. Furthermore performance indicators can be linked to the elements which are required for the IT management approach underlying ADOit. In figure 3.78 an intuitive example for an IT production architecture is presented. As can be seen from the symbol set and the example, the use of expressive icons greatly eases the understanding of the underlying model in this approach.

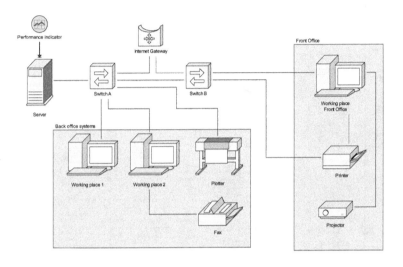

Figure 3.78: Example for an ADOit Production Architecture Model (created with ADOit)

Generic	Buildings	Airplanes	Information Systems
Ballpark	Bubble charts	Concepts	Scope/objectives
Owner's representation	Architect's drawings	Work breakdown structure	Model of the business or business description
Designer's representation	Architect's plans	Engineering design/bill-of-materials	Model of the information system (or information system description)
Builder's representation	Contractor's plans	Manufacturing engineering design/bill-of-materials	Technology model (or technology-constrained description)
Out-of-context representation	Shop plans	Assembly/-fabrication drawings	Detailed description
Machine language representation	-	Numerical code programs	Machine language description (or object code)
Product	Building	Airplane	Information system

Table 3.1: Architectural Representations by Zachman [Zac87](p.282)

4 Analysis of Visualisations

Based on the survey of existing visualisation approaches in business, computer science, and business informatics the underlying principles of these visualisations shall now be investigated. The purpose of this chapter is therefore to reveal how the presented visualisations are actually created, which concepts form the basis and which theories and technologies are available that can lead to successful IT based implementations. To achieve this goal two paths for an analysis can be chosen: The first path is based on the author's subjective experiences when exploring the various forms of visualisations that have been included in this work. Due to the many different types of visualisations and the range of tools that have been used for their creation it is estimated that a well founded practical insight is possible. However, there exist also theoretical and technical approaches for the creation of visualisations that might underlie particular approaches. It is thus obvious to revert to these existing and scientifically established approaches in a second path of analysis. The combination of the subjective path and the insights gained by the examination of the available scientific theories will then form the basis for identitifying potential extensions to the existing approaches for visual representations and their creation. The chapter is thus structures as follows: At first the subjective experience of the author in regard to the creation of the visualisation used in this work will be outlined, then the scientific concepts that are available for the definition of visualisation are discussed and finally a derivation of possible extensions to the current ways of visualisations and their creation process will be given.

4.1 Subjective Experience

The creation of the visualisations shown in chapter 3 has been conducted by the author in three different ways: The first, and probably most often used procedure for publications dealing with visualisations from other sources, is the scientific citation[1] of the visualisation in terms of a digital copy from an existing source. Depending on the type of source the actual graphic can either be copied in a *pixel format* – which in general leads to lower quality as most pixel based graphics are

---

[1] Note: As permitted by current copyright regulations.

only available in compressed formats that do not satisfy proper printing requirements – or as a *vector graphics*. The latter is often available in electronically available scientific publications and practically does not occur in the case of graphics
that have to be taken from the internet (although open source graphics standards
such as SVG would technically allow for it).

As the pure citation of visualisations is therefore either limited due to the available quality of the graphical representation or does not satisfy the pragmatical
requirements of the context where it shall be integrated, i.e. although the basic
type of visualisation is appropriate (e.g. an ER diagram) the available instances do
not fit, another path has to be chosen. The second possibility which is available
today for creating visualisations is to create them by oneself – the possibility of
employing someone else who creates the visualisation upon request would only
shift the task[2]. In the case of IT based visualisations as they are discussed within
this work this involves the interaction with some kind of information technology
and therefore requires sufficient knowledge of the utilised hardware and software
applications.

Again, this procedural path has various options: For a lot of visualisation requirements it is sufficient to revert to image editing software where one can draw
different types of graphical primitives, adjust their painting attributes such as colour,
line thickness or line style and save the resulting graphical representation in a wide
variety of formats (which can be proprietary to a software vendor or open source).
To enhance the quality of the representations vector graphics software may be used
that records the types of primitives that a user has selected and the modifications of
their graphical attributes and is thus capable of a posterior modifcation of the primitives in the picture without losing quality. An often used approach for generating
vector graphics is to use libraries of pre-defined graphical representations that can
be inserted into the representation and modified in their attributes (cf. the primitive
objects in a software like Powerpoint or various clipart collections). This approach
has for example been applied for the creation of the figures 3.1 on page 40 and 3.18
on page 62.

For IT based visualisations that are too complex to create by hand or by the use
of pre-defined objects it has to be turned to specialised visualisation software. This
comprises for example most of the chart visualisations (some of which can be created by standard office packages) and the examples for information visualisations

---

[2]Although a detailed discussion of this *outsourcing* of the visualisation procedure is at this
point not considered it is a common solution for many enterprises that hire specialised staff
for this purpose (e.g. as for example successfully done by the global consulting company
McKinsey with their Visual Graphics Computing Services subsidiary in Kerbala, India – see
http://www.mckinsey.com/locations/india/vgi/).

that not only require specific algorithms for their creation but also an underlying data set which they represent. For example the heatmap in figure 3.46 on page 108 has been created using specialised applications from the area of information visualisation. Although the underlying algorithms can become very complex, the process of creating a visualisation is largely handled by the software so that the user only has to point to the required data source and adjust some attributes of the representation. The actual creation of the graphical primitives and the specific adjustments of their graphical attributes subject to the visualisation algorithm for the data set are usually handled by the software. In case the available software does not meet the visualisation requirements a user would have to engage in the programming of an application where he or she could make use of several application programming interfaces (APIs) that are available for realising visualisation software (e.g. the InfoVis Toolkit[3] or TGS OpenInventor [4]).

However, even if it might be concluded that the programming of visualisations resembles the last imaginable step in the process of generating IT based visualisations another aspect has not yet been considered. The approaches discussed so far have not considered the semantic issues that are on the one hand inherently related to visualisations and that can on the other hand also be represented by visualisations. The semantics conveyed by a visualisation, i.e. the meaning of the representation, are responsible for their successful pragmatic use as well as the syntactic aspects of how e.g. the data is mapped to graphical primitives and their attributes. Visualisation semantics are therefore related to questions such as *What may a user associate with the resulting graphical representation?* or *Is the intended meaning of the visualisation correctly transfered to the user or would another type of representation better fit?*. Although these are obvious questions, very often they are not considered (cf. the discussions of Zelazny on these aspects [Zel92]). When creating visualisations in the aforementioned ways it would thus be necessary to take this into account as well and refer to semiotic, psychological (for theories of perception) and design issues to assure that the visualisations are created in the correct way.

The second semantic issue is that of expressing semantic relationships by visualisations. Several examples have been discussed in chapter 3 that are not built from sets of data but are actually used to represent domain semantics. This includes for example ER diagrams which are used to structure entity types and relations of a domain or the different types of business process visualisations that explicate the procedural knowledge of employees in an enterprise. In contrast to visualisation approaches that are initiated based on a given data set and the approaches that pro-

---

[3] See http://ivtk.sourceforge.net/ accessed 13-05-2006.
[4] See http://www.tgs.com/ accessed 13-05-2006

duce graphical representations with drawing software, these types of visualisations build upon a particular model that determines the rules for the combination of the graphical objects and is semantically described.

After this description of the subjective experiences of the process of creating visualisations it shall now be turned to an analysis of the scientific concepts that can be consulted for a further step in the cognitive process.

4.2 Scientific Concepts

Based on the insights gained by the subjective experiences for the process of generating visualisations the focus shall now be put on the existing scientific elaborations that underlie IT based visualisations. Although it would be an acknowledged approach to discuss the creation of IT based visualisations entirely from a technical point of view and solely revert to the field of computer graphics, the path chosen here aims to take a broader view, including the "pre-technical" aspects which are inherent in every approach for creating visualisations – even though they are often not explicitly mentioned.

It has therefore been recognised as an essential point in the creation of visualisations to investigate the mechanisms that take place before the actual drawing, configuration or implementation of a visual representation. Several paths could be chosen to discuss this stage, including philosophical and psychological aspects to highlight the principles of human cognition and perception. The approach that has been selected for this work at first takes up principles from *general model theory* that combines aspects from philosophy, linguistics, and natural as well as technical sciences [Sta73] to identify the basic principles of the model aspects of visualisations. The second part of the scientific elaboration is then devoted to reviews of the current *meta approaches* for defining IT based visualisations to give an insight into the current state of the art. Finally, a *meta model based* analysis of representatives from the survey of visualisation approaches will be conducted.

Model Aspects of Visualisations

The survey of the existing visualisation approaches in chapter 3 and the illustration of the subjective experiences have clearly revealed that visualisations are not an arbitrary combination of graphical objects but that they are built upon a distinct conception of a domain. To detail the structure of these conceptions it can be reverted to general model theory [Sta73] that proposes a high level view on the basic constituents and relationships of models that is largely independent of a specific branch of science.

According to this theory[5] a model can be generally defined by three main types of characteristics:

- Mapping characteristics
- Reduction characteristics
- Pragmatic characteristics

The mapping characteristics state that a model is always a *model of something*, i.e. a mapping or representation of an original that can be natural or artificial, and that can also be models themselves. In general model theory both originals and models are regarded as *classes of attributes*. The mapping relation between an original and a model of this original is therefore a mapping between the attributes of the original and the attributes of the model (in the sense of the understanding of mapping in mathematical set theory).

The second characteristic of models is that they usually do not take over all attributes of the original but only those attributes that are perceived as relevant by the creator of the model and/or for the users. An interesting remark is that the knowledge which attributes of the original are part of the model requires the knowledge about all attributes both of the original as well as the model. As Stachowiak highlights, already the reduction characteristics of models reach a pragmatic level by the choice of the model attributes [Sta73](p.132).

The pragmatic characteristics deepen these aspects by declaring that models are not assigned to originals per se but that they replace the original for the purpose of distinct subjects within a distinct time interval and by restrictions to distinct theoretical or actual operations.

The elements of which models are composed are fundamentally divided into *individuals* and *attributes*. The term *attribute* in the sense of general model theory can be further defined as "characteristics of individuals, relations between individuals, characteristics of characteristics, characteristics of relations and so forth" [Sta73](p.134)[6]. Attributes that belong to an original and cannot be further decomposed are denoted as *zero order attributes*, attributes that describe properties and relations of individuals are *first order attributes*, attributes that describe the properties of properties are *second order attributes* and so on.

The mapping characteristics of models can be divided by the type of the adaptation of the model to the original into *structural/formal adaptation, material adaptation / adaption of the content*, and *spatial and temporal metric* models.

---

[5]In the following it will be relied on the elaborations by Herbert Stachowiak in [Sta73].

[6]Free translation by the author from German.

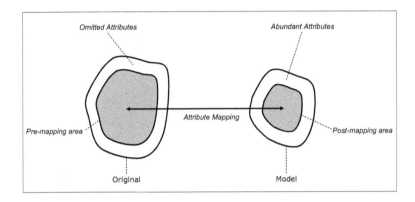

Figure 4.1: Mapping between Original and Model (redrawn after [Sta73](p.157))

The type of structural/formal adaptation describes which formal attributes remain on the side of the original and which are taken over to the model (see figure 4.1 for an illustration). For the case of *atomic models* the class[7] of all conceived attributes of the original are reduced to exactly one individual in the model. An attribute class (or an original, a model or a system) that contains exactly one individual is defined to be *monadic*.

In *isomorphic models* the number of individuals and the number of attributes of the original are equal to the number of individuals and the number of attributes in the model. Relations between inviduals of the original and relations between individuals of the model are therefore exactly mapped and the mapping also persists if the original and the model and therefore also the pre-mapping area and the post-mapping area (see figure 4.1) are swapped.

When some of the attributes of the original are not mapped to the model this is denoted as *omittance of attributes*[8]. In some cases the model contains attributes that do not have an equivalent in the original which are denoted as *abundant attributes*.

The material adaptation concerns the adapatation of material attributes of the model to material attributes of the original. The differentiation between material and formal/structural attributes depends on the pragmatic aspects that encompass the mapping and can be be based on the availability of a semantic meta language. An attribute can therefore be considered as formal/structural if the mapping be-

---

[7]Class is hereby implicitly understood as a collection of things that share a common attribute.
[8]Note: Stachowiak terms this "Präterition" in the original German version [Sta73](p.155).

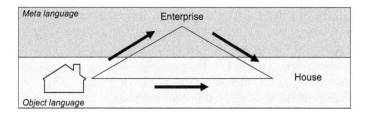

Figure 4.2: Object Language vs. Meta Language

tween the original attribute and the model attribute takes place on the basis of a formalised object language (that may be defined in a meta language). If a formal attribute is described by a semantic meta language, i.e. a meaning (also denoted as referent or code in terms of semiotics) is assigned to the attribute, the attribute is considered as a material attribute in the model. These concepts are illustrated by figure 4.2 that is built upon the concept of the semiotic triangle and exemplifies these relations for a visual representation: The mapping between the graphical icon on the left and the term *House* on the right would correspond to the mapping of formal attributes in the object language, whereas the addition of the semantic meta language on top allows for the semantic exact description of the icon as representing an enterprise.

On the basis of these concepts again two extreme types of material adaptations can be described: The first is the *analog model* where the meaning (coding) of every attribute of the original is reinterpreted for the model. The second is the type of an *isohylic model* where the material consistence of the attributes of the original is fully preserved in the model. For both cases the structural adaptation is presupposed and independent of the material adaptation (e.g. also in an isohylic model groups of attributes may for example be combined in one model attribute).

Another type of models are *equate* models or *copies* of originals that combine the properties of isomorphic and isohylic models. When the isohylic aspect is omitted they are denoted as *structural copies*. A subtype of equate models are *spatial metric models* that are fully congruent to their originals in the sense of Euclidean geometry and dimensions. If the metric dimensions of the model are scaled down in relation to the original they are termed *spatial contractional models*, if the dimensions are scaled up *spatial dilatational models*. The same considerations can be applied to temporal relations by *temporally variable spatial models* and accordingly *temporally contractional models* and *temporally dilatational models*.

To detail the role of semantics in regard to general model theory Stachowiak discusses two concepts: The first is the *categorisation of meaning and sense* after Gottlob Frege[9] and the second is the *theory of semantic levels* that is part of the general model theory.

The categories by Frege (cited after [Sta73](p.147ff.)) describe a cascaded structure for distinguishing between the following entities that lead to the formal explication of meaning:

(a.) The medium carrying a sign
(b.) Sign
(c.) Meaning
(d.) Sense
(e.) Association

The first is the medium that carries a sign which can be a material substrate or an energetic state. Stachowiak exemplies this by a visually perceivable configuration of letters made up of black colour on a white paper. The second entitity is the sign which is the basis for a combination of signs that is the expression for something (a predicate statement). For the creation of a predicative statement indvidual constants are combined with unsaturated predicates as attributed signs. These predicate statements are defined as being equal to syntax. The example that Stachowiak gives in this relation could not be directly translated to English and has therefore been slightly modified to the following: The individual constant *The Jupiter* (which is the name for a Roman god and for the fifth planet in our solar system) is combined with the unsaturated, i.e. containing an empty position, predicate *is illuminated by the sun*. This results in the predicative statement *The Jupiter is illuminated by the sun* where the predicate has been saturated by the supplementation of the constant.

The third level in the cascade is the meaning that is expressed by a sign and that leads to the definition of semantics. As before for the definition of syntax this part is divided into the meaning of the individuals and the meaning of the attributes that are then combined to form a logical value. Continuing with the example from above this implies the determination of the semantic referendum for *The Jupiter* by *the fifth planet of the solar system* and the specification of the content of the predicate *is illuminated by the sun* by a mathematical function that returns for every valid value whether the logical values of *true* or *false*.

---

[9]Stachowiak refers to the original publications by Frege in 1891 and 1892 which are available as reprints in [FT02]. The elaborations here will be based on Stachowiaks interpretation of Frege's arguments [Sta73](p.147ff.).

By the fourth level (sense) it is expressed how semantics in a broader sense (also denoted as noetics[10]) are assigned to the signs and attributes. This concerns the literal sense of the individual and the unsaturated predicate that goes beyond the meaning of the item. The saturation of the predicate takes place in analogy to above by the combination of the sense of the individual and the sense of the predicate in the thought that is phrased by the predicative statement. Turning to the example this means that the individual *The Jupiter* and *is illuminated by the sun* have a literal sense that goes beyond the meaning of the third level and is e.g. also invariant in regard to an adequate translation into another language. It is perceived that this level therefore contains the area of emotions, feelings, and intuition - which constitutes an indispensable aspect also in regard to visualisation. As Stachowiak remarks there also exist signs that do not have a meaning according to the previous argumentation but which nevertheless have a sense [Sta73](p.150).

The fifth and last level (that is already part of pragmatics) is designated to the subjective association that is evoked in an individual when perceiving the individual, the attribute and also the predicative statement as a whole. For example the evocation of the mental picture of a red coloured planet patterned by horizontal stripes when reading the predicative statement *The Jupiter is illuminated by the sun*. Similar to the fourth level the association might occur directly without the intermediate levels.

A special type of the conceptions by Frege is the part of general model theory that describes how the information processing of humans in regard to models takes place. It is denoted as the theory of semantic levels [Sta73](p.196ff.) and will serve as the basis for a linkage of the theoretical and universally applicable concepts of general model theory to the area of visualisation. The meta model of the theory of semantic levels contains three main levels and one basic level. The *basic level* acts as the carrier of the most basic entities that can be perceived which are denoted as *taxes*[11]. *Taxems* are an equivalent class of *taxes* that are similar in regard to their colour, shape etc. in the way that they are perceived as identical by most users. *Morphs* define the smallest sequence of taxes that carry a meaning and can be subsumed again as *morphems*. The *morphems* can be in the same combined to more complex structures, the *lexems*. The smallest semantic entity that can be used to describe morphems and lexems are *semems* resp. *semantems*.

---

[10]Based on the definition in the Brockhaus encyclopedia *noetics* is the doctrine of thinking, comprehension, and cognition that is not only directed towards correct thinking but also towards genuine cognition (http://www.brockhaus-enzyklopaedie.de).

[11]The terms used for the following structures stem from the field of linguistics, as many approaches from the area of computer science and (as will be shown later) also visual language theory.

The same considerations of the structuring of most basic entities has been applied to the area of visualisation: Based on research results from psychology and neural visual processing the smallest, visually perceivable distinct entities are denoted as *graphems* [War00](p.174). To identify graphems of visual representations one approach is to revert to work in the area of *pre-attentive* processing[12]. This approach from psychological research has identified certain features of visual information that are processed by the human brain much faster than others and which can therefore be regarded as elementary. Figure 4.3 shows an overview of the categories of pre-attentively processed features. In the context of visualisation morphems are therefore the smallest sequences of graphems for assigning meaning. For visual morphems the assignment of the semems depends (just as in linguistics) on specific conventions that are either explicitly or implicitly available (similar to the legend of a map) and are as well subject to cultural factors.

Form	• Line orientation	• Curvature
	• Line length	• Spatial grouping
	• Line width	• Added marks
	• Line collinearity	• Numerosity
	• Size	
Colour	• Hue	• Intensity
Motion	• Flicker	• Direction of motion
Spatial Position	• 2D position	• Convex/concave shape from shading
	• Stereoscopic depth	

Figure 4.3: Categories of Pre-Attentively Processed Features (redrawn after [War00])

The first semantic level that follows the basic level reflects the *internal model of an individual* that is made up of the information received from the outside world. These models that are created from perception form the basis for all types of semantic constructions as they lead to the creation of internal, non-perceptual models such as imaginations, concepts, thoughts etc. (also denoted as cogitative models). The main characteristics (mapping, reduction, and pragmatic) of models as stated at the beginning of this section are also applicable to these models.

On the second level the so called *self communication* takes place: The internal models from the first semantic level are explicated into models that are built from the elementary constructs (taxems resp. graphems). Thereby an *internal commu-*

---

[12] Another approach that will be elaborated in chapter 5 on page 223 would be to revert to the concept of graphical primitives.

nication system (or first order communication system) is created that may be of an auditive, visual or tactile nature.

The third level characterises a further step of modelling where the models for self communication are transfered to models that can be exchanged with other individuals which is the basis for *general communication systems* (or second order commmunication systems).

Before being able to investigate the visualisation approaches based on the considerations of general model theory, a fundamental view on the generation of visualisations shall be given derived from the concepts developed so far. It can be concluded that for creating visualisations it is not sufficient to stick to the simple conception of one visual model that represents an original as it is implied by Stachowiak for his view on graphical models [Sta73](p.168). It is rather necessary to distinguish between two types of models and two originals in this case: On the one hand a model of an original is created that defines which attributes are conveyed into the model space and which structural and material adapations are applied. This first abstraction from the original cannot however yet constitute a visualisation. The reason for this is that on the other hand visualisations can themselves be regarded as originals with a number of attributes that is too large to be handled in their original form. Therefore, also a model of the visualisation is created that represents the visualisation and makes it manageable (e.g. in the same way as an architect has to determine which visual model he wants to use for creating the plan of a house, may it be two or three dimensional, artistic or technical). Nevertheless the model of the visualisation and the model of the original have to correspond to each other if the visualisation is to be used for any kind of application in regard to the original. Again, reverting to the example of the architect this would mean that the visual model the architect has chosen has to correspond to a model that contains all necessary attributes for building a house. These relationships are depicted in figure 4.4 on the next page.

The subsequent analyses will take up the concepts of general model theory in the following way to provide a scientifically sound procedure: At first the pragmatic aspects of the visualisations will be analysed to investigate the goals and potential uses of the visualisations. In a next step the main types of models (of the originals) that precede the visual models (as illustrated in figure 4.4 on the following page) will be discussed before it will be turned to the meta approaches for the specification of visualisations as representatives of models of visualisations.

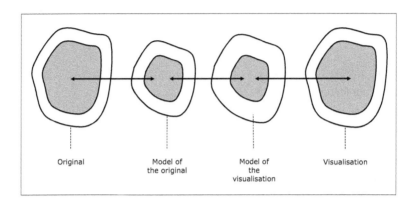

Original   Model of   Model of   Visualisation
                  the original   the
                                    visualisation

Figure 4.4: Model Theoretical Relationships for Visualisations

Pragmatic Aspects of Visualisations

To analyse the pragmatic aspects of the surveyed visualisations an approach from the area of knowledge management shall be applied as visualisations can be regarded as an essential supportive mechanisms in this field (see the formation of the field of knowledge visualisation in the last years that focuses on exactly these aspects [Bur04a, Bur04b, Epp04]). Four basic aims of visualisations have therefore been derived:

– Knowledge explication
– Knowledge transfer
– Knowledge creation
– Knowledge application

The goal of *knowledge explication* as it shall be understood here[13] is to explicate knowledge that resides in the heads and minds of people and express it by a visualisation. A typical example are business process models where procedural knowledge is explicitly laid down in the form of graphs. The same principle applies for example to the cause effect models of Balanced Scorecards where the influences between strategic goals are laid down, as well as to Entity Relationship models where relationships of a domain are depicted. The key characteristic of this aspect is the human creation of the visualisation based on his/her knowledge, thoughts and attitudes. In terms of the model of semantic levels this would

---

[13]In contrast to knowledge representation in the context of machine processing in section 3.2 on page 78 that will be taken up again for the discussion of the models of the application domain.

correspond to the transformation of the internal model of the user that he/she has developed based on his/her perceptions (e.g. when working in an enterprise) to an internal communication system for his/her own purposes (e.g. in the form of an individual sketch of the business process) and then further to a second order communication system that is commonly semantically defined (e.g. a representation in BPMN notation). Obviously, the process of knowledge explication does not have to be restricted to a single user but can involve several persons who commonly develop a visualisation that matches their own views on a task.

After the knowledge has been explicated by a visualisation a *knowledge transfer* between one or more individuals can be conducted on the basis of the graphical representation. By turning to the field of group support systems that study the enhancement facilities of intra-group processes a number of tasks can be identified where visualisation applications can facilitate group communication and reasoning (following an idea by [Epp04] who derived the tasks from [BVNT01](p.2)):

- Diverge – moving from having fewer concepts to having more concepts
- Converge – moving from having many concepts to focusing on a few concepts deemed worthy of further attention
- Organise – moving from less understanding to more understanding of the relationships among concepts
- Elaborate – moving from having concepts expressed in less detail to having concepts expressed in more detail.
- Abstract – moving from having concepts expressed in more detail to having concepts expressed in less detail.
- Evaluate – move from less understanding of the value of concepts for achieving a goal to more understanding of the value of concepts for achieving a goal.
- Build Consensus – moving from having less agreement among stakeholders to having more agreement among stakeholders.

The task of *Diverge* is for example clearly supported by the visualisation of ontologies (see e.g. figure 3.47) where additional related concepts can be directly identified. Other examples would be the various types of enterprise models in section 3.3 on page 117 that can give groups of users a better overview of the concepts that surround them and help them as well for *Organise* tasks (e.g. from the different business process representations showing the embedding of an employee's tasks into a broader environment). The *Converge* task becomes apparent by the various types of charts that aggregate a lot of information in one visual representation as well as the specific visualisations from the field of information visualisation (e.g. the treemap of a filesystem that lets one directly discover the relatively biggest files).

A good example for *Elaborate* tasks are the three dimensional representations that have been shown for various approaches (e.g. figure 3.9 showing a 3D logistics application, the 3D circuit board representation in figure 3.25 on page 75 or the business process visualisation approach of ProVision3D (see chapter 3.3). These virtual reality like visualisations can be used in addition to the standard two dimensional representations and thereby reveal previously unknown details supplied by other users. For the *Abstract* tasks these considerations for 2D and 3D representations can be made the other way round, i.e. by moving from the complex three dimensional view to a two dimensional view. Actually, most of the visualisations abstract from the related originals in the sense of the reduction characteristic of general model theory, i.e. by either not mapping all attributes (structural or material) of the original to the models or by combining structural attributes and preserving their semantics. A visualisation that deviates from this principle and comes close to an equate model, i.e. that is both isomorphic and isohylic, is given by the circuit board layouts and also by similar CAD applications: In this case the exact representation of the original is necessary for a later implementation of the components.

Evaluate tasks as described in the listing above are supported for example by the various enterprise cockpit approaches (page 130ff.): The achievement of strategic goals is evaluated by the visualisation of the corresponding performance indicators. The tasks for *Building Consensus* are facilitated by all types of visualisations that are created by humans. Information visualisations that are based on data can therefore not be directly included in this task - however, also these types of visualisation might be used for argumentation purposes and lead to consensus building.

The *discovery of knowledge* becomes apparent by the visualisation of ontologies that can support the discovery by related concepts. An interesting aspect of modelling for knowledge discovery is expressed by [GGM+04] for the case of legacy systems where the knowledge about the functioning of an application may be re-discovered by creating static and behavioural models (e.g. by the use of UML models as shown on page 98ff). The *creation of new knowledge* by visualisations cannot only occur in the analysis phase of enterprise models (e.g. by gaining insight into explicit process structures, the dependencies of strategic goals etc.) but also by the techniques from information visualisation which put a special focus on these aspect in the way that they aim to exploit all possibilities that are theoretically and practically available to comprehend existing data structures and discover new properties and relations.

Visualisations supporting the *application of knowledge* are for example enterprise models in a prescriptive sense, e.g. as apparent by reference models for process structures (cf. [BDK04, FL04]). In the same way also the visualisations of circuit board layouts can be regarded as the basis for the application of the knowledge how to build the circuit board.

Explicit Models

After the discussion of the pragmatic aspects the different types of models of an original (as shown in figure 4.4 on page 172) which precede the models of visualisations will now be investigated. Founded on the considerations in general model theory a distinction is made between *explicit* and *implicit* models: Explicit models correspond to models of second order communication systems of the third semantic level, i.e. models that can be exchanged with other individuals based on established conventions. Furthermore, explicit models are here characterised as models that are represented in an IT processable format and have therefore to be expressed in a formal or semi-formal way to be implementable. The term implicit model will be used to describe models that reside on the third semantic level but which lack the second aspect of being formalised or implemented.

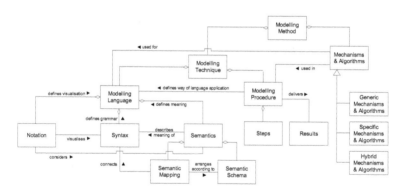

Figure 4.5: Components of Modelling Methods (Source: [KK02])

To further detail explicit models it can be reverted to the terminology as used in enterprise modelling (see figure 4.5)). According to Karagiannis et al. [KK02] *modelling methods* reflecting the pragmatic aspects of models consist of two components:

(a.) A *Modelling Technique* and

(b.) *Mechanisms and Algorithms*

Modelling techniques can be further divided into a *modelling language* and a *modelling procedure*. The modelling language contains the elements for generating models and is described by its syntax, semantics, and notation (e.g. textual or graphical). The modelling procedure explains how the modelling language is applied to generate instances of models [KK02]. The semantics of a modelling language are defined by the semantic mapping of the modelling syntax to a semantic schema. As can be immediately perceived by figure 4.5 on the preceding page the visualisation part concerns the notation of the modelling language and is defined by the modelling language. It visualises the syntax of the modelling language and considers at the same time its semantics. This terminology allows for a positioning of the subsequently discussed approaches for explicit models as well as the subsequently discussed meta approaches for specifying visualisations.

Relational Models   The first type of explicit models that has been identified to form a basis for visual models are relational models. According to their original conception by Codd in 1970 [Cod70] they can characterised as follows: Starting from a number of sets $S_1, S_2, \ldots, S_n$ a relation R is defined on these n sets if it is itself a subset of the Cartesian product $S_1 \times S_2 \ldots \times S_n$. The subset as described by Codd is derived by assigning the first element of S_1, to the first tuple, the first element of S_2 to the second tuple and so on up to n-tuples. A common representation of relations is in the form of arrays or tables - as shown in figure 4.6. Sets may be of different data types, including integer, float, string or date, as well as they may contain binary objects.

R	S_1	S_2	S_3	S_4	...	S_n
	V_{11}	V_{21}	V_{31}	V_{41}	...	V_{n1}
	V_{12}	V_{22}	V_{32}	V_{42}	...	V_{n2}
	...	...	...	...	...	...

Figure 4.6: Illustration of the Relational Model

Several operations can be performed on the relations, including join, projection, permutation, composition, and restriction as well as various types of normalisations[14].

Relational models are typical to act as a basis for visualisations in statistics and information visualisation. Due to their goal to gain insight into large data sets and the requirement to handle these amounts of information, they require efficient and proven approaches for coping with the data. The relational model and its enhancements over the last more than thirty years provide these benefits, especially due to the availability of high performance database applications (which is also a reason why semantically more expressive models have not been favoured in the past [BM04b]). Additionally, several other models can be translated into the relational model (see [EN94]) making it a good starting point for all visualisation ventures that deal with large amounts of data. By the examples for heat maps (figure 3.46 on page 108) and parallel coordinates (see page 107ff.) visualisations the underlying relational models even become directly visible.

Conceptual Models Conceptual models have been identified as the second type of explicit models for deriving visual models. They can be defined as a formal description of some aspects of the physical and social world for purposes of (human) understanding and communication [Myl92]. In contrast to knowledge representation models conceptual models do not focus on reasoning aspects in the sense of an expert system for example but are concerned with "life-size models of portions of the world" [Myl92](p.3) for human users. Conceptual models themselves can be represented by string grammars (as e.g. for the classical Telos approach [Myl92]) or by visual models such as Entity relationship diagrams as well as UML class diagrams. To express the specifity of the conceptual model for a concrete application domain (also denoted as domain specific models) the concrete instances of abstract conceptual models may be enhanced with particular graphical notations (as it is the case for the approaches of meta modelling that will be discussed in detail below).

Typical representatives for conceptual models are the meta models underlying the different types of visual models in section 3.3 on page 117 that all share the goal to be understood by humans and are all based on a formal or semi-formal based view of the world. Although these types of models are not primarily directed towards reasoning, they can be complemented by specific elements to allow for certain reasoning mechanisms (e.g. as it is the case in the notation of the Ado-

---

[14]For a discussion of the operations see the original publication [Cod70] or standard literature on relational databases

nis standard method for the simulation of business processes - see section 3.3 on page 140). Although the visualisations in enterprise cockpits can also be based on relational models alone (for the case of data driven business monitoring [Lic05]), some of them (e.g. the ADOscore cockpit, see section 3.3 on page 121) is also implicitly based on the conceptual meta model of a Balanced Scorecard.

Knowledge Representation Models   Whereas conceptual models are oriented towards the human understanding and communication another type of models can be found that seems to be (at first sight) equal to conceptual models but actually differs in its pragmatic aspect: Knowledge representation models. The purpose of knowledge representation models that have their foundations in artificial intelligence and are widely based on logical formalisms (e.g. including first-order predicate logic, description logic or temporal logic – for an in-depth discussion see [Sow00]) is to represent parts of the world in a machine interpretable way, including the machine understandable representation of semantics. Included here are also semantic data models, that can be positioned between conceptual and knowledge representation models but have a stronger affinity to implementation aspects [Myl92], and abstract representations such as algorithms that need not have a counterpart in the original world but that represent the knowledge of the designer of the algorithm.

The most obvious example for a knowledge representation model is given by the visualisation of ontologies (figure 3.47 on page 110) that originate themselves from the area of artificial intelligence. Although it has not been directly verifiable also for the visualisations of circuit board layouts, network animations, and visualisations in the context of algorithms knowledge representation models are assumed to assure the logically correct and machine interpretable configuration of the models.

Implicit Models

As mentioned above implicit models characterise models of originals that may in fact reside on the third semantic level, expressing that they are semantically communicable to other indviduals, but that have not been explicitly formalised so that the model itself could be processed by an IT system for the assignment to an IT based visual model. The case of implicit models is assumed for the types of drawings that are generated in a software application for illustrating entities and their attributes (in a very general sense) but where the entities and attributes are not part of an underlying explicit model. Nevertheless, the user generating these drawings might have conceived them in an implicit model that describes the syntactic and semantic aspects of the model and that he/she is able to communicate to others. From a pragmatic point of view also visual models that are based on implicit models may be sufficient for certain scenarios. This includes aspects of visual design (cf. [Bon99, Sta94]) as well as illustrations that are autonomous in regard to different usage scenarios (e.g. a slideshow presentation showing business processes that need not be simulated subsequently).

However, from a general point of view visualisations that build upon implicit models are questionable for business applications in the way that the actual realisation depends on the knowledge, skills, and abilities of the individual designer and is not intersubjectively exchangeable which makes the know-how for their creation difficult to be transfered.

Meta Approaches for the Specification of IT-Based Visualisations

To analyse the creation and structure of models of visualisations (again referring to figure 4.4 on page 172) the following remarks concern the definition of IT based visualisations as seen from a meta level. This means that the focus is not put on the definition of the graphical representation itself but rather on the techniques that can be used for defining the syntax and semantics of graphical representations. Three basic approaches have been identified how this can be achieved:

– Technical descriptions
– Informal descriptions
– Formal descriptions

Technical descriptions – such as the subsequently discussed visualisation pipeline – constitute the very basic, implementation dependent creation of IT based visualisations. Their consideration is to varying extents necessary for any kind of implementation of visualisations using information technology. This concerns especially the research fields of scientific visualisation and information visualisation, which strongly focus on technical implementations for creating visualisations. Nevertheless, also for the creation of complex two dimensional and three dimensional visualisations in other fields it may be necessary to revert to technical aspects for creating visualisations (e.g. to harness the range of visualisation capabilities integrated in modern graphic cards).

The use of informal decriptions precedes in many cases the formal descriptions. A prominent example for informally described visualisations is the first description of Entity Relationship diagrams by Chen [Che76] where he speaks of the representation in the way that "Each entity set is represented by a rectangular box, and each relationship set is represented by a diamond-shaped box" [Che76](p.19). Informal descriptions have the advantage of being (in most cases) easily understandable also to users that are not familiar with formal methods. When referring to a classification of diagrams as outlined by [CM98], informally described visualisations would correspond to an *uninterpreted diagramming model* where no constraints of the syntactic definition of the visualisation are imposed on a user creating a visualisation.

On the other hand the great exactness that can be achieved by formal approaches allows for additional usage scenarios as for example prevalent by the field of diagrammatic reasoning that enables the full interaction of users and machines on the basis of formal languages (for a further discussion see e.g. [WBJ00]). In this area two basic approaches can be distinguished (again based on [CM98]): A specification based on the *syntax directed model* that enforces a strict syntax checking and only allows a user to act within the rules and constraints preset by the syntax definitions or a visualisation based on the *intelligent diagram model* that unites the advantages of the strict syntax directed model and the uninterpreted model by first allowing the user to freely edit all graphical presentations and then perform the syntax check afterwards.

The Visualisation Pipeline

The discussion of technical visualisation aspects on computer hardware will be restricted in this work to a brief overview of the main concept. For this purpose it can be reverted to the description of the visualisation process in the form of the *visualisation pipeline* [Grö01] as described in computer graphics. The area of computer graphics deals with computer supported methods and techniques to process images, animation sequences, and visual information and comprises aspects such as generative computer graphics or image processing [Grö01, HB97].

As shown in figure 4.7 on the facing page the visualisation pipeline is composed of several consecutive steps: As in these steps mainly the technical aspects of visualiation are taken into account at first the data for the visualisation has to be acquired. In the area of scientific visualisation this data may originate from measurements or simulations and in the area of business informatics this data may refer for example to the objects in a business process model or the relational data underlying a bar chart. In the second step this data is enhanced for the purposes of visualisation. Again, in information visualisation this could be the application of filters or resampling to different measurement units. Translated into the area of business informatics also filtering methods could be applied to select for example only a specific section of a large model or data set. After the data has been

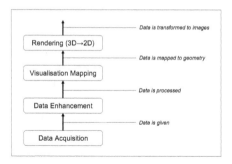

Figure 4.7: The Visualisation Pipeline (adapted from [Grö01])

processed it is mapped to a geometry. Thereby visual properties are assigned to the data and the resulting image of the data is determined. In the case of the various types of visual models that have been discussed in chapter 3 on page 39 this mapping is essential for the conveying of the meaning of the visualisation, i.e. the semantics, and therefore has to be exactly specified. However, some degrees of freedom may still exist for the mapping without interfering with the visualisation semantics (as will be highlighted in section 4.3 on page 211). After the mapping the last step in the pipeline is reached where images or animation sequences are produced by using computer graphics techniques (e.g. projections, visibility, shading, etc.). In the case of three dimensional graphics a 2D representation has to be derived for showing the visualisation on a screen.

Based on these considerations about the technical visualisation process in the following subsections approaches for *uninterpreted, pattern based* (as an extension to the uninterpreted model) and *visual language* definitions of visualisations will be discussed. These approaches will implictly detail the first three steps of the visualisation pipeline by providing concepts for the provision of data and their mapping to geometric objects.

Uninterpreted Generation

For the *uninterpreted generation* of visualisations no specific requirements exist: They are not technically derived from any kind of underlying model and the user is free to create any type of graphical representation and modify the attributes of the representation in any regard (corresponding to an implicit model as described above). Typical applications that represent such a proceeding are all types of graphical editors, whether they are based on pixel graphics (such as Adobe Photoshop, Corel Photopaint or the opensource editor Gimp[15]) or on vector graphics (such as Adobe Illustrator, CorelDraw or Inkscape[16]).

The usage of these tools is merely for design purposes as e.g. very often it is required for presentation slides to highlight specific aspects of visualisations or for professionally printed brochures where specific graphic formats and properties are needed, as well as for the captialisation of visual effects that are not provided by visualisation software as discussed in the following or would require large programming effort for a simple illustration. Therefore, the meta level, i.e. the model of the visualisation of drawing approaches based on pixel graphics is joined with the visualisation itself. Only for vector graphics based approaches a visualisation model is created which is however usually not further specified by syntactic or semantic constraints.

Pattern-Based Approaches

The second type for creating visualisations are *pattern-based approaches*. This type of visualisation model extends the uninterpreted generation by providing patterns that the user can select from for creating the visualisation. The pattern may be just an assembly of several graphical primitives (e.g. as common by cliparts) that represent a common entity or may be assembled on the basis of an algorithm. The main characteristics of patterns are that they are usually pre-defined and that the user can in general only modify certain attributes of the pattern. Patterns are therefore a concrete visualisation model that can be reused and adjusted to a user's needs.

By this characterisation of patterns not only pre-defined symbols where the user can adjust their size, colour, orientation etc. are comprised but also visualisations such as typical statistical charts, information visualisations or user interface components where the user assigns a data set to the visualisation pattern, adjusts a number of attributes and receives the final visualisation.

In the sense of model theory the concept of a pattern corresponds to a predefined visualisation model or a subset thereof that can be linked to an explicit or implicit model of an original. An important aspect of this linkage is that there is no exchange of semantics between the model and the visualisation model. This mapping of material attributes from the model to the visualisation model would necessitate the availability of a meta language level in the sense of semiotics as shown in figure 4.2 on page 167. To illustrate the principle of the pattern approach

---

[15]The selection of these tools is exemplarily, see the websites of the manufacturers: http://www.adobe.com, http://www.corel.com and http://www.gimp.org

[16]Again see the websites, additionally http://www.inkscape.org

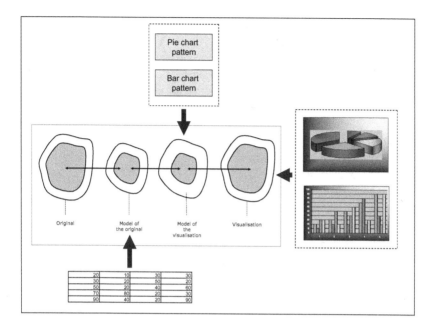

Figure 4.8: Illustration of Pattern-Based Visualisation Approaches

figure 4.8 gives an example of two patterns that are mapped to a simple relational model and the resulting visualisations of a pie and a bar chart.

Apart from the visual patterns that are assigned to data (as statistical charts and information visualisations), similar approaches for visual patterns will be discussed in the context of visual languages (cf. the approach described in [SK03]) and meta modelling (cf. [KK02, Fil04]).

Visual Language Approaches

The third group of approaches for specifying the generation of visualisations are the *visual language approaches*. In contrast to uninterpreted generation and pattern based approaches this type strongly relies on formal respectively semi-formal theoretical specifications. The basic motivation underlying the classical approaches from the area of visual languages is to provide a theoretical basis for the generation of visual representations that is similar to the existing theories for textual languages. Although the term "visual language" is sometimes restricted to visual programming languages or program visualisation [Wan95](p.11) it shall here be used in a broader sense.

Visual language approaches in general are based on the following definition [CDOP02]: Visual languages are composed of a collection of *visual sentences* which are determined by graphical objects that are arranged in a two or higher dimensional space. To formally express these concepts at first an application domain (*AD*) for a visual language is regarded[17]. The *AD* contains objects O, attributes A and relationships R^n to describe the state S of a domain, i.e. $S = \{O, A, R^n\}$.

A visual language (*VL*) is defined to be composed of a set of visual sentences (*VS*). The vocabulary V of the visual sentences consists of a set P of visual primitives, that have visual dimensions D, and a set of visual relations V^n that can exist between two or more primitives, i.e. $V = \{P, D, V^n\}$. The visual dimensions directly lead to the field of semiotics that deals with the meaning of signs and visual expressions and how they convey information. Bertin [Ber82] lists eight visual dimensions that can be used to transcribe similarity, ordinal relations and proportionality in a two dimensional space: The *position*, given by the two dimensions of a plane (X,Y), *size*, *brightness*, *texture*, *colour*, *orientation*, and *shape*.

The sentences of the visual language can be mapped to a state of the domain *AD*, thereby specifying the semantics of the language. The mapping takes place e.g. by $O \leftrightarrow P$, $A \leftrightarrow D$ and $R^n \leftrightarrow V^n$ or a combination of these (in line with the abovely step in the visualisation pipeline).

To classify the different approaches for specifying visual languages it is differentiated between two fundamental views:

– Formal specifications and
– Meta model based specifications

The formal specifications are largely based upon mathematical concepts and theories and are necessary for the exact and fully machine interpretable definition of visualisations. However, not all types of diagrams can be fully formally specified due to their complexity. Meta model based approaches have, as will be shown in the following a different approach to the process of specifying visual languages. By the separation of the model of the application domain and the corresponding notation of a visual language they take advantage of the benefit of independent modifications of the two parts. It has to be noted that there exist also attempts for a formal specification of meta modelling approaches (cf. in this regard the formal specifications of the meta meta model of the Meta Object Facility [OMG02]).

---

[17]The following considerations are based on a formalisation in [NH98] which has also been used in [Fil06a].

At first, the formal approaches for the specification of visual languages will be outlined, following a widely used classification as discussed by Costagliola [CDOP02] and Marriot [MMW98] who distinguish between *Grammatical*, *Logical*, and *Algebraic* approaches. Thereafter, meta-models based approaches as used in business informatics [KK02] and also recently discussed in the Visual Language community [BG04] will be investigated.

Formal Specifications   The formal specification of visual languages has a long history and has been discussed in many contexts and for a variety of different languages. When analysing the different approaches for formalisations a criterion of differentation lies not only in the varying underlying fields as expressed in [CDOP02] and Marriot [MMW98] but can also be expressed by

- linear versus
- non-linear

approaches, depending on the way of application of the formal definitions. The formalisations discussed in the following will be additionally differentiated by this criterion. By this discussion of formal approaches it is intended to highlight the main ideas of their contribution to the specification of visualisations. For detailed mathematical comparisons and further specialised and sometimes extensive discussions of the particular approaches it is referred to the respective literature sources.

One common approach for a formalisation is to regard a visual language as being specified by a *grammar* that is composed of a set of production rules which determine the composition of grammatical components, e.g. a visual sentence. The semantics of the sentence can be derived from the lookup of the meaning of the words in the sentence in a dictionary and the combination of these meanings by following the structure of the sentence [MMW98]. This is in analogy to the specification of sequential textual languages which has a long tradition both in linguistics as well as in computer science. For the case of visual languages it is assumed that the primitive objects (i.e. the terminal symbols) are distinct graphical primitives (e.g. lines, circles, text labels and so on) that are arranged on the basis of production rules that specify how complex graphical objects are composed of simpler graphical objects and in the end the primitive objects. Grammar based approaches are based on a linear application of the production rules. The identification of concepts defined in the grammar therefore requires to follow this linear procedure.

An example for a grammar based formalisation approach is illustrated in the following (based on an example in [MMW98]). The approach defines four types of concatentation operations for graphical primitives (as shown in 4.9 for the prim-

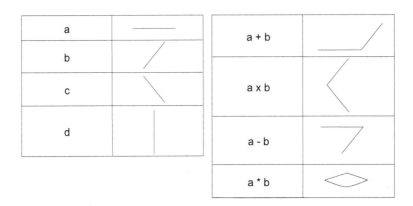

Figure 4.9: Primitives and Their Concatentation Operators (cf. [MMW98]

itives a, b, c, and d). Furthermore, a unary negation operator $\sim$ that reverses the head and tail of a primitive and a unary composition operator \ that overlays primitives that have the same label are defined. By the use of a context-free grammar these operators can be used to define pictures, e.g. by:

$$S \quad \to \quad House \tag{4.1}$$

$$House \quad \to \quad (((\sim d) + (a + d) * Triangle \tag{4.2}$$

$$Triangle \quad \to \quad ((b + c) * a) \tag{4.3}$$

Thereby the complex objects of a triangle and a house can be composed as shown in figure 4.10 on the facing page. These types of generalised string grammars can be further extended by the integration of operators for spatial and geometrical relationships, e.g. such as *contains* or *above*, which allow for even more detailed declarations.

A further extension are *positional grammars* that generalise the idea of concatenation by defining constructs for arbitrary spatial relations that give information about the relative position of the next symbol with respect to the current symbol. Productions in positional grammars are expressed by the subsequent rule [MMW98] where A is a non-terminal symbol, $\alpha_{1...n}$ are terminal or non-terminal symbols and REL_i determines the relative position of symbol α_{i+1} in regard to α_i. :

$$A \quad \to \quad \alpha_1 \; REL_1 \; \alpha_2 \; REL_2 \; \cdots \; REL_{n-1} \; \alpha_n$$

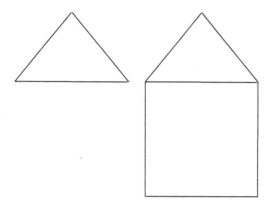

Figure 4.10: Example for a Picture Based on a String Grammar

The symbols used in positional grammars have x,y coordinates that determine their position on a grid and are not contained in the production rules explicitly (as the positions are determined by the REL_i symbols).

Another type of formalisation that is also based upon a grammar based approach are *graph grammars* which have a tradition of more than thirty years[18]. In figure 4.11 on the next page an intuitive example for the application of a graph transformation rule to a statechart diagram is shown. The rule expresses that the pointer indicating the current position in a statechart (on state s1) is moved to the subsequent state s2 and that in the second graph (with node 0) a node is inserted before the current node (which is marked by *end*).

Graph grammars thus provide a possibility to describe the syntax of graph diagrams by specifying transformation rules for defining how the elements in a graph are to be arranged. By figure 4.11 another aspect for the usage of graph transformations can be seen: By the definition of a second graph that is generated while walking through the first graph, a sequence of the steps undertaken is generated: This sequence corresponds to the *operational semantics* of the graph. This approach for defining operational semantics by graph grammars can also be applied to (the graphs) of meta models which are discussed below.

Besides the illustrative representations of graph transformation rules, graph grammars can also be defined by textual production rules. This shall be illustrated by

---

[18]See the proceedings of the international workshops on graph transformation published by Springer and recently the proceedings of the International Conferences on Graph Transformation [CEKR02, EEPPR04].

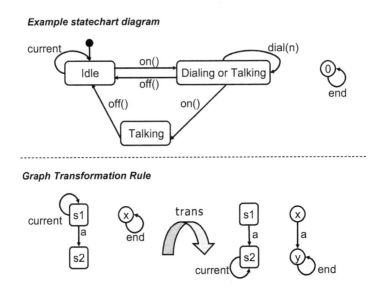

Figure 4.11: Example for the Application of Graph Transformation Rules (Source: Reiko Heckel)

an example in a *plex grammar* that is one of the many existing forms of graph grammars. Plex grammars are composed of primitive objects called NAPEs (non-attaching-point entity) that are grouped together in the form of *plex structures* [MMW98].

The following example (taken from [MMW98](p.18f.)) shall show the basic procedure of context free plex grammars[19]. The production rules 4.4 to 4.7 are a plex grammar for the specification of simple flowchart diagrams. They contain the non-terminal symbols *Prog* and *End* as well as the terminal symbols *Start*, *Halt*, *Funct*, and *Pred*. For each non-terminal symbol a NAPE is defined in the way shown in figure 4.12 on the next page: *Start* and *Halt* each have one attaching point, *Funct* has two and *Pred* has three. In the equations every production rule is followed by two pairs of brackets: The content of the first brackets determines how

---

[19] A deviation to the example in [MMW98] occurs in equation 4.7 which is described by Marriot et al. as $End(1) \rightarrow PredEndEnd(210,201)(100)$. It is assumed that the form depicted here with the formal parameters $(210,301)(100)$ is the one that was intended to describe the sequence as shown in the example in figure 4.12 on the facing page.

the attaching points of the involved NAPEs are combined and the second defines which attaching points are available after the application of the production rule.

Therefore, the rule in 4.7 states that an *End* symbol with one attaching point is rewritten by *Pred* and two *End* symbols where the attaching point number 2 of *Pred* is connected to the attaching point 1 of the first *End* symbol (expressed by *210*) and the attaching point 3 of *Pred* is connected to point 1 of the second *End*. The right side of figure 4.12 shows an example flow chart that can be composed based on this grammar.

$$Prog() \quad \rightarrow \quad StartEnd(11)() \tag{4.4}$$

$$End(1) \quad \rightarrow \quad Halt()(1) \tag{4.5}$$

$$End(1) \quad \rightarrow \quad FunctEnd(21)(10) \tag{4.6}$$

$$End(1) \quad \rightarrow \quad PredEndEnd(210,301)(100) \tag{4.7}$$

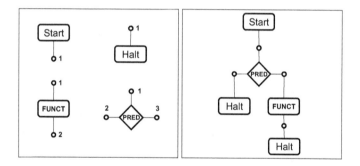

Figure 4.12: Example for the Elements of a Plex Grammar (Redrawn after: [MMW98]

Apart from the simple example for a plex grammar shown above, graph grammars can be used to specify complex diagram types and are also suitable for defining non graph based diagrams. This can either be achieved by creating a transformation of a non-graph diagram to a graph structure (see figure 4.13 on the next page for an example how a Nassi-Shneiderman diagram can be transformed into a hypergraph structure) or by referencing to the meta structure of the diagram (e.g. to the geometric definition of the graphical primitives as nodes and the spatial relations between the primitives as edges) and transforming these structures to graph structures.

The last type of grammar formalism that shall be presented are *attributed multiset grammars*. The central aspect of these grammars is that the productions

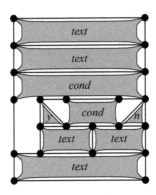

Figure 4.13: Hypergraph of a Nassi-Shneiderman Diagram (Source: [MV95](p.2))

rewrite sets or multisets of symbols with associated geometric or semantic attributes. Constraints over these attributes on the right hand sides of the productions control how the rewriting is performed, additional functions determine how the attributes of the non-terminal are computed in terms of the symbols on the right hand side [MMW98]. A sub type of attributed multiset grammars are *constraint multiset grammars* that permit the integration of existentially quantified symbols and allow symbols to occur in negative constraints. The terminal symbols in constraint multiset grammars refer to graphical primitives that are detailed by geometric attributes.

Listings 4.1 and 4.2 on the next page show examples for production rules in constraint multiset grammars that have been conceived for the Penguin system [CM98]. The first listing shows the rule for a state in a statechart diagram that is defined by two circles and a text label as terminal symbols. The constraints express that the midpoint of circle one has to be equal to the midpoint of the second, that the midpoint of circle one has to be equal to the midpoint of the text label and that the radius of the first circle has to be equal or smaller than the radius of the second. Furthermore, functional definitions for the attributes of the non-terminal state S are given. The centerpoint of S is set equal to the centerpoint of the first circle, the radius of S equal to the radius of the second circle, the label of S to the label of the text and the kind of S is set to final, thereby indicating that the described type of the state element is a final state.

Listing 4.1: Production rule based on a constraint mulitset grammar, Source: [CM98]

```
S:state()  ::=  C1:circle,C2:circle,
    T:text
            where (C1.mid == C2.mid
            C1.mid == T.mid
            C1.radius <= C2.radius
  ) {
            S.mid = C1.mid;
            S.radius = C2.radius;
            S.label = T.label;
            S.kind = "final";

  }
```

The second example in listing 4.2 is an extension to the first and is required to explicitly differentiate between a normal state and a final state in a state chart diagram (for a detailed discussion see the original source [CM98]). Therefore, it makes use of a negative application constraint to define that there does not exist a second circle primitive that has the same center as the first. As can be derived from the presented example for recognising states in statechart diagrams, the purpose of the approach of constraint multiset grammars lies mainly in the recognition of sketches and their semantic interpretation and is an example how an editor based on the intelligent diagram model can derive the drawn visual language.

Listing 4.2: Negative existential quantifier in a constraint multiset grammar, Source: [CM98]

```
S:state()  ::=  C:circle,T:text where (
            not exist M:circle where (M.
                mid == C.mid) &&
            T.mid == C.mid
  ) {
            S.mid = C.mid;
            S.radius = C.radius;
            S.name = T.text;
            S.kind = "normal";

  }
```

The second major area for the formal mathematical specification of visual languages is the area of *logic*. The basic aims of logic specification approaches are to improve the expressiveness and utility of specifications and to provide a single unified framework to overcome the deficiencies of sometimes semantically imprecisely specified elements and relations in grammatical approaches (e.g. in regard to the exact meaning of spatial relations) [MMW98]. The elementary constructs in logic and more specifically logic programming are *programs* which consist of rules that define first-order predicates. A rule is defined by a *premise* (or condition) and a *conclusion* (or action) [KT01](p.60). The premises may be extended by *conjunctions* and *disjunctions* leading to rules as exemplarily shown in equation set 4.8: On the left hand side of the rules premises that are concatenated with conjunctions (first rule) and disjunctions (in the second rule) are shown. The premises are composed of first order predicates p_i with the terms S_i^j. The conclusions are depicted on the right hand side.

$$p_1\left(S_1^1,\ldots,S_1^n\right) \wedge \cdots \wedge p_m\left(S_m^1,\ldots,S_m^n\right) \quad \rightarrow \quad p\left(T_1,\ldots,T_n\right) \qquad (4.8)$$

$$p_1\left(S_1^1,\ldots,S_1^n\right) \vee \cdots \vee p_m\left(S_m^1,\ldots,S_m^n\right) \quad \rightarrow \quad p\left(T_1,\ldots,T_n\right) \qquad (4.9)$$

By defining rules that consists only of premises it is indicated that they are unconditionally true. These rules are then called *facts*. Facts can be evaluated by the set of rules (also denoted as the knowledge base) and new facts can be generated. Logic based specification approaches can be classified as non-linear approaches as the sequence of the application of the rules defining the concepts is not pre-determined: A rule is here selected depending on the premise that matches an input wherafter the rule matching the new statement is selected and so on.

Without going into the details of logic theory[20] the following example from description logics shall provide an intuitive illustration how logic approaches can be applied to define a visual language[21]. Description logics statements basically consist of single unique term names on the left hand side of an equation and descriptions about sets of individuals on the right hand side. The elements of descriptions are *concepts*, *roles*, and *constructors* [Haa98]. To define rules in descriptions logics at first a set of names for concepts and roles is determined which is then used to form more complex terms by applying description constructors. The constructors can be of numerous types, including unary and binary operators (e.g. $\neg$, $\wedge$, $\vee$). The roles may be filled with concepts and the number and values can be restricted. Numbers can be restricted to maximum and minimum values and values by defining individuals of a specific concept. The semantics of descriptions logics can be formally described in denotational form by using a set Δ of domain values and a mapping ξ from the concept or role descriptions to subsets of Δ [Haa98](p.265)[22]. The following example (taken from [MMW98](p.40) and

---

[20] A general introduction is provided in [KT01, RN04] and specifically for description logics [BHS04].

[21] For further discussions and an overview of logic based visual language specifications it is reverted to [MMW98]

[22] For further details of the semantic specification see [Haa98](p.265ff.)

also explained in [Haa98](p.277)[23]) may illustrate these definitions (based on the visual representation of a simple Entity Relationship diagram in figure 4.14):

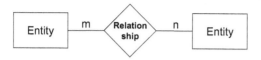

Figure 4.14: Example for an Entity Relationship Diagram based on Description Logic Specifications

In equation 4.10 the concept of a *relationship* is defined which may be described in natural language as follows: A *diamond* and a *named_region* and the role *linked_with* which is restricted to a maximum of two fillers and two concepts of the type *entity* and the role *touching* that is also restricted to two fillers and to the concept of the type *relationship_entity* and another role *touching* restricted to two or less occurrences and the text value 1 and two roles *touching* restricted to one or less occurrences and the text values *m* respectively *n*. It has to be added that this formalisation is based on the assumption of a set of geometric primitives (e.g. points, line segments, polygons, etc.), a number of high level relations (e.g. *disjoint, touching, intersecting, linked_with* etc.) and externally defined concepts (e.g. *relationship_connector*) - see [Haa98](p.270f.).

$$
\begin{aligned}
relationship \quad \equiv_{def} \\
(diamond \wedge named\_region \wedge \\
(\exists_{=2} linked\_with) \wedge (\forall linked\_with\ entity) \wedge \\
(\exists_{=2} touching \wedge (\forall touching\ relationship\_connector) \wedge \\
(\exists_{\leq 2}((touching.textvalue) = 1) \wedge \\
(\exists_{\leq 1}((touching.textvalue) = m) \wedge \\
(\exists_{\leq 1}((touching.textvalue) = n) \wedge \qquad\qquad (4.10)
\end{aligned}
$$

Based on these logic statements it is possible to apply three different types of *visual reasoning* to a graphical representation [MMW98](p.40): An existing representation may either be *parsed* on the basis of the rules whereby the defined concepts and roles are identified in the graphics by selecting matching rules. Or,

---

[23]The approach used in the example has been implemented in the GenEd project, see http://www.sts.tu-harburg.de/ mi.wessel/gened/gened.html for further information.

secondly an example picture may be constructed from the specifications (also denoted as *inverse parsing*. Or, thirdly the specifications can be used to *hypothesise missing information* for incomplete pictures (e.g. it could be derived which graphical primitives or modifications in their spatial positioning are required to construct a valid statement in the visual language).

The third group of formal visual language specifications are approaches based on *algebraic formalisms*. In the context of visual language specification the goal of an algebraic specification has generally been described as "to map the domain to be defined into typed abstract data structures and to define typed functions and predicates operating on these structures that specify the operations of the application domain" [MMW98](p.45). This implies the existence of two separate areas: Namely on the one hand the domain part and on the other hand a collection of data structures, functions and predicates that is mapped to the domain. This is remarkable in regard to the so far discussed approaches of formal visual language specification as these have not distinguished between two parts but rather integrated both aspects into one specification. Similar to the previously discussed logic based approaches also algebraic approaches are classified as non-linear specification approaches. However, algebraic specifications of visual languages may become linear when the application domain they are mapped to would imply such a procedure. In the following an often discussed approach for an algebraic specification by Wang et al. [WZ98, Wan95] shall be briefly outlined to illustrate the main idea.

The approach for picture description languages described in [WZ98] differentiates between a *graphical signature* and a *graphical theory*. The graphical signature defines the syntax of the picture description language, i.e. the symbols and their relationships, the graphical theory (or graphical inference) assigns geometrical algorithms to the graphical expressions in the language (e.g. for actually computing an expression such as *overlap*).

More specifically the graphical signature consists of three sets of elements: *Graphical sorts with a partial order*, *Graphical functions*, and *Graphical predicates*. Graphical sorts S are collections of graphical objects (e.g. Circle, Line, Arrow, Rectangle) and can be divided into *normal sorts* S_N and *relational sorts* S_R that are used to represent objects expressing relations (e.g. an arrow). Graphical objects may also be assigned to both types of sorts, depending on the intended usage of the object. To characterise subsort relations between the elements of the sorts *partial orders* $\leq$ are introduced. Thereby, a square can for example be defined as a subsort of rectangle (square $\leq$ rectangle). This corresponds to the concept of classes and subclasses as it has been discussed in section 3.2 on page 78.

The graphical functions $\mathscr{F}$ stand for the operations over graphical objects and are divided into constants $\mathscr{F}_C$ that represent the basic graphical objects, natural functions $\mathscr{F}_N$ that represent emergent graphical objects (e.g. to define a polygon by several overlapping rectangles), artificial functions $\mathscr{F}_A$ to create new graphical objects out of existing ones and attribute functions $\mathscr{F}_{At}$ to specify attributes of graphical objects (e.g. to calculate the length of a line).

Graphical predicates $\mathscr{P}$ can then be used to define formulas representing spatial relations between graphical objects (e.g. *overlap*(a,b) indicates that object a overlaps object b.

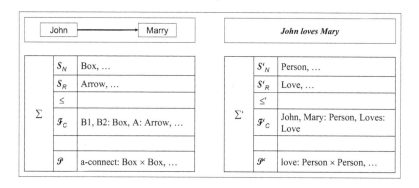

Figure 4.15: Example for an Algebraic Picture Description (after [WZ98])

In figure 4.15 an example for a graphical signature Σ on the left hand side and the corresponding application domain signature Σ' on the right hand side are shown. The *a-connect* predicate in the graphical signature expresses that two boxes are connected by an arrow. For defining a mapping between the graphical and the application domain signature a *signature morphism* between the two has to exist. This signature morphism (or interpretation) maps the normal sorts of the first signature to the normal sorts of the second signature, as well as the relational sorts, functions and predicates. For example by Box $\mapsto$ Person, Arrow $\mapsto$ Love, $B_1 \mapsto$ John, $B_2 \mapsto$ Mary, A $\mapsto$ Loves, a-connect $\mapsto$ love.

For using picture description languages to visualise concepts and relationships of a domain it is essential that the interpretation, i.e. the mapping between the application domain signature and the graphical signature, is not only syntactically correct but also conveys the correct semantics. Wang states that this semantic correctness "can only be achieved by the user through a good understanding of the application domain as well as the picture description language" [Wan95](p.50). He further gives three criterions that have to be satisfied for this purpose: *Consistency*, *Soundness*, and *Conservativity*. By consistency he states that the information derived by the interpretation of a picture may not lead to contradictions to the domain theory. Soundness expresses that all properties that an interpretation carries from a picture are derivable in the domain theory. Conservativity determines that the properties of an interpretation of a picture include all properties of the corresponding objects in the domain theory. Additionally he postulates that "semantic correctness cannot be automatically checked" [Wan95](p.54), mainly due to insufficient knowledge of a technical system about the semantics of the application domain. The approach developed in chapter 5 on page 223 will focus on exactly this point and provide a resolution to overcome these problems. The following section will show alternative approaches for the specification of visual languages which focus on the aspects of the underlying application domains.

Meta Model based Approaches   Apart from the formal approaches originating from the field of visual language theory another view to specify visualisations is taken by the approach of meta modelling. The term *meta modelling* can be found in many areas related to computer science with different connotations [Str98]: Basic definitions of meta models range from "a model that describes other models", "a model of a higher abstraction level" to "abstractions or models of the semantics of a modelling technique" and "model of the concepts used for modelling" (cited after [Str98](p.14)). Furthermore, the recent developments in regard to the open Meta Object Facility standard by OMG [OMG02] imply a focus on the aspect of metadata by the definition of "..an abstract language for some kind of metadata.." [OMG02](p.xi).

To narrow the meaning of the term it will be in the following relied on the views on meta modelling as expressed in the area of enterprise modelling and more specifically as discussed in [Küh04, KK02, Str98]. As will become apparent by the following definitions meta models in this view are strongly related to the area of conceptual models (as discussed above) and are usually described in a semi-formal way. Other views on meta models including formal definitions that are related to these approaches can be found in software engineering [SVJ01], requirements engineering (in [GBM86] after [Myl92]), conceptual modelling [Myl92] or reference modelling [BDK04].

Meta models will be used as a basis to describe the model of a domain which forms the basis for creating models of visualisations that can adequately represent the meta models. It has to be remarked that also approaches exist that use meta models to classify the different types of visual languages [BG04] - these approaches are not included here. To distinguish meta model based visualisation approaches from the previously discussed visual language approaches it can be again reverted to the definition of modelling methods (figure 4.5 on page 175): Although also the approaches of visual languages provide solutions to create visualisations of domain models – e.g. has been shown for Nassi-Shneiderman diagrams for the domain of algorithm development – they do not differentiate between the domain model language and the model of the visualisation (notation) but rather integrate both views in one model (see e.g. listing 4.2 on page 191 and equation 4.4 on page 189 that directly integrate the syntactic domain specification into the visual specification). The visualisation is therefore tightly coupled to the domain model. In contrast, the approach of meta modelling as described subsequently performs a clear separation between the modelling language and the notation. To make clear the aspects of meta modelling based visualisation approaches the aspects of meta models are detailed in the following.

To describe a modelling language (according to the relations in figure 4.5) one approach is to define a *metamodel* as a model of the modelling language [Str98]. Thereby a hierarchy of modelling languages is built where a (meta-)modelling language in one layer describes the modelling language in the underlying layer [Str98]. The hierarchy of these modelling languages is theoretically not limited to a certain level, nevertheless a useful level of abstraction has to be found [KK02]. Illustration 4.16 on the following page depicts these relationships graphically where the bottom level is the original that symbolises the target point for all modeling ventures. This hierarchy is used in a similar form for the foundations of UML, which is today accomplished by the Meta-Object Facility [OMG02].

Meta-modelling techniques define elements and possible relations between these elements within a certain domain. The elements may contain attributes and can represent abstract or concrete parts of the real-world. One of the advantages of meta-modelling is the abstraction of a part of the real world to allow for an easier understanding of complex relationships. Furthermore, typical meta-modelling approaches such as the meta-object-facility [OMG02] or ADONIS[24] [Jun00b] allow for arbitrary, not necessarily formally specified elements and relations (see [Jar92a]), which eases the definition of individual meta-models. Nevertheless, this higher degree of freedom also limits the usage of the models: Inferencing and consistency checking methods require additional (semantic) information[25].

The semantics of the elements and relations specified in a meta model are defined by the mapping of the syntactic elements and relations to a *semantic schema*. Although this semantic schema is for many meta-modelling approaches not ex-

---

[24] ADONIS is a registered trademark and commercial product of BOC GmbH.

[25] Similar results can be achieved via the use of constraint languages such as the Object Constraint Language in the UML 2.0 specification [OMG03] or the ADONIS scripting language AdoScript.

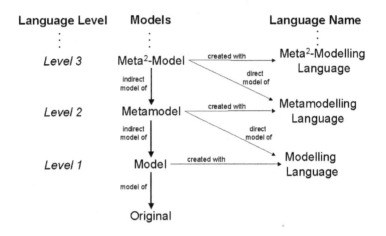

Figure 4.16: Relationship of Meta Models and Meta Languages [KK02]

plicitly defined so that the semantics are expressed in textual form (as it is e.g. the case for the UML specification [OMG04a]) recent attempts have been made to use machine processable definitions of semantic concepts and relationships. In this context ontologies have been discussed as an approach for such an explicit semantic schema [Küh04](p.35).

In contrast to meta models ontologies have a slightly different objective of representing the concepts and relationships of a domain: They have originally been proposed in computer science as a specification mechanism to enhance knowledge sharing and reuse across different applications with the aim of enabling machines to make automatic interpretations (inferences) of given facts [BA97]. They define "the basic terms and relations comprising the vocabulary of a topic area as well as the rules for combining terms and relations to define extensions to the vocabulary" [NFF+91](p. 40). Ontologies are currently widely discussed in relation to the Semantic Web [BLHL01] that aims to extend today's methods of representing information on the Internet by annotating the information semantically. A typical ontology language that is used for these purposes is the open accessible Web Ontology Language OWL [W3C04] which uses the basic constructs of resources, properties, and values to describe the objects in a domain.

Ontologies in general do not abstract to such a high degree from the original terms as meta models but are rather used for representing a highly detailed view on concepts of the real world. Whereas the elements of a meta-model are usually limited to a manageable number, the quality of an ontology increases with the multitude of its contained or referenced items and relations, i.e. its expressiveness. To combine the advantages of both approaches recent attempts strive for an integration of meta-modelling and Semantic Web technologies [OMG05]. This aspect of a higher expressiveness of ontologies together with their strictly formal specification qualifies them to be used as a semantic meta language for describing the elements of meta models.

Furthermore, by the definition of an *enterprise ontology* that structures the terms and relates the concepts that are used within a business not only a semantic definition of the meta models but also a semantic integration of different meta models can be achieved (see figure 4.17 for an illustration).

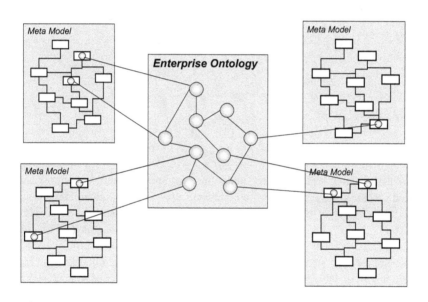

Figure 4.17: Conceptual Meta Model Integration based on an Ontology

A concrete example for an integration of two meta models is given in figure 4.18 on the following page. It shows an excerpt of a meta model for a cause effect model as it is used for the representation of the relationships between strategic goals in the balanced scorecard paradigm (see also section 3.3 on page 119) and an excerpt of a meta model for business processes (section 3.3 on page 129). The integration is performed by the denotation of two equivalent classes to the common concept *performance indicator* in the ontology. Thereby the semantics of the meta model classes are defined and an integration of the two meta models on a semantic level is possible.

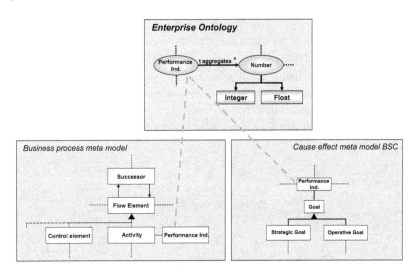

Figure 4.18: Concrete Integration of two Meta Models

With the elaboration of these foundations it can now be shown how meta model based visualisation approaches are conducted: To ease the human interaction one important aspect of the meta-modelling approaches as discussed here [Küh04, KK02] is the use of a graphical notation for the modelling language. The graphical notation is determined by the modelling language and its specific syntax. Two basic approaches for the notation can be identified: On the one hand the use of *static* notations where exactly one graphical symbol is assigned to each syntactic construct. And on the other hand *dynamic* notations that add control structures to the graphical representation for influencing the appearance of the symbol based on the state of the modelling construct.

A visual language that is specified by a meta model based approach – see also [Fil04] – can thus be characterised as follows: The syntax of the visual language is defined by the syntax of the meta model. The syntactic constraints for the arrangement of the symbols therefore directly correspond to the constraints of a domain. However, the visual representation of the symbols is defined separately by the notation. Thereby the notation can be changed without changing the meta model and the meta model may be modified without changing the graphical representation. The integration of dynamic notations additionally permits to visualise the state of attributes of the meta model. The semantics of the visual language is equally determined by the meta model. Depending on the approach used for the semantic definition of the meta model (e.g. via an ontology) also semantic definitions can be assigned to the elements of the visual language. In the following section an analysis of the surveyed visualisation will be discussed on the basis of this meta model based approach for visual language specification.

Meta Model Based Specification of Visualisations

To analyse the visualisations in chapter 3 from a scientific point of view it is necessary not only to take into account the visualisations and their underlying visualisation models themselves but also the models of the domains that are established independently of the visualisations. Based on the different approaches for specifying visualisations shown in the previous section this analysis could be performed in a variety of ways: The visualisations could either be regarded from the field of graph grammars so that every type of visualisation is transformed into a graph structure that can then be investigated by mathematical methods. Or an attempt could be made to apply a pattern based approach to the various kinds of visualisations (which has been successfully done by [SK03, Jun00a] for visual languages) and determine how the patterns are influenced by a particular domain model. However, as has already been stated these approaches do not separate the model of the domain from the model of the visualisation which makes it in some cases rather difficult to undertake an analysis of the visualisation aspects on their own and then determine the domain influences.

Therefore, the analysis approach taken here will be based on meta models that allow for this separation and provide similar functionality as the methods from visual language theory. To conduct the analysis at first a distinction between two major types of visualisations is made based on the insights gained in chapter 3: On the one hand several visualisation approaches can be identified that are based on *graphs*. This includes for example network plans (figure 3.5 on page 48), the Lab-View Block diagrams (figure 3.27 on page 77), network animations (figure 3.28 on page 78), as well as flowcharts or the modelling languages in software engineering and business informatics (e.g. figure 3.62 on page 137).

The second major type of visualisations that occurred were the various types of *charts* (figure 3.18 on page 62), *metaphoric visualisations* that used concrete symbols (e.g. the LabView panels in figure 3.26 on page 76 or the enterprise cockpit visualisations in figures 3.58 on page 129 and 3.59 on page 130 as well as the virtual reality approaches, e.g. in figure 3.9 on page 52), and *abstract visualisations* such as treemaps or parallel coordinates that could also be regarded as charts but do not adhere to the standard chart types (see chapter 3.2). This leads to the general differentiation between *graph based visualisations* and *other types of visualisations*.

Graph Based Visualisations

To show how graph based visualisation can be realised by using meta models an example from the area of business process management is presented in the following. At first the conceptual foundation for a view on business processes is described in the form of *business graphs*. From these basic elaborations a meta model for business processes can be derived which can in turn be used for defining visualisations for business process models.

A Business Graph is a formal representation of a clearly structured and comprehensible design of a business process including all important elements [KJS96]. These elements are structured in two components: A business process model and a working environment model. The business process model contains *activities*, i.e. atomic units of a process (e.g. the working units which cannot or should not be divided any more), *subprocesses*, i.e. the combination of activities in order to achieve reusability and a higher level of abstraction which are both necessary for distinctly structuring the process, and a *control flow* which is characterised by variables and predicates to determine the logical subsequence of the activities and allow for the description of parallelisms (or synchronisations), decisions, sequences and loops.

To provide a simplified view which is sufficient for the subsequent discussions of visualisations the control flow is limited to three elements (*start*, *end*, and *decision*). The working environment model consists of *actors* (persons), that represent the performers of activities, *groups* which are used to describe organisational structures such as positions, functions, roles, responsibilities and units of organisations, and *resources* which are defined as all means that are necessary for the realisation of activities such as documents, data or services. Between the business process and the working environment model mappings can be established such as *responsibilities*, i.e. the definition who is carrying out an activity or *requirements*, i.e. the regulations which resources are required to perform an activity.

Formally Business Graphs can be described as follows: Let $\Gamma = \{\beta_j, \omega, \rho_{ij}\}$ be a Business Graph with

- a number of i business processes $\beta_i = \{\theta_i, \kappa_{ij}\}$ in which θ_i signifies process element $i, i \in \{1,2,3,\ldots,n\}$ and κ_{ij} stands for a control connector $ij, i \in \{1,2,3,\ldots,n\}$, $j \in \{1,2,3,\ldots,n\}$ between process elements. Process elements are defined as $\theta_i = \{A_i, \beta_j, \sigma, \eta, \delta_k\}$ where A_i signifies activity

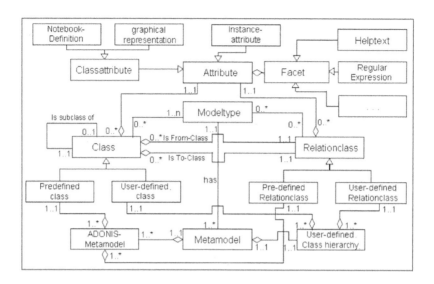

Figure 4.19: Adonis Meta^2 Model [JKSK00]

$i, i \in \{1, 2, 3, \ldots, n\}$, β_j signifies subprocess $j, j \in \{1, 2, 3, \ldots, m\}$, σ signifies start, η signifies end, and δ_k signifies decision where $k \in \{1, 2, 3, \ldots, l\}$.
– a working environment $\omega = \{P_i, G_j, R_k, \pi_{ij}\}$, with $i \in \{1, 2, 3, \ldots, n\}$, $j \in \{1, 2, 3, \ldots, m\}$, $k \in \{1, 2, 3, \ldots, o\}$ and where P_i signifies a person $i, i \in \{1, 2, 3, \ldots, n\}$, G_j signifies a grouping $j, j \in \{1, 2, 3, \ldots, m\}$, R_k signifies a resource $k, k \in \{1, 2, 3, \ldots, o\}$ and π_{ij} the relations between the elements of P_i, G_j and R_k with $i \in \{1, 2, 3, \ldots, n\}$, $j \in \{1, 2, 3, \ldots, m\}$
– and the relations ρ_{ij} between the elements of β_i and ω.

Business Graphs are a syntactical conceptualisation of the domain of business process models. For a concrete usage the semantics of the entities of a Business Graph have to be specified e.g. by mapping them to an ontology and distinct rules for the arrangement of the elements in the business process models have to be defined. For the purposes of illustrating the relation to the visualisation of the models the formal concepts have been instantiated to a meta-model (figure 4.20) that defines the cardinalities between the entities and can also provide a basic definition of syntax and operational semantics via a meta-meta model.

The meta^2 model has been taken from the approach used in Adonis [Fil04] and is shown in figure 4.19. It defines *classes* and *relationclasses* as the basic elements

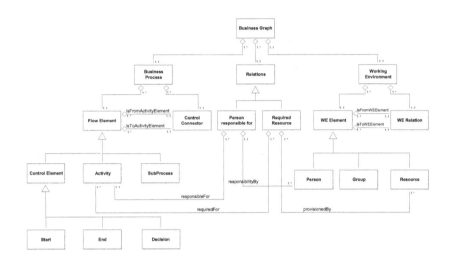

Figure 4.20: Meta Model for Business Graphs

of meta models. Both elements can further contain a range of attributes, including the graphical representation. In the approach of the meta modelling plattform Adonis the graphical attributes are described in a proprietary language (GRAPHREP) that may also contain variables and control structures. Thereby the aspect of dynamic notations as described above can be realised. Furthermore, by the definition of a graphical attribute each syntactic entity of a meta model is directly linked to a graphical representation. In listing 4.3 an excerpt of the Adonis Library Language (ALL) is shown to concretely point out these relationships: Two definitions of classattributes are shown, one for the GraphRep definition and one for the definition of cardinalities (Klassenkardinaliät[sic!]). The GraphRep defines an ellipse and an optional textual representation of an attribute value by the ATTR command. Due to the IF clause surrounding the command it is only executed of the expression (d = 'mit Namen') evaluates to true.

Listing 4.3: Excerpt of the Adonis ALL definition, Source: [Fil04]

```
. . .
CLASSATTRIBUTE <GraphRep>
        VALUE "
                GRAPHREP
                SHADOW off FILL
                color:black
```

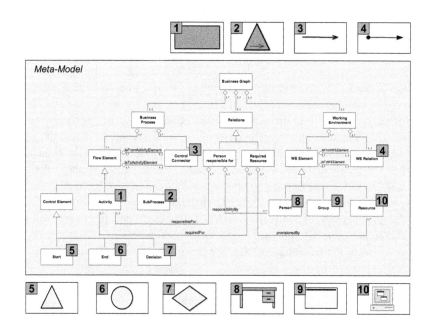

Figure 4.21: Assignment of Symbols to the BP Meta Model

```
ELLIPSE rx:0.15cm ry:0
      .15cm AVAL
      d:'Darstellung'
IF (d = \"mit Namen\")
         ATTR \"Name\"
               y:-.2cm w:c
                  h:b
      ENDIF"
...
CLASSATTRIBUTE <Klassenkardinaliät>
      VALUE "CARDINALITIES
            RELATION \"has
                  successor\"
            max-outgoing:1
            max-incoming:0"
...
```

The assignment of the symbols to the syntactic entities of the business process meta model is illustrated in figure 4.21 on the preceding page: The numbers that are attached to each symbol correspond to the numbers in the meta model and thus determine the assignment. As the approach of business graphs does not determine a specific layout of the resulting visual model only the syntactic relationships between the model elements are relevant for the positioning of the elements. It can, therefore, be derived that the symbol representing the *control connector* (no.3 in figure 4.21) may only connect *flow elements* or subclasses of it. Should the graphical representation of the connector be changed no modification of the elements or relations of the meta model would be necessary. For the case that the structure of the meta model is changed the graphical attributes may have to be adapted. But still this adaptation could be performed independently of the meta model change.

With the approach of using meta models almost every type of graph based visualisation can be directly specified. Additional mechanisms are however necessary if the layout of the resulting visualisation has to be conform to requirements that are not expressed by the meta model. This could be for example the case for automatically generated models where no human user specifies the positions of the elements. It then has to be reverted to additional mechanisms and algorithms working on the modelling language (see figure 4.5 on page 175) to satisfy these additional constraints. Another shortcoming of the approach presented here is the derivation of the meta models from the abovely shown meta^2 model in regard to the graphical attributes: Although this approach already allows for the implementation of dynamic notations and the inclusion of control structures the graphical representation is still encapsulated in a specific meta model attribute. The approach discussed in chapter 5 on page 223 will present a further step towards a complete loose coupling of the domain model and the visualisation.

Other Visualisations

Apart from the graph based visualisations the meta model based approach also permits to specify other types of visualisations. Again, the advantage is to specify the visualisation independently of the domain model and then establish a link between the domain and the visualisation specifications. For illustrating the procedure for a metaphoric visualisation in an enterprise cockpit a meta model for balanced scorecards is taken as basis.

This meta model (shown in figure 4.22 on the next page) contains elements and relations to describe models of balanced scorecards similar to the models that have been shown in figure 3.52 on page 123: The central meta model elements are the *strategic* and *operational goals* that are derived from the *goal* element.

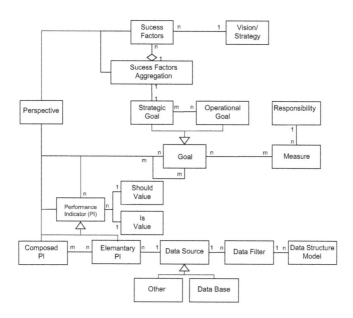

Figure 4.22: Metamodel for Balanced Scorecards (Source: [LKK02])

Several *goal* elements can be related to several other goal elements and linked to performance indicators. The performance indicators are described by an *is value* and a *should value* and can be detailed by *composed* and *elementary* indicators. The elementary performance indicators are linked to a *data source* that can either be a *database* or another source. The *data source* reverts to one or more *data filters* that are linked to one or more *data structure models*.

In contrast to the abovely shown meta model for business graphs the meta model for balanced scorecards is not derived from an explicit meta^2 model. It could however be complemented by such a model and extended to instantiate e.g. cause effect models as shown in figure 3.52 on page 123. For the generation of non-graph based visualisations from this meta model the meta^2 model is however not absolutely required. To create a visualisation as has been shown in section 3.3 on page 119 for depicting the *is* and *should* values of a performance indicator the meta model elements are linked to a visualisation (see figure 4.23 on the next page). The model of the visualisation can either be described as above by an attribute of the meta model or generated externally. In the case of an external generation the link

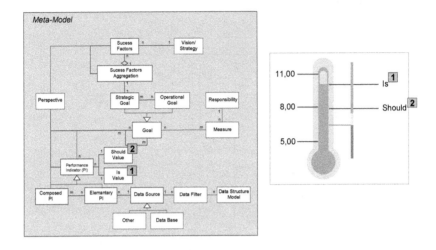

Figure 4.23: Assignment of a Thermometer Visualisation to a BSC Meta Model

between the meta model and the model of the visualisation has to be separately specified.

```
...
<ATTRIBUTES NAME="Status" TYPE="valueattribute">
     <STATUS>green</STATUS>
     <SHOULDVALUE>44</SHOULDVALUE>
     <ISVALUE>42,86</ISVALUE>
     <TOLERANCE_RY>4,40</TOLERANCE_RY>
     <TOLERANCE_YG>1,76</TOLERANCE_YG>
     <THRESHOLD_TYPE>from bottom</THRESHOLD_TYPE>
     <SCORE>74</SCORE>
     <MEASURETYPE>%</MEASURETYPE>
     <TOLERANCE_TYPE>relative</TOLERANCE_TYPE>
</ATTRIBUTES>
...
```

Figure 4.24: Excerpt of the ADOscore cockpit.xml (adapted)

In figure 4.24 such a specification is depicted. It has been taken from the ADOscore cockpit.xml format that contains an XML serialisation of the model information used in the ADOscore balanced scorecard toolkit. ADOscore implements and extends the abovely shown meta model (figure 4.22 on the previous page) and provides a Java-based enterprise cockpit application (see also section 3.3

on page 120). The ADOscore cockpit parses the XML information and visualises the values by different metaphoric representations. As the model of the visualisation is implemented directly in the Java programming language a modification of the visualisation would currently require a re-compilation. It could however be shown in a student project[26] that a graphical representation designed in the Scalable Vector Graphics (SVG) standard can be extended to allow for dynamic modifications. In contrast to several approaches for generating SVG graphics with XML transformations (see e.g. [Ger05, Cam03]) this approach does not require the definition of a transformation specification for generating the SVG representation but integrates definitions of variables in an existing SVG code. Therefore, the design of the graphics can be accomplished in any graphics editor that is capable of generating SVG and does not require programming effort. To add the possibility of a linkage of the SVG representation to the serialisation of a meta model variable definitions containing XPath links to the modifiable values are integrated.

```
<?xml version="1.0" encoding="UTF-8"?>
<svg
        xmlns:svg="http://www.w3.org/2000/svg"
        xmlns:atsw="http://www.dke.univie.ac.at/semantic"
        xmlns:dc="http://purl.org/dc/elements/1.1/" ... >
...
<atsw:var id="ActualValue">
        <atsw:set expression="$inputvalue$"
                xpath="//rect[@id='Fuellbalken']/@height| |0| "/>
        <atsw:set
                expression="$xpath[/svg/g[@id='layer1']/rect[@id='Fuellbalken_gesamt'
                ]/@y| |0|y]$ +
                $xpath[/svg/g[@id='layer1']/rect[@id='Fuellbalken_gesamt']/@height|
                |0|y]$ - $inputvalue$" xpath="//rect[@id='Fuellbalken']/@y| |0|y"/>
        ...
        <atsw:set
                expression="$xpath[/svg/g[@id='layer1']/rect[@id='Fuellbalken_gesamt'
                ]/@y| |0|y]$ +
                $xpath[/svg/g[@id='layer1']/rect[@id='Fuellbalken_gesamt']/@height|
                |0|y]$ - $inputvalue$ + 8" xpath="//text[@id='IstText']/@y| |0|y"/>
</atsw:var>
...
```

Figure 4.25: Sample Code of the SVG Extension for Adding Variables

In figure 4.25 the extensions of the SVG structure are shown: By the definition of the additional namespace atsw variables (atsw:var) can be introduced directly in the SVG code that contain a set of references (atsw:set) to the elements of the

---

[26]Implemented by Andreas Hornich, David Waldhans and Bernhard Scholz.

SVG. Although another choice would have been to revert to the ECMA scripting language[27] of SVG to handle the modification of the SVG structure the integration of separate variables has been chosen for performance reasons (i.e. the evaluation of the variables does not depend on the client side performance constraints as the client only receives a simple SVG graphics without additional code structures).

```
...
<rect style="fill:#1aea18;opacity:1.0000000;fill-opacity:0.82710284;stroke:#000000;
       stroke-width:0.34945816;stroke-linejoin:bevel;stroke-
       miterlimit:4.0000000;stroke-dasharray:none;stroke-
       opacity:1.0000000;display:inline"
     id="Fuellbalken"
     width="53.593906"
     height="172.20241"
      x="51.302727"
      y="15.689260"
      rx="6.1828303"
      ry="6.1828303"
      inkscape:label="#rect11806" />
...

</svg>
```

Figure 4.26: Sample Code of the extended SVG for Defining Graphical Primitives

Figure 4.26 depicts an SVG element that has been complemented with an ID attribute to allow for the unambiguous identification of the element by the links of the variable sets. With the expression in figure 4.25 on the previous page `//rect[@id='Fuellbalken']/@height` the height of the rectangle can thus be directly referenced without knowing about the complete (and sometimes highly complex) structure of the XML document. The calculations for the adaptation of the value originating from the meta model (e.g. the *is* value of a performance indicator) to the height of the rectangle in the visualisation has in this approach still to be performed externally. Despite this requirement the approach marks a first step towards a decoupling of the visualisation model from the domain model also for non-graph based visualisations.

---

[27]ECMA: European association for standardizing information and communication systems. An international standardisation organisation that defined (a.o.) the specification of a scripting language that can be integrated in XML documents.

4.3 Derivation of Possible Extensions

The discussion of the different aspects of visualisations both from a pragmatic point of view in chapter 3 and from an analytical point of view in the previous sections can be used to identify a range of extensions for the visualisations themselves as well as the models underlying the visualisations and the ways how they are created. Therefore, three main groups of extensions will be elaborated in the following:

- The aspects of visualisations in regard to their exploitation of graphical attributes for encoding information.
- Syntactic enhancements for defining visualisations.
- And the integration of aspects of service orientation in the process of visualisation.

These considerations will be used for the creation of the framework of visualisation that is discussed in the next chapter.

Exploitation of Graphical Attributes

The first possibility for deriving extensions for visualisations is seen in the way how visualisations encode information. This aspect is primarily discussed in the area of information visualisation where several approaches exist to analyse the ways how information can be encoded visually and how the encoding can be best perceived. At some stages it will also be highlighted which prerequisites have to be taken into account for (partly) automating the generation of visualisations as is elaborated in regard to service oriented aspects. For this purpose Bertin [Ber82] lists eight visual dimensions to assign information to a two dimensional graphical representation:

- The position, given by the two dimensions of a plane (X,Y)
- Size
- Brightness
- Texture
- Colour
- Orientation
- Shape

These dimensions will be used in the following to review the visualisations of chapter 3 and derive possible extensions. Additionally, the *role of spatial dimensions* will be regarded including the possibilities of adding a time dimension.

Position

The dimension of *position* (or the spatial arrangement) is exploited by most of the visualisations. Especially, the visualisations of charts (figure 3.18 on page 62) strongly rely on the arrangement of elements to determine the values and dimensions of the underlying figures. In the visualisations of Nassi-Shneiderman diagrams (see figure 3.31 on page 83) the *relative* positions of the elements to each other decide which element is part of which other elements (e.g. for representing the sequences following a control element). This aspect of relative positions (or containments) is also used by the concept of swimlanes (e.g. see the process diagram in figure 3.65 on page 141) and for the treemap visualisations where it defines the hierarchies of elements.

Furthermore for some of the graph based visualisation approaches the position plays an important role: In the case of the enterprise models that are created by human users and not automatically (e.g. the business process diagrams, the cause effect models or to some extent also the models in software engineering) the position of the elements and the relations determines the *mental map* of a user (as also discussed in the graph drawing literature [MELS95, DiB97]). Although the layout of the elements may not be decisive for the underlying method (as for the mathematical concept of a graph the visual position of the nodes and edges is not relevant) it can therefore not be directly used for further information encoding. If the graph based visualisation has been created automatically additional information can be included by the positions of the elements as has for example been shown for the ontology visualisations (figure 3.47 on page 110). Otherwise it has at least to be understandable to a user how the visualisation he created is altered by the modification of the positions (e.g. by animations between the different layouts).

Colour

The aspect of *colour* is despite its outstanding advantage for displaying category information a difficult field for encoding information due to the limited number of distinguishable colours. It has been found that this number is limited to about five to twelve values [War00].

The use of colour is particularly exploited in the approaches of circuit board layouts (figure 3.25 on page 75), heatmaps (figure 3.46 on page 108), parallel coordinates (see page 106ff.), tree maps, charts (figure 3.18 on page 62) and specialised visualisations in enterprise cockpits (e.g. by the colour of the thermometers in the ADOscore cockpit in figure 3.59 on page 130). It is partly used in the process models of Adonis (figure 3.65 on page 141) and EPCs (figure 3.64 on page 139) as well as for the visualisations of cause effect models (e.g. figure 3.57 on page 128). In the latter approaches colour is however only used to additionally differentiate between certain types of elements (e.g. the control, activity and variable elements in the Adonis business process models). For the basic differentiation it would be sufficient in most of these visualisations to revert to the shape based encoding.

The dimension of colour could therefore be additionally integrated into the visualisation of business process models, the diagrams of the UML family or the cause effect diagrams. In the BPMN specification [BPM04] this possibility is actually explicitly mentioned and will be taken up again in chapter 6 on page 269. What has to be considered additionally when using colours is the meaning that is assigned to a colour on its own. Besides the obvious distinction between for example dark and light colours some colours or combinations thereof have specific, often culture based connotations. An example where this becomes directly apparent are the visualisations of the enterprise cockpit of ADOscore (figure 3.59 on page 130) where the colours red, yellow and green carry a meaning besides their primary function of being easily distinguishable: The meaning originates from the relation to the colours of traffic lights that have the culturally established semantics for "<stop>", "<attention>" (or middle position) and "<go>".

The regard of such additional connotations can play an important role and is often strongly dependent on national or group culture [Mar01]. Besides the field of cross-cultural user interface design where it is aimed for an IT based view on these relationships other fields from the area of semiotics such as heraldry[28] and in particular also vexillology[29] have discussed these aspects for a long time and provide important historic and cultural foundations.

It can however be assumed that most visualisations shown here implicitly obey these relationships. The reason can be identified in the human users who designed the visualisations and were either by distinct studies or upon their intuition aware of the connotations (at least for their cultural group). A case where these semantics have to be made explicit is the automatic generation of visualisations (as will be discussed below) where a human user may only be partly or not at all involved in the final design of the visualisation. For this purpose it would have to be necessary

---

[28]Heraldry is the "the science and the art that deal with the use, display, and regulation of hereditary symbols employed to distinguish individuals, armies, institutions, and corporations." (Source: Encyclopedia Britannica Online, http://www.britannica.com/ access 09-06-2006)

[29]Vexillology can be described as the scholarly study of flags. Encyclopedia Britannica explains the origin for these studies as "..the colours and designs of national flags are usually not arbitrarily selected but rather stem from the history, culture, or religion of the particular country. Many flags can be traced to a common origin, and such "flag families" are often linked both by common traditions and by geography." (Source: Encyclopedia Britannica Online, http://www.britannica.com/ access 09-06-2006)

to formalise such aspects or make them IT processable in another way. A solution how this can be achieved will be discussed in section 5.3 on page 245 in the context of Ontological Visualisation Patterns that can be described by a semantic meta language including such cultural aspects.

Size

The encoding of information in regard to *size* is exploited in the example for ontology/cluster map visualisations by Fluit and Harmelen (figure 3.47 on page 110), the two and three dimensional charts (in relative terms for the case of pie charts and absolute terms for bar charts), and treemaps. For the other graph based visualisations besides the cluster maps shown in chapter 3 the dimension of size has so far not been considered and could therefore be investigated. When using size to code information one important constraint is the limited space that is available for a visualisation, especially on computer screens and even more importantly on mobile devices. Furthermore the size dimension can only show gross differences between values and might therefore have to be combined with other dimensions or textual annotations.

Brightness

Similar to the dimension of colour also the dimension of *brightness* has a limited range of values. Additionally, from the viewpoint of human perception colour and brightness cannot be exactly separated as the colour of representations with extreme positive or negative brightness values cannot be optimally perceived. Brightness has only been exploited in the approaches for heatmapes (figure 3.46 on page 108) and geocharts (figure 3.15 on page 58).

Texture

In the visualisations discussed here the dimension of *texture* could only be found to act as an additional criterion of differentiation but not for the purpose of coding information alone. The use of textures can be seen in the visualisations of emPlant (figure 3.9 on page 52) and CASUS (figure 3.1) where it supports the realistic representation of machines, buildings and human actors. In the example of geon diagrams (figure 3.42 on page 103) texture is also applied to three dimensional objects but again only for better distinguishing the objects.

Orientation and Shape

As for the dimension of *orientation* no particular examples could be found in the investigated visualisations it is jointly discussed with the dimension of *shape*. Shapes are a major criterion for differentiation in most diagrams in computer science and business informatics. This becomes apparent by the various symbol tables that have been shown in sections 3.2 on page 78 and 3.3 on page 117. Similar to the considerations for colour also the use of shapes has to take into account the possible meanings of a shape as such. The field of semiotics can again provide useful input for these aspects (cf. [Ber95, Kaz95, Sch97]).

As has been remarked for the dimension of colour the introduction of systems that can automatically generate visualisations independently of a human user also requires that the choice which shape is appropriate for a given context has to obey these conditions. The specific difficulty that arises in the case of shapes is the semantical indefiniteness of shapes. Although sets of basic primitive shapes can be set up (which can for example be the primitives "<circle">, "<square"> and "<triangle"> and their derivations [Kaz95]) many variations of the basic primitives can occur that each need a specific description.

The rhomb shapes in ER diagrams and the BPMN notation can serve as an example for illustrating the different meanings assigned to a shape: Although for both visualisations the shape is exactly the same they have entirely different meanings. In contrast, although the shapes are the same the traffic sign for a priority road is sufficiently different due to the addition of the yellow filled rhomb (see figure 4.27). It could however be the case that for a specific group of users (e.g. designers of road signs) that are confronted with the BPMN visualisation the connotation of the traffic sign influences their perception so that a different sign may be more appropriate.

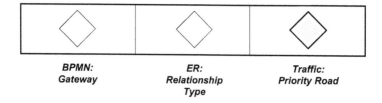

BPMN:	ER:	Traffic:
Gateway	Relationship Type	Priority Road

Figure 4.27: Comparison of Three Different Meanings of the Rhomb Shape

Another aspect of shapes concerns their *focal meaning*. This relates to the common meanings that are most frequently assigned to shapes. For example the focal meaning assigned to circular symbols have been found to be *sun, warmth, beginning, source, center, god, perfection* or *homogeneity* and for square shapes *neutrality, matter, stability, durability* (excerpt taken from [Kaz95](p.148) – similar assessments have been made for horizontal, vertical, diagonal and right angled lines). To present an example how these aspects influence the visualisations in business informatics a closer look is taken on the different shapes used to represent the graphs in cause effect diagrams. In the visualisation of Strat&Go (figure 3.55) as well as in the Hyperion scorecard (figure 3.56 on page 127) the edges are drawn as curves whereas in the Business Objects Scorecard (figure 3.57 on page 128) and the ADOscore approach (figure 3.52 on page 123) edges are drawn as right-angled lines with straight segments.

To highlight these difference figure 4.28 shows two visualisations of the same mathematical graph. Due to the mathematical isomorphism both types of visualisation could in principle be used for a cause effect diagram. But the connotations of the shapes are different. For Graph A they could be described as 'a vague relation between homogenous entities' and for Graph B as 'a very decisive, clear relation between three objects'. Although these connotations have not been empirically founded (which is not the goal of this work) they can give a hint to the subtle different perceptions that are implicitly triggered by the choice of the shapes.

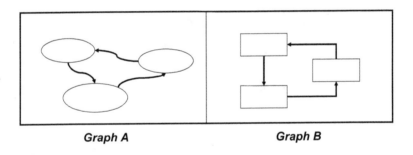

Graph A   **Graph B**

Figure 4.28: Comparison of Different Shapes for the Same (Mathematical) Graph

For the realisation of automatic or semi-automatic generations of visualisations it therefore seems necessary to develop easily manageable but still formal enough approaches for assigning established or invidually determined meanings to shapes. Ideally such an approach also allows for the definition of abstract shapes that are part of other shapes and contribute to their meaning. On the basis of such formal descriptions rules could be established which shape is adequate for a particular purpose based on research in semiotics and human perception.

Spatial and Time Dimensionality

By the analysis of *spatial and time dimensionality* it is determined which visualisation approaches use additional dimensionalities to encode information, either by the usage of the third dimension or by the integration of time based variations. The use of the third dimension can be found in certain chart types. It has to be further differentiated in this regard between real three dimensional representation where for example the viewpoint or the objects could be changed in all three dimensions and so called 2.5D visualisation where the three dimensional effect is only simulated by graphical effects. Typical representatives for real 3D visualisations are found in CASUS (figure 3.1 on page 53), emPlant (figure 3.9 on page 52), the NYSE trading floor visualisation (figure 3.19 on page 63), the circuit board layout approaches (figure 3.25 on page 75), ProVision3D ((see chapter 3.3)), 3D business process gadgets (figure 3.71 on page 149), GRADE-3D (figure 3.76 on page 155) and the Interactive Process Visualiser (figure 3.3 on page 151) as well as in some chart types. An example for a 2.5D visualisation is the representation of computer hardware in the ADOit approach (figure 3.78 on page 158).

Time based variations or animations are defined as the change in one or more of the abovely outlined visual dimensions over time. This aspect is particularly important in the approaches of network animations (figure 3.28 on page 78), CASUS, emPlant, and algorithm animations (figure 3.32 on page 87). Also for simulations in business process management that have not been expclicitely addressed in chapter 3 but that are described for several tools (e.g. ProVision3D, Adonis and the 3D business process gadgets) animations are used to illustrate the behaviour of elements over time.

As has been remarked earlier the integration of three dimensional representations and animations has become much easier realisable by the advent of powerful and at the same time affordable computer hardware. It is estimated that this trend will prevail and that more visualisation applications integrate these aspects in the future. However, a major factor whether this integration will be successful is not only seen in the provision of the appropriate computing power (e.g. also for large visualisations with many hundreds of single elements) but also in the human-computer interaction: The perception and effective interaction with three dimensions on a two dimensional computer screen still poses a challenge to many people. Although the success of three dimensional computer games in the last years indicates ways how the interaction can be successfully optimised, the application to professional uses such as 3D business process representations cannot yet be observed on a broad level. Despite these open questions the use of more than two dimensions has to be further investigated because of the increasing amounts of information that have to be handled and in turn visualised.

Common Syntax for Visualisations

The second possibility for extending visualisations has been identified in the way visualisations are described. Although many international graphical standards currently exist - both for vector and pixel graphics (e.g. SVG[30], PNG[31], SMIL[32]) - no attempt can be found that addresses the standardisation of visual languages or visualisations in general. The major difference to the aforementioned graphical standards is on the one hand the possibility for the definition of syntactic relationships as well as the assignment of semantic definitions to the static syntax and behaviour of the representations. Additionally, the linkage to data would have to be specifically addressed to realise the majority of currently existing information visualisations.

Standards that point towards such directions are the various standards for describing graphs, e.g. GraphXML (for graphs and their visualisations) [HM00], GraphML [BEH+02] or GXL [HSSW02]. Despite their benefits for describing graphs (and some of them also the corresponding visualisations) in exchangeables formats their limitation is the restriction to graph structures. A description of other types of visualisations is not possible with these standards.

The definition of a common syntactical standard for describing visualisations would not only enable the exchange of the abstract specifications of visualisations but also provide the basis for a semantic descriptions. Both of these aspects are seen as prerequisites for the realisation of service oriented visualisation architectures as described in the next section.

Integration of Service-Oriented Aspects

The final aspect of an extension that builds upon the previous sections is the vision of a *service oriented visualisation architecture*. Such an architecture can be described as a composition of software components that permit the automatic or semi-automatic generation of visualisations based on machine or human input. The properties and basic mechanisms of the architecture are similar to the currently

---

[30] SVG: Scalable Vector graphics [FFJ03].

[31] PNG: Portable Network Graphics is is "an extensible file format for the lossless, portable, well-compressed storage of raster images" (http://www.w3.org/Graphics/PNG/ accessed 10-06-2006)

[32] SMIL: Synchronized Multimedia Integration Language is "used for 'rich media'/multimedia presentations which integrate streaming audio and video with images, text or any other media type" (http://www.w3.org/AudioVideo/ accessed 10-06-2006)

widely discussed service oriented architectures for business solutions: Through an automated discovery of services that match the requirements of a certain business task a description of the service including its access point and operations is made available to the requesting client. The client can then access the functionality of the service based on a standardised protocol without having to know about the exact implementation of the service (see figure 4.29). Today this kind of functionalities is typically implemented based on a variety of standards from the area of web services [TBB03].

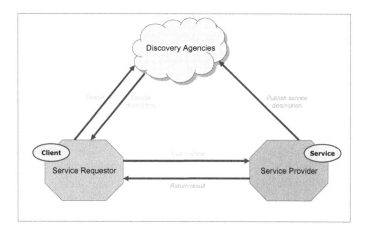

Figure 4.29: Roles in a Service-Oriented Environment

Although a standard for a directory and discovery of web services is available by UDDI[33] [CHRR04] it has yet not been widely adopted. Instead, specific standards for web service descriptions (e.g. via WSDL [CCMW01]) and the standardised exchange of information (e.g. via SOAP [Mit03]) can today be found in many business solutions. The syntactic basis for these standards is the extensible markup language XML [BPSM+04].

Similar considerations can be made for visualisations: With the many different approaches and tools for visualisation that are available today, it would be of a major benefit to realise *web based visualisation services*. The goal of these services would be the standardised and therefore universally applicable web based access to visualisations without having to know about their specific implementation. In the case of a *semi-automatic* generation a human user could then easily *choose*

---

[33]UDDI: Universal Description Discovery & Integration.

between different visualisations based on the services that match his requirements. In analogy to the pattern based characterisation of visualisations (see section 4.2 on page 182) visualisation services would only provide a set of parameters to describe their functionality and hide their concrete implementation. A user may thus be able to create a new visual modelling method by choosing visualisations from a variety of services and without having to design or maybe even code the visualisation herself.

The basis for these services is a common syntax for *accessing* the visualisation. In the case of a common syntax for *describing* the visualisations itself as proposed in the previous section even the exchange and individual adaptation of the visualisation could be achieved. In the light of the upcoming of cooperative web applications (as e.g. Wikipedia[34] or flickr.com[35]) a similar *cooperative visualisation platform* could also be realised.

When further extending the services by semantic descriptions (as it is likewise discussed for semantic web services [BFM02, BLHL01]) even the fully *automatic* generation of visualisations could be realised. A machine may then automatically present a visualisation based on a machine processable semantic specification without additional human input. As it has been outlined in the previous section above this full automation requires several pieces of information about the user: Not only his individual preferences and the task that the visualisation is used for but also his knowledge and cultural background are necessary to determine the appropriate and adequate visualisation [Gra01].

An important remark has to be made for separating the meaning of *automatic visualisation services* from other approaches: The design of theories and systems that support the automatic graphical representation of data has been particularly addressed in the past by two authors [Gra01]: The first is the article (and according PhD thesis by Mackinlay [Mac86]) and the second the publication (and PhD thesis) by Casner [Cas91]. The vision of (semantic) visualisation services can be distinguished from these approaches in the following way: Whereas the major contribution of Mackinlay lies in the provision of formal graphical languages that have the same precise syntax and semantics as other formal languages and Casner's approach adds the formal specification of tasks to determine the design of the visualisation both approaches are limited to relational models. Furthermore, this limitation leads to the fact that both approaches only discuss visualisations of quantitative data in the form of charts - e.g. bar, line and scatterplots in [Mac86] - and additional types of charts (e.g. for an airplane load visualisation) in [Cas91]. Graphs are not shown in either of the two publications and it is not clear whether

---

[34] A cooperative online encyclopedia, see http://www.wikipedia.org/
[35] A platform for storing, sharing, and searching pictures commonly - see http://www.flickr.com/

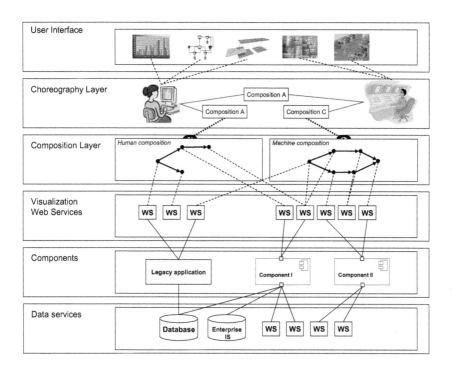

Figure 4.30: Vision of a Generic Service-Oriented Visualisation Architecture

the approaches could be adapted for visualisations of conceptual models for example. However, their focus is put on the automated design of a graphical presentation whereas semantic visualisation services shall provide a ready made visualisation that is selected as it is upon a match of requirements. The visualisation itself could be generated automatically (e.g. with systems described in [Mac86, Cas91]) thereby expanding the range of possible matches or be designed by a human user and then exposed as a service.

To show in detail how visualisation services can be integrated in a service oriented architecture as currently used for business applications figure 4.30 on the preceding page presents an overview of the relationships. It incorporates both the aspect of semi-automatic as well as fully automatic generations of visualisations. On the bottom layer (*data services*) the different types of data sources are shown. These can either be traditional databases, enterprise information systems in general (including for example conceptual models of a business) as well as internal and external web services. The *component layer* accesses the data and performs the generation of the visualisations. This can either be accomplished by existing (legacy) applications or newly created components. Both types of applications are exposed via web service interfaces on the layer of *visualisation web services*. Thereby a uniform access to both legacy visualisation applications as well as new components is ensured.

On the composition layer two approaches are conceived: For the case of the semi-automatic generation of the visualisation a human user is involved. Depending on the process (or concrete task) the visualisation is used for (as described by the *choreography layer*, her individual preferences and knowledge the user can revert to one or more visualisation services for composing a visualisation. If the generation of the visualisation is fully-automated a machine takes over these choices. This configuration of a visualisation also includes the aspects of visual modelling: Based on a meta model in an enterprise information system that is made available via a web service components can be used to provide visualisation services for these models. The composition layer then acts as modelling layer where a concrete visual model is realised. The final visualisation is then made available via a *user interface*.

5 A Framework for Visualisation in IT-based Management

After the survey of the existing visualisations in the areas of business, computer science, and business informatics and the analysis of the approaches for creating these visualisations in the previous chapter a new way for the creation of visualisations will be presented in this chapter. The approach taken here will rely on some basic conceptions including a theoretical framework for procedures. Based on this framework a visualisation framework has been derived for integrating the different views that have so far been discussed in relation to visualisation. The core part of the framework which is directed towards the integration of a semantic view into the visualisation process will then be discussed in detail. The chapter will conclude with the presentation of a first prototype implementation that has been created for facilitating user interaction in this new visualisation environment.

5.1 Basic Conceptions

As has been shown in chapters 3 and 4 several different views exist as to what constitutes a visualisation and how it is created. This includes the very exact specifications of the syntax and semantics of visual languages as well as methods from information visualisation and statistics that deal with aspects of data exploration and the derivation of hypotheses by visual means. As all the discussed approaches deal with visualisation it would seem obvious to search for a way to integrate these different views and develop a kind of *unified foundation for IT based visualisation*. Although it might be argued that the *visualisation* pipeline (as discussed in section 4.2 on page 180) takes into account all relevant aspects for IT based visualisations, several factors can be quoted that are not considered: This includes for example the consideration of the physiological *personal abilities* of a specific user in regard to the perception of a visualisation, the influence of the *pragmatic aspects* of the visualisation (i.e. the context the visualisation is embedded in) as well as the *semantics* (i.e. the meaning) of a visualisation for a particular individual or a group of individuals. Other frameworks for visualisation that are discussed in the scientific literature besides the visualisation pipeline partly take these additional factors into account. In the work by [Chi00] a framework is described that provides a general basis for visualisation systems that transform data into visualisations. Its contribution is mainly the review of a large number of visualisation approaches and their analysis in regard to the underlying data set, the transformation of the data, their analytical abstraction, their visual mapping transformation, and the possibilities of interaction with the final view. The concept of the visualisation pipeline is extended in this approach in the way that a visualisation method can be chosen based on its concrete application characteristics which corresponds (at least partly) to an integration of contextual factors.

The framework outlined by Kamada et al. [KK91] presents a view on the procedural steps of the visualisation pipeline from a visual language perspective. Their visualisation framework starts with the input of an original textual representation which is analysed and transformed into a relational (semantic) structure. This universal representation contains abstract objects and relations which are then translated into graphical objects and relations based on user defined mapping data. From the visual structure the target pictorial representation is generated. It therefore takes into account both the view of visual languages (by explicitly specifying the structure of the graphical objects) as well as the sequential procedure of the visualisation pipeline and the partly integration of user specifications (due to the mapping definition).

Based on models from human computer interaction Kennedy et al. [KMB96] describe an information visualisation framework consisting of four components: The user, the database, the visualisation, and the interaction. The user is characterised by his expertise with the data to be visualised, the tasks she wishes to perform, and her authority to view or modify data. In the visualisation component the metaphors used to represent the items of the data and the physical layout on the screen are considered. The interaction component takes into account how the user may alter the visualisation or the data itself. It therefore considers user's intentions, the medium for realising these intentions and the effects of user actions. Although this approach integrates already most of the abovely mentioned additional factors it is primarily directed towards data based information visualisations (cf. similar frameworks in [GKW04] and in [War00](p.)) and does not seem to be applicable to visual language approaches.

The taxonomic framework by [PHP01] also originates from the area of information visualisation but takes an even broader view than the framework by Kennedy et al.: It describes both the skills of the user (by a range from novice to expert), the contextual factors (e.g. the user's life experience, her intent, needs, and devices), the type of task and interactivity, as well as the data and the visualisation itself. Although this framework considers a large number of visualisation aspects it lacks the definition of a concrete procedure for creating visualisations based on these factors[1]. Furthermore, its origin in the area of information visualisation leads to the strong focus of data based visualisations. The creation of visualisations that directly stem from human thinking without an intermediate data layer are not explicitly covered.

Therefore, a set of basic requirements can be derived that are necessary for establishing a framework for IT based visualisations that unites the aspects mentioned in the various areas. Although for some specific applications additional aspects may have to be considered the following necessary and sufficient factors have been identified:

- The framework has to be open in regard to different existing and ideally also future views on visualisation.
- It therefore has to integrate both the data based view on visualisations as it is performed in information visualisation as well as views that position the individual user at the origin for visualisations.
- It has to consider the influence of contextual factors such as the type of task (including for example economic factors and aspects of the application domain) that is related to the visualisation as well as aspects of human diversity in regard to physiological and cognitive abilities.
- It has to allow for the creation of both strictly formally described visualisations (as typical in the visual language area) as well as semi- or non-formally described visualisations.
- It should separate the methodological and technical implementation of visualisations to allow for an easy adaptation of each part to new requirements.
- It should express a procedural advancement for creating visualisations that takes into account the influence of the abovely described requirements.

Based on these requirements at first a meta model for procedures will be presented that serves as a generic basis for a view on the process of visualisations. This meta model will then be used to describe a visualisation framework that incorporates several new aspects in comparison to the abovely discussed approaches.

A Meta Model for Procedures

When creating visualisations not only the technical aspects of the visualisation procedure have to be considered as it is done by the visualisation pipeline but also the embedding of the procedural advancement has to be taken into account.

---

[1]The phases of user interaction discussed at the beginning of [PHP01] which could be considered as such a procedure only express a very general view.

Therefore a meta framework for procedures has been designed that provides a holistic view on the environment of the procedure (see figure 5.1).

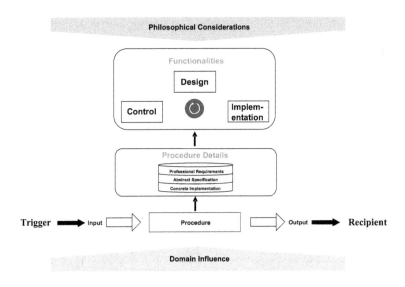

Figure 5.1: Meta Framework for Procedures

Two main factors of influence surround the environment of a procedure: On the top philosophical considerations and on the bottom the domain where the procedure is applied. Philosophical considerations can be theoretical derivations that lead to the conception of the procedure as well as concerns what impact the procedure might have in a general sense (e.g. ethical, social or cultural aspects) and how these consequences take effect on the procedure itself. The influence of the domain is a central factor for every type of procedure. It not only determines the concrete applicability but also sets the contextual requirements and constraints. Whereas one procedure might be suitable for a problem in one domain, it could be totally useless in another despite the same problem characteristics.

The procedure itself is triggered from the outside, receives input and transforms it to an output for the purpose of a recipient. The procedure can be further detailed by professional requirements (e.g. for a specific use case), an abstract specification that describes the detailed working of the procedure and a concrete implementation of the procedure that is available for a distinct usage. To achieve the actual working of the procedure it reverts to three types of functionalities which are influenced by the procedure details: *Control functionalities* that are responsible for the behaviour of the procedure in relation to the outside world, *design functionalities* that define the abstract elements and their relationships of the procedure that can be instantiated to a concrete implementation, and *implementation functionalities* that instantiate the procedure to a technical context by obeying its constraints and implementation facilities.

Theoretical Considerations

From the meta model for procedures the visualisation framework as shown in figure 5.1 has been instantiated. It's aim is to provide a basis for an integration of the different types of visualisations that currently exist and that might come into existence in the future in the area of business informatics and the related fields of business and computer science. The framework is therefore on the one hand generic enough to allow for different approaches to visualisation as well as it fulfills specific requirements that will be relevant in the near future. It further provides a conceptual model for assessing the possible application domains and ranges of technologies in the context of visualisation.

The framework is based on the notion that every visualisation comes into existence through a. a specific *input* and b. a specific *visualisation procedure*. This view is obviously characterised by the human act of volition to represent something concrete or to receive a result in visual form by a certain action (procedure). Everything else is not considered to be a visualisation in the scope of this framework. The input may contain both technical and human aspects. It can therefore consist of human knowledge, i.e. information that only persists in the head of a person and that can only be partly explicated to the outside world, as well as technical data for example (e.g. stemming from a database or being encoded in an electronic document). The procedure is regarded to be a sequence of steps that turns the input into a graphical representation and is open to all technologies and methods that produce results in this respect. With these basic components a multitude of different visualisation approaches can be described, spanning from manual techniques (such as drawing an image that represents a mental conception), combinations of manual and technical approaches (e.g. by the arrangement or configuration of visual patterns as described in section 4.2 on page 182) or purely technical realisations (e.g. an automated generation of a statistical chart).

The visualisation procedure, its input and the visualisation itself are directly influenced by an environment that is seen as external to this framework. It is here characterised as *domain influence* that describes the tasks that motivate the need for a visualisation in a certain context and further lead to the input, determine which procedures are suitable and, therefore, also has an impact on the outcome that has to be compatible to the external facts. Included in the domain influence are also contextual factors such as the user group that shall be addressed by the visualisation and their characteristics, e.g. the cultural factors of the group. The classification of the domain influence as external therefore implies that its requirements are considered for the visualisation procedure but that the domain descriptions itself is not specifically described by the framework.

The output of the process is a graphical representation that may be available as hard-copy or in an electronic format. The output is generated by the abstract concept of a visualisation procedure (which will be detailed in the following) and is directed towards a recipient. As visualisation has been defined for this work in section 1.5 on page 19 to amplify human cognition the recipient could also be equated with human recipient[2].

When using information technology for creating visualisations the exact steps for the creation of a visualisation can be described by the visualisation pipeline of computer graphics (as discussed in section 4.2 on page 180) which is therefore shown above the generic visualisation process in figure 5.1. It describes the transformation of data to visualisations by assigning the enhanced data to visual properties and then rendering them on computer graphics hardware so that an image or a sequence of images are shown. The integration of the visualisation pipeline into the visualisation procedure is optional in the respect that it is only necessary for IT based visualisations.

With the framework concepts discussed so far the primary elements for creating visualisations would have already been sufficiently integrated. However, what has not been considered up to this point is the integration of the task requirements into the visualisation procedure as well as the separation of the visualisation methodology and the technical implementation. Furthermore, also the elements of visualisations themselves have until now only been very generally described by the concept of the visualisation pipeline. The visualisation procedure is therefore detailed by so-called *Semantic Visualisation Functionalities* that complete the visualisation procedure in regard to its *professional requirements*, the *abstract specification* and the *concrete implementation*. The professional requirements of the visualisation procedure are the requirements specified by the domain influence, the trigger of the procedure and its input to the procedure as well as the output and the recipient of the visualisation. The abstract specification designates a solution for a visualisation procedure that is derived from these requirements in the sense

---

[2]To maintain the framework as open as possible the term *recipient* has nevertheless been found to be more appropriate. Although not discussed in this work there also exist graphical representations that are not addressed to humans (as e.g. the EAN barcodes) and that could also be classified as visualisations in other contexts.

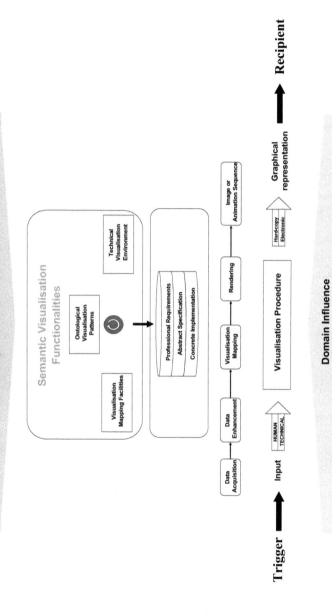

Figure 5.2: Visualisation Framework

of a visualisation template. For realising a visualisation the abstract specification has to be transformed to a concrete implementation that is responsible for actually generating the graphical representation from the input to the procedure. The derivation of the concrete implementation from professional requirements and the resulting abstract specification constitutes an essential distinguishing feature of this framework. Especially the abstract specification raises the procedure of generating visualisations to a meta level which is often only implicitly assumed. It resembles to a certain extent the pattern based approaches described in section 4.2 on page 182 but is not focused on a specific implementation (as most pattern based approaches are in effect).

To realise a visualisation procedure in this way and specify a visualisation meta model three concepts have been developed that can serve for this purpose and act as a kind of meta-meta model for visualisations. These are:

- Ontological Visualisation Patterns
- Visualisation Mapping Facilities
- Technical Visualisation Environment

Ontological Visualisation Patterns: For specifying the types of visualisations generated by the framework the concept of Ontological Visualisation Patterns is introduced to describe how visual objects are composed and to specify the meaning of the this composition. Visual objects consist of one or more graphical primitives, variables and control structures and can be altered depending on the variables exposed by the object. Also an invidual visual object may be semantically described. The semantic description of the visual object can serve for example to differentiate between the symbol for multiplication as shown in the context of ADOscore (see figure 3.50 on page 122) and the symbol for a Cancel event in BPMN (see figure 3.61 on page 136) which contain very similar graphical primitives but have very different associated meanings. Ontological visualisation patterns are the main element for realising an abstract specification of a visualisation and can be either mapped to a data set or used directly by a user to generate a visualisation.

Visualisation Mapping Facilities: As Ontological Visualisation Patterns are only responsible for the specification of the representation of the visual objects (including their composition also in terms of layout) a mechanism is required to establish the mapping between the visualisation model and the underlying model of the original world (cf. figure 4.4 on page 172). Additionally, Visualisation Mapping Facilities take into account the professional requirements for a visualisation and determine the appropriate Ontological Visualisation Pattern in terms of the domain influence, the trigger of the procedure and the recipient.

Technical Visualisation Environment: To deploy concrete instances of visualisations a technical environment is necessary that is flexible and powerful enough to meet all requirements as demanded from the professional requirements and allows for an easy adaptation to new technical standards. It therefore has to provide an interface for the abstract specification of the visualisation that is capable of translating the information of the specification to a variety of concrete technical implementations.

In the following sections the characteristics of the Semantic Visualisation Functionalities will now be detailed and also partly formalised: Starting with the structure of visual objects it will be shown how they can be combined and semantically described to realise Ontological Visualisation Patterns. For the Visualisation Mapping Facilities a set of core dimensions will be derived that are crucial for their realisation. Finally, the Technical Visualisation Environment will be detailed by an interface specification that has to be provided for implementing the visualisations.

5.2 The Structure of Visual Objects

As has been shortly described above visual objects are basically a composition of graphical primitives enriched with additional constructs such as variables and control structures. The considerations underlying this definition are however more deeply founded and originate from the attempt to identify the most elementary elements of every kind of visualisation. A first step in this direction has already been described in section 4.2 on page 164 with the discussion of the aspects of model theory and the formal explication of meaning. Translating these considerations to the field of visualisation it has been reverted to graphems as the most basic entities of visual perception based on psychological research. Although the pre-attentively attributes of graphical representations play an important role for visualisations it would be difficult to take them as a starting point for creating graphical representations. The steps of the formal explication of meaning (as described on page 168) also occur however in other forms that seem to be more appropriate for specifying visualisations. By reverting to the field of knowledge representation that deals with comparable approaches for identifying the basic entities that can convey meaning a more directly usable way can be found for such a description.

According to a widely used concept by North [Nor02] *signs and symbols* form the basic entities for the definition of knowledge in information and communication technology. When adding syntax to signs and symbols North denotes this as *data*,when adding semantics North speaks of *information*. In North's model knowledge is located on top of information that requires (human) capabilities for the linking of information in face of certain contexts and the derivation of according actions. This view is directly compatible with the levels of Frege (Sign-Meaning-Sense-Association) in the context of model theory.

In North's structure *knowledge representation* is regarded to be a process starting at the top level and ranging down to the bottom level. This process is not assumed to convey all information available at the top level (knowledge level) down to the bottom level and therefore does not claim to represent knowledge solely in the form of signs and symbols. On the other hand it is assumed that starting from the bottom level knowledge can be generated out of information, information out of data and data out of symbols. In the context of IT based management this upward process shall is denoted as *knowledge generation*.

The different forms of visualisation that currently exist in IT based management can be analysed on the basis of this structure thereby making a first step towards an investigation of their composition. Starting from the bottom it has to be found out which are the elementary concepts that are common for all visualisations (and not graphical representations alone as with the graphems). In terms of North this would be a search for the *symbols of visualisations* in the sense of being entities that are so universal that they exist in every form of visualisation. It can then be examined how these symbols are structured for generating the actual visualisation, corresponding to the *syntax of the visualisation* and how *semantics* can be assigned to this structure.

Basic Requirements

As has been shown by the survey of existing visualisations in chapter 3 visualisations occur in many different forms, ranging from formally specified visual languages, three dimensional representations to metaphoric representations as used for example in enterprise cockpits. It therefore depends very much on the context of the visualisation and its intended use how a visualisation is described and what are the symbols of the visualisation. For three dimensional representations these symbols may be complex objects such as cones, cubes or spheres and in two dimensional representations symbols may be defined as different variants of curves and faces.

Despite these differences one dominating aspect can be found for any kind of IT based visualisation. That is that it has to be *technically implementable*. Therefore, whatever the structure of a visualisation might be there has to be a method that allows for a formalisation in terms of computer science to process the visualisation data electronically either for output purposes (e.g. on a display, computer screen or on a printing device) or for manipulations (e.g. for the data mapping, geometric calculations etc.). It thus seems obvious to consult the technical aspects of computer graphics to determine necessary basic requirements that allow for a technical realisation.

In the area of computer graphics pictures and therefore also visualisations can be described in several ways [HB97]: Under the assumption of a rasterised display (e.g. as prevalent in CRT[3] or LCD[4] monitors) a picture is specified by the set of intensities of the pixel positions in the display.

On the other hand a picture can be described by objects that abstract from their technical realisation on a display (e.g. trees, terrain or furniture). For a technical implementation every part of these objects (e.g. the leaf of a tree) can now either be described by pixel arrays or with sets of basic geometric structures (e.g. lines, boxes, polygones etc.)[5]. The pixel arrays can be directly technically displayed (by sending them to the framebuffer of a graphics card), the geometric structures in contrast have to be first scan converted to pixel arrays and can then be processed by hardware as well.

When solely describing visualisations in the form of sets of pixel arrays difficulties arise when using different resolutions respectively when an image has to be scaled to a different size (as the information is limited to the amount of pixels specified cf. [UAE95]). In practice this occurs very often as there exist not only many heterogenous display devices but it is also necessary for many complex visualisations to be able to scale pictures to different sizes (e.g. for inspecting a particular aspect of a visualisation in detail). For achieving an optimal quality of visualisations in all resolutions it is therefore necessary to describe them by basic geometric objects (vector graphics) that are also referred to as *graphical or output primitives*.

Graphical Primitives

Which objects are classified as primitives mainly depends on the viewpoint of the designer. In some contexts a point might be the only valid primitive, in others such as for example often seen in technical realisations of three dimensional graphics a triangle is the source of all graphical objects and again for other cases triangles, squares and circles might be regarded as primitives. Besides the usually discussed two and three dimensional representations the number of dimensions may also be

---

[3]CRT: Cathode Ray Tube.

[4]LCD: Liquid crystal display.

[5]In the case of three dimensional objects a projection to the two dimensional space first has to be performed.

higher (see table 5.2) [Dow96]. The types of graphical primitives might then have
to be adjusted to take the higher dimensions into account appropriately (e.g. for a
six dimensional visualisation that integrates speech also phonetic primitives might
have to be integrated).

Table 5.1: Seven Dimensions in Graphics According to [Dow96]

Dimension	Explanation
0D	Pixel or point
1D	Line or vector
2D	Shapes
2-1/2D	2D graphics that simulate three-dimensionality
3D	True three.dimensional graphics using geometrical models
3-1/2D	2D or 3D graphics that simulate or -imply movement
4D	Moving or animated graphics
5D	Graphics with added psychological or emotional content
6D	Graphics combined with other media, especially sound or speech
7D	Graphics that interact with humans or computer systems

In the scope of this work the discussion will be restricted to two dimensional
representations. Nevertheless the extension to the third or higher dimensions will
not be significantly impeded by this restriction.

For defining graphical primitives from a geometrical/mathematical point of view
one of the most (if not the most) influential work in geometry has been performed
by Euclid in his famous book *Elements* [ET96]. Euclid bases all his statements on
three graphical primitives: Points, lines and circles. The definitions for the geometric shapes of Euclid can be regarded as an ontological foundation for geometry.
An excerpt of his statements is exemplarily presented in the following[6]:

---

[6]The English translation has been taken from D.E. Joyce from Clark University, see
http://aleph0.clarku.edu/~djoyce/java/elements/bookI/bookI.html

- A *point* is that which has no part.
- A *line* is breadthless length.
- The ends of a line are points.
- A *straight line* is a line which lies evenly with the points on itself.
- ...
- A *figure* is that which is contained by any boundary or boundaries.
- A *circle* is a plane figure contained by one line such that all the straight lines falling upon it from one point among those lying within the figure equal one another.
- And the point is called the *center of the circle*.
- ...

Besides their relevance for geometry the definitions by Euclid can also be regarded as a semantic description of graphical primitives and in some way the first approach to exactly describe graphical representations. What makes his definitions even more valuable for a discussion within this work is the fact that the semantic descriptions he offers directly correspond to the abovely expressed requirement of computer graphics to express every graphical representation in the form of points. So, to define graphical primitives the *point* has been selected as the very basic graphical primitive as it is not only a technical requirement but it furthermore seems to be universally applicable to all visualisation approaches: If a visualisation can be traced back to a set of points it will be describable by the hereby developed theory.

Formalisation of Graphical Primitives

Points can have different dimensionalities: A visually displayable point has to contain at least two coordinates (x- and y-axis). In three dimensional space it contains three coordinates and when adding time it might even contain four or more coordinates[7].

Besides coordinate and time values a point has another attribute that has to be defined explicitly or implicitly for a visualisation: Its colour. The coordinate, time and colour attributes are (in technical environments) usually specified by integer values which might be positive or negative for coordinates and positive for colours (typically in a limited range such as for example a 24-bit range that allows for approx. 16.7 million different colours). It shall be noted that this approach of treating visualisation has been substantially influenced by considerations of com-

---

[7]By adding more coordinates for time issues such as the display duration, the position of a point related to a certain point in time or the movement of a point over time may be specified

puter graphics. Aspects such as the shapes or maybe even patterns of a point that might be of high importance to applications in the science of art are therefore not taken into account at this stage. This assumption also applies to the color values that might also be regarded differently from an aristic point of view (for a detailed discussion of the artistic issues see the work of Johannes Itten for color [Itt00] and Anton Stankowksi [Sta94].

Describing these relationships formally leads to the following statement: A Point P in its basic form consists of a pair of coordinates x, y and an attribute for its colour c which is specified by pointing to a number from the set of the 24-bit colour range, i.e.

$$P = \{x, y, c \mid (x, y) \in \mathbb{R}^2, \ c \in \{1, 2, \ldots, 2^{24}\}\} \tag{5.1}$$

From a technical viewpoint it would already be sufficient to use this concept together with a specification of the valid ranges for x and y (i.e. the definition of the canvas) to define a visualisation by applying it to every possible combination of x and y. This procedure would result in a pixel graphic (i.e. a definition of a certain colour for every pixel on a computer screen) that can be almost directly processed on computer graphics hardware.

By combining points more complex graphical objects can be created. A *line* can therefore be seen as a composition of points. In the case of a straight line this composition is equal to the shortest connection between two distinct points (which corresponds to the geometric definition of Euclid). Curved lines are non-linear connections of points where a non-linear mathematical function is used to specify the arrangement of the positions of the in-between points. When adding lines to each other objects that shall be denoted as *polylines* can be created (e.g. a zigzag line). Furthermore *images* can be described as sets of points thus also acting as a direct derivation of a single point. Based on lines *shapes* like triangles, squares or circles can be expressed. These can either consist of solely straight or curved lines or of compositions of them (e.g. a pie-shaped circle segment consisting of two straight and one curved line). In a three dimensional environment shapes can also be arranged spatially to construct *geometric bodies* such as for example the platonic bodies.

In the following formal expressions are given for lines L, curves C, ovals O, polylines *POL*, and rectangles *RECT* that can all be based on the point primitive[8]:

---

[8] It shall be remarked that also analytical geometry would provide a range of formalisations for geometry with a long historical tradition and in fact many of the algorithms underlying the IT based creation of the primitives are based on analytical geometry. For the purposes here it is nevertheless sufficient to abstract from these analytical details. The formalisations based on points have

$$L = (P_1,P_2 \mid P_1,P_2 :: P) \qquad (5.2)$$

$$C = (P_1,P_2,P_3,P_4 \mid P_{1...4} :: P) \qquad (5.3)$$

$$O = (P_1,P_2 \mid P_1,P_2 :: P) \qquad (5.4)$$

$$POL = (P_1,P_2,...,P_n \mid P_{1...n} :: P) \qquad (5.5)$$

$$RECT = (P_1,P_2 \mid P_1,P_2 :: P) \qquad (5.6)$$

Curves C are defined by four points from which two define the start and the end of the curve and two more act as control points. The control points influence the curvature and can be created by cubic spline algorithms (cf. [HB97]). Ovals O are the general form of circles and are defined by their bounding rectangle (in the case of a bounding square a circle is created). Rectangles *RECT* are defined by their bottom left and their top right corner[9]. As can be directly seen by these formalisations the following generalisation can be made for the definition of any kind of shape S based on points:

$$S = \{P_{1...\lambda} \mid P_{1...\lambda} :: P\} \qquad (5.7)$$

So far the graphical properties of the primitives such as different colours for the points of a line have been neglected. Also, variations in the style of the lines for example or the opacity of the representations have not been considered. One additional primitive however needs to be introduced for the subsequent elaborations that deviates from the structure expressed in equation 5.7:

$$TEXT = \{P_1,P_2,T \mid P_1,P_2 :: P, T :: String\} \qquad (5.8)$$

The *TEXT* primitive contains besides two points for specifying a bounding box an object of the type *String* to represent arbitrary alphanumeric characters. It is furthermore assumed that the bounding box also determines the size of the generated text. The reason for adding this primitive is that in most visualisations discussed so far textual information is integrated into visual representations either for explanation or additional information purposes.

---

been found as a suitable way for showing the following extensions in regard to visual objects and Ontological Visualisation Patterns.

[9] For the creation of concrete IT based graphical representations based on these formalisations it would be necessary to define algorithms for calculating the intermediate points. As most programming languages today contain already pre-defined methods for this purpose this step is not further treated for developpinf the theory here.

Symbols in Visualisation

When mapping the structure of visualisations to the concept by North what one would be looking for are basic objects that have neither a syntax (i.e. ordering rules) nor semantics (i.e. any meaning) assigned to them. This holds true for graphical primitives as described above as long as they do not carry an inherent meaning. An example would be a simple line which can be aligned to other objects according to syntactic rules or that can be assigned a semantic connotation e.g. to be a very simplistic representation of a person. Problems might occur in the case of more complex objects that might already have a specific connotation (although they might still be aligned to a syntactic rule and be put in a more specific semantic context). An example would be a polyline in the shape of an arrow: Although this representation can be regarded as a basic 'symbol' without any syntax nor semantics it still carries a certain connotation i.e. to point to a certain direction. This connotation might probably not be intended by the creator of the object who might have envisaged to use this arrow-like shape (pointing of bottom to top) for the representation of a tree (e.g. a fir) which could also be a valid interpretation.

As a consequence the equivalent in visualisation to 'symbols' in terms of North would only be the single point as the very basic graphical primitive (as it is also done in visual language theory [MM98]). Already a line as the composition of points can express a certain meaning (e.g. depending on whether it's a horizontal line that might resemble a dash, a vertical line that might represent a separator, an upward pointing line that could indicate an upward movement etc.).

Addition of Syntax

Following the concept by North the symbols can be structured in the form of specific rules. In visual language theory several approaches exist that focus on this syntactic structuring (as has been discussed in section 4.2 on page 183). With the theory described here it is not intended to disregard the sometimes highly elaborated and sound approaches existing in visual language theory. They are positioned as an additional and for some application purposes better suited approach for defining the syntax of visualisations. However, in the context here syntax does not yet refer to the syntax of a visual language but rather to the syntax of the graphical representation. As described above the concept of Semantic Visualisation Functionalities separates the model from the visualisation model. Therefore visualisation models have their own syntax that can then be mapped to the syntax of the model. To build up visual representation the point itself would not be sufficient. Similar to the concept of 'Data' that is defined by North as symbols plus syntax (i.e. ordering rules for the arrangement of the symbols), there is also an equivalent for visualisations. By adding rules to the entity of the point further graphical primitives can be constructed that can again be assembled by applying rules to create even more complex objects.

For the purposes here the basic syntax of a visual object is defined as the ordered set $\mathscr{D}$ of instances *PRIM* of the basic graphical primitives line, curve, oval, polyline, rectangle, and text (see equations 5.9 and 5.10). The position in the set thereby determines the occlusion of the underlying primitives (i.e. the first object may be occluded by the subsequent primitives). By the combination of these primitives already a large number of graphical representations can be realised. In contrast to the approaches in visual language theory the spatial arrangement of the graphical primitives is not formally specified on the basic level. Instead, two constructs are introduced to allow for the establishing of the necessary functionalities for expressing relations between primitives: *Variables* and *Control structures*.

$$PRIM \quad :: \quad P \mathbin{\dot\vee} L \mathbin{\dot\vee} C \mathbin{\dot\vee} O \mathbin{\dot\vee} POL \mathbin{\dot\vee} RECT \mathbin{\dot\vee} TEXT \tag{5.9}$$

$$\mathscr{D} \;=\; \{PRIM_1, PRIM_2, \ldots, PRIM_n \mid PRIM_i :: PRIM\} \tag{5.10}$$

Addition of Variables

Similar to the definition of programming languages variables are integrated into the definition of the graphical representation. For keeping the resulting specification of the representation as simple as possible variables can only be of the three types: *Integer*, *Float*, and *String*. Additionally, variables contain three standard values that have to be specified upon their instantiation: A minimum value, a maximum value and a default value. Similar to the concept of arrays variables contain an ordered set of values that can be addressed by an integer index value and that is of arbitrary size. For taking into account the scaling of graphical representations variables also contain a boolean value *SCALE*. The exposition of variables to the outside (the reason will be given below) is also defined by a boolean value *EXPOS*. To differentiate between different variables also a *NAME* attribute is assigned.

$$V \;=\; (NAME, TYPE, MIN, MAX, DEF, SCALE, EXPOS, \mathscr{V}) \tag{5.11}$$

$$NAME \quad :: \quad String \tag{5.12}$$

$$TYPE \quad :: \quad Integer \mathbin{\dot\vee} Float \mathbin{\dot\vee} String \tag{5.13}$$

$$MIN \quad :: \quad TYPE \tag{5.14}$$

$$MAX \quad :: \quad TYPE \tag{5.15}$$

$$
\begin{aligned}
DEF &:: TYPE & (5.16)\\
SCALE &= true \ \dot\vee \ false & (5.17)\\
EXPOS &= true \ \dot\vee \ false & (5.18)\\
\mathcal{V} &= \{ VAL_1, VAL_2, \ldots, VAL_n \mid VAL_{1\ldots n} :: TYPE \} & (5.19)
\end{aligned}
$$

The purpose of the introduction of variables in this form is to assign elements of the set $\mathcal{V}$ to coordinates of points P. Thereby the representation of a graphical primitive can be influenced via the modification of the variable value. To restrict the range of possible modifications minimum and maximum values are introduced. The default value is integrated for the purpose of a standard representation of the visual object for the case that no values have been assigned to a variable. The *SCALE* switch is necessary for the correct spatial behaviour of the representation when it is scaled. The uniform scaling of a vector graphics representation is usually performed by multiplying all coordinate values of the points by the scaling factor. For the definition of a relative spatial arrangement between objects the resulting effect might however not be beneficial: An object that was lying close to another object would be moved further away from this object due to the scaling. With the definition of a variable and the setting of *SCALE* to false the variable is not scaled together with the coordinate values and the spatial position can be preserved. The *EXPOS* switch is needed for distinguishing between variables that are used for internal purposes of the visual object and variables that can be modified from outside the visual object.

The values of the variables of a visual object may furthermore be controlled in the following ways: Upon their instantiation a set of values can be assigned to the set $\mathcal{V}$; the values may be modified and deleted and new values may be added. To include variables in the definitions of primitives the point primitive is extended so that the point coordinates and colour can contain a reference to a variable value and variables are integrated into the set $\mathcal{Q}$ as follows:

$$
\begin{aligned}
P_{ext} &= \{x,y,c \\
& \quad \mid x \in (\mathbb{R} \cup \mathcal{V}_a), y \in (\mathbb{R} \cup \mathcal{V}_b), \\
& \quad c \in (\{1,2,\ldots,2^{24}\} \cup \mathcal{V}_c)\} & (5.20)\\
\forall P &\rightarrow P_{ext} & (5.21)\\
\mathcal{Q}_{VAR} &= \{ VAR_1, VAR_2, \ldots, VAR_m, PRIM_1, PRIM_2, \ldots, PRIM_n \\
& \quad \mid VAR_{1\ldots m} :: V, PRIM_{1\ldots n} :: PRIM \} & (5.22)
\end{aligned}
$$

Addition of Control Structures

To complete the specification of visual objects four types of control structures are integrated: *IF* clauses, *WHILE* loops, and assignment operations *ASSIGN*. They are subsumed under the term *STATEMENT* which contains either one or more of these control structures or one or more primitives (from the set $\mathscr{D}$) or a combination of these (as expressed by the non-exclusive *or* in the following formal description). The *expression* term signifies an arbitrary combination of variable, numeric and string values that may be related to each other by mathematical (e.g. multiplication, division, etc.) and string operators (e.g. concatenation, substrings, replacement, etc.) as well as arithmetical functions (e.g. sinus(), tangens(), pi(), squareroot(), etc.). The *condition_expression* terms are special expressions that additionally contain comparison operators (e.g. $<$, $>$, $==$, $!=$, etc.) for numerical and string values and return a boolean value as a result.

$$STATEMENT \;=\; E_{1...w} \in \mathscr{D} \vee IF \vee WHILE \vee ASSIGN \tag{5.23}$$

$$IF \;=\; (condition\_expression, STATEMENT_{true},$$
$$STATEMENT_{false}) \tag{5.24}$$

$$WHILE \;=\; (condition\_expression, STATEMENT) \tag{5.25}$$

$$ASSIGN \;=\; (\mathscr{V}_\alpha, expression) \tag{5.26}$$

To fully formally specify these constructs it would be necessary to revert to syntax descriptions such as EBNF[10] and define sets of production rules (cf. [HMU02]). As the exact description of the syntax will not be necessary for the following elaborations and as the main elements as characterised in equations 5.23 to 5.26 directly correspond to expressions that can be found in every standard programming language this step is omitted here. The meaning of these constructs is as follows: *IF* clauses are used to test the *condition_expression* and perform the $STATEMENT_{true}$ if the result of test is *true* and $STATEMENT_{false}$ if the result is *false*. As the statement elements may contain further *IF* clauses also complex decision structures are possible. The *WHILE* loop characterises a set of statements that are performed as long as the *condition_expression* equals *true*. The *ASSIGN* operation allows for the assignment of an expression result to a variable value $\mathscr{V}_\alpha$.

With these constructs the set $\mathscr{D}_{VAR}$ can be further extended to the set $\mathscr{D}_{CTRL}$ by:

$$\mathscr{D}_{CTRL} \;=\; \{VAR_1, VAR_2, \ldots, VAR_m, \; E_1, E_2, \ldots, E_n$$

---

[10]EBNF: Extended Backus Naur Form.

$$| \ VAR_{1...m} :: V, E_{1...n} :: PRIM \ \dot{\vee} STATEMENT \} \qquad (5.27)$$

The visual objects that are based on the set $\mathscr{Q}_{CTRL}$ are regarded to be powerful enough from a functional perspective to act as a basis for a large variety of visualistions. Indeed, even a complete visualisation could be specified on the basis of these objects, either by using the point primitives and variables for realising a pixel based representation or a vector graphics with the basic primitives. For some applications it might be necessary to integrate more complex graphical primitives such as filled primitives as well as additional operations for creating sophisticated curve objects etc. For the following elaborations the set of primitives included here is nevertheless comprehensive enough to illustrate the central ideas.

Signature and Recursive Definition

Before continuing with the discussion of Ontological Visualisation Patterns one more intermediate step needs to be taken. As has been stated above the variables of visual objects are differentiated between internal and external variables via the *EXPOS* switch. The reason for this exposition is to *hide* the the structure of the visual object from the outside and provide only defined accessors to influence the object. This corresponds to the encapsulation mechanisms in object orientation and is a requirement for utilising objects in the context of a service oriented architecture (as has been discussed in section 4.3 on page 218). The accessible variables can be pooled in the form of a *visual object signature* (termed *SIG*) that characterises the object:

$$
\begin{aligned}
SIG \ = \ & \{ VAR_1, VAR_2, \ldots, VAR_n \ | \\
& \forall VAR \in \mathscr{Q}_{CTRL} \\
& \wedge \ \forall EXPOS_{VAR_{1...n}} : true \}
\end{aligned} \qquad (5.28)
$$

The explicit definition of this signature allows for another purpose that is useful to better structure complex visual objects. By the integration of a *recursive* definition of visual objects one object may be nested in another one. The inclusion of an object takes place by using the signature whose contained variables are then accessible in the same way as the other variables in the object. The scope of the *EXPOS* switch is assumed to be limited to one level above the original object, i.e. for a further exposition of the variables of a nested object the variables would have to be linked to variables of the parent object which could then in turn be exposed. These relationships are also illustrated in figure 5.3 on the next page. The integration of one visual object in another one further requires to specify the size and position of the contained visual object. This is for the moment assumed to be covered by the variables of the signature and will be further detailed in section 5.3 in the context of layouting the visual objects of an Ontological Visualisation Pattern.

$$\mathcal{D}_{REC} = \{VAR_1, VAR_2, \ldots, VAR_m, E_1, E_2, \ldots, E_n$$
$$| VAR_{1\ldots m} :: V, E_{1\ldots n} :: PRIM \; \dot{\vee} STATEMENT \; \dot{\vee} \; SIG\} \quad (5.29)$$

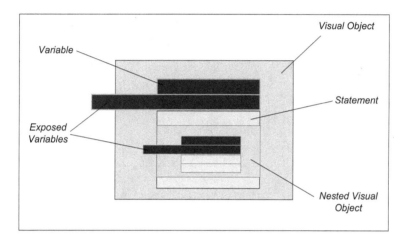

Figure 5.3: Illustration of the Nesting of Visual Objects and the Scope of Variables

Wrapping of Visualisations

Besides the recursive definition of visual objects another path for the definition of the actual visualisation can be chosen. Due to the sometimes highly complex algorithms for creating visualisations and the large amounts of data that are required (especially in information visualisation) the structure of visual objects as outlined here may not suffice. Therefore a reference to an external component can be integrated in the definition of visual objects. By the definition of an interface between this component and the structure of the visual object the visual object acts as a *wrapper* to the separately defined visualisation. Although this approach does not allow for the utilisation of the complete functionality of visual objects (e.g. for identifying the primitives used in an object for comparing it to other objects as will be discussed subsequently) it marks an important step towards a *service-oriented visualisation architecture* (SOVA). As one crucial point for the realisation of service oriented architectures in general is the integration of legacy data and systems (cf. [SS03]) the same mechanism can thereby be applied to visualisations.

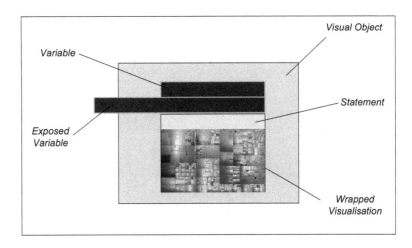

Figure 5.4: Wrapping of Visualisations in Visual Objects

As shown in figure 5.4 a visual object contains a complex visualisation (e.g. here the treemap visualisation as discussed in section 3.2 on page 106) and exposes one or more variables to the outside of the object. The contained visualisation is thus only accessible via the variables of the visual object which may also be semantically described (as will be elaborated in the next section). The formal characterisation of visual objects has to be equally adapted by integrating a reference call to an external visualisation component $VC()$ that receives a number of variables. Among these variables have to be declarations of the size VAR_{size} and position VAR_{pos} of the embedded visualisation to determine its positioning within the visual object.

$$
\begin{aligned}
\mathscr{D}_{WRAP} \;=\; & \{VAR_1, VAR_2, \ldots, VAR_m, \; E_1, E_2, \ldots, E_n \\
& \mid VAR_{1\ldots m} :: V, E_{1\ldots n} :: PRIM \;\dot\vee\, STATEMENT \;\dot\vee\, SIG \\
& \dot\vee\; VC(VAR_{pos}, VAR_{size}, VAR_1 \ldots, VAR_w \mid VAR_{pos,size,1\ldots w} :: V)\}
\end{aligned}
$$

$$(5.30)$$

The wrapping of complex visualisations in this way furthermore leads to a unification of the approaches of visual languages and of information visualisation: Through a common accessor mechanisms based on the exposed variables of the visual object both specifications from visual languages (e.g. to represent particular symbols) as well as from information visualisation can be described and uniformly used.

5.3 The Concept of Ontological Visualisation Patterns

Based on the concept of visual objects it will now be discussed how Ontological Visualisation Patterns are composed of one or more visual objects and what specific characteristics they have. Ontological Visualisation Patterns constitute a new way for defining visualisations. Ontological Visualisation patterns contain several features that have not been conceptualised before: They are the main factor for fulfilling the requirements of a service oriented visualisation architecture where small (software) components can be accessed for providing a specific visualiation functionality. Furthermore they contain abstract specifications of visualisations that are semantically specified and can be directly used by intelligent agents if the semantics are available in a machine processable format (cf. [BLFM05]).

For illustrating their relation to concrete graphics the subsequent illustration has been created in analogy to the well known semantic web stack (see figure 5.5). On its bottom layer it contains the core elements of any visualisation: *Points* as the smallest visual entity and *Graphical Primitives* that are composed of a finite number of points as has been shown in the previous section. On the next layer reside *Graphical Representations* in the form of vector graphics that are composed of graphical primitives[11].

To allow for a dynamic change of the graphical representations the *Visual objects* layer adds variable properties and control structures for these properties to the graphical representations as has been describe above. Thereby a representation can be changed according to a variably assigned value.

On the *Ontological Visualisations Patterns* layer one or more visual objects are combined and positioned according to a *layout procedure*. The variables of the visual objects are either directly exposed as variables of the pattern or via a transformation function. The ontological visualisation pattern therefore also has to contain

---

[11]Although it would theoretically be possible to include pixel graphics as well for the reason of quality (see section 5.2 on page 232) only the aspects of vector graphics are treated in this context.

control structures and variables, but in contrast to the visual objects the variables
as well as the pattern itself are enriched with a *semantic specification* on the basis of a *semantic meta language*. This semantic meta language can then also be
used for inferencing mechanisms working on the visualisation such as *Logic*, *Proof*
and *Trust*. The last three layers are not further discussed within this work. They
are regarded as extensions that can be developped upon the theories laid out here
and could build partly upon the approaches in visual and diagrammatic reasoning
(cf. [WBJ00]).

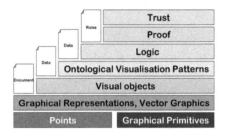

Figure 5.5: Semantic Visualisation Stack

Adding Semantics to Visualisations

The use of a semantic meta language for describing visualisations has so far not
been explicitly discussed in the scientific literature. The publications that partly
address such aspects can be seen in the publication by [DBD04] in the context
of the creation of a visualisation ontology and in approaches for adding metadata
to graphical representations (as e.g. proposed in the SVG specification [FFJ03][12].
Although a variety of approaches exist that focus on the formal semantic specification of visual languages (e.g. [Erw98, Haa95, Wan95]) and picture description
languages (e.g. [HM91]) these approaches do not explicitly consider the third semantic level in the sense of Stachowiak (see section 4.2 on page 164), i.e. of a
general communication system. The viewpoint of the semantic specification approaches for visual languages is therefore only limited and would correspond in
the context of the theory described in this work to the semantic specification of
the composition of visual objects. Although this could be regarded as an extension
to the specification of visual objects as shown above it would still not give any
information of the use of the visualisation from a pragmatic point of view.

---

[12] And more detailed in http://www.w3.org/TR/2003/REC-SVG11-20030114/metadata.html

So, what is addressed here is, how a visualisation can be semantically described in a general sense. An example would be to take an arbitrary visual language that is completely specified within itself in terms of syntax and semantics and relate this type of visual language to the specification of a domain. Or, more concretely, one could take the visual model of the business process modelling notation BPMN (as described in section 3.3 on page 135) and relate its elements to the elements of a general model for specifying business processes. The syntax and semantics of the BPMN visual language itself are determined on the basis of its elements, i.e. how the elements are composed of graphical primitives, how the elements may be spatially related to each other and what the meaning of these rules for the spatial arrangement is in terms of the BPMN specification. The additional semantical specification of the constructs of the BPMN by a more general model (which could for example be an ontology such as the Open Source Business Management Ontology[13]) would mean that a further level of abstraction is added to the visualisation. By aligning the model of the original world as well to this general specification it could be directly derived which element of the model can be linked (and in which way) to the model of the visualisation. If several types of visualisations are mapped to the general model it would not only become clear which solution a visualisation proposes for representing a particular domain but also how translations between different visualisation take place.

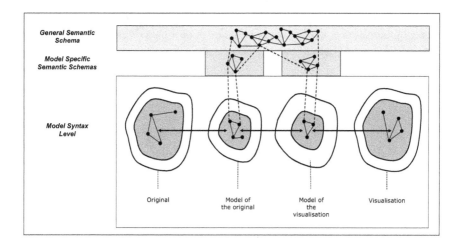

Figure 5.6: Illustration of the Mappings of Semantic Schemata

---

[13]See http://www.bpiresearch.com/Resources/RE_OSSOnt/re_ossont.htm

In figure 5.6 on the previous page these relationships are illustrated: Starting from the view of separated models for an original and for the visualisation *model specific semantic schemata* are depicted in the level above the syntactic model space. These are used as semantic reference constructs to define the meaning of the syntax of the models. Traditionally, there would only be one common semantic schema for both models so that a semantic integration takes place directly on this level (which could e.g. be a mathematical algebraic specification as e.g. shown in [Erw98](p.465f.)). This is however regarded to be only a semantic definition of the second level (self-communication) in regard to the explication of the semantics.

Based on the BPMN example this would mean that the conceptual model for business processes as described in the BPMN specification is itself syntactically described in the way which elements may be combined with each other (e.g. that activity elements may be linked with a sequence flow element) and semantically described in the sense that an activity stands for a generic term of work that a company performs and a sequence flow shows the order how activities are performed in a process. The visual model (i.e. the notation part of BPMN) is syntactically described by spatial arrangement possibilities of a rectangle specified by two points and an arrow composed of e.g. three lines. The semantic description of the visual model is then achieved by linking the syntactic visual elements to the semantic description, i.e. by stating that the arrow stands for a sequence flow. However, with this description another semantic aspect has been implicitly described: That is that the combination of for example the three lines already stands for something, namely an arrow that has the connotation of indicating a direction. If one would have only described in this context an object consisting of three lines and linking it to the semantic description of the BPMN it would have not been understandable in the same way. Therefore it seems essential to also explicitly semantically describe the model of the visualisation as it is done in the approaches for describing the formal semantics of visual languages.

But despite the formal description of the visual model (as e.g. illustrated by the various approaches in section 4.2 on page 183) the application purposes of these descriptions are not included. Although the syntax and the semantics of both the models and their mappings are explicitly laid down an intersubjective exchange of this information is not possible. To enable this exchange the level of a *General Semantic Schema* is required that allows to semantically describe both models. The visualisation approaches discussed in chapter 3 of course need to refer to such a general semantic schema as they would otherwise not be understood by other individuals than their creators. However, this schema has not been made explicit so far, i.e. the general semantic schema is usually described in natural language (which is the case for most notation specifications in the area of business informatics, cf.

section 3.3 on page 117) or mathematical formalisms. Ontological Visualisation Patterns mark a solution to overcome this deficiency of abstracting from the meaning of a visualisation (as has also been noted in section 4.2 on page 195 in the context of the work by [Wan95]). By linking the semantic schema of the visualisation model to an explicit general semantic schema the semantics of the visualisation can be raised to the third level. For this purpose the concept of ontologies as "explicit specification(s) of a (shared[14]) conceptualisation" [Gru95](p.908) provide an appropriate solution.

The formal representation of these aspects will be based on the formalisations for visual objects in the previous chapter. Additionally an ontology O is introduced which is characterised by sets of classes $\mathscr{C}$, object properties $\mathscr{OP}$, datatype properties $\mathscr{DP}$ and a set $\mathscr{V}$ of values VAL[15]. By the subsequent formal expressions a sample ontology consisting of two concept classes C_1, C_2 which are interlinked by one object property OP_1 is described. The concept C_2 is furthermore linked to a value VAL_1 by the datatype property DP_1.

$$\mathscr{O} = \{\mathscr{C}, \mathscr{OP}, \mathscr{DP}, \mathscr{V}\} \tag{5.31}$$

$$\mathscr{C} = \{C_1, C_2 \mid C_1, C_2 :: C\} \tag{5.32}$$

$$\mathscr{OP} = \{OP_1 \mid OP_1 :: OP\} \tag{5.33}$$

$$\mathscr{DP} = \{DP_1 \mid DP_1 :: DP\} \tag{5.34}$$

$$OP_1 = (C_1, C_2) \tag{5.35}$$

$$VAL_1 \quad :: \quad VAL \tag{5.36}$$

$$DP_1 = (C_2, VAL_1) \tag{5.37}$$

$$\tag{5.38}$$

The elements of the ontology can be instantiated and then linked in the simplest case to a visual object VO_1 (which stands for a specific instance of the set $\mathscr{D}_{REC}$) and a variable of the visual object VAR_1 as shown in equations 5.40 and 5.41. Thereby a semantic relationship is established between the visual object and the second concept of the ontology as well as between the datatype property and the variable. In figure 5.7 on the following page these linkages are shown in visual

---

[14] The addition of the aspect of a *shared* specification does not turn up in the original citation. It is however regarded to be essential for the characterisation of ontologies as they are understood in the context of Semantic Web.

[15] This would correspond to a simplified conception of the Web Ontology Language OWL [W3C04] which is often referenced in literature as being the current internationally aligned standard for describing ontologies.

form. Additionally, figure 5.7 also contains another link between the variable of the visual object and the value attached to the datatype property. This corresponds to the syntactic relation between these two elements that is required to actually assign the value to the variable and satisfy the syntactic consistency (i.e. also in terms of consistent datatypes).

$$VO_1 \quad : \quad \mathcal{D}_{REC}^{VO_1} \tag{5.39}$$

$$C_2 \quad \leftrightarrow \quad VO_1 \tag{5.40}$$

$$VAL_1 \quad \leftrightarrow \quad VAR_1 \tag{5.41}$$

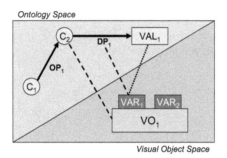

Figure 5.7: Semantic Linkage between an Ontology and a Visual Object

To complete the concept of Ontological Visualisation Patterns in the way as indicated by figure 5.6 on page 247 the semantics of the visual model have to be further detailed. In the case of an Ontological Visualisation Pattern that only consists of one visual object the model specific semantic schema refers to the elements of the set $\mathcal{D}_{REC}$. This has been described in section 5.2 on page 238 by detailing the meaning of graphical primitives, variables, control structures and recursion and relating their meaning to the semantics of standard programming languages, e.g. as has been noted for expressions. Thereby the semantics of the visual model, i.e. the 'construction plan' for the visualisation, have been defined.

For the realisation of Ontological Visualisation Patterns that contain more than one visual object additional mechanisms have been identified to be necessary: With the existence of several visual objects it needs to be determined how these objects are arranged in relation to each other and how linkages between different visual objects are realised. For both kinds of mechanisms it is necessary to provide particular algorithmic and data structures as the concepts inherent in visual objects as discussed above would not be sufficient to fulfill these purposes. Therefore also variables and control structures are introduced for Ontological Visualisation Patterns.

Pattern Variables and Control Structures

Similar to the specification of visual objects also Ontological Visualisation Patterns can be defined by an ordered set containing an arbitrary number of objects. The objects of this set $\mathscr{P}$ are in the first step the visual objects VO_i (again under the same assumption as laid down in equation 5.39 on the preceding page):

$$\mathscr{P} = \{VO_1, VO_2, \ldots, VO_n \mid VO_{1\ldots n} :: VO\} \qquad (5.42)$$

The integration of variables can therefore be performed in the same way as for visual objects (by referring to the same assumptions for variables as in equation 5.11 on page 239):

$$\mathscr{P}_{VAR} = \{VAR_1, VAR_2, \ldots, VAR_m, VO_1, VO_2, \ldots, VO_n$$
$$\mid VAR_{1\ldots m} :: V, VO_{1\ldots n} :: VO\} \qquad (5.43)$$

And with the extension to control structures for the patterns (referring to the assumptions in 5.23 on page 241:

$$\mathscr{P}_{CTRL} = \{VAR_1, VAR_2, \ldots, VAR_m, E_1, E_2, \ldots, E_n$$
$$\mid VAR_{1\ldots m} :: V, E_{1\ldots n} :: VO \lor STATEMENT\} \qquad (5.44)$$

Based on these additional constructs for Ontological Visualisation Patterns the model of the visualisation can be further detailed: By using the same approach as for visual objects a signature can be specified for Ontological Visualisation Patterns that abstracts from the inner structure of the pattern: Similarly, only specific variables of the pattern are exposed to the outside which are linked to internal variables and statements and that can thus influence in turn the contained visual objects and the visualisation. A specific aspect of the inner structure is the positioning of the visual objects.

Layouting of Visual Objects

The aspect of positioning several visual objects can be circumscribed by *layouting* and turns up in several fields related to visualisation: The most general mechanisms of positioning objects on a canvas are found in the area of *user interface design* where the single user interface components have to be positioned based on conceptual as well as technical constraints. The conceptual constraints concern aspects such as the optimal positioning for an efficient interaction or the traceability by the user when the position of the components changes (i.e. for understanding why the visualisation has changed). From the technical side the limited space on a computer screen has to be efficiently used by the components so that all necessary components can be displayed correctly.

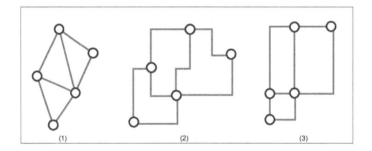

Figure 5.8: Example for Three Different Layouts of the Same Graph (Source: [CT98])

Besides user interface design also the scientific field of *graph drawing* [DiB97, MJL01] is concerned with the positioning of objects. The focus here is, as the name already implies, put on graph structures and their visualisation. Two basic directions can be identified to classify the approaches in graph drawing from a high level perspective: On the one hand several approaches are presented that are based on a mathematical definition of a graph and calculate the positioning of nodes and vertices based on a variety of aesthetics criteria [Pur97, CT98] such as the minimisation of crossings, the total area of the graph, the number of bends or slopes as well as the maximisation of the smallest angle (to achieve orthogonal drawings) or the display of symmetries. To illustrate these mechanisms figure 5.8 shows three different layouts of the same mathematical graph that can be automatically computed. The second direction for drawing graphs takes a different view: As graphs are for some applications not primarily considered as visual representations of a mathematical structure but rather as representations of knowledge that has been explicated in a visual format the position of the nodes and edges depends on a human specification. Therefore the layout of the graph cannot be changed without considering these aspects. This preservation of the *mental map* is also addressed in graph drawing and several suggestions have been discussed how this can be successfully achieved [FE02, MELS95]. For the purposes of multi-object Ontological Visualisation Patterns two possibilities are therefore deemed as essential for realising the correct layout of the objects: The first is to take over the specifications by the user which are linked to the model of the original world and that may already include layout coordinates. This would be the case if the user creates a new visualisation based on a given Ontological Visualisation Pattern or if a different pattern is applied to an existing visualisation. The second possibility is that the layout is solely determined by the type of Ontological Visualisation Pattern that is used. In that case the layout may either be computed by a specific layout component or by the control structures of the pattern itself. The reference to an external layout component is required as some of the automatic layout algorithms might not be efficiently computed or not even realisable with the comparatively simple algorithmic structures contained in Ontological Visualisation Pattern.

To integrate these views into the formal description of Ontological Visualisation Patterns it is necessary to slightly extend the description of visual objects as well as the pattern structure: So far, visual objects have been conceived only for the single object case where neither the positioning nor the size or the structure of the objects had to be explicitly specified. The determination of these aspects had been implicitely assumed to be handled by the Technical Visualisation Environment based on concrete user preferences (e.g. the screen resolution and the application purpose of the visual object). The conception based on vector graphics had also permitted to satisfy the quality requirements of the resulting graphics. To allow for the application of layout mechanisms that influence the position of visual objects relative to other objects on a canvas as well as the size and in some cases also the structure of the objects (e.g. for representing several bendpoints for edges in graphs) these visual object variables have to be made available in a generic way to the containing pattern and further to the layout mechanisms. The structure of visual objects $\mathcal{Q}_{WRAP}$ is therefore extended to $\mathcal{Q}_{MULT}$ by an identity variable VAR_{ident}, a position VAR_{pos}, a size VAR_{size} and a reference VAR_{ref} variable.

$$
\begin{aligned}
\mathcal{Q}_{MULT} \ = \ & \{ VAR_{ident}, VAR_{pos}, VAR_{size}, VAR_{ref}, VAR_1, VAR_2, \ldots, VAR_m, \\
& E_1, E_2, \ldots, E_n \mid VAR_{ident,pos,size,ref,1\ldots m} :: V, \\
& E_{1\ldots n} :: PRIM \ \dot{\vee} STATEMENT \ \dot{\vee} \ SIG \\
& \dot{\vee} \ VC(VAR_{pos}, VAR_{size}, VAR_1 \ldots, VAR_w \mid VAR_{pos,size,1\ldots w} :: V),
\end{aligned}
$$

$$EXPOS_{VAR_{ident,pos,size,ref}} : true\}$$ (5.45)

The meaning of these extensions can be described as follows: The position and size variables each contain in the case of two dimensional visualisations (as discussed here) two values: The position equals the x- and y-coordinates for the top left corner of a virtual *bounding box* for the visual object that corresponds to a rectangular transitive closure of the graphical representation. The first value of the size variables thus contains the width of the bounding box and the second the height as measured from the position point (see figure 5.9). The reference variable is used to express linkages between visual objects based on their identity variables. Thereby it can be specified which visual objects are for example connected by an edge object in a graph.

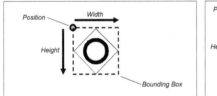 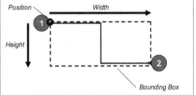

Figure 5.9: Bounding Boxes for Visual Objects

The structure of Ontological Visualisation Patterns has to be adapted in a similar way so that the size that is available for the visualisation of the pattern can be determined as well as external components for layout algorithms can be integrated. Therefore two additional elements are added to the set $\mathscr{P}_{CTRL}$: The exposed variable VAR_{size} and the abstract definition of a layout component $LAYC()$ that receives the signatures $SIG_{1...n}$ of the contained visual objects.

$$
\begin{aligned}
\mathscr{P}_{LAYT} = \ & \{VAR_{size}, VAR_1, VAR_2, \ldots, VAR_m, E_1, E_2, \ldots, E_n, \\
& LAYC(SIG_1, SIG_2, \ldots, SIG_n) \\
& \mid VAR_{size,1...m} :: V, E_{1...n} :: VO \ \dot{\vee} STATEMENT, \\
& SIG_{1...n} :: SIG\}
\end{aligned}
$$ (5.46)

The complete view on the relationships of Ontological Visualisation Patterns and visual objects is shown in figure 5.10 on the facing page. Based on these foundations in the following section it will be discussed how the concepts can be put into practice. The model for Ontological Visualisation Patterns in figure 5.10

on the next page can furthermore be seen as an approach for a meta model for visualisations in general that is independent from a specific visualisation approach but still concrete enough to be implemented.

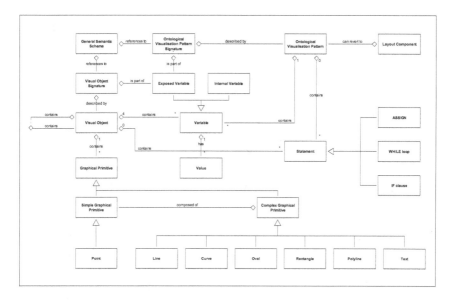

Figure 5.10: Relationship of the Elements of Ontological Visualisation Patterns

5.4 The Composition of Ontological Visualisation Patterns

To illustrate the theoretical concepts that have been elaborated in the previous sections it shall now be shown how a concrete realisation could be performed. Therefore at first the case of Ontological Visualisation Patterns containing only one visual object (*Single-object-patterns* will be looked at and then the version of patterns containing several visual objects (*multi-object patterns*) is discussed.

Single-Object Patterns

In chapter 3 several visualisation approaches have been shown that can be realised by the simplest case of single object patterns. Although the choice of how many visual objects are part of a pattern is left to the designer of the Ontological Visualisation Pattern (due to the possibility of recursion for visual objects that permits to subsume all objects under a single visual object) the visualisation approaches for enterprise cockpits (see section 3.3 on page 119) provide a good starting point for practically illustrating the concepts. Therefore it will be worked out in the following how a thermometer visualisation as used for example in the enterprise cockpit of ADOscore can be generated. In figure 5.11 the steps for creating an Ontological Visualisation Patterns are illustrated.

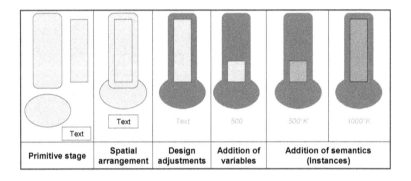

| Primitive stage | Spatial arrangement | Design adjustments | Addition of variables | Addition of semantics (Instances) |

Figure 5.11: Advancement Steps in the Definition of Ontological Visualisation Patterns

At the *primitive stage* the graphical primitives are created. This requires to determine which primitives will be needed to realise the visualisation and to specify the relative size of the objects. At the second stage of *spatial arrangement* the objects are positioned relative to each other to achieve the desired basic design of the visual object. The design can then be detailed by *design adjustments* which will not be regarded in detail here as the conceptions for visual objects shown in the subsequent section do not contain possibilities for these adjustments (e.g. to change the colour)[16]. After the design phase it needs to be derived what functionality shall be assigned to the object in terms of *variables*. For the representation of a thermometer as in figure 5.11 it is necessary to adjust the middle rectangle and the text depending on the temperature that shall be visualised by the object. This includes the specification of the upper and lower bounds of the rectangle as well as the consideration of the size of the text. The final step is the *addition of semantics* so that the meaning of the visualisation is exactly described. To achieve

---

[16]The concepts of visual objects could be extended for these purposes but to illustrate the basic functionalities they are not necessary.

this another variable for containing a temperature value and its relation to the inner rectangle as well as the text have to be added.

```xml
<?xml version="1.0" encoding="UTF-8"?>
<visualobject id="thermometer"
xmlns="http://www.dke.univie.ac.at/~fill/example_vo.xml#">
    <variable name="temperature" type="float" min="-50" max="50" default="0"
exposed="true" scale="false"/>
    <variable name="bar_size" type="integer" min="15" max="115" default="115"
exposed="false" scale="true"/>
    <assign variable="bar_size" expression="((bar_size.max-
bar_size.min)/(abs(temperature.max-temperature.min)))*temperature.[0]"/>
    <oval>
            <point x="100" y="100"/>
            <point x="200" y="150"/>
    </oval>
    <rectangle>
            <point x="125" y="120"/>
            <point x="175" y="10"/>
    </rectangle>
    <rectangle>
            <point x="130" y="115"/>
            <point x="170" y="15"/>
    </rectangle>
    <text>
            <point x="100" y="150"/>
            <point x="200" y="180"/>
            <textstring value="concat('Temperature: ', temperature.[0])"/>
    </text>
</visualobject>
```

Figure 5.12: Example XML Code for a Visual Object definition

To show in more concrete form how the visual object of a thermometer would have to be described figure 5.12 contains a sample syntactic specification in XML syntax[17] based on the definition of visual objects $\mathcal{D}_{REC}$ (equation 5.29 on page 243). Thereby it becomes directly visible how the variables of the visual object influence the graphical representation. It has to be noted that the values of variables are accessed by adding a dot and the number of the accessed value in brackets. Similarly the standard values of variables are accessed (e.g. *bar_size.max*). In the expressions *abs()* stands for a function returning the absolute value and *concat()* (in the specification of the text string) means the concatentation of a number of strings. The graphical primitives are specified based on points as laid out in the previous sections.

For the completion of Ontological Visualisation Patterns it is finally necessary to link the variable values of the visual object to the concepts and datatype properties of an ontology. For this purpose a sample ontology in the web ontology language

---

[17]The XML syntax shown in the following examples is only for illustrative purposes and would require the addition of references to the corresponding XML Schemata or Document Type Definitions.

```
<?xml version="1.0" encoding="UTF-8"?>
<rdf:RDF xmlns:rdf="http://www.w3.org/1999/02/22-rdf-syntax-ns#"
xmlns:rdfs="http://www.w3.org/2000/01/rdf-schema#"
xmlns:owl="http://www.w3.org/2002/07/owl#"="http://www.dke.univie.ac.at/~fill/tempe
rature/temperature.owl#"
xml:base="http://www.dke.univie.ac.at/~fill/temperature/temperature.owl">
        <owl:Ontology rdf:about="http://www.dke.univie.ac.at/~fill/temperature"/>
        <owl:Class rdf:ID="Temperature_Celsius">
            <rdfs:subClassOf>
                <owl:Class rdf:ID="Temperature"/>
            </rdfs:subClassOf>
        </owl:Class>
        <owl:Class rdf:ID="Temperature_Fahrenheit">
            <rdfs:subClassOf>
                <owl:Class rdf:about="#Temperature"/>
            </rdfs:subClassOf>
        </owl:Class>
        <owl:Class rdf:ID="Temperatur">
            <owl:sameAs>
                <owl:Class rdf:about="#Temperature"/>
            </owl:sameAs>
        </owl:Class>
        <owl:Class rdf:about="#Temperature">
            <owl:sameAs rdf:resource="#Temperatur"/>
        </owl:Class>
        <owl:DatatypeProperty rdf:ID="Temperature_in_Celsius">
            <rdfs:range rdf:resource="http://www.w3.org/2001/XMLSchema#float"/>
            <rdfs:domain rdf:resource="#Temperature_Celsius"/>
        </owl:DatatypeProperty>
</rdf:RDF>
```

Figure 5.13: A sample Temperature Ontology

OWL is shown in figure 5.13. It contains four classes to specify the concept *Temperature*, its equivalent concept *Temperatur* in German and two sub classes *Temperature_Fahrenheit* and *Temperature_Celsius*. The latter also contains a datatype property *Temperature_in_Celsius* that is of the range float as specified by the XML Schema datatype.

The description of the Ontological Visualisation Pattern is shown in figure 5.14 on the facing page. It is composed of a variable that is exposed and a visual object. The visual object contains an XLink Reference[18] to the specification of the visual object (as in figure 5.12 on the previous page). The exposed variable of the visual object (*thermometer.temperature.[0]*) is then assigned to the variable of the pattern.

The linkage of the Ontological Visualisation Pattern to the ontology is realised by a separate definition (depicted in figure 5.15 on the facing page). Although the mapping definition could also be integrated into the pattern specification the separate definition allows for a higher flexibility (which will be further extended

---

[18]XLink is a generic reference syntax for XML documents, see http://www.w3.org/TR/xlink/

```
<?xml version="1.0" encoding="UTF-8"?>
<ontologicalVisualisationPattern
xmlns="http://www.dke.univie.ac.at/~fill/example_pattern.xml#">
        <variable name="temperature" type="float" min="-50" max="50" default="0"
            exposed="true" scale="false"/>
        <visualobject id="thermometer" xlink:type="locator"
            xlink:href="http://www.dke.univie.ac.at/~fill/example_vo.xml#"/>
        <assign variable="thermometer.temperature.[0]"
            expression="temperature.[0]"/>
</ontologicalVisualisationPattern>
```

Figure 5.14: Sample Ontological Visualisation Pattern

```
<?xml version="1.0" encoding="UTF-8"?>
<mappingDefinition xmlns:xlink="http://www.w3.org/1999/xlink" xlink:type="extended"
xmlns="http://www.dke.univie.ac.at/~fill/mapping_definition.xml">
        <pattern xlink:type="locator"
            xlink:href="http://www.dke.univie.ac.at/~fill/example_pattern.xml#"
            xlink:label="pattern1" />

        <visualobject xlink:type="locator"
            xlink:href="http://www.dke.univie.ac.at/~fill/example_pattern.xml#xpoint
            er(visualobject[@id='thermometer'])" xlink:label="vo1" />

        <patternvariable xlink:type="locator"
            xlink:href="http://www.dke.univie.ac.at/~fill/example_pattern.xml#xpoint
            er(variable[@name='temperature'])" xlink:label="var1" />

        <ontologyConcept xlink:type="locator"
            xlink:href="http://www.dke.univie.ac.at/~fill/temperature/temperature.owl
            #xpointer(owl:Class[@rdf:ID='Temperature_Celsius'])"
            xlink:label="concept1" />

        <ontologyDataType xlink:type="locator"
            xlink:href="http://www.dke.univie.ac.at/~fill/temperature/temperature.owl
            #xpointer(owl:DatatypeProperty[@rdf:ID='Temperature_in_Celsius'])"
            xlink:label="datatype1" />

        <mapping xlink:type="arc" xlink:from="vo1" xlink:to="concept1" />
        <mapping xlink:type="arc" xlink:from="var1" xlink:to="datatype1" />
</mappingDefinition>
```

Figure 5.15: Mapping Definition for Relating the Ontology and the Ontological Visualisation Pattern in the following section) in regard to relating different ontologies to one pattern definition. The mapping at first defines references to the Ontological Visualisation pattern, the visual object (as contained in the pattern), the variable of the pattern that is exposed as well as to the owl:Class *Temperature_Celsius* and the datatype property *Temperature_in_Celsius*. These references are again defined on the basis of the XLink syntax that includes XPointer expressions[19]. Finally, the mappings between visual object (referenced by the label *vo1*) and the ontology class (referenced by *concept1*) and the variable of the visual object (*var1*) and the datatype property (*datatype1*) are established.

Recursive Composition and Abstraction

To allow for a better re-use of visual objects and thereby support the designers of visual objects and Ontological Visualisation Patterns a second approach for the abovely described example would involve recursive visual objects. This allows to create abstract visual objects that fit to a large variety of ontological concepts and can then be individually adapted to specific requirements. From the survey in chapter 3 sets of basic visual objects thus can be derived that occur in several visualisations. To illustrate this approach it shall be reverted to the *rhomb* symbol that is used in flowcharts (see figure 3.29 on page 80), ER diagrams (figure 3.34 on page 91), UML activity diagrams (figure 3.39 on page 100), the BPMN notation (figure 3.61 on page 136) and Adonis business process models (figure 3.65 on page 141). In figure 5.16 on the facing page the different variants of this symbol are compiled.

By using the abstract visual object of a rhomb for creating the different variants a relationship between the original symbol and the variant can be established. Similar to the approaches for visual language specifications that aim for an identification of pre-defined objects in a drawing to determine their meaning (see section 4.2 on page 183) the use of common abstract visual objects allows a designer to investigate which meanings a specific symbol has in other contexts. The benefit of this functionality is to support the design of new visual languages in the way that it can be queried which meanings have already been assigned to specific symbols or in which other symbols a particular symbol is used. The same approach could also be applied to the level of graphical primitives, i.e. it could be searched for similar primitive constellations in other visual objects. The greatest benefit of these operations can be achieved if the conception of visual objects and Ontological Visualisation Patterns could be raised to the level of an open international

---

[19] XPointer is a language to define fragment identifiers for arbitrary URI (Uniform Resoruce Identifier) references - see http://www.w3.org/TR/xptr/

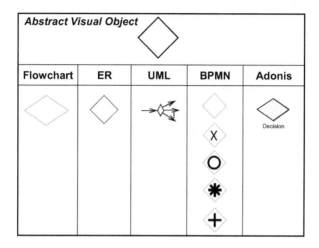

Figure 5.16: Identification of Abstract Visual Objects

standard for defining visualisations. It might be argued that such an undertaking could already be performed by existing graphical standards such as Scalable Vector Graphics (SVG) [FFJ03] and the integrated scripting languages. However, the exposition of variables and the linkage to ontologies for semantically defining visualisation has so far not been initiated.

To detail the argument of using variables and semantic descriptions a second example for the use of recursion in visual objects can be described. When coming back to the example of the creation of the Ontological Visualisation Pattern for visualising the temperature by a thermometer like representation it can be discovered that the semantic linkage as described here would not allow for a use of the pattern in an enterprise cockpit (as shown in figure 3.59 on page 130). The reason is that the semantic description that the pattern is linked to determines the restriction to temperature values. A visualisation of turnover rates for example could not be directly derived from this conception. However, the visualisation of the thermometer can be abstracted so that it does not only describe a thermometer but that it is rather left undefined which semantic concept is assigned. To allow for a search on this basis however the pattern has to be somehow identifiable. The solution is to only take into account the syntactic signature of the pattern and determine whether it fits to the syntax structure of the data that is to be assigned.

For the case of the Ontological Visualisation pattern specified in figure 5.14 on page 259 this means to address the exposed variable as a float value with the bounds -50 and 50. If the corresponding data can be adequately mapped to this syntactic characterisation the pattern can be used for the intended purpose. More concretely, the mapping of turnover values to this pattern could then be success-fully realised if the magnitudes can be transformed to the range of -50 and 50. The underlying transformation function for numerical values is similar to the one required for linking the exposed variable of a visual object to an internal variable for creating the visualisation (see figure 5.12 on page 257).

$$f(x) = \frac{|target.max - target.min|}{|source.max - source.min|} * x \qquad (5.47)$$

Equation 5.47 defines the basic transformation function between two different continous scales: At first the absolute range of the target scale is subdivided by the absolute range of the source scale. The result (i.e. the transformation multiplier) can then be multiplied by a value of the original scale. What has not been consid-ered up to this point is the representation of the textual value in the visual object. In the example of figure 5.12 on page 257 the text had been linked to the exposed variable and would therefore not correctly represent the source value (which is usu-ally intended). To overcome this problem the introduction of a separate variable for displaying the text would be necessary.

Multi-Object Patterns

Despite the many types of visualisations that can be realised with single-object patterns the extension to multi-object patterns is necessary for two reasons: On the one hand it allows for a *clearer structure* of an Ontological Visualisation Pattern than would be the case if the pattern is entirely specified by one visual object that contains several recursively integrated objects. On the other hand it eases the specification of complex patterns that would require several layers for exposing the variables of the recursively specified visual objects.

A typical example for a multi-object pattern shall therefore be discussed in detail in the following. The basis for the example is a simple business process diagram (in a variant of the Adonis notation as shown in section 3.3 on page 143) that depicts a business process as a sequence of activities which are enclosed in a start and end object (see figure 5.17 on the facing page). The elements are connected with arrows so that the resulting structure can be characterised as a directed graph.

To create visualisations in this style four visual objects have been created (see figure 5.18 on the next page) which can be referenced by unique resource iden-tifiers. To take into account the special role of the visual object representing the arrows it is assumed that this object may contain two references to other visual

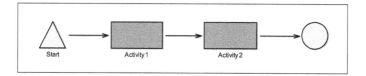

Figure 5.17: Business Process Diagam composed of Multi-Object Pattern

objects. Furthermore all visual objects are assumed to be defined on the basis of $\mathscr{Q}_{MULT}$ (see equation 5.45 on page 254), i.e. that all objects contain particular exposed variables for their size and position.

Visual Object Representation	URI
 △ Start	http://www.dke.univie.ac.at/~fill/start_vo.xml#
 ▭ Activity 1	http://www.dke.univie.ac.at/~fill/activity_vo.xml#
 →	http://www.dke.univie.ac.at/~fill/successor_vo.xml#
 ○	http://www.dke.univie.ac.at/~fill/end_vo.xml#

Figure 5.18: Visual Objects of the Multi-Object Pattern

The first step in the definition of the Ontological Visualisation Pattern is the definition of the required variables (see figure 5.19 on the next page). In total seven variables are necessary: The *startID* and *endID* variables contain the unique identifiers for the start and end objects, the *activityIDs* and *successorIDs* variables contains as many IDs as there are activities and succesor relationships in the process and the *fromSuccessorID* and *toSuccessorID* variables contain the referenced objects for each successor object. The *index* variable is an internal variable which will be needed for the definition of loops.

```
<?xml version="1.0" encoding="UTF-8"?>
<ontologicalVisualisationPattern
xmlns="http://www.dke.univie.ac.at/~fill/example_multipattern.xml#">
        <variable name="startID" type="string" exposed="true" scale="false"/>
        <variable name="endID" type="string" exposed="true" scale="false"/>
        <variable name="activityIDs" type="string" exposed="true" scale="false"/>
        <variable name="successorIDs" type="integer" exposed="true" scale="false"/>
        <variable name="fromSuccessorID" type="string" exposed="true"
            scale="false"/>
        <variable name="toSuccessorID" type="string" exposed="true" scale="false"/>
        <variable name="index" type="integer" default="0" exposed="false"
            scale="false"/>
```

Figure 5.19: Multi-Object Pattern: Variable Definition

```
<visualobject id="startID.[0]" xlink:type="locator"
        xlink:href="http://www.dke.univie.ac.at/~fill/start_vo.xml#"/>
<visualobject id="endID.[0]" xlink:type="locator"
        xlink:href="http://www.dke.univie.ac.at/~fill/end_vo.xml#"/>
```

Figure 5.20: Multi-Object pattern: Definition of Start and End Visual Objects

Following the variable definitions two visual objects can be defined (figure 5.20) whose occurence is for the example here assumed to be fixed. Although this already relies on the syntax of an underlying model for business processes (i.e. that a business process must contain a start and an end object to be valid) the additional necessary control structures for ensuring the occurence are omitted for simplicity - to make the pattern independent of such an assumption it would have to be checked whether e.g. the variable *startID* contains a string so that the visual object is only created if this is the case. The IDs of the resulting visual objects are set equal to the variables handed over to the pattern.

The creation of the visual objects for representing activities is shown in figure 5.21 on the next page. It involves the usage of a while-loop that iterates over the creation of visual objects for representing activities. The value of the index variable is raised by one with every loop. The expression of the while loop includes an XML specifity: As the $<$ signs in XML are used to define the bounds of elements they have to be replaced by escape characters (in this case <). After the while loop has ended the *index* variable is resetted to zero. The same procedure of creating multiple visual objects is applied to the *successorIDs* variable to bring the necessary objects for the successor objects into existence.

For defining the references to visual objects the reference variable of the *successor* visual objects have to be filled with the values from the *fromSuccessorID* and *toSuccessorID* values. This is shown exemplarily for the first case in figure 5.22

```
<while expression="index &lt; activityIDs.length">
    <visualobject id="activityIDs.[index]" xlink:type="locator"
        xlink:href="http://www.dke.univie.ac.at/~fill/activity_vo.xml#"/>
        <assign variable="index" expression="index++"/>
</while>
<assign variable="index" expression="0"/>
```

Figure 5.21: Multi-Object Pattern: Definition of Activity Visual Objects

```
<while expression="index &lt; fromSuccessorID.length">
    <assign variable="(concat(successor, '-', index)).ref[0]"
        expression="fromSuccessorID.[index]"/>
        <assign variable="index" expression="index++"/>
</while>
<assign variable="index" expression="0"/>
```

Figure 5.22: Multi-object Pattern: Assignment of References to Successor Visual Objects

on the facing page. For this procedure to work correctly it is assumed that every successor must have a from- and a to-value which again would depend on the underlying business process model.

Finally, the layout of the created visual objects is determined. This is realised by the call of an external layout service that receives the the IDs of the visual objects representing the nodes and the IDs representing the edges (see figure 5.23). This service then calculates the positions and styles of the objects to achieve the final version of a diagram like in the example (figure 5.17 on page 263). As has been shown in the context of single-object patterns also the visual objects and the pattern itself can be linked to an external semantic schema by a mapping definition. Besides the mapping aspect between the visual representation and the semantic schema the following section will discuss the mapping of the Ontological Visualisation Patterns to the model of a specific domain.

```
<callLayoutComponent xlink:type="locator"
    xlink:href="http://www.dke.univie.ac.at/~fill/ProcessLayoutService#"
    nodes="startID.[0], endID.[0], activityIDs" edges="successorIDs"/>
</ontologicalVisualisationPattern>
```

Figure 5.23: Multi-Object Pattern: Call of an External Layout Component

5.5 Core Dimensions of Visualisation Mapping Facilities

To fully realise the vision of a Semantic Visualisation, which is seen in the availability of semantically described visualisation services that can on demand and automatically create dynamic visualisations that are appropriate for a specific use case the mapping between Ontological Visualisation Patterns and a domain conceptualisation via a semantic schema has to be further specified. For this purpose four dimensions have been identified that characterise this mapping: The *Functional Implementation*, the level of *Standardisation*, the type of *Deployment*, and the *Time Reference* (see figure 5.24).

The Functional Implementation describes whether the mapping takes place fully automatically (e.g. through intelligent agents that receive a request for a visualisation and deliver the result), semi automatically (e.g. by offering visualisation alternatives that can be chosen by the user) or manually (e.g. when the visualisations for the mapping are manually selected based on the subjective assessment of a user). The Standardisation dimension determines to which amount the mapping is performed by using standardised technology for the description of the conceptualisation of the Ontological Visualisation Patterns, the description of the domain conceptualisation and the mapping itself. Again, for fully realising Semantic Visualisation standardised technologies are required to enable the direct cooperation of all three parts. The two types for the Deployment reflect whether the visualisation can be dynamically altered after the deployment (whereby e.g. the change of an attribute status in the domain conceptualisation can influence the visualisation after the mapping has been defined) or whether the mapping is static and cannot be changed. The Time Reference dimension expresses whether the visualisation is assembled on demand (i.e. directly upon the request of a user) or is pre-configured and then accessed at a later point in time.

Functional Implementation	*Automatic*	*Semi automatic*	*Manual*
Standardization	*Fully Standards based*	*Partly Standards based*	*Proprietary*
Deployment	*Static*		*Dynamic*
Time Reference	*On demand*		*Pre-configured*

Figure 5.24: Core Dimensions of the Visualisation Mapping Facilities

Although no explicit standard is yet available for the realisation of this mapping it can be reverted to XML as a wide spread syntactic standard. Thereby at least the syntactic interaction can be based on a common standard. For the semantic definition also standards such as RDF or RDFS could be used, however a proprietary semantic schema would have to be defined to which the concepts of these standards can relate to.

For the case that the visualisation can be altered after the deployment it is necessary to either provide the corresponding interaction facilities for the user or integrate an automatic update procedure for the visualiation. The interaction facilities for the user are regarded to be part of the particular user interface that presents the visualisation. This aspect is not explicitly covered here. The automatic update of the visualisation corresponds to a re-creation that is either triggered by the user when re-invoking the visualisation procedure or by the technical input for the procedure.

An aspect that has to be taken into account if the visualisation is not created on demand is the storage of the actual graphical representation. This can either be accomplished by storing the state of a visualisation procedure or the output of the procedure. The choice between the two possibilities depends on the complexity of the visualisation procedure and the output. For a complex procedure it may be more effective to store the output in terms of a static picture whereas for a complex output, e.g. an animation or a large image, it may be more favourable to retain the state and re-create the output as needed.

5.6 Requirements for the Technical Visualisation Environment

The Technical Visualisation Environment is responsible for the actual creation of the visualisation. It therefore has to provide technical functionalities to implement Ontological Visualisation Patterns, the Visualisation Mapping facilities as well as the interaction with the output devices for the graphical representation. In detail the following requirements have to be met:

- The technical environment has to be able to represent visual objects and Ontological Visualisation Patterns in computer language.
- It must be able to access external components and services as it is required for wrapping visualisations and layout services.
- It has to be adaptable to a wide variety of output devices.

- The environment is ideally web based and provides interfaces which are described by international standards, e.g. by the Web Service Description Language (WSDL).
- It must specify an exchange format for defining visual objects, Ontological Visualisation Patterns and the mapping between Ontological Visualisation Patterns and the semantic schema.

- It has to take into account performance aspects that are important for realising complex visualisations. It may therefore be necessary to provide interfaces to high performance computers or grid systems.

As has been shown by the examples in section 5.3 on page 245 the abstract specifications of visual objects and Ontological Visualisation Patterns can be directly translated to an XML [BPSM$^+$04] format. Thereby the requirements of using international standards as well as the provision of an exchange format can be satisfied. The representation of the concepts in a concrete programming language will be shown in chapter 7 on page 291 by the Java programming language. Based on an XML exchange format similar implementations in other programming languages can also be easily achieved. This is of special importance for the consideration of performance aspects: For generating complex visualisations that are based on large datasets – as it occurs often in the area of information visualisation – other computational environments such as the access to grid technologies [FKNT02] may be required. Despite the specific adaptations that would be required for such environments the XML serialisations shown here are in any case an appropriate starting point. This also applies to the use of standard interface technologies such as WSDL [CCMW01] that have counterparts in the area of grid technologies, e.g. by the OGSI[20] specification.

---

[20]OGSI: Open Grid Services Infrastructure defines WSDL interfaces for Grid services [TCF$^+$03].

6 Application Scenario for Semantic Visualisation Functionalities

With the establishment of the framework for visualisation and a concrete method for realising semantic visualisation functionalities it shall now be turned to a concrete application scenario. The purpose of this scenario will be to give an integrated view on semantic visualisation functionalities and their embedding by instantiating them to a concrete visualisation task. The field that has been selected for this purpose is *enterprise risk management*. The following remarks will present a new approach for dealing with this subject that has been elaborated in a joint cooperation of Prof. Dr. Hans Ulrich Buhl, Prof. Dr. Robert Winter and Prof. Dr. Dimitris Karagiannis. First results of this research have been published in [FB05]. For the IT support of the concepts presented in this approach another publication is currently being worked out[1]. The discussion here will primarily focus on these IT aspects.

6.1 Integrated Enterprise Balancing

The concept of Integrated Enterprise Balancing (IEB) describes a new approach for an IT-based management that enables financial service providers and corporate finance departments to control the return and risk aspects of their business activities based on innovative information systems [FB05]. For the optimisation of the corporate return and risk positions the prevailing and future regulatory constraints and reporting obligations such as Basel II, Kon-TraG[2] or the Sarbanes-Oxley-Act have to be taken into account depending on the particular branch. Upcoming new reporting obligations often lead to new, isolated controlling systems for a single specific purpose. The provision of an integrated data model as well as the measuring of return and risk contributions on different aggregation levels has so far not been particularly addressed in business informatics. The realisation of such

---

[1] Working paper by Fill, H.-G., Karagiannis, D., Winter, R. (2006): Method & Process Engineering for the 4R Framework, University of Vienna and University St. Gallen.

[2] KonTraG: Gesetz zur Kontrolle und Transparenz im Unternehmensbereich (Corporate Sector Supervision and Transparency Act)

a data model depends both on the availability of adequate financial methods and performance indicators as well as their integration into the design of the business processes and IT services and their organisational embedding.

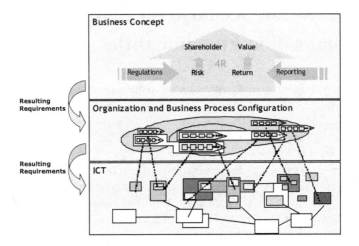

Figure 6.1: The 4R Framework cf. [FB05]

The vision of an *Integrated Enterprise Balancing* is therefore directed towards an integration of the IT based return and risk management to enable enterprises to conduct their business activities upon consistent and uniform return and risk indicators for achieving the compliance to internal and external control requirements [FB05]. For taking optimal decisions the influence of reporting obligations as well as regulatory constraints have to be taken into account. This is reflected by a *4R control methodology* where 4R stands for: Risk, Return, Regulation, and Reporting. As shown in figure 6.1 the 4R control methdology is positioned as a top level concept from which resulting requirements are derived for the *organisation and business process configuration* and further for the underlying *information and communication technologies* (ICT).

For supporting the 4R framework a 4R IT-Framework has been derived. It provides components for achieving the fulfillment of reporting requirements and regulatory constraints by reverting to a meta model based approach. In figure 6.2 on the facing page the three layers of the 4R IT-Framework and their relation to the 4R Framework are depicted: The *Enterprise Template Integration* layer provides functionality for the support of the business concept, the *Enterprise Method Integration* layer supports the organisation and business process configuration and the

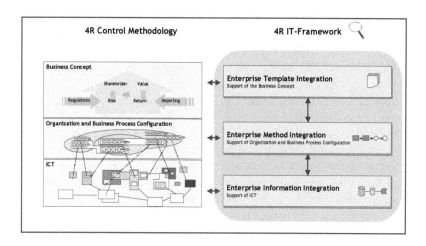

Figure 6.2: The 4R IT-Framework

Enterprise Information Integration layer the handling of information in regard to information and communication technologies.

Each layer of the 4R IT-Framework can be described by one or more meta models. Through the integration of these meta models a holistic and consistent IT concept for the 4R Framework is provided. The instantiation of the meta models to concrete models is based on the specific domain requirements of the 4R layers. In the following section two meta models will be discussed that mark a first approach towards a realisation of the 4R IT-Framework. Based on these domain conceptualisations the approach of semantic visualisation functionalities can then be applied accordingly.

6.2 Domain Conceptualisation

The first meta model has been conceived for the Enterprise Template Integration layer. *Enterprise Templates* are an innovative approach for supporting the requirements of the 4R business concept in a generic way: A template is generally characterised as a method to separate form and content by an abstract specification. Typical representatives for templates can be found in the context of web based presentation formats: Through the use of stylesheets an arbitrary XML document that matches the style specifications can be rendered to a specific presentation format [Cla99]. The stylesheets in this example thereby act as the template specification. For Enterprise Templates this concept is extended in the way that the aspect of a specific *methodology* is added to form and content. The template therefore not only defines the resulting presentation based on a specific content but is also composed of a specific, explicitly defined methodology.

In figure 6.3 on the next page the first conception of an Enterprise Template meta model is shown. The three core concepts *form*, *content* and *methodology* are represented as parts of an Enterprise Template. The template content consists of compliance information that is determined by the *reporting obligations* and the *regulatory constraints*. The compliance information is specialised into *qualitative* and *quantitative* compliance information. By qualitative compliance information all aspects that concern the existence or specific implementation of procedures in an enterprise are encompassed and by quantitative compliance information all figures and performance indicators. The content has a direct relationship to the methodology that is the provider of the necessary information. A methodology reverts to a *foundation* that can either be a *scientific theory* (as in the case of Enterprise Balancing), *experience* or an *agreed standard*. The methodology refers to a *metamodel* that is also the basis for the realisation of the *implementation*. Meta models may be *pre-defined* or *user-defined*. The form of the Enterprise Template has to respect the compatibility to the meta model of the methodology and contains both *textual* and *visual representations*. The form itself may also be *pre-defined* or *user-defined*.

In direct relation to the first meta model a second meta model is introduced that corresponds to the second layer of the 4R IT-Framework. The link to the Enterprise Template meta model is established via the meta model element of the enterprise templates that stands for the characterisation of the used methodology. The foundation for the methodology is the scientific theory for Integrated Enterprise Balancing as discussed in [FB05] together with the subsequently discussed derivations for business processes.

Faisst and Buhl have described a procedure for aggregating the return and risk figures of uncertain financial flows both from a product and a customer perspective on a portfolio basis [FB05]. This advancment is independent of a specific regulatory constraint or reporting obligation but turns up in many regulations in this field (e.g. KontraG). The result of these aggregations is illustrated by figure 6.4 on page 274: On the top level the portfolios for the products P and Q are shown with their attached return (RE) and risk figures (RI). The return figures are equal to the expected present values of the uncertain future financial flows and the risk figures evaluate the variations of this present value. The relations between the product portfolios and the overall portfolio of the enterprise are additionally described by

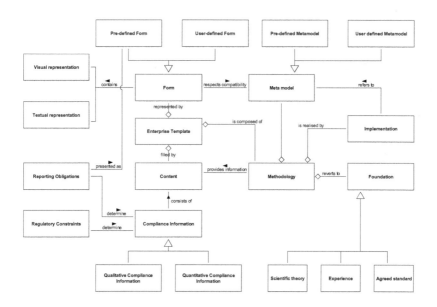

Figure 6.3: Enterprise Template Meta Model

their correlations (ρ). Thereby the dependencies between the different portfolios can be investigated. On the right hand side the portfolios for the customers of an enterprise are shown. For realising the multi-dimensional aggregation both the dimension of products and the dimension of customers are broken down to level of portfolios of single business transactions. As for the other portfolios also on this level the return and risk figures are estimated.

For deriving from this approach the necessary requirements for the organisation and business process configuration the portfolios of the single business transactions have been replaced by business processes. Thereby the transactions can be detailed to the level of single process elements as well as their organisational embedding. These replacements are illustrated by figure 6.5 on page 275. The same considerations as for the business transactions portfolios in regard to the estimation of return and risk values can now be applied to the business process level. For this purpose the concept of traditional business processes has to be extended as traditionally most approaches for describing business processes include considerations of the cost, time and sometimes the return of a process but not the assessment of risks.

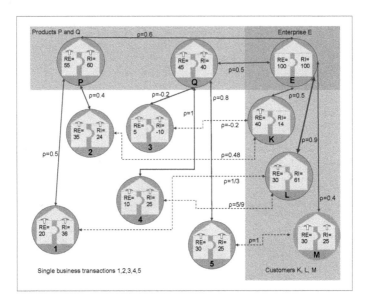

Figure 6.4: Multi-Dimensional Aggregation of Return and Risk Figures in a Multi-dimensional Tree Structure (Translated from [FB05])

To narrow the discussion of the domain conceptualisation to the very essential points for the basis of the application of semantic visualisation functionalities only the consideration of the integration of risk assessments will be taken up in the following. The Enterprise Method Integration (EMI) meta model that comes into play at this stage is based on the meta model for business graphs that has been described in section 4.2 on page 204. For integrating the assessment of risks in business processes it has been extended as follows[3]: As shown in figure 6.6 on page 276 the *activity* element is additionally associated to an *event* element. This event element is further specialised into a *positive* and a *negative* event. Events in this context influence the way an activity of a business process is accomplished. This concerns the factors that are relevant for the determination of the return of a business transaction: *time, cost* and *quality*. If a single business activity is not performed under the given time constraints a potential direct or indirect decrease of return may occur. The same is true for the factors of the estimated costs for an activity and its quality, i.e. if the expected output of an activity is not satisfying and

---

[3]These extensions are based on ideas in an internal best practice report by Schwab, M. (2006): A Framework to the Sarbanes Oxley Act of 2002, BOC Group, Ireland.

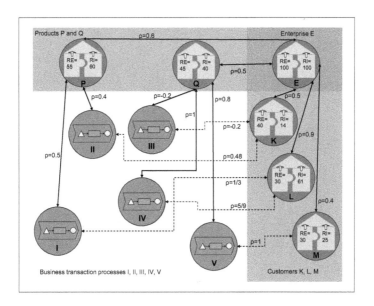

Figure 6.5: Replacement of Business Transactions by Business Processes

might have to be repeated in the worst case. These negative effects that may come up are denoted as *risks*. Although also positive effects can be integrated, e.g. for the case that a process activity is executed in less time than specified, these effects are not considered here.

On the basis of these conceptions the meta model can now be directly implemented on a meta modelling platform (e.g. such as Adonis or Meta Edit). Thereby a first level for an IT support of Integrated Enterprise Balancing can be realised. Figure 6.7 on page 277 shows how the EMI meta model elements are derived from the Adonis meta^2 model. Two model types (M) are defined for the element business process and working environment. Additionally several classes (C), relationclasses (R) and attributes (A) are defined. By this mapping the EMI meta model is adapted to the syntactical structure of a directed graph: The classes correspond to the nodes and the relationclasses to the edges whereby the associations both in the EMI metamodel and the Meta^2 model stand for the implied directions of the edges (e.g. by *IsFromClass*, *IsToClass*).

Up to now the IT support would however only work on an implementation level without the consideration of visual models or specific semantics of the meta models. Therefore the mapping between the meta model and a general seman-

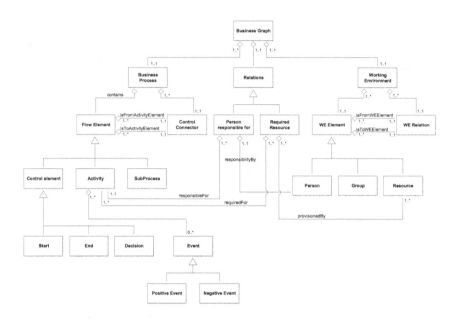

Figure 6.6: Extended Business Graph Meta Model

tic schema is established. This description will not only permit the exchange of the meta model information on a semantic level but also provide the necessary basic foundations for applying semantic visualisation. The traditional step to assign visual representations to the objects of the meta model – as it is necessary for example on the Adonis plattform [Fil04] – can then either be accomplished automatically or supported to a large extent by semantic visualisation functionalities. In figure 6.8 on page 278 the mapping between the domain conceptualisation, i.e. the meta model and an ontology is illustrated. Although this mapping could also be automated, e.g. by determining synonyms on the basis of the WordNet ontology[4] it will here be done manually for simplicity purposes. Furthermore, this mapping may involve specific assumptions that have not been made explicit so that a human user is required in any case.

The ontology that has been chosen for the mapping is the open source Business Management Ontology (BMO). This ontology is freely available for commercial and non-commercial applications. It is provided on the internet by the consulting

---

[4]See http://wordnet.princeton.edu/

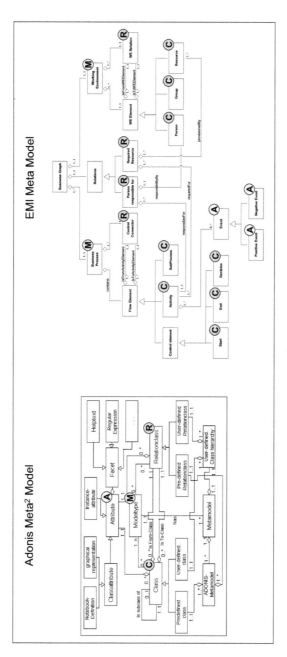

Figure 6.7: Derivation of the Meta Model Elements from the Adonis Meta^2 Model

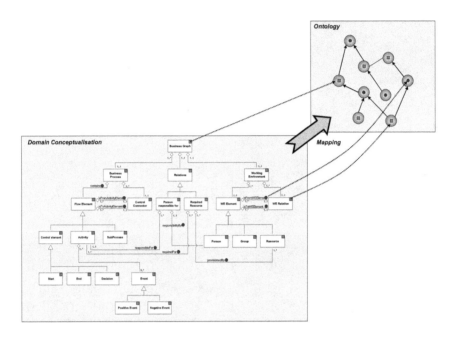

Figure 6.8: Mapping of the Domain Conceptualisation to an Ontology

firm Jenz&Partner in the web ontology language[5]. Other ontologies that could have been used for this purpose are the Enterprise Ontology maintained by the Artificial Intelligence Applications Institute at the University of Edinburgh[6] or the Obelix E-Business ontology developed in an EU project under the leadership of the Foundation for Scientific and Industrial Research at the Norwegian Institute of Technology [Gor02]. The assignment of the elements of the meta model to the open source business management ontology is done in the following way: For each meta model element it is attempted to find a semantically equivalent concept in the ontology (see figure 6.9 on the next page). Thereby the meta model can be described in terms of the general ontology.

On the basis of this semantic description of a domain conceptualisation the approach of Semantic Visualisation can now be applied in the following.

---

[5]See http://www.bpiresearch.com/Resources/RE_OSSOnt/re_ossont.htm accessed 13-06-2006.
[6]See http://www.aiai.ed.ac.uk/project/enterprise/ (accessed 23-02-2006).

IEB – EMI Meta Model	Ontology Classes BMO
Business Process	bpmcore:PrivateProcess
Control connector	bpmcore:PrivateProcessConnectableNode
Start	bpmcore:PrivateProcessStartEvent
End	bpmcore:ProcessEndEventTerminate
Decision	bpmcore:PrivateProcessGateway
SubProcess	bpmcore:PrivateProcessSubProcess
Activity	bpmcore:PrivateProcessTask
Positive Event	bpmcore:PrivateProcessIntermediateEvent
Negative Event	bpmcore:PrivateProcessIntermediateEventErrorTriggered
Resource	*- No direct equivalent found -*
Working Environment Relation	*- No direct equivalent found -*
Person	Org:Person
Group	Org:Workgroup
Required Resource	*- No direct equivalent found -*
Person responsible for	*- No direct equivalent found -*

Figure 6.9: Mapping of Concepts between the EMI Meta Model and the BMO Ontology

6.3 Application of Semantic Visualisation

For realising visualisations of the domain conceptualisations on the basis of Semantic Visualisation two fundamental assumptions are made here: The first assumption is that all visualisations and symbols shown in chapter 3 are available in the form of ontological visualisation patterns and the underlying visual objects. In detail this means that visual objects are for example available for the symbol for a strategic goal shown in figure 3.50 on page 122 as well as for an entity type as shown in figure 3.34 on page 91. Ontological visualisation patterns are further assumed to be existent as single object patterns (according to section 5.4 on page 255) for these visual objects and as multi-object patterns for the shown diagram types (e.g. an Ontological Visualisation Pattern for ER diagrams).

At this point the second assumption comes into place: It states that the semantic schema that the assumed Ontological Visualisation Patterns are related to is – as far as possible – the Business Management Ontology that has been discussed above and that the remaining items are grouped in the form of a taxonomy as a semantically weaker form of an ontology (see section 2.2 on page 27). This leads for example to the fact that the symbol for an entity type is now referenced by the concept *metadefs:EntityType* of the Business Management Ontology and the symbol of an event type as present in an EPC by *bpmcore:PrivateProcessProcessEvent*.

For some of the symbols and diagrams no equivalent may be found in the BMO. For these elements the taxonomy is used that contains the description of the element as given in the symbol tables in chapter 3 and a reference to the corresponding visual object.

Therefore the subsequently discussed methods can revert to the totality of this space of visual objects either by the reference to the BMO or to the separately defined taxonomy. The first way for linking visualisations to the domain conceptualisation of Integrated Enterprise Balancing will make use of the BMO as a domain ontology. The second will refer to the visual objects themselves and thereby extend the existing visualisations in regard to the exploitation of graphical attributes as discussed in section 4.3 on page 211.

Domain Schemata-Based

Based on the abovely elaborated domain conceptualisation and the previous assumptions the most obvious application of Semantic Visualisation is to use it for (semi-)automatic generation of visual modelling elements. The traditional approach for this generation would be to integrate visual elements directly in the meta model (as e.g. discussed in section 4.2 on page 201). The shortcoming of this proceeding is however that this integration could not be automated as no common machine understandable descriptions are assigned and that a change of a visual element would again require customisation or even progamming effort.

With the mapping of some of the elements of the domain conceptualisation to a general ontology this step can be machine supported in the following way (see figure 6.10 on the facing page): If one or more Ontological Visualisation Pattern can be found that reference the same concept as an element of the domain conceptualisation it can be proposed as a possible representation. For example for the *Start* element of the EMI metamodel that references *bpmcore:PrivateProcessStartEvent* the symbols of other modelling languages and visualisations may be retrieved: E.g. the start symbol of a flowchart, the initial node symbol of UML activity diagrams (figure 3.39 on page 100) or the start symbol of the BPMN (figure 3.61 on page 136).

In case that no pattern can be found by using the ontology either because the meta model element could not be referenced by the ontology or there exists no pattern that is referenced to the particular concept also the taxonomy of patterns can be consulted. Here, again two principle approaches can be identified: Either the search for an appropriate pattern is performed on the basis of a *syntactical* match or partial match. Or the search is conducted *semantically*, e.g. by the match of synonyms of the name of the meta model element and the taxonomy entry for the

Ontological Visualisation pattern (e.g. on the basis of the WordNet ontology). An example for such a syntactic match is as follows: The element *Required Resource* in the EMI meta model has e.g. not been found to be explained by the BMO. A syntactical search in the visualisations contained in the taxonomy then returns a symbol of the organisational models in Adonis named *has resource* (see figure 3.66 on page 142) due to the partial match of *resource*.

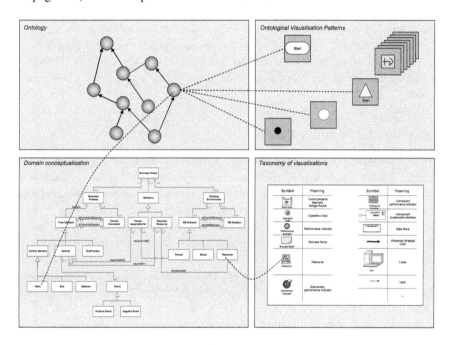

Figure 6.10: Mapping of the Domain Conceptualisation to Visualisations by Ontologies

To fully automate the assignment of visualisations to the elements of the domain conceptualisation three criteria have to be fulfilled: At first it is required that the semantic schema that is used as a reference is able to cover all elements of the conceptualisation. Otherwise no exact match of the visualisation and the domain conceptualisation can be established. Secondly, there has to be at least one visualisation for every element of the semantic schema. Although an alternative solution would be to define a default visualisation that is used in case no matching Ontological Visualisation Pattern can be found, this is regarded only as a second best solution. The third requirement is that the visual objects contained in an Ontological Visualisation Pattern are flexible enough to be used in different scenarios.

Although the assignment of the visualisations to a semantic schema already determines its basic properties (e.g. whether a visual object acts as a relation between objects can be specified by linking it to an object property of an ontology) it must be adaptable to different layout requirements and technical environments (e.g. for being properly displayed on a monochrome screen). Furthermore, the ontology must allow for the automatic determination of different user requirements so that the type of user and the task the visualisation is used for can be derived (similar to the approach by [Cas91] as discussed in section 4.3 on page 218).

However, this full automation may not be required for exploiting the advantages that are available with the introduction of Semantic Visualisation. Therefore another approach for the application of Semantic Visualisation is discussed subsequently.

Individual Schemata-Based

An alternative way for applying Semantic Visualisation is to develop an individual semantic schema for detailing the domain conceptualisation and then manually assign Ontological Visualisation Patterns to this schema. This means that it can be assured that every element of the conceptualisation can be referenced by a concept of the semantic schema and that there exists at least one Ontological Visualisation Pattern for every concept. The additional benefit of this approach is on the one hand that further domain conceptualisations that are built on the same semantic schema can reuse the visual elements and that this reuse is also semantically correct. Furthermore, the Ontological Visualisation Patterns can be adapted to new visualisation requirements independently of the domain conceptualisation but by maintaining the correct semantical reference to the elements of the conceptualisation. Figure 6.11 on the next page presents an excerpt of a sample ontology for the domain conceptualisation of Integrated Enterprise Balancing. In contrast to the meta model shown in figure 6.6 on page 276 that defines the syntactic structure of the elements the ontology details the semantics of the relations between the elements. With this information also semantical inferences can be performed. It can thus be derived that the actual work that is done in a business process also encompasses the making of phone calls or the computer interaction.

The aspect that the visualisation can be changed independently of the domain conceptualisation leads to the possibility of defining *transformations* of visualisations. These transformations are characterised by the fact that the semantic mapping between the visualisation and the domain conceptualisation is fully maintained but that the visualisation itself is altered. The main benefit that can be attained by this approach is the enabling of an adaptation of the visualisations to

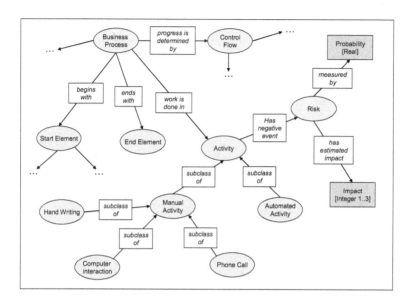

Figure 6.11: Excerpt of a Sample Ontology for the IEB Domain Conceptualisation

human diversity as discussed in the context of user interface design [Shn93]: Due to the possibility of providing different types of visualisations for a particular domain conceptualisation the individual requirements of a user or a group of users can be taken into account. This concerns all graphical attributes of a visualisation (as discussed in section 4.3 on page 211) and ranges from *physiological requirements*, e.g. for respecting disabilities such as colour blindness, *cultural aspects*, e.g. for using shapes that have a specific meaning in a particular group to *analysis aspects*, e.g. by encoding additional information by a visualisation.

In figure 6.12 on the following page the basic concept of the mapping between an individual ontology for the domain conceptualisation and different Ontological Visualisation Patterns is depicted. The assignment of the domain conceptualisation as well as the visualisation to an ontology is thereby only illustrative. The actual mapping would have to take into account all elements of either part. The first Ontological Visualisation Pattern on the right hand side (A) is a multi-object pattern containing a range of visual objects. For the following explanations the first four visual objects are used. The pattern presents a simplified version of the Adonis notation for business processes that is assumed to be adapted to the specific needs of the domain conceptualisation for Integrated Enterprise Balancing and a corresponding ontology. The second pattern (B) is a slightly modified version of the first pattern. The third visual object has been extended in the way that an exposed variable of the object is used to influence its colour shading. In the third pattern (C) the third visual object also contains an exposed variable. This is used to change the representation to three pre-defined images.

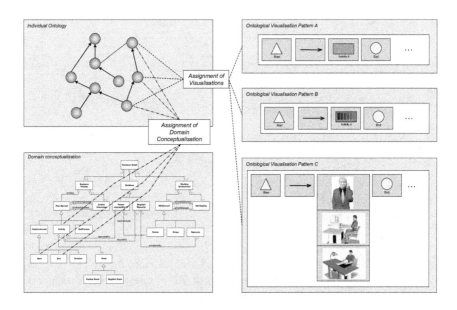

Figure 6.12: Semantic Visualisation Based on an Individual Ontology

Due to the separation of the visualisation from the domain conceptualisation the change in the representation of a concrete instance of the domain conceptualisation can be performed at any time: Therefore at the design time of an instance, e.g. a concrete model that is derived from the meta model as the domain concept, a different type of visualisation may be used then for example during the analysis stage of the model. An important factor to allow for such a degree of freedom is the integration of appropriate layout services into the Ontological Visualisation Patterns (as described in section 5.4 on page 262) which is not explicitly treated here. This is required due to the different sizes and relationship behaviours of the visual objects: The layout service has to ensure that both the mental map of the user who uses the visualisation as well as the optimal graphical representation are satisfied.

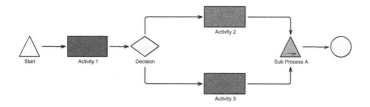

Figure 6.13: Application of the B-Pattern

In figure 6.13 an example for the application of the second pattern is shown. The variable that is responsible for the colour shading (from black to light red) is thereby connected to the data type *Probability* of the ontology in figure 6.11 on page 283 which is in turn connected to the *negative event* element of the EMI meta model that has been set as an attribute of the *activity* class by derivation from the meta^2 model (figure 6.7 on page 277). These details are illustrated in figure 6.14 on the next page that contains excerpts of the EMI meta model, the Adonis meta^2 model, the Ontological Visualisation Pattern and the individual ontology. The purpose of this pattern can therefore be seen in the encoding of the probability of a negative event of a process activity. The different shadings thereby indicate the value of the probability estimate. The encoding via the colour attribute is possible due to the fact that the differentiation between the symbols in this pattern is primarily based on the shape attribute. Another way of encoding additional information in this type of processes by using the size attribute is discussed in [Fil06a].

Another way for the exploitation of graphical attributes is to use specific textures. As shown by the C-pattern and in figure 6.15 on the following page these textures can also be images or even animations. When using images as shown in figure 6.15 it is necessary to design the visual objects in close relation to the domain conceptualisation. Based on the ontology shown above the three images can be directly related to the concepts *Phone call*, *Computer interaction* and *Hand writing*. As the conceptualisation of the EMI meta model does not contain an explicit detailing of the activity element this type of pattern is however not directly applicable.

Apart from the addition of an according attribute to the conceptualisation also two other possibilities are available: The choice of the image could either be handled only by the user interface, e.g. for the purpose of a visual demonstration that does not need to be related explicitly to the domain conceptualisation, or the selection of the image could be derived from other attributes (e.g. the name of the activity) or the particular embedding in relation to other objects (e.g. when

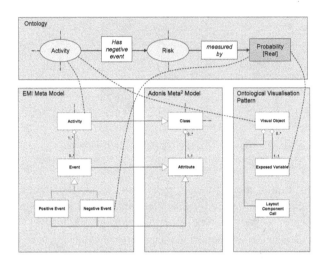

Figure 6.14: Excerpt of the Mappings for the B-Pattern

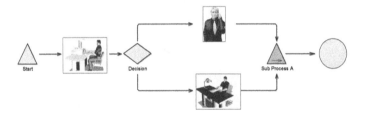

Figure 6.15: Theoretical Application of the C-Pattern

a person and a phone resource are assigned to an activity the corresponding image could be shown). These features have to be separately conceived and require – similar to the additional constraint specifications for meta models – additional mechanisms. In the meta modelling specifications such constraints are expressed in distinct languages (e.g. the OCL specification [OMG02, OMG03] for MOF or AdoScript [KK02] for the Adonis plattform). Based on these augmented domain conceptualisations the application of Ontological Visualisation Patterns can then be realised by extending the mapping between the semantic schema and the domain conceptualisation to constraint checked elements: The mapping then for example reverts to the constraint expression of "activity elements that directly follow a decision element".

6.4 Evaluation

When reviewing the abovely described application scenario the following insights can be gained: Although generally referencable semantic schemata and ontologies in particular are estimated to be more and more widespread with the forthcoming of the Semantic Web, the consistent provision of these references can so far not be guaranteed. Therefore the use of individual schemata that are either created for a specific domain conceptualisation or derived from generally available schemata currently seems to be more effective.

However, the recently upcoming cooperative approaches which are subsumed under the catch word *folksonomy* could provide an alternative solution. Folksonomy is made up of the word *folk* and *taxonomy* and characterises the joint, web based creation of common taxonomies. The free online encyclopedia Wikipedia is a well known example for such an approach. Also a currently introduced service by Google makes use of such an approach for creating arbitrary, freely accessible individual information profiles[7].

To evaluate at which stages service oriented aspects can be realised in the application scenario figure 6.16 on the next page takes up the service oriented architecture for visualisations discussed in section 4.3 on page 218. On the bottom level a database, an enterprise information system and a web service are shown that deliver data for a component that handles the domain conceptualisations. In the case of a meta model based approach this component would be a meta modelling plattform that hosts the meta models and the corresponding instances and is able to assign data to the models from the enterprise information system or external web services. The information (e.g. the meta models and model instances) of this component can be accessed via web services shown on the subsequent layer. The same applies to two components that are responsible for hosting the visual objects. These are also stored in a database and exposed via visualisation web services. On the composition layer the assembly of the Ontological Visualisation Pattern takes place as well as their relation to the domain conceptualisations and its instances. The choreography layer concerns the observable interactions of the visualisations with their users. Therefore a particular visualisation has to be selected by the user. This is then displayed on the user interface.

---

[7]See https://www.google.de/base

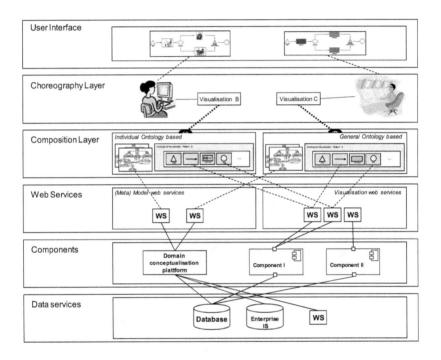

Figure 6.16: Detailed View on the Service-Oriented Generation of Visualisations

It has to be noted that the architecture shown here does not take into account the interaction of a user with the visualisation. This would be required if the user is authorised to change for example an instance of the domain conceptualisation. Therefore the relations between the different layers have to be regarded as being asymmetric.

6.5 Benefit of Semantic Visualisation

The separation of the visual representations from the domain model and the semantic linkage require in any case additional effort. Therefore, the question has to be posed which benefits arise from this undertaking.

Apart from the benefit of being able to describe a visualisation semantically and allow for a *semantic-based search* for appropriate visualisations the presented approach is particularly valuable for the purpose of *analyses*. Through the provision of different types of visual objects for one semantic concept the models of a domain can be displayed in different notations. As has been shown above thereby for example a visualisation that is specifically focused on the analysis of attribute values can be applied without having to modify the domain model. In the case of the traditional approaches where the visualisation is tightly coupled to the domain model specialised knowledge would be required to change the representation. The loose syntactic coupling of the visualisation together with the semantic assignment is able to abstract from this specialised knowledge in the way that the user who wishes to apply another visualisation does not have to possess knowledge about the concrete implementation of the visualisation. Instead she can work on the pragmatic level whereby the information system implementing Semantic Visualisation provides the applicable, semantically correct visual representations.

7 Prototypical Implementation

For showing how the previously elaborated theoretical considerations can be practically realised a prototypical implementation is discussed in the following. Included in this discussion is an overview of the relevant technical frameworks that can be consulted for the implementation of visualisation procedures.

7.1 Technical Frameworks and Standards

The related technical frameworks and standards that can be used for the creation of visualisations have been classified into three categories:

- Application Programming Interfaces (APIs)
- Open standards
- Specialised software

In this classification *Application Programming Interfaces* comprise all software components that can be used for creating graphical representations on computer hardware. This can be both open source as well as commercial components. Typically, these components have to be permanently linked to the actual implementation. Although the advent of web services would allow to realise the loose coupling of implementations to programming functionalities so far no generally available web services can be found that offer the functionality required for implementing graphical representations in the same way as traditional APIs. An approach that is directed towards such functionality is the remote rendering service of OpenInventor - which is however not freely accessible but restricted to OpenInventor based applications[1]. The elaborations on service oriented visualisation architectures in the previous chapters of this work therefore also mark an important advancement in this respect.

Existing APIs that can be used for the creation of graphics on computer hardware are either contained in the development kits of the programming languages themselves – as e.g. the Java Graphics2D[2] package or the graphics device inter-

---

[1] See http://www.tgs.com/pro_div/oiv_highli_features.htm (last accessed 20-06-2006).
[2] See http://java.sun.com/j2se/1.5.0/docs/api/ (accessed 20-06-2006).

face[3] in Windows and more recently DirectX[4] – or available as additional libraries such as the Java3D API[5], the OpenGL library[6], the Batik Toolkit[7] or OpenInventor[8].

In figure 7.1 a classification for the different types of APIs is presented. The *plattform dependency* expresses whether a particular API is plattform independent such as the Java Graphics2D API, Java 3D or Batik, available for multiple plattforms as e.g. the OpenGL API or bound to a specific operating system as the GDI and DirectX. The *access* dimension states whether the API is freely available under an open source licencse (e.g. the Java APIs, Batik and OpenGL) or a commercial product (as GDI, DirectX, and OpenInventor). The *supported dimensionality* distinguishes between APIs that only support 2D representations (e.g. Java2D and GDI), three dimensional representations (e.g. Java3D and OpenInventor) and animations (4D). The support of animations is however mostly not explicitly defined but is left to the application using the API by changing the parameters of the graphical representation. By *programming language dependency* it is defined whether an API can only be used in relation with a specific language (as e.g. the Java2D API for Java and GDI for C/C++) or independently of a language (as e.g. the OpenGL core commands).

Plattform Dependency	Plattform Independent	Available for multiple plattforms		Plattform Bound
Access	Open Source		Commercial	
Supported Dimensionality	2D	3D		Animation (4D)
Programming Language Dependency	Language Independent		Language Dependent	

Figure 7.1: Classification of APIs

---

[3] "The graphics device interface (GDI) enables applications to use graphics and formatted text on both the video display and the printer. Windows-based applications do not access the graphics hardware directly. Instead, GDI interacts with device drivers on behalf of applications." (Source http://msdn.microsoft.com, accessed 20-06-2006)

[4] "Microsoft DirectX is an advanced suite of multimedia application programming interfaces (APIs) built into Microsoft Windows operating systems." (Source http://msdn.microsoft.com, accessed 20-06-2006)

[5] See http://java.sun.com/products/java-media/3D/reference/api/index.html (accessed 20-06-2006).

[6] See http://www.opengl.org/ (accessed 20-06-2006).

[7] See http://xmlgraphics.apache.org/batik/ (accessed 20-06-2006)

[8] See http://www.tgs.com/ (accessed 20-06-2006).

Besides the APIs also *standardised data formats* are available to define graphical representations independent of a specific implementation. It can be differentiated between *open accessible* and *proprietary* standards. For the realisation of visualisation services in particular the open accessible standards are relevant to enable the interoperability between different systems. The most often mentioned open standard for defining graphical representations is the XML based *Scalable Vector Graphics (SVG)* standard [FFJ03]. Besides the definition of graphics based on a number of primitives and drawing styles this standard also allows for the integration of a scripting language. Thereby the interaction of a user with the graphics as well as the manipulation of the graphics can be performed at run time. In contrast to SVG that only permits to define two dimensional representations the open *X3D* standard provides an XML vocabulary for defining three dimensional graphics. Further standards that can be mentioned in this context are the upcoming open standards for defining user interfaces as discussed in section 3.2 on page 106.

The third category that is relevant for the implementation of visualisations is *specialised software* that is explicitly directed towards visualisation applications. This includes the large number of tools for defining visual languages (e.g. DiaGen [MV95], VL-Eli [SK03]) as well as toolkits for creating information visualisations (e.g. the InfoVis Toolkit [Fek04]) and graph representations (e.g. the open JGraph toolkit[9]).

For the specific needs of the theory for visualisations that has been developed in this work no appropriate standard nor a specialised software application could be found. Although the SVG standard could be partly used as a basis for the generation of visual objects it would have required very profound knowledge of the elements of the standard by the user (e.g. to integrate variables into the SVG source code and link them to the graphical primitives). The same applies to the different approaches for specifying visual languages that are either restricted to specific patterns that have to be used as e.g. in [SK03] or demand from the user to generate different types of source code for the specification (e.g. [MV95]). Therefore the decision has been made to implement a prototypical application that is both easy to handle by users who are not familiar with programming but still provides all required functionalities.

7.2 An Editor for Visual Objects

In the following an editor for the creation of visual objects is described that has been implemented in the Java programming language (excerpts of the source code

---

[9]See http://www.jgraph.com/ (last accessed 19-06-2006).

are shown in the appendix). It makes use of the Java Graphics2D functionalities as well as of the Java Swing [LEW02] extensions for creating the user interface. The aim for the implementation of the editor was to abstract from the underlying technical specification to the highest degree possible but maintain at the same time the technical functionality.

The structure of the editor is very closely related to the elaborations in chapter 5. Therefore a hierarchy of graphical primitives is implemented that is entirely based on the *point* as the very basic primitive. The advantage of this approach compared to other approaches that use points and spatial measures for defining primitives is the uniform access to all primitive definitions as well as the direct relationship to the interaction with the user: When creating a primitive on a computer screen the typical input device which is used today is a mouse. As a mouse only delivers coordinate values in the form of points on the screen it seems a natural approach to use these values directly for specifying the primitives. The user can thereby and with no additional effort determine if for example a primitive is exactly aligned to another primitive without having to perform calculations (e.g. by adding or sub-tracting the spatial values from the coordinate values).

In figure 7.2 a class diagram is shown that represents an abstract primitive class which contains common basic functionality for all primitives and seven types of primitives that are derived from this class. In contrast to the specifications in chapter 5 the style of the primitives is not determined by separate primitives (e.g. for a filled and a non-filled rectangle) but influenced by a specific *Render Modifier*.

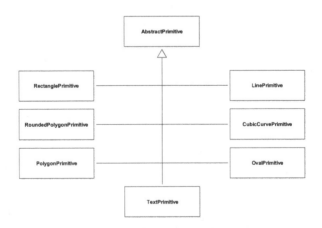

Figure 7.2: Class Hierarchy of AbstractPrimitive

The screenshot of the visual object editor in figure 7.3 gives an overview of the user interface: On the left hand side a tree component shows the variables and primitives defined for the current visual object and on the right hand side the drawing area is depicted. Below the tree component are several buttons for influencing the tree of primitives and variables and on top of the tree component the type of primitive to be drawn can be selected from a list. Besides the menu a checkbox is shown to toggle between drawing and edit mode.

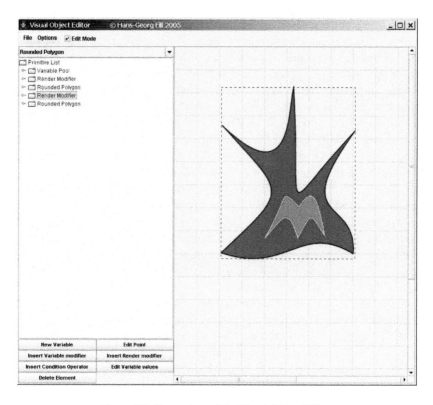

Figure 7.3: Screenshot of the Visual Object Editor

When the drawing mode is enabled the user can choose from the list of primitives and create them by simple mouse interaction on the drawing pane. After switching to the edit mode the drawn primitives can be selected and the points defining the primitives can be changed. Correspondingly the tree component lists the hierarchy of primitives drawn so far. The bottom primitive in the list thereby stands for the last primitive drawn. In the first picture in figure 7.4 on the next page the primitive list is shown in more detail. The first element in the list is the *Variable Pool* that contains all variables defined for a visual object. For every visual object the variables for the size, position and the hull of the object are integrated by default.

When a primitive is selected a dialogue for editing its points can be invoked by pressing the corresponding button. This dialogue is shown in the second picture of figure 7.4 on the facing page. It allows to exactly specify the point values by entering them in the textfield as well as to link variables to the point coordinates. As defined by the concepts in chapter 5 the variables may contain multiple values. Therefore not only the variable but also the intended index has to be selected. The editing of variables is performed in a separate dialgue that is shown in the third picture. Depending on the type of the variable (integer, string or float) either a value or an expression can be entered. The evaluation of the expressions has been realised by reverting to the Beanshell API[10]. This permits to use arbitrary Java code in the expressions, e.g. for performing mathematical calculations. Before the expression is evaluated the contained variables are replaced by their current values so that they can be integrated in the expressions as well.

In figure 7.5 on page 298 the first picture shows a render modifier dialogue. Render modifiers can be inserted at every stage of the primtive list to influence the style and fill of the primitives. They include functionalities for defining the line and the fill colour of primitives, the antialiasing, the transparency and the line width. The second picture depicts a variable modifier. This element can also be inserted in the primtive list and changes a value of a variable. If necessary the change can be defined to be based on the old value and/or an expression. The third picture shows a condition operator dialgue. Condition operators determine the control flow in the visual object and may be of the types *WHILE_TYPE*, *IF_TYPE* or *ARRAY_LOOP_TYPE*. The first two types correspond to If-clauses and While-loops as in standard programming languages, the last type is used to iterate over a number of values of a variable. To determine the indices of the values a second variable then has to be specified as the index variable.

After a visual object has been designed a *compile* function can be invoked from the menu. The specifications of the visual object are then translated into Java source code and automatically compiled with the Java compiler. The resulting component is created as a Java Swing component and implements a common interface for accessing the variables values. Thereby it can be directly integrated in any type of user interface or further processed.

---

[10]See http://www.beanshell.org/ (last accessed 20-06-2006).

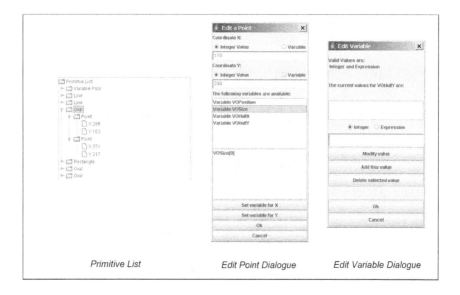

Primitive List   Edit Point Dialogue   Edit Variable Dialogue

Figure 7.4: Screenshots of the Primitive List, the Edit Point Dialogue and the Edit Variable Dialogue

To realise a webservice offering the functionalities and representations of the visual object the Swing component can be immediately exposed. To link the visual object to a semantic schema it can then also be reverted to the Java component or a corresponding serialisation, e.g. in XML.

7.3 Further Extensions

To further extend the shown prototypical implementation functionalities for the *scaling*, *rotation*, and *grouping* could also be integrated. Thereby additional possibilities for the manipulation and structure of visual objects could be added.

In a similar way as shown here for the two dimensional case the concept could also be directly applied to three dimensional representations. However, the construction of three dimensional objects not only requires a highly developed spatial sense of the designer but also becomes more complex due to the additional amount of data that has to be specified.

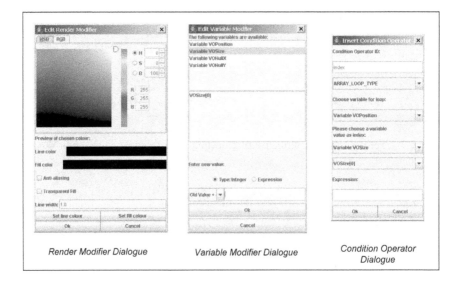

Render Modifier Dialogue   *Variable Modifier Dialogue*   *Condition Operator*
                                                                        Dialogue

Figure 7.5: Screenshots of the Edit Render Modifier Dialogue, the Edit Variable Modifier and the Inser Condition Operator Dialogue

8 Summary and Outlook

In this work it has been investigated which types of visualisations are currently used in the area of business informatics. Therefore the three sub-fields of business, computer science, and business informatics have been structured according to a framework based approach. Within this structure a search for visualisations has been conducted and the basic elements and symbols of these visualisations have been described.

Upon this survey the generation and the content of the visualisations has been analysed. Therefore it has been reverted to the concepts of general model theory and in particular the fields of visual language theory and meta modelling. As a result of this analysis derivations for possible extensions of the visualisations themselves as well as the process of their creation have been formulated.

The framework for visualisation in IT based management has subsequently been presented as an approach to unite different aspects of visualisations. Besides the technical generation of visualisations this framework also encompasses the organisational embedding of the visualisation procedure. Furthermore, the concept of Semantic Visualisation has been developed that allows for the semantic definition of visualisations on the basis of a semantic schema.

To show the practical applicability a concrete application scenario for Semantic Visualisation has then been outlined. For this purpose a domain model in the area of enterprise risk management and its semantic description via an ontology have been derived. On this basis the assignment of visualisations to the domain model have been shown by relating the visualisations to the ontology. With this scenario it could be shown that the effort for defining visualisations semantically provides advantages in regard to the use of visualisations for analysis purposes.

Finally, a prototypical implementation has been presented that allows for an intuitive design of visual objects and the inclusion of variable statements.

With this research it could be shown how the semantic description of visualisations can be achieved and what impact such a description can have in a concrete application setting. Other applications of the approach would include the semantic animation of visualisations by applying a fourth dimension to the visual objects and Ontological Visualisation Patterns as well as the extension to the three dimensional space.

Despite the successful implementation which could proof the general working of the concept several open questions remain. This includes in particular the further research that is required concerning the role of semantics. This is regarded as just being at the beginning. The vision of a Semantic Web will still need a lot of effort to be put into practice and so will the concept of Semantic Visualisation that largely depends on insights from this field. However, at this stage of research the convergence of manual and (semi-)automatic approaches for the generation of visualisations is clearly visible and is estimated to be continued in the future.

Bibliography

[AAB⁺03]   J. Aliprand, J. Allen, J. Becker, M. Davis, M. Everson, A. Freytag, J. Jenkins, M. Ksar, R. McGowan, E. Muller, L. Moore, M. Suignard, and K. Whistler, editors. *The Unicode Standard - Version 4.0.* Addison-Wesley, Boston et al., 2003. http://www.unicode.org/versions/Unicode4.0.0/ accessed 02-01-2006.

[AAW99]   J. Arnott, N. Alm, and A. Waller. Cognitive prostheses: communication, rehabilitation and beyond. In *IEEE International Conference on Systems, Man, and Cybernetics*, volume 6, pages 346–351. IEEE Press, 1999.

[ACN05]   ACNielsen. The Nutrition-Conscious Global Shopper - Consumer Attitudes Towards Nutritional Labels on Food Packaging in Europe - August 2005, 2005.

[AK00]   G. Armstrong and P. Kotler. *Marketing: An Introduction.* Prentice-Hall International (UK) Limited, London, 2000.

[AL04]   J. Angele and G. Lausen. Ontologies in F-logic. In S. Staab and R. Studer, editors, *Handbook on Ontologies*, pages 29–50. Springer, Berlin et al., 2004.

[Alt96]   G. Altrogge. *Netzplantechnik.* Oldenbourg, München, Wien, 3rd edition edition, 1996.

[Ama71]   S. Amarel. Computer science: a conceptual framework for curriculum planning. *Communications of the ACM*, 14(6):391–401, 1971.

[ARR⁺97]   B. Andalman, K. Ryall, W. Ruml, J. Marks, and S. Shieber. Design Gallery Browsers based on 2D and 3D Graph Drawing (Demo). In G. DiBattista, editor, *Graph Drawing*, pages 322–329. Springer, Rome, 1997.

[BA97]   P. Borst and H. Akkermans. Engineering ontologies. *International Journal of Human-Computer Studies*, 46:365–406, 1997.

[Bac69]   C. W. Bachman. Data structure diagrams. *ACM SIGMIS Database*,
            1(2):4–10, 1969.

[Bal98]   H. Balzert. *Lehrbuch der Software-Technik: Software Management,
            Software-Qualitätssicherung, Unternehmensmodellierung*. Spek-
            trum Akad. Verlag, Heidelberg, 1998.

[BCLT96a]   J. E. Baker, I. F. Cruz, G. Liotta, and R. Tamassia. Algorithm an-
            imation over the World Wide Web. In T. Catarci, M. F. Costabile,
            S. Levialdi, and G. Santucci, editors, *Proceedings of the workshop
            on Advanced visual interfaces*, pages 203–212, Gubbio, Italy, 1996.
            ACM Press.

[BCLT96b]   J. E. Baker, I. F. Cruz, G. Liotta, and R. Tamassia. The Mocha algo-
            rithm animation system. In T. Catarci, M. F. Costabile, S. Levialdi,
            and G. Santucci, editors, *Proceedings of the workshop on Advanced
            visual interfaces*, pages 248–250, Gubbio, Italy, 1996. ACM Press.

[BDK04]   J. Becker, P. Delfmann, and R. Knackstedt. Konstruktion
            von Referenzmodellierungssprachen - Ein Ordnungsrahmen zur
            Spezifikation von Adaptionsmechanismen für Informationsmodelle.
            Wirtschaftsinformatik, 46(4):251–264, 2004.

[BdWH+03]   I. Burnett, R. Van de Walle, K. Hill, J. Bormans, and F. Pereira.
            MPEG-21: Goals and Achievements. *IEEE Multimedia*, 10(4):60–
            70, 2003.

[BEF+00]   L. Breslau, D. Estrin, K. Fall, S. Floyd, J. Heidemann, A. Helmy,
            P. Huang, S. McCanne, K. Varadhan, Y. Xu, and H. Yu. Advances
            in Network Simulation. *IEEE Computer*, (May 2000):59–67, 2000.

[BEH+02]   U. Brandes, M. Eiglsperger, I. Herman, M. Himsolt, and M. S. Mar-
            shall. GraphML Progress Report: Structural Layer Proposal. In
            *Procceddings of the 9th International Symposium on Graph Drawing
            (GD '01)*, volume LNCS 2265, pages 501–512. Springer, 2002.

[Ber82]   J. Bertin. *Graphische Darstellungen und die graphische Weiterver-
            arbeitung der Information*. De Gruyter, Berlin, New York, 1982.

[Ber95]   J. Bernard, editor. *Bildsprache, Visualisierung, Diagrammatik : Ak-
            ten zweier internationaler Symposien Wien 1991 & 1993*, volume 19
            of *Semiotische Berichte*. 1995.

[BETT99]   G. Battista, P. Eades, R. Tamassia, and I. G. Tollis. *Graph Drawing - Algorithms for the visualization of graphs.* Prentice Hall, London, 1999.

[BFM02]   C. Bussler, D. Fensel, and A. Maedche. A Conceptual Architecture for Semantic Web Enabled Web Services. *SIGMOD Record,* 31(4):24–29, 2002.

[BG04]   P. Bottoni and A. Grau. A Suite of Metamodels as a Basis for a Classification of Visual Languages. In *IEEE Symposium on Visual Languages and Human Centric Computing (VLHCC'04)*, page 8p., Rome, Italy, 2004. IEEE.

[BGJ⁺05]   D. Bulterman, G. Grassel, J. Jansen, A. Koivisto, N. Layaïda, T. Michel, S. Mullender, and D. Zucker. Synchronized Multimedia Integration Language (SMIL 2.1) - W3C Recommendation 13 December 2005. Technical report, W3C, 2005. http://www.w3.org/TR/2005/REC-SMIL2-20051213/ accessed 23-12-2005.

[BHS04]   F. Baader, I. Horrocks, and U. Sattler. Description Logics. In S. Staab and R. Studer, editors, *Handbook on Ontologies.* Springer, Berlin - Heidelberg, 2004.

[BJ66]   C. Böhm and G. Jacopini. Flow diagrams, turing machines and languages with only two formation rules. *Communications of the ACM,* 9(5):366–371, 1966.

[BK05]   J. Bajnai and D. Karagiannis. Platform Independent Instruction Design - The Tool ADVISOR. In M. Auer, U. Auer, and R. Mittermeir, editors, *Interactive Computer aided Learning ICL 2005*, Villach, Austria, 2005. Kassel University Press.

[BKM01]   P. Bertolazzi, C. Krusich, and M. Missikoff. An Approach to the Definition of a Core Enterprise Ontology: CEO. In *International Workshop on Open Enterprise Solutions: Systems, Experiences, and Organizations*, Rome, Italy, 2001. http://cersi.luiss.it/oesseo2001/papers/9.pdf access 23-09-2006.

[BKM04]   F. Bayer, D. Karagiannis, and C. Moser. ITIL: Modellgestützte Umsetzung mit ADOit. In F. Victor and H. Günther, editors, *Optimiertes IT-Management mit ITIL.* Vieweg, 2004.

[BLFM05]   T. Berners-Lee, R. Fielding, and L. Masinter. Uniform Resource Identifier (URI): Generic Syntax. Technical Report Request for Comments 3986, The Internet Society - Network Working Group, 2005. http://www.gbiv.com/protocols/uri/rfc/rfc3986.html accessed 03-01-2006.

[BLHL01]   T. Berners-Lee, J. Hendler, and O. Lassila. The Semantic Web - A new form of Web content that is meaningful to computers will unleash a revolution of new possibilities. *Scientific American*, May 2001, 2001.

[BM04a]   D. Beckett and B. McBride. RDF/XML Syntax Specification (Revised) - W3C Recommendation 10 February 2004. Technical report, W3C, 02-10-2004 2004. http://www.w3.org/TR/ rdf-syntax-grammar/ accessed 02-01-2006.

[BM04b]   A. Borgida and J. Mylopoulos. Data Semantics Revisited. In *Proc. of 2nd Int. Workshop on Semantic Web and Databases (SWDB 2004)*, pages 9–26. Springer, 2004.

[BN93]   M. H. Brown and M. A. Najork. Algorithm animation using 3D interactive graphs. In *Proceedings of the 6th annual ACM symposium on User interface software and technology*, pages 93–100, Atlanta, Georgia, United States, 1993. ACM Press.

[Bon99]   P. Bonnici. *Visual language - the hidden medium of communication*. Rotovision, Crans-Près-Céligny, 1999.

[BPM04]   Business Process Management Initiative BPMI. Business Process Modeling Notation - Specification Version 1.0. Technical report, 2004. http://www.bpmn.org/Documents/BPMN%20V1-0% 20May%203%202004.pdf.

[BPSM⁺04]   T. Bray, J. Paoli, C. M. Sperberg-McQueen, E. Maler, and F. Yergeau. Extensible Markup Language (XML) 1.0 (Third Edition) - W3C Recommendation 04 February 2004. Technical report, W3C, 2004. http://www.w3.org/TR/2004/REC-xml-20040204/ accessed 29-12-2005.

[BRB03]   J. Bovey, P. Rodgers, and F. Benoy. Movement as an Aid to Understanding Graphs. In *Seventh International Conference on Information Visualization (IV03)*, pages 472–478. IEEE, 2003.

[Bri04]   D. Brickley. RDF Vocabulary Description Language 1.0: RDF Schema. Technical report, W3C, 2004. http://www.w3.org/TR/rdf-schema/ (accessed 18-05-2005).

[Bro91]   M. H. Brown. Zeus: a system for algorithm animation and multi-view editing. In *Proceedings of the IEEE Workshop on Visual Languages, 1991*, pages 4–9, Kobe, Japan, 1991. IEEE.

[BRS95]   J. Becker, M. Roseman, and R. Schütte. Grundsätze ordnungsmäßiger Modellierung. *Wirtschaftsinformatik*, 37:435–445, 1995.

[Bry96]   S. Bryson. Virtual Reality in Scientific Visualization. *Communications of the ACM*, 39(5):62–71, 1996.

[BS84]   M. H. Brown and R. Sedgewick. A system for algorithm animation. *ACM SIGGRAPH Computer Graphics*, 18(3):177–186, 1984.

[Bur04a]   R. A. Burkhard. Learning from Architects: The Difference between Knowledge Visualization and Information Visualization. In *Draft for 8th International Conference on Information Visualization (IV04)*, London, 2004.

[Bur04b]   R. A. Burkhard. Visual Knowledge Transfer between Planners and Business Decision Makers - A Framework for Knowledge Visualization. In J. P. Van Leeuwen and H. J. P. Timmermans, editors, *Developments in Design & Decision Support Systems in Architecture and Urban Planning*, pages 193–208. Eindhoven University of Technology, Eindhoven, 2004.

[BVNT01]   R. Briggs, G. De Vreede, J. J. Nunamaker, and D. Tobey. ThinkLets: Achieving Predictable, Repeatable Patterns of Group Interaction with Group Support Systems (GSS). In *34th Annual Hawaii International Conference on System Sciences (HICSS-34)*, volume 1, page pp. 1057, 2001.

[BW00]   B. Braune and R. Wilhelm. Focusing in Algorithm Explanation. *IEEE Transactions on Visualization and Computer Graphics*, 6(1), 2000.

[Cam03]   O. Campesato. *Fundamentals of Svg Programming: Concepts to Source Code*. Charles River Media, 2003.

[Cas91]   S. M. Casner. Task-analytic approach to the automated design of
             graphic presentations. *ACM Transactions on Graphics*, 10(2):111 –
             151, 1991.

[CB01]   R. Chawla and A. Banerjee. A virtual environment for simulating
             manufacturing operations in 3D. In B. A. Peters, J. S. Smith, D. J.
             Medeiros, and M. W. Rohrer, editors, *Winter Simulation Conference*,
             2001.

[CCMW01]   E. Christensen, F. Curbera, G. Meredith, and S. Weerawarana. Web
             Services Description Language (WSDL) 1.1 - W3C Note 15 March
             2001. Technical report, W3C, 2001. http://www.w3.org/TR/2001/
             NOTE-wsdl-20010315 accessed 29-12-2005.

[CDOP02]   G. Costagliola, A. Delucia, S. Orefice, and G. Polese. A Classifica-
             tion Framework to Support the Design of Visual Languages. *Journal
             of Visual Languages and Computing*, 13:573–600, 2002.

[CE03]   K. Casey and C. Exton. A Java 3D implementation of a geon
             based visualisation tool for UML. In *Proceedings of the 2nd in-
             ternational conference on Principles and practice of programming
             in Java*, pages 63–65. Computer Science Press, Inc., Kilkenny City,
             Ireland, 2003.

[CEKR02]   A. Corradini, H. Ehrig, H.-J. Kreowski, and G. Rozenberg. *Proceed-
             ings of the First International Conference on Graph Transformation*.
             Springer, Barcelona, Spain, 2002.

[CG04]   P. Chamoni and P. Gluchowski. Integrationstrends bei Business-
             Intelligence-Systemen - Empirische Untersuchung auf Basis des
             Business Intelligence Maturity Model. *Wirtschaftsinformatik*,
             46(2):119–128, 2004.

[Che76]   P. P.-S. Chen. The Entity-Relationship Model-Toward a Unified
             View of Data. *ACM Transactions on Database Systems*, 1(1):9–36,
             1976.

[Che99]   C. Chen. *Information Visualisation and Virtual Environments*.
             Springer, London - Berlin - Heidelberg - New York, 1999.

[Chi00]   E. H. Chi. A taxonomy of visualization techniques using the data
             state reference model. In *IEEE Symposium on Information Visual-
             ization*, pages 69–75. IEEE, 2000.

[CHRR04]   L. Clement, A. Hately, C. Von Riegen, and T. Rogers. UDDI Version 3.0.2 - UDDI Spec Technical Committee Draft, Dated 20041019. Technical report, OASIS, 19-10-2004 2004. http://uddi.org/pubs/ uddi-v3.0.2-20041019.htm accessed 29-12-2005.

[Cla99]   J. Clark. Associating Style Sheets with XML documents Version 1.0. Technical report, W3C, 1999. http://www.w3.org/TR/ xml-stylesheet/ (accessed 20-11-2005).

[CM98]   S. S. Chok and K. Marriot. Automatic construction of intelligent diagram editors. In *Proceedings of the 11th annual ACM symposium on User interface software and technology*, pages 185–194. ACM Press, 1998.

[CM01]   A. Cockburn and B. McKenzie. 3D or not 3D?: evaluating the effect of the third dimension in a document management system. *Proceedings of the SIGCHI conference on Human factors in computing systems*, pages 434–441, 2001.

[CMS99]   S. K. Card, J. D. Mackinlay, and B. Shneiderman. *Readings in Information Visualization - Using Vision to Think*. Morgan Kaufmann, San Francisco, CA, 1999.

[Coa05]   Workflow Management Coalition. Workflow Management Coalition: Workflow Standard Process Definition Interface – XML Process Definition Language, 2005. http://www.wfmc.org/standards/ docs/TC-1025_xpdl_2_2005-10-03.pdf accessed 27-09-2006.

[Coc04]   A. Cockburn. Revisiting 2D vs 3D implications on spatial memory. *Proceedings of the 5th ACM conference on Australasian user interface*, 28:25–31, 2004.

[Cod70]   E. F. Codd. A relational model of data for large shared data banks. *Communications of the ACM*, 13(6):377–387, 1970.

[Con05]   Web3D Consortium. X3D Framework, Components, Profiles, Language Bindings, Encodings, and Amendments per 2005-11-20. Technical report, Web3D Consortium, 2005. http://www.web3d.org/ x3d/specifications/X3DPublicSpecifications.zip.

[Cor01]   IBM Corporation. IBM MQ Series Workflow: Concepts and Architecture Version 3.3, 2001. ftp://ftp.software.ibm.com/software/

integration/mqfamily/library/books/fmcg0mst.pdf accessed 30-06-2004.

[Cor05]   M. Corp. Windows Presentation Foundation, 2005. http://msdn.microsoft.com/windowsvista/building/presentation/ accessed 22-12-2005.

[CS01]   T. Chen and T. Sobh. A tool for data structure visualization and user-defined algorithm animation. In *Frontiers in Education Conference (FIE 2001)*, Reno, Nevada, 2001. IEEE.

[CT98]   I. F. Cruz and R. Tamassia. Graph Drawing Tutorial. Technical report, Worcester Polytechnic Institute, Brown University, 1998. http://www.cs.brown.edu/people/rt/papers/gd-tutorial/gd-constraints.pdf accessed 2006-06-02.

[Dal05]   K. Dalkir. *Knowledge Management in Theory and Practice*. Elsevier Butterworth-Heinemann, Oxford, UK, 2005.

[DBD04]   D. J. Duke, K. W. Brodlie, and D. A. Duce. Building an Ontology of Visualization. In *IEEE Visualization 2004*, Austin, Texas, 2004. IEEE.

[Del99]   B. Delaney. The NYSE's 3D Trading Floor. *IEEE Computer Graphics and Applications*, 19(6):12–15, 1999.

[Deu66]   Deutsches Institut für Normung. DIN66001-1966, 1966. http://www.fh-jena.de/~kleine/history/software/DIN66001-1966.pdf accessed 07-04-2006.

[Deu83]   Deutsches Institut für Normung. DIN66001-1983, 1983. http://www.cabeweb.de/fun/images/din66001dez1983.pdf access 07-04-2006.

[DFM93]   E. Dengler, M. Friedell, and J. Marks. Constraint-Driven Diagram Layout. In *IEEE Symposium on Visual Languages*, pages 330–335, Bergen, Norway, 1993. IEEE.

[DGK03]   J. Dedrick, V. Gurbaxani, and K. L. Kraemer. Information Technology and Economic Performance: A Critical Review of the Empirical Evidence. *ACM Computing Surveys*, 35(1):1–28, 2003.

[DiB97]   G. DiBattista. Graph Drawing. In *5th International Symposium on Graph Drawing*, Rome, Italy, 1997. Springer.

[Die00]   R. Diestel. *Graphentheorie*. Springer, Heidelberg, 2000.

[Dij59]   E. W. Dijkstra. A Note on Two Problems in Connexion with Graphs. *Numerische Mathematik*, 1:269–271, 1959.

[Dij68]   E. W. Dijkstra. Letters to the editor: go to statement considered harmful. *Communications of the ACM*, 11(3):147–148, 1968.

[DJA93]   N. Dahlbäck, A. Jönsson, and L. Ahrenberg. Wizard of Oz studies: why and how. In *Proceedings of the 1st international conference on Intelligent user interfaces*, pages 193–200. ACM Press, Orlando, Florida, United States, 1993.

[Dow96]   D. Dowhal. A seven-dimensional approach to graphics. In A. P. SIGDOC, editor, *Annual ACM Conference on Systems Documentation*, pages 149–160, Research Triangle Park, North Carolina, USA, 1996.

[DSW06]   M. Dumas, M. Spork, and K. Wang. Adapt or Perish: Algebra and Visual Notation for Service Interface Adaptation. In S. Dustdar, J. L. Fiadeiro, and A. Sheth, editors, *Business Process Management*, volume LNCS 4102, pages 65–80, Vienna, Austria, 2006. Springer.

[Dwy01]   T. Dwyer. Three Dimensional UML Using Force Directed Layout. In P. Eades and T. Pattison, editors, *Conferences in Research and Practice in Information Technology*, volume 9. Australian Symposium on Information Visualization, Sydney Dec 2001, 2001.

[ECH97]   P. Eades, R. F. Cohen, and M. L. Huang. Online Animated Graph Drawing for Web Navigation. In G. DiBattista, editor, *Graph Drawing*. Springer, Rome, 1997.

[EEPPR04]   H. Ehrig, G. Engels, F. Parisi-Presicce, and G. Rozenberg. *Proceedings of the Second International Conference on Graph Transformation ICGT 2004*. Springer, Rome, Italy, 2004.

[EHH+00]   D. Estrin, M. Handley, J. Heidemann, S. McCanne, Y. Xu, and H. Yu. Network Visualization with Nam, the VINT Network Animator. *IEEE Computer*, 33(11):63–68, 2000.

[EN94]   R. Elmasri and S. B. Navathe. *Fundamentals of Database Systems*. Addison-Wesley World Student Series. Benjamin/Cummings Publications, Redwood City, CA, USA, 1994.

[Ent06]   Oracle Peoplesoft Enterprise.   Peoplesoft Enterprise Customer Scorecard, 2006.   http://www.oracle.com/applications/performance-management/ent/module/cust_scorecard.html   accessed 25-01-2006.

[Epp03]   M. J. Eppler. The Image of Insight: The Use of Visual Metaphors in the Communication of Knowledge.   In K. Tochtermann and H. Maurer, editors, *Proceedings of the I-KNOW '03, 3rd International Conference on Knowledge Management*, Graz, Austria, 2003. Springer.   http://i-know.know-center.tugraz.at/previous/i-know03/papers/ivkm/Eppler_IVKM.pdf accessed 03-01-2006.

[Epp04]   M. J. Eppler. Facilitating Knowledge Communication through Joint Interactive Visualization. In *I-KNOW '04*, Graz, Austria, 2004.

[Erw98]   M. Erwig.   Abstract Syntax and Semantics of Visual Languages. *Journal of Visual Languages and Computing*, 9:461–483, 1998.

[ES05]   M. Erwig and A. Schürr. *Proceedings of the 2005 IEEE Symposium on Visual Languages and Human Centric Computing*.   IEEE Computer Society, 2005.

[ET96]   Euclides and C. Thaer.   *Die Elemente (Bücher I-XIII)*.   Deutsch, Thun, 1996.

[FB66]   E. F. Fama and M. E. Blume. Filter Rules and Stock-Market Trading. *Journal of Business*, 39(1):226–241, 1966.

[FB05]   U. Faisst and H. U. Buhl.   Integrated Enterprise Balancing mit integrierten Ertrags- und Risikodatenbanken. *Wirtschaftsinformatik*, 47(6):403–412, 2005.

[FE02]   C. Friedrich and P. Eades.   Graph Drawing in Motion. *Journal of Graph Algorithms and Applications*, 6(3):353–370, 2002.

[Fek04]   J.-D. Fekete. The InfoVis Toolkit. In *Proceedings of the IEEE Symposium on Information Visualization*. IEEE Press, Austin, Texas, 2004.

[FFJ03]   J. Ferraiolo, J. Fujisawa, and D. Jackson. Scalable Vector Graphics (SVG) 1.1 Specification - W3C Recommendation 14 January 2003. Technical report, W3C, 2003. http://www.w3.org/TR/2003/REC-SVG11-20030114/ accessed: 23-12-2005.

[FG97]   M. S. Fox and M. Grüninger. On Ontologies and Enterprise Modelling. In *International Conference on Enterprise Integration Modelling Technology 97*. Springer, 1997. http://www.eil.utoronto.ca/enterprise-modelling/papers/fox-eimt97.pdf accessed 23-09-2006.

[FG98]   M. S. Fox and M. Grüninger. Enterprise Modeling. *AI Magazine*, 19(3):109–121, 1998.

[FH06]   H.-G. Fill and P. Höfferer. Visual Enhancements of Enterprise Models. In F. Lehner, H. Nösekabel, and P. Kleinschmidt, editors, *Multikonferenz Wirtschaftsinformatik 2006*, pages 541–550, Passau, Germany, 2006. GITO Verlag.

[Fil04]   H.-G. Fill. UML Statechart Diagrams on the ADONIS Metamodeling Platform. In *International Workshop on Graph-Based Tools (GraBaTs 2004)*, pages 27–36, Rome, Italy, 2004. Elsevier, Electronic Notes in Theoretical Computer Science.

[Fil06a]   H.-G. Fill. Semantic Visualisation of Heterogenous Knowledge Sources. In K. Hinkelmann and U. Reimer, editors, *Modellierung für Wissensmanagement - Workshop im Rahmen der Modellierung 2006*, volume 2006-W01, pages 17–27. Sonderdrucke der Fachhochschule Nordwestschweiz, Innsbruck, Austria, 2006.

[Fil06b]   H.-G. Fill. Semantic Visualization for Business Process Models. In *Proceedings of the Twelth International Conference on Distributed Multimedia Systems - International Workshop on Visual Languages and Computing 2006*, pages 168–173. Knowledge Systems Institute, Grand Canyon, USA, 2006.

[Fis96]   E. O. Fischer. *Finanzwirtschaft für Anfänger*. Lehr- und Handbücher zur entscheidungsorientierten Betriebswirtschaft. Oldenbourg, München, Wien, 1996.

[FKNT02]   I. Foster, C. Kesselman, J. Nick, and S. Tuecke. The Physiology of the Grid: An Open Grid Services Architecture for Distributed Systems Integration, 2002.

[FKT01]   I. Foster, C. Kesselman, and S. Tuecke. The Anatomy of the Grid: Enabling Scalable Virtual Organizations. *Lecture Notes in Computer Science*, 2150:1, 2001.

[FL03]   P. Fettke and P. Loos. Model Driven Architecture (MDA). *Wirtschaftsinformatik*, 45(5):555–559, 2003.

[FL04]   P. Fettke and P. Loos. Referenzmodellierungsforschung. *Wirtschaftsinformatik*, 46(5):331–340, 2004.

[Fox92]   M. S. Fox. The TOVE Project: A Common-sense Model of the Enterprise. In F. Belli and F. J. Radermacher, editors, *Industrial and Engineering Applications of Artificial Intelligence and Expert Systems*, volume LNCS 604 of *Lecture Notes in Artificial Intelligence*, pages 25–34. Springer, 1992.

[Fra99]   U. Frank. Memo: Visual Languages for Enterprise Modelling (Working paper). Technical report, Institut für Wirtschaftsinformatik, University of Koblenz, 1999.

[Fri90]   J. Friedrichs. *Methoden empirischer Sozialforschung*, volume 28. Westdeutscher Verlag, 14th edition edition, 1990.

[FS93]   O. K. Ferstl and E. Sinz. Der Modellierungsansatz des Semantischen Objektmodells (SOM). *Bamberger Beiträge zur Wirtschaftsinformatik*, 18:1–20, 1993.

[FSH03]   C. Fluit, M. Sabou, and F. Van Harmelen. Ontology-based Information Visualization. In V. Geroimenko and C. Chen, editors, *Visualizing the Semantic Web - XML-based Internet and Information Visualization*, pages 36–48. Springer, London - Berlin - Heidelberg, 2003.

[FT02]   G. Frege and M. E. Textor. *Funktion, Begriff, Bedeutung*. Vandenhoeck und Ruprecht, Göttingen, 2002.

[FW04]   D. C. Fallside and P. Walmsley. XML Schema Part 0: Primer Second Edition. Technical report, W3C, 2004. http://www.w3.org/TR/xmlschema-0/ (accessed 20-05-2005).

[FWR99]   A.-H. Fua, M. O. Ward, and E. A. Rundensteiner. Hierarchical Parallel Coordinates for Exploration of Large Datasets. In *10th IEEE Visualization 1999 (VIS'99)*, page pp. 4. IEEE, 1999.

[GBM86]   J. Greenspan, A. Borgida, and J. Mylopoulos. A requirements modelling language. *Information Systems*, 11(1):9–23, 1986.

[Gee05]   D. Geer. Chip makers turn to multicore processors. *Computer*, 38(5):11–13, 2005. TY - JOUR.

[Geo00]   P. M. Georges. The Management Cockpit - the human interface for management software: reviewing 50 user sites over 10 years of experience. *Wirtschaftsinformatik*, 42(2):131–136, 2000.

[Ger05]   V. Geroimenko, editor. *Visualizing information using SVG and X3D - XML-based technologies for the XML-based web*. Springer, London, 2005.

[GGKZ85]   K. J. Goldman, S. A. Goldman, P. C. Kanellakis, and S. B. Zdonik. ISIS: interface for a semantic information system. *Proceedings of the 1985 ACM SIGMOD international conference on Management of data*, 14(4):328–342, 1985.

[GGM⁺04]   A. Gerber, E. Glynn, A. MacDonald, M. Lawley, and K. Raymond. Modeling for Knowledge Discovery. In *EDOC workshop on Model-Driven Evolution of Legacy Systems (MELS)*, Monterey, USA, 2004.

[GHJV95]   E. Gamma, R. Helm, R. Johnson, and J. Vlissides. *Design Patterns - Elements of Reusable Object-Oriented Software*. Addison-Wesley, Reading, MA, 1995.

[GKW04]   G. Grinstein, D. Keim, and M. O. Ward. Tutorial at IEEE Visualization 2004 Conference: Information Visualization and Visual Discovery. In *Visualization 2004*, page 58p. IEEE, 2004.

[Gor02]   J. Gordijn. E-Business ontology, 2002. http://www.cs.vu.nl/~obelix/ D5.1.pdf accessed 2006-02-23.

[Grö01]   E. Gröller. Insight into Data through Visualization. In P. Mutzel, M. Jünger, and S. Leipert, editors, *GD2001*. Springer, 2001.

[Gra01]   B. Grawemeyer. User adaptive information visualization. In S. o. C. a. C. S. University of Sussex, editor, *5th Human Centred Technology Postgraduate Workshop*, Brighton, 2001.

[Gru93]   T. Gruber. A translation approach to portable ontologies. *Knowledge Acquisition*, 5(2):199–220, 1993.

[Gru95]   T. Gruber.   Toward principles for the design of ontologies used for knowledge sharing. *International Journal of Human-Computer Studies*, 43:907–928, 1995.

[GT97]   H.-O. Günther and H. Tempelmeier.   *Produktion und Logistik*. Springer, Berlin, 3rd revised and extended edition edition, 1997.

[Gur99]   C. A. Gurr.   Effective Diagrammatic Communication: Syntactic, Semantic and Pragmatic Issues. *Journal of Visual Languages and Computing*, 10:317–342, 1999.

[GW00]   V. Gruhn and U. Wellen.   Process Landscaping - eine Methode zur Geschäftsprozessmodellierung. *Wirtschaftsinformatik*, 42(4):297–309, 2000.

[Haa95]   V. Haarslev.   Formal Semantics of Visual Languages Using Spatial Reasoning.   In V. Haarslev, editor, *11th IEEE International Symposium on Visual Languages*, pages 156–163, Darmstadt, Germany, 1995. IEEE.

[Haa98]   V. Haarslev.   A Fully Formalized Theory for Describing Visual Notations. In K. Marriot and B. Meyer, editors, *Visual language theory*, pages 261–291. Springer, New York, 1998.

[Har87]   D. Harel.   Statecharts: A visual formalism for complex systems. *Science of Computer Programming*, 8:231–274, 1987.

[HB97]   D. Hearn and P. M. Baker. *Computer graphics - C version*. Prentice Hall, Upper Saddle River, New Jersey, 1997.

[Hel01]   H.-J. Hellberg. *Aktiv investieren: der systematische Einstieg in die Technische Analyse*. TM Börsenverlag AG, Rosenheim, 1st edition september 2001 edition, 2001.

[HF02]   G. Häubl and P. Figueroa.   Interactive 3D Presentations and Buyer Behavior. In *CHI'2002*, Minneapolis, Minnesota, USA, 2002. ACM.

[HGD+93]   T. Hubing, P. Grover, T. Van Doren, J. Drewniak, and L. Hill. An algorithm for automated printed circuit board layout and routing evaluation. In *IEEE International Symposium on Electromagnetic Compatibility*, pages 318–321, 1993.

[HH93]   J.-M. Hasemann and T. Heikkila. An embedded monitoring system for intelligent robots. In *IEEE/RSJ International Conference on Intelligent Robots and Systems*, volume 2, pages 1431–1438. IEEE, 1993.

[Hib99]   S. L. Hibino. Task Analysis for Information Visualization. In D. P. Huijsmans and A. W. M. Smeulders, editors, *VISUAL'99*. Springer, Berlin Heidelberg, 1999.

[Hil03]   C. A. Hillbrand. *Inferenzbasierte Konstruktion betriebswirtschaftlicher Kausalmodelle zur Unterstützung der strategischen Unternehmensplanung.* Phd thesis, University of Vienna, 2003.

[HK99]   M. Hitz and G. Kappel. *UML@Work - Von der Analyse zur Realisierung.* dpunkt.verlag, Heidelberg, 1999.

[HM81]   M. Hammer and D. McLeod. Database description with SDM: a semantic database model. *ACM Transactions on Database Systems (TODS)*, 6(3):351–386, 1981.

[HM91]   R. Helm and K. Marriot. A declarative specification and semantics for visual languages. *Journal of Visual Languages and Computing*, 2:311–331, 1991.

[HM00]   I. Herman and M. S. Marshall. GraphXML - An XML Based Graph Interchange Format. Technical Report Report INS-R0009, Centrum voor Wiskunde en Informatica, 2000. http://ftp.cwi.nl/CWIreports/INS/INS-R0009.pdf accessed 10-06-2006.

[HMU02]   J. E. Hopcroft, R. Motwani, and J. D. Ullman. *Introduction to automata theory, languages, and computation.* Addison-Wesley, Boston, MA, 2nd edition edition, 2002.

[Hol97]   M. B. Holbrook. Three-Dimensional Stereographic Visual Displays in Marketing and Consumer Research. *Academy of Marketing Science Review*, 11(1), 1997.

[HSSW02]   R. Holt, A. Schürr, S. E. Sim, and A. Winter. Graph eXchange Language, 2002. http://www.gupro.de/GXL/ accessed 10-06-2006.

[Ins00]   IT Governance Institute. Cobit Framework 3rd edition, 2000. http://www.isaca.org access 18-07-2005.

[Ins05]   IT Governance Institute. Cobit 4.0 - Deutsche Ausgabe, 2005. http://
            www.isaca.at/Ressourcen/CobiT%204.0%20Deutsch.pdf access 28-
            09-2006.

[Itt00]   J. Itten. *Kunst der Farbe - subjektives Erleben und objektives Erken-
            nen als Wege zur Kunst*. Ravensburg, 13th edition edition, 2000.

[IW00]   P. Irani and C. Ware. Diagrams based on structural object perception.
            In *Working Conference on Advanced Visual Interfaces*, Palermo,
            Italy, 2000. ACM Press SIGCHI, SIGMULTIMEDIA.

[Jab95]   S. Jablonski. On the complementarity of workflow management and
            business process modeling. *ACM SIGOIS Bulletin*, 16(1):33–38,
            1995.

[Jar92a]   M. Jarke. Metamodellierung: Werkzeuge für das Engineering von
            Unternehmensprozessen. In K.-W. Hansmann and A.-W. Scheer,
            editors, *Praxis und Theorie der Unternehmung*. Gabler, Wiesbaden,
            1992.

[Jar92b]   M. Jarke. Organizing software information: a concept-based ap-
            proach. *ACM SIGOIS Bulletin*, 13(2):13–27, 1992.

[JKSK00]   S. Junginger, H. Kühn, R. Strobl, and D. Karagiannis. Ein
            Geschäftsprozessmanagement-Werkzeug der nächsten Generation -
            ADONIS: Konzeption und Anwendungen. *Wirtschaftsinformatik*,
            42(5):392–401, 2000.

[JLMM04]   A. Jonen, V. Lingnau, J. Müller, and P. Müller. Balanced IT-
            Decision-Card: Ein Instrument für das Investitionscontrolling von
            IT-Projekten. *Wirtschaftsinformatik*, 46(3):196–203, 2004.

[JMS04]   M. B. Juric, B. Mathew, and P. Sarang. *Business Process Execution
            Language for Web Services*. PACKT Publishing, 2004.

[JOO01]   J.-A. Johannessen, J. Olaisen, and B. Olsen. Mismanagement of tacit
            knowledge: the importance of tacit knowledge, the danger of infor-
            mation technology, and what to do about it. *International Journal of
            Information Management*, 21:3–20, 2001.

[Jun00a]   M. Jung. *Ein Generator zur Entwicklung visueller Sprachen*. Phd
            thesis, Universität Paderborn, 2000.

[Jun00b]   S. Junginger. Modellierung von Geschäftsprozessen. Report of the bpms group, Institut für Informatik und Wirtschaftsinformatik, University of Vienna, June 2000 2000.

[Jun01]   S. Junginger. *Workflowbasierte Umsetzung von Geschäftsprozessen.* Phd thesis, University of Vienna, 2001.

[JW95]   R. Jamal and L. Wenzel. The applicability of the visual programming language LabVIEW to large real-world applications. In V. Haarslev, editor, *11th International IEEE Symposium on Visual Languages*, pages 99–106, Darmstadt, Germany, 1995. IEEE.

[Kar95]   D. Karagiannis. BPMS: Business Process Management Systems. *SIGOIS Bulletin*, 16(1):10–13, 1995.

[Kaz95]   E. Kazmierczak. Universals in Visual Codification. In J. Bernard, editor, *Bildsprache – Visualisierung – Diagrammatik, Special Issue of 'Semiotische Berichte', Institute for Socio-Semiotic Studies Vienna*, volume 19, pages 131–152. Vienna, Austria, 1995.

[Kel05]   S. Kelly. Domänenspezifische Modellierung mit MetaEdit+. *Objektspektrum*, (1/2005):1–5, 2005.

[KGM99]   H. Krallmann, F. Gu, and A. Mitritz. ProVision3D - Eine Virtual Reality Workbench zur Modellierung, Kontrolle und Steuerung von Geschäftsprozessen im virtuellen Raum. *Wirtschaftsinformatik*, 41(1):48–57, 1999.

[Küh04]   H. Kühn. *Methodenintegration im Business Engineering*. Phd thesis, University of Vienna, 2004.

[KJS96]   D. Karagiannis, S. Junginger, and R. Strobl. Introduction to Business Process Management Systems Concepts. In B. Scholz-Reiter and E. Stickel, editors, *Business Process Modelling*, pages 81–106. Springer, Berlin et al., 1996.

[KK91]   T. Kamada and S. Kawai. A General Framework for Visualizing Abstract Objects and Relations. *ACM Transactions on Graphics*, 10(1):1–39, 1991.

[KK02]   D. Karagiannis and H. Kühn. Metamodelling Platforms. In K. Bauknecht, A. Min Tjoa, and G. Quirchmayer, editors, *Third*

International Conference EC-Web 2002 – Dexa 2002, LNCS2455, page 182, Aix-en-Provence, France, 2002. Springer Verlag.

[KKK⁺06]   G. Kappel, E. Kapsammer, H. Kargl, G. Kramler, T. Reiter, W. Retschitzegger, W. Schwinger, and M. Wimmer. On Models and Ontologies - A Layered Approach for Model-based Tool Integration. In H. C. Mayr and R. Breu, editors, *Modellierung 2006*, volume GI-Edition-Lecture Notes in Informatics (LNI), P-82, pages 11–27, Innsbruck, 2006.

[KMB96]   J. B. Kennedy, K. J. Mitchell, and P. J. Barclay. A Framework for Information Visualization. *SIGMOD Record*, 25(4):30–34, 1996.

[KN96]   R. S. Kaplan and D. P. Norton. Using the Balanced Scorecard as a Strategic Management System. *Harvard Business Review*, January-February 1996:75–85, 1996.

[KNS92]   G. Keller, M. Nüttgens, and A.-W. Scheer. Semantische Prozeß-modellierung auf der Grundlage "Ereignisgesteuerter Prozeßketten (EPK)". *Veröffentlichungen des Instituts für Wirtschaftsinformatik (IWi), Universität des Saarlandes*, Heft 89:29p., 1992. http://www.iwi.uni-sb.de/nuettgens/Veroef/Artikel/heft089/heft089.pdf.

[Kos95]   K. Kosanke. CIMOSA - Overview and status. *Computers in Industry*, 27:101–109, 1995.

[Krö02]   D. Krömker. CASUS Anim – Ein objektorientiertes, dreidimensionales Animationssystem für ereignisorientierte Simulatoren. Technical report, Fraunhofer Institut für Graphische Datenverarbeitung, 2002.

[KS00]   H. Kyllönen and M. Salmela. VRP Creator - A Process Modelling Tool for Building Smart Virtual Prototypes. In *The Ninth Nordic Workshop on Programming and Software Development Environment Research*, Lillehammer, Norway, 2000. http://www.ifi.uib.no/konf/nwper2000/.

[KT01]   D. Karagiannis and R. Telesko. *Wissensmanagement - Konzepte der Künstlichen Intelligenz und des Softcomputing*. Oldenbourg, München - Wien, 2001.

[KVZ99]   K. Kosanke, F. Vernadat, and M. Zelm. CIMOSA: enterprise engineering and integration. *Computers in Industry*, 40:83–97, 1999.

[KZA06]   B. Karakostas, Y. Zorgios, and C. C. Alevizos. The Seman-
           tics of Business Service Orchestration. In J. Eder and S. Dust-
           dar, editors, *Business Process Management Workshops*, volume
           LNCS4103, pages 435–446, Vienna, Austria, 2006. Springer.

[Laa93]   W. Laatz. *Empirische Methoden - Ein Lehrbuch für Sozialwis-
           senschafter*. Verlag Harri Deutsch, Thun und Frankfurt am Main,
           1993.

[LB97]   V. Luckas and T. Broll. CASUS; an object-oriented three-
           dimensional animation system for event-oriented simulators. In
           Computer Animation '97, pages 144–150, 1997. TY - CONF.

[LeB99]   B. LeBaron. Technical trading rule profitability and foreign
           exchange intervention. *Journal of International Economics*,
           49(1):125–143, 1999.

[Lei00]   S. Leinenbach. *Interaktive Geschäftsprozessmodellierung: Doku-
           mentation von Prozesswissen in einer virtual-reality-gestützten Un-
           ternehmensvisualisierung*. Dt. Univ.-Verlag, Gabler, Wiesbaden,
           2000.

[LEW02]   M. Loy, R. Eckstein, and D. Wood. *Java Swing*. O'Reilly Media,
           2002.

[Lic05]   C. Lichka. Strategic Monitoring and Alignment to Achieve Business
           Process Best Practices. In *16th International Workshop on Database
           and Expert Systems Applications (DEXA '05)*, pages 914–918. IEEE,
           2005.

[Lie95]   H. Lieberman. The visual language of experts in graphic design. In
           V. Haarslev, editor, *11th International IEEE Symposium on Visual
           Languages*, pages 342–349, Darmstadt, Germany, 1995. IEEE.

[Lin01]   T. Lindh. Embedded monitoring of QoS parameters in IP-based vir-
           tual private networks. In *IEEE/IFIP International Symposium on
           Integrated Network Management*, pages 289–292. IEEE, 2001.

[LKK02]   C. Lichka, H. Kühn, and D. Karagiannis. ADOscore - IT gestützte
           Balanced Scorecard. *wisu-Das Wirtschaftsstudium*, (7):915–918,
           2002.

320   *Bibliography*

[LL96]   K. C. Laudon and J. P. Laudon. *Management Information Systems -
            Organisation and Technology*. Prentice Hall, 1996.

[LLS06]   K. C. Laudon, J. P. Laudon, and D. Schoder. *Wirtschaftsinformatik
            - Eine Einführung*. Pearson Education, München et al., 2006.

[LM98]   Y.-H. Lui and D. Mole. The use of fundamental and technical anal-
            yses by foreign exchange dealers: Hong Kong evidence. *Journal of
            International Money and Finance*, 17(3):535–545, 1998.

[LSTT97]   S.-P. Lahtinen, E. Sutinen, A.-P. Tuovinen, and J. Tarhio. Object-
            Oriented Visualization of Program Logic. In *Tools-23: Technology
            of Object-Oriented Languages and Systems*, pages 76–89, 1997.

[LSW97]   P. Langner, C. Schneider, and J. Wehler. Prozeßmodellierung
            mit ereignisgesteuerten Prozeßketten (EPKs) und Petri-Netzen.
            Wirtschaftsinformatik, 39(5):479–489, 1997.

[LW05]   V. S. Lai and B. K. Wong. Business Types, E-Strategies, and Perfor-
            mance. *Communications of the ACM*, 48(5):80–85, 2005.

[Mac86]   J. D. Mackinlay. Automating the Design of Graphical Presenta-
            tions of Relational Information. *ACM Transactions on Graphics*,
            5(2):110–141, 1986.

[Mar01]   A. Marcus. Cross-Cultural User-Interface Design for Work, Home,
            Play, and on the Way. In *SIGDOC'01*, pages 221–222, Sante Fe,
            New Mexico, USA, 2001. ACM.

[Mar06]   A. Marcus. Visualizing the future of information visualization. *in-
            teractions*, 13(2):42–43, 2006.

[MB05]   C. Moser and F. Bayer. IT Architecture Management: A Framework
            for IT Services. In J. Desel and U. Frank, editors, *Proceedings of the
            Workshop on Enterprise Modelling and Information Systems Archi-
            tectures*. Lecture Notes in Informatics - Gesellschaft für Informatik
            (GI), Klagenfurt, Austria, 2005.

[Mef00]   H. Meffert. *Marketing - Grundlagen der Absatzpolitik*. Gabler,
            Wiesbaden, 9th edition edition, 2000.

[MELS95]   K. Misue, P. Eades, W. Lai, and K. Sugiyama. Layout Adjustment
            and the Mental Map. *Journal of Visual Languages and Computing*,
            6(2):183–210, 1995.

[Mer05]   P. Mertens. Gefahren für die Wirtschaftsinformatik – Risikoanalyse eines Faches. In O. K. Ferstl, E. J. Sinz, S. Eckert, and T. Isselhorst, editors, *Wirtschaftsinformatik 2005*, pages 1733–1754. Heidelberg, 2005.

[MH05]   E. Miller and J. Hendler. Web Ontology Language (OWL), 2005. http://www.w3.org/2004/OWL/ (accessed 08-07-2005).

[Mit03]   N. Mitra. SOAP Version 1.2 Part 0: Primer - W3C Recommendation 24 June 2003. Technical report, W3C, 24-06-2003 2003. http://www.w3.org/TR/2003/REC-soap12-part0-20030624/ accessed 29-12-2005.

[MJL01]   P. Mutzel, M. Jünger, and S. Leipert. Graph Drawing. In G. Goos, J. Hartmanis, and J. Van Leeuwen, editors, *9th International Symposium, GD 2001*, Vienna, Austria, 2001. Springer.

[MK03]   X. Ma and G. S. Kuo. Optical Switching Technology Comparison: Optical MEMS vs. other technologies. *IEEE Communications Magazine*, 41(11):16–23, 2003.

[MKN04]   B. Mathiak, A. Kupfer, and K. Neumann. Using XML Languages for Modeling and Web-Visualization of Geographical Legacy Data. In C. Iochpe and G. Câmara, editors, *Proceedings of the 6th Brazilian Symposium on GeoInformatics: GeoInfo 2004*, pages 265–280. Instituto Nacional de Pesquisas Espaciais, Campos do Jordão, 2004.

[MKP02]   J. M. Martínez, R. Koenen, and F. Pereira. MPEG-7: The Generic Multimedia Content Description Standard. *IEEE Multimedia*, 9(2):78–87, 2002.

[MM98]   K. Marriott and B. Meyer, editors. *Visual language theory*. Springer, New York, 1998.

[MM05]   J. Mukerji and J. Miller. MDA Guide Version 1.0.1, 2005. http://www.omg.org/docs/omg/03-06-01.pdf accessed 07-07-2005.

[MMW98]   K. Marriot, B. Meyer, and K. B. Wittenburg. A Survey of Visual Language Specification and Recognition. In K. Marriot and B. Meyer, editors, *Visual language theory*, pages 5–85. Springer, New York, 1998.

[Mol94]   K.-R. Moll. *Informatik-Management*. Springer, Berlin et al., 1994.

[Mon00]   R. D. Montasser. *Technische Analyse verstehen: Ansätze - Metho-den - Weiterentwicklungen.* Technical Investor. FinanzBuch Verlag, 2000.

[Moo03]   G. E. Moore. No exponential is forever: but "Forever" can be delayed! [semiconductor industry]. In *Solid-State Circuits Conference, 2003. Digest of Technical Papers. ISSCC. 2003 IEEE International*, pages 20–23 vol.1, 2003. TY - CONF.

[Mos04]   P. D. Mosses. Formal Semantics of Programming Languages. In R. Heckel and J. H. Hausmann, editors, *School on Foundations of Visual Modelling Techniques*, page 260p. Dagstuhl, Germany, 2004. http://wwwcs.upb.de/cs/ag-engels/ag_engl/Segravis/school/html/Segravis%20School%202004%20Handout.pdf accessed 22-05-2006.

[MS95]   K. Mullet and D. J. Schiano. 3D or not 3D: "More is better" or " Less is more"? In *CHI'95 Mosaic of creativity*, pages 174–175, 1995.

[Mur97]   J. J. Murphy. *Visuelle Aktienanalyse: mit Charts Börsentrends frühzeitig erkennen.* Fachbuchreihe Vereinigung Technischer Analysten Deutschlands. Campus Verlag, Frankfurt/Main, New York, 1997.

[MV95]   M. Minas and G. Viehstaedt. DiaGen: A generator for diagram editors providing direct manipulation and execution of diagrams. In V. Haarslev, editor, *11th IEEE International Symposium on Visual Languages (VL'95)*, pages 203–210, Darmstadt, Germany, 1995. IEEE Computer Society Press.

[MWJ02]   W. Mueller-Wittig and R. Jegathese. Virtual Factory - Highly Interactive Visualisation for Manufacturing. In E. Yücesan, C.-H. Chen, J. L. Snowdon, and J. M. Charnes, editors, *Proceedings of the 2002 Winter Simulation Conference*, 2002.

[Mye90]   B. Myers. Taxonomies of visual programming and program visualization. *Journal of Visual Languages and Computing*, 1(1):97–123, 1990.

[Myl92]   J. Mylopoulos. Conceptual Modeling and Telos. In P. Loucopoulos and R. Zicari, editors, *Conceptual Modelling, Databases and CASE: An Integrated View of Information Systems Development*, pages 49–68. Wiley, 1992.

[MZK03]   M. Meyer, R. Zarnekow, and L. M. Kolbe. IT-Governance - Begriff, Status quo und Bedeutung. *Wirtschaftsinformatik*, 45(4):445–448, 2003.

[Naj01]   M. A. Najork. Web-based Algorithm Animation. In *DAC 2001*, pages 506–511, Las Vegas, Nevada, USA, 2001. ACM.

[NFF⁺91]   R. Neches, R. Fikes, T. Finin, T. Gruber, R. Patil, T. Senator, and W. R. Swartout. Enabling Technology for Knowledge Sharing. *AI Magazine*, 12(3):36–56, 1991.

[NH98]   N. H. Narayanan and R. Hübscher. Visual Language Theory: Towards a Human-Computer Interaction Perspective. In K. Marriott, editor, *Visual language theory*. Springer, New York, 1998.

[Noh00]   H. Nohr. Wissen und Wissensprozesse visualisieren. Technical report, Fachhochschule Stuttgart, 2000.

[Nor02]   K. North. *Wissensorientierte Unternehmensführung: Wertschöpfung durch Wissen*. Gabler, Wiesbaden, 2002.

[NS73]   I. Nassi and B. Shneiderman. Flowchart techniques for structured programming. *ACM SIGPLAN Notices*, 8(8):12–26, 1973.

[NT95]   I. Nonaka and H. Takeuchi. *The Knowledge-Creating Company*. Oxford University Press, New York, Oxford, 1995.

[Obr03]   L. Obrst. Ontologies for semantically interoperable systems. In *Proceedings of the 12th International Conference on Information and Knowledge Management*, New Orleans, 2003. ACM Press.

[oC02]   Library of Congress. Sarbanes-Oxley Act of 2002 (Enrolled as Agreed to or Passed by Both House and Senate), 2002. http://thomas.loc.gov/cgi-bin/query/z?c107:H.R.3763.ENR: accessed 29-09-2006.

[Oes04]   B. Oestereich. *Objektorientierte Softwareentwicklung - Analyse und Design mit der UML 2.0*. Oldenbourg, München - Wien, 6th edition edition, 2004.

[oGCO]   Office of Government Commerce (OGC). ITIL - IT Service Management. http://www.itil.co.uk/ accessed 28-09-2006.

[OMG02]   Object Management Group OMG.   Meta Object Facility (MOF)
            Specification 1.4.   Technical report, 2002.   http://www.omg.org/
            cgi-bin/apps/doc?formal/02-04-03.pdf accessed 14-09-2005.

[OMG03]   Object Management Group OMG.   UML 2.0 OCL Specification.
            Technical report, 2003. http://www.omg.org/docs/ptc/03-10-14.pdf
            accessed 20-09-2005.

[OMG04a]   Object Management Group OMG. Unified Modeling Language: Su-
            perstructure version 2.0. Technical report, 2004. http://www.omg.
            org/docs/formal/05-07-04.pdf accessed 12-03-2006.

[OMG04b]   Object Management Group OMG.   Unified Modeling Language
            (UML) Specification: Infrastructure version 2.0. Technical report,
            2004. http://www.omg.org/docs/ptc/04-10-14.pdf accessed 12-03-
            2006.

[OMG05]   Object Management Group OMG. Ontology Definition Metamodel,
            Third Revised Submission to OMG/ RFP ad/2003-03-40. Technical
            report, 2005.   http://www.omg.org/docs/ad/05-08-01.pdf accessed
            16-09-2005.

[OST04]   T. Okamura, B. Shizuki, and J. Tanaka. Execution Visualization and
            Debugging in Three-Dimensional Visual Programming. In *Eighth
            International Conference on Information Visualisation (IV'04)*, page
            6p. IEEE, 2004.

[Par04]   J. Park. Information Systems Interoperability: What Lies Beneath?
            ACM Transactions on Information Systems, 22(4):595–632, 2004.

[Par06]   Jenz & Partner.   The Open Source Business Management On-
            tology (BMO), 2006. http://www.bpiresearch.com/Resources/RE_
            OSSOnt/re_ossont.htm accessed 13-06-2006.

[PHP01]   D. Pfitzner, V. Hobbs, and D. Powers. A Unified Taxonomic Frame-
            work for Information Visualization. In J. Weckert, editor, *2nd Aus-
            tralian Institute of Computer Ethics Conference (AICE2000)*, vol-
            ume 1, Canberra, 2001.

[Por85]   M. Porter. *Competitive advantage - creating and sustaining superior
            performance*. Free Pr., New York, 1985.

[Pos04]   H. Poser. *Wissenschaftstheorie: Eine philosophische Einführung.* Reclam, Stuttgart, 2004.

[PPL04]   H. Peyret, A. Parker, and G. Leganza. Trends 2005: Business Process Modeling And Enterprise Architecture Tools. Technical report, Forrester Research, November 8, 2004 2004.

[PSV04]   J.-Y. Potvin, P. Soriano, and M. Vallée. Generating trading rules on the stock markets with genetic programming. *Computers & Operations Research*, 31, 2004.

[Pur97]   H. Purchase. Which Aesthetic has the greatest effect on human understanding? In G. DiBattista, editor, *Graph Drawing*. Springer, Rome, 1997.

[RBdBT94]   W. Ribarsky, J. Bolter, A. Op den Bosch, and R. Van Teylingen. Visualization and Analysis using Virtual Reality. *IEEE Computer Graphics and Applications*, (January 1994), 1994.

[RBP+91]   J. Rumbaugh, M. Blaha, W. Premerlani, F. Eddy, and W. Lorensen. *Object-oriented modeling and design.* Prentice-Hall, Englewood Cliffs, New Jersey, 1991.

[Res01]   P. J. Restle. Technical visualizations in VLSI design. In *Proceedings of the Design Automation Conference, 2001.* IEEE, 2001.

[RF02]   G. Rössling and B. Freisleben. Animal: A System for Supporting Multiple Roles in Algorithm Animation. *Journal of Visual Languages and Computing*, 13(3):341–354, 2002.

[RJB99]   J. Rumbaugh, I. Jacobson, and G. Booch. *The Unified Modeling Language Reference Manual.* Addison Wesley Longman, Reading, MA, 1999.

[RMC91]   G. G. Robertson, J. D. Mackinlay, and S. Card. Cone Trees: animated 3D visualizations of hierarchical information. In *Proceedings of the SIGCHI conference on Human factors in computing systems: Reaching through technology*, pages 189–194. ACM Press, New Orleans, Louisiana, United States, 1991.

[RN04]   S. Russell and P. Norvig. *Künstliche Intelligenz - Ein moderner Ansatz (Original english title: Artificial Intelligence - A modern approach).* Pearson Education Deutschland, München, 2004.

[Ron05a]   F. Ronaghi. A Modeling Method for Integrated Performance Man-
            agement. In *16th International Workshop on Database and Expert
            Systems Applications (DEXA'05)*, pages 972–976, 2005.

[Ron05b]   F. Ronaghi. *Integrated performance management*. Phd thesis, Uni-
            versity of Vienna, 2005.

[Ros04]   P. S. Rosenbloom. A New Framework for Computer Science and
            Engineering. *Computer*, 37(11):23–28, 2004.

[RTW04]   H. Rushmeier, G. Turk, and J. J. Van Wijk. *Proceedings of the 2004
            IEEE Visualisation Conference*. IEEE Computer Society, Austin,
            TX, USA, 2004.

[SA95]   R. E. Shiffler and A. J. Adams. *Introductory Business Statistics with
            Computer Applications*. Duxbury Press, Belmont, California, 2nd
            edition edition, 1995.

[SAKW02]   B. Stolk, F. Abdoelrahman, A. Koning, and A. Wielinga. Mining
            the Human Genome using Virtual Reality. In D. Bartz, X. Pueyo,
            and E. Reinhard, editors, *Fourth Eurographics Workshop on Parallel
            Graphics and Visualization*. The Eurographics Association, 2002.

[SB98]   R. Schütte and J. Becker. Subjektivitätsmanagement bei Informa-
            tionsmodellen. Technical report, GI-Workshop, 1998.

[sB00]   H. Österle and D. Blessing. Business Engineering Model. In
            H. Österle and R. Winter, editors, *Business Engineering - Auf dem
            Weg zum Unternehmen des Informationszeitalters*, pages 61–81.
            Springer, Berlin, 2000.

[SBE00]   B. Schönhage, A. Van Ballegooij, and A. Eliens. 3D Gadgets for
            Business Process Visualization - a case study. In *VRML 2000*, Mon-
            terey, CA USA, 2000. ACM.

[SCC05]   Supply-Chain-Council. Supply-Chain Operations Reference-model
            Version 7.0 Overview, 2005. http://www.supply-chain.org/galleries/
            default-file/SCOR%207.0%20Overview.pdf.

[Sch91]   A.-W. Scheer. *Architektur integrierter Informationssysteme -
            Grundlagen der Unternehmensmodellierung*. Springer, Berlin,
            1991.

[Sch96]   A.-W. Scheer.   ARIS-House of Business Engineering: Von der Geschäftsprozeßmodellierung zur Workflow-gesteuerten Anwendung; vom Business Process Reengineering zum Continuous Process Improvement. *Veröffentlichungen des Instituts für Wirtschaftsinformatik, Universität des Saarlandes*, 133:34, 1996.

[Sch97]   A. Schelske. *Die kulturelle Bedeutung von Bildern: Soziologische und semiotische Überlegungen zur visuellen Kommunikation.* Deutscher Universitäts Verlag / Gabler, Vieweg, Westdeutscher Verlag, Wiesbaden, 1997.

[Sch00]   A. Schwarzhaupt. *Grundkurs Technische Analyse - Chartformationen.* FinanzBuch Verlag München, 2000.

[SGR05]   C. T. Silva, E. Gröller, and H. Rushmeier. *Proceedings of the 2005 IEEE Visualisation Conference.* IEEE Computer Society, Minneapolis,MN, USA, 2005.

[SH02]   P. Stahlknecht and U. Hasenkamp. *Einführung in die Wirtschaftsinformatik.* Springer, Berlin et al., 10th edition edition, 2002.

[Shn92]   B. Shneiderman. Tree visualization with tree-maps: 2-d space-filling approach. *ACM Transactions on Graphics (TOG)*, 11(1):92–99, 1992.

[Shn93]   B. Shneiderman. *Designing the user interface - strategies for effective human-computer interaction.* Addison-Wesley, Reading, MA, USA, 2nd edition edition, 1993.

[Shn01]   B. Shneiderman. Inventing Discovery Tools: Combining Information Visualization with Data Mining. In K. P. Jantke and A. Shinohara, editors, *DS 2001, LNAI 2226*, pages 17–28. Springer, Berlin Heidelberg, 2001.

[Sii04]   H. Siirtola. Interactive Cluster Analysis. In *Eighth International Conference on Information Visualisation (IV'04)*, pages 471–476. IEEE, 2004.

[SK03]   C. Schmidt and U. Kastens. Implementation of visual languages using pattern-based specifications. *Software - Practice and Experience*, 33:1471–1505, 2003.

[SLB97]   F. Steinfath, B. Lange, and K. Böhm. 3D-graphische Werkzeuge zur Analyse komplexer CSP-basierter Modelle. *Informatik Forschung und Entwicklung*, 12(3):128–142, 1997.

[SM96]   J. Stasko and J. Muthukumarasamy. Visualizing Program Executions on Large Data Sets. In *IEEE Symposium on Visual Languages*, 1996.

[Sow00]   J. F. Sowa. *Knowledge representation - logical, philosophical, and computational foundations*. Brooks/Cole, Pacific Grove, CA, USA, 2000.

[SS77]   J. M. Smith and D. C. P. Smith. Database abstractions: aggregation and generalization. *ACM Transactions on Database Systems (TODS)*, 2(2), 1977.

[SS03]   H. M. Sneed and S. H. Sneed. Creating Web Services from Legacy Host Programs. In *5th International Workshop on Web Site Evolution*, page pp. 59. IEEE, 2003.

[SS04]   S. Staab and R. Studer, editors. *Handbook on Ontologies*. International Handbooks on Information Systems. Springer, Berlin et al., 2004.

[Sta73]   H. Stachowiak. *Allgemeine Modelltheorie*. Springer, 1973.

[Sta90]   J. Stasko. Tango: a framework and system for algorithm animation. *IEEE Computer*, 23(9):27–39, 1990.

[Sta94]   A. Stankowski. *Visuelle Kommunikation - ein Design-Handbuch*. Reimer, Berlin, 2nd edition edition, 1994.

[Str98]   S. Strahringer. Ein sprachbasierter Metamodellbegriff und seine Verallgemeinerung durch das Konzept des Metaisierungsprinzips. Technical report, Modellierung'98, 1998.

[SVJ01]   A. Sreenivas, R. Venkatesh, and M. Joseph. Meta-Modelling for Formal Software Development. *Electronic Notes in Theoretical Computer Science - Computing: The Australasian Theory Symposium (CATS 2001)*, 42(January 2001):1–11, 2001.

[SVM⁺99]   M. M. Sebrechts, J. Vasilakis, M. S. Miller, J. V. Cugini, and S. J. Laskowski. Visualization of search results: a comparative evaluation of text, 2D, and 3D interfaces. In *22nd annual international ACM SIGIR conference on Research and development in information retrieval*, Berkeley, California, USA, 1999. ACM Press SIGIR.

[SWND05]   D. Shreiner, M. Woo, J. Neider, and T. Davis. *OpenGL Programming Guide - The Official Guide to Learning OpenGL Version 2*. Addison-Wesley Professional, 2005.

[SZ92]   J. F. Sowa and J. A. Zachman. Extending and formalizing the framework for information systems architecture. *IBM Systems Journal*, 31(3):590–616, 1992.

[TA92]   M. P. Taylor and H. Allen. The use of technical analysis in the foreign exchange market. *Journal of International Money and Finance*, 11(3):304–314, 1992.

[TBB03]   M. Turner, D. Budgen, and P. Brereton. Turning Software into a Service. *IEEE Computer*, 36(10):38–44, 2003.

[TCF⁺03]   S. Tuecke, K. Czajkowski, I. Foster, J. Frey, S. Graham, C. Kesselman, T. Maquire, T. Sandholm, D. Snelling, and P. Vanderbilt. Open Grid Services Infrastructure (OGSI) Version 1.0. Technical report, Global Grid Forum, 2003.

[TK04]   J.-P. Tolvanen and S. Kelly. Domänenspezifische Modellierung. *Objektspektrum*, (4/2004):30–34, 2004.

[TP06]   V. Torres and V. Pelechano. Building Business Process Driven Web Applications. In S. Dustdar, J. L. Fiadeiro, and A. Sheth, editors, *Business Process Management*, volume LNCS 4102, pages 322–337, Vienna, Austria, 2006. Springer.

[Tud03]   M. E. Tudoreanu. Designing Effective Program Visualization Tools for Reducing User's Cognitive Effort. In *Symposium on Software Visualization*, pages 105–114, 213, San Diego, CA, USA, 2003. ACM.

[Tuf83]   E. R. Tufte. *The visual display of quantitative information*. Graphics Press, Chesire, Connecticut, USA, 1983.

[UAE95]   M. Unser, A. Aldroubi, and M. Eden. Enlargement or Reduction of Digital Images with Minimum Loss of Information. *IEEE transactions on Image Processing*, 4(3):247–258, 1995.

[UKMZ98] M. Uschold, M. King, S. Moralee, and Y. Zorgios. The Enterprise
          Ontology. *The Knowledge Engineering Review*, 13(Special Issue
          on Putting Ontologies to Use (eds. Mike Uschold and Austin Tate)),
          1998.

[Ull82]   J. D. Ullman. *Principles of Database Systems*. Computer Software
          Engineering Series. Computer Science Press, 2nd edition edition,
          1982.

[Vol05]   K. Vollmer. Trends 2006: Integration-Centric Business Process
          Management. Technical report, Forrester Research, October 24,
          2005 2005.

[W3C04]   W3C. OWL Web Ontology Language - Overview W3C Rec-
          ommendation 10 February 2004, 2004. http://www.w3.org/TR/
          owl-features/ accessed 16-09-2005.

[WAK96]   J. Wilson, R. Aiken, and I. Katz. Review of animation systems for al-
          gorithm understanding. *ACM SIGCSE Bulletin*, 28(1):75–77, 1996.

[Wan95]   D. Wang. *Studies on the Formal Semantics of Pictures*. Phd thesis,
          University of Amsterdam, 1995.

[War00]   C. Ware. *Information Visualization - Perception for design*. Morgan
          Kaufman, 2000.

[WB99]   S. Waite and M. Bendame. An introduction to Electronics Work-
          bench for designing circuits and PCBs. In *IEE Colloquium on Ef-
          fective Microwave CAD Tools*, pages 6/1–6/4, London, 1999.

[WBJ00]   D. Winterstein, A. Bundy, and M. Jamnik. A Proposal for Automat-
          ing Diagrammatic Reasoning in Continuous Domains. In M. An-
          derson, P. Cheng, and V. Haarslev, editors, *Diagrams 2000*, volume
          LNAI1889, pages 286–299. Springer Verlag, 2000.

[WdB92]   W. Van Waterschoot and C. Van den Bulte. The 4P Classification of
          the Marketing Mix Revisited. *Journal of Marketing*, 56(4):83–93,
          1992.

[Wef00]   M. Wefers. Strategische Unternehmensführung mit der IV-
          gestützten Balanced Scorecard. *Wirtschaftsinformatik*, 42(2):123–
          130, 2000.

[Wes96]   D. B. West. *Introduction to Graph Theory*. Prentice Hall, Upper Saddle River, 1996.

[WJ94]   T. Wickham-Jones. *Computer graphics with Mathematica*. Springer, New York, 1994.

[WK04]   T. Williams and C. Kelley. GNUPLOT - An Interactive Plotting Program. Technical report, 2004. http://www.gnuplot.info/docs/gnuplot.html accessed 20-12-2005.

[WOCD97]   C. D. Wickens, O. Olmos, A. Chudy, and C. Davenport. Aviation display support for situation awareness. Technical Report ARL-97-10/LOGICON-97-2, University of Illinois at Urbana-Champaign - Aviation Research Lab Institute of Aviation, July 1997 1997.

[Woi04]   R. Woitsch. *Process Oriented Knowledge Management: A Service Based Approach*. Phd thesis, University of Vienna, 2004.

[WPCM02]   C. Ware, H. Purchase, L. Colpoys, and M. McGill. Cognitive Measurements of Graph Aesthetics. *Information Visualisation*, 1(2):103–110, 2002.

[WZ98]   D. Wang and H. Zeevat. A Syntax-Directed Approach to Picture Semantics. In K. Marriot and B. Meyer, editors, *Visual language theory*, pages 307–323. Springer, New York, 1998.

[Zac87]   J. A. Zachman. A framework for information systems architecture. *IBM Systems Journal*, 26(3):276–292, 1987.

[Zac98]   Zachman Institute (zifa.com). The Framework for Enterprise Architecture - Cell Definitions, 1998. http://www.zifa.com/cgi-bin/download.cgi?file_name=ZIFA03.pdf&file_path=/home/zifa.com/friends/ZIFA03.pdf&size=174147 accessed 30-01-2006.

[Zac06]   J. A. Zachman. The Framework for Enterprise Architecture: Background, Description and Utility. Technical report, Zachman Institute for Framework Advancement, 2006. http://www.zifa.com/cgi-bin/download.cgi?file_name=ZIFA07.pdf&file_path=/home/zifa.com/friends/ZIFA07.pdf&size=209368 accessed 30-01-2006.

[ZB03]   R. Zarnekow and W. Brenner. Auf dem Weg zu einem produkt- und
           dienstleistungsorientierten IT-Management. In A. Meier, W. Bren-
           ner, and R. Zarnekow, editors, *Strategisches IT-Management*, vol-
           ume 232 of *HMD Praxis der Wirtschaftsinformatik*. dpunkt.verlag,
           2003.

[ZB04]   R. Zarnekow and W. Brenner. Integriertes Informationsmanage-
           ment: Vom Plan, Build, Run zum Source, Make, Deliver.   In
           R. Zarnekow, W. Brenner, and H. H. Grohmann, editors, *Informa-
           tionsmanagement - Konzepte und Strategien für die Praxis*, pages
           3–24. dpunkt.verlag, 2004.

[Zel92]   G. Zelazny. *Wie aus Zahlen Bilder werden (engl. Say it with charts)*.
           Gabler, Wiesbaden, 1992.

[ZVK95]   M. Zelm, F. Vernadat, and K. Kosanke. The CIMOSA business mod-
           elling process. *Computers in Industry*, 27:123–142, 1995.

GPSR Compliance
The European Union's (EU) General Product Safety Regulation (GPSR) is a set
of rules that requires consumer products to be safe and our obligations to
ensure this.

If you have any concerns about our products, you can contact us on

ProductSafety@springernature.com

In case Publisher is established outside the EU, the EU authorized
representative is:

Springer Nature Customer Service Center GmbH
Europaplatz 3
69115 Heidelberg, Germany